FOND DU LAC PUBLIC LIBRARY

32 SHEBOYGAN STREET

FOND DU LAC, WI 54935

Closing with the Enemy

Closing with the Enemy

HOW GIS FOUGHT THE WAR IN EUROPE, 1944–1945

Michael D. Doubler

 University Press of Kansas

Published by the University Press of Kansas (Lawrence, Kansas 66049), which was organized by the Kansas Board of Regents and is operated and funded by Emporia State University, Fort Hays State University, Kansas State University, Pittsburg State University, the University of Kansas, and Wichita State University

Library of Congress Cataloging-in-Publication Data

Doubler, Michael D. (Michael Dale), 1955–
    Closing with the enemy : how GIs fought the war in Europe,
1944–1945 / Michael D. Doubler.
        p.   cm. — (Modern war studies)
    Includes bibliographical references and index.
    ISBN 0–7006–0675–0 (hardcover : acid free paper)
    1. World War, 1939–1945—Campaigns—France.   2. World War,
1939–1945—Campaigns—Germany.   3. World War, 1939–1945—United
States.   I. Title.   II. Series.
    D761.D64   1995
    940.54′21—dc20   94-25067

British Library Cataloguing in Publication Data is available.
Printed in the United States of America
10 9 8 7 6 5 4 3 2

To my father
Alvin F. Doubler
A veteran of World War II
who made the march from Normandy to Bavaria

CONTENTS

List of Illustrations and Tables   ix

Acknowledgments   xi

Glossary   xiii

Introduction   1

1 Lessons Learned in the North African and Mediterranean
   Campaigns   10

2 Busting the Bocage   31

3 The Air-Ground Battle Team   63

4 Battles of Buildings and Cobblestones   87

5 Struggles against Steel and Concrete   110

6 In Spite of Hell and High Water   141

7 Confusion and Slaughter among the Firs   172

8 Defense in the Ardennes   198

9 The American Soldier   227

10 The Schoolhouse of War   265

Appendix A U.S. Army Organization and Weaponry   301

Appendix B U.S. Army Doctrine and Tatics   304

A Note on Sources   307

Notes   313

Bibliography   335

Index   343

ILLUSTRATIONS AND TABLES

Maps

2.1 The Advance Inland, 1 July 1944   33
2.2 29th Infantry Division Attack on St. Lo   52
4.1 The Advance to the West Wall, 31 July 1944–3 January 1945   89
5.1 The Siegfried Line Campaign   117
5.2 XX Corps' Capture of Metz, 8–21 November 1944   128
6.1 80th Infantry Division Attempts to Cross the Moselle River,
        5–10 September 1944   146
6.2 The Remagen Bridgehead, 7–18 March 1945   161
7.1 The Second Attack on Schmidt, 28th Infantry Division   176
8.1 The Defense of the Elsenborn Ridge, 16–22 December 1944   204
8.2 Bastogne, 25–26 December 1944   215

Figures

2.1 German Hedgerow Defense   37
2.2 29th Infantry Division Hedgerow Tactics   50
2.3 3d Armored Division Hedgerow Tactics   55
4.1 2d Armored Division Fire and Maneuver Tactics   103
5.1 30th Infantry Division Pillbox Reducing Tactics   122
6.1 U.S. River Crossing Doctrine, 1943   143
9.1 Battlefield Maneuver: Doctrine and Practice   231
9.2 Orchestration of American Firepower, 1944–1945   234

Photographs

Sherman tank equipped with flail device and bangalore torpedoes   16
Sherman tank equipped with a hedgerow cutter   45
P-47 Thunderbolts   71
Infantrymen advance on Brest   94
Tank-infantry team clears Aachen   99

GIs use a flame thrower on a German pillbox   119
Officers supervise work on "snake" explosive devices   132
Soldiers crossing a river   151
The bridge at Remagen   162
Infantrymen clad in snowsuits   206
Infantrymen in assault boat during a river crossing   255

TABLES

9.1 Comparative Statistics of Army Divisions in the ETO   236

ACKNOWLEDGMENTS

It is impossible to complete a major research and writing project without the support and assistance of many wonderful people. It was my great fortune to find such persons in abundance during the time it took to complete this book.

Professor Allan R. Millett of Ohio State University in Columbus, Ohio, has served as teacher, friend, and mentor. From inception, through writing, research, and final publication, I have benefited from Allan Millett's encouragement, advice, and camaraderie. Dr. Harold R. Winton of the U.S. Air Force's School of Advanced Airpower Studies, Air University in Montgomery, Alabama, provided valuable insights and recommendations that helped make the final product much more analytical than it might otherwise have been.

A number of researchers and archivists guided me through their collections with great courtesy and competence. A very special note of thanks must go to John Slonaker and David A. Keough of the U.S. Army Military History Institute at Carlisle Barracks, Pennsylvania. Without their assistance, the research for this project might not have been completed. Betty Van Sickle of the Donovan Technical Library at the U.S. Army Infantry School made my research at Fort Benning, Georgia, extremely worthwhile. Special mention must also be made of the staffs of the Pentagon Library in Washington, D.C., the Eisenhower Presidential Library in Abilene, Kansas, the U.S. Army Armor Center Library at Fort Knox, Kentucky, and the U.S. Army Combined Arms Research Library at Fort Leavenworth, Kansas, for providing research materials.

The administrative tasks involved in completing a book can be daunting. Special thanks go to my co-workers Bertha A. Starr and Larry Bergquist for their support and assistance in preparing the manuscript. Sherry L. Dowdy of the U.S. Army Center of Military History deserves special thanks for the professionalism and quality she put into selected maps and figures. The editors and staff of the University Press of Kansas also deserve a special salute for the diligence and care they displayed during the stages of production and publication.

A special note of gratitude must go to my mother, Mary Macon Doubler, for all of the love and encouragement she has given over the years. Without her constant and unqualified caring, this book might not have been completed. I would also like to express sincere thanks to my brothers—Bernard, Robert, Paul, and John—and my sister Kathleen for their support.

And on a final note . . . for all of those who chided me that it took me longer to complete this book than it took our fathers and grandfathers to fight World War II, all I can say is there was more of them than there was of me.

Alexandria, Virginia
June 6, 1994

GLOSSARY

AAF	Army Air Forces
ACC	Armored column cover
AGF	Army Ground Forces
BAR	Browning automatic rifle
CAS	Close air support
CC	Combat command
COMZ	Communications zone
D-Day	The day designated for the commencement of a specific military operation
ETO	European Theater of Operations
FAC	Forward air controller
FM	Field manual
FO	Forward observer
FSCL	Fire support coordination line
GHQ	General Headquarters
H-hour	The exact hour of the beginning of a specific military operation
HORSEFLY	Air control system of aerial FACs
IP	Initial point
JCS	Joint Chiefs of Staff
KIA	Killed in action
LC	Line of contact
LD	Line of departure
LD/LC	Line of departure/line of contact
LOC	Line of communications
LP	Listening post
MIA	Missing in action
MLR	Main line of resistance
MSR	Main supply route
NCO	Noncommissioned officer
OP	Observation post
OP/LP	Observation post/listening post
PW	Prisoner of war
RAF	Royal Air Force
SHAEF	Supreme Headquarters, Allied Expeditionary Force

TAC   Tactical Air Command
TD   Tank destroyer
TF   Task force
TOT   Time-on-target
WIA   Wounded in action

Introduction

The old saying "live and learn" must be reversed in war, for there we
"learn and live"; otherwise, we die. It is with this learning, in order to live,
that the Army is so vitally concerned.
— *"Lessons Learned and Expedients Used in Combat,"*
War Department Pamphlet no. 20-17, July 1945

From a hillside north of Singling, France, on 6 December 1944, Generalleutnant Fritz Bayerlein, commander of Nazi Germany's crack Panzer
Lehr Division and one of the Third Reich's premier panzer leaders,
watched intently for an attack to begin. Suddenly, tanks broke out of a
distant tree line and, with close infantry support, pushed across open hills
in an assault on Singling. The attack's precision and violence made a great
impression on Bayerlein. After the war, he recalled the action and spoke
of it with professional enthusiasm as "an outstanding tank attack, such as
I have rarely seen, over ideal tank terrain." Bayerlein's pronouncement
was uniquely impartial, for at Singling he had observed not panzer grenadiers and Panther tanks but American M4 Sherman tanks supported by
American infantry. The combined arms attack he had observed with such
animation was carried out by tankers and infantrymen of Maj. Gen. Hugh
M. Gaffey's 4th Armored Division of Lt. Gen. George S. Patton's Third
Army. In December 1944 the 4th Armored was just one of many American divisions trying to close with the enemy, smash its opponents, and
end World War II.[1]

Bayerlein watched the Singling attack just one day short of the anniver-
sary of the U.S. entry into World War II. Only three short years had passed
since Pearl Harbor, yet the United States was standing on Germany's door-
step with powerful land and air forces. Although getting U.S. troops overseas and into the fight had been difficult, the most formidable challenges
came on the battlefield. One of the great lessons American soldiers had to
learn in World War II was the need for an integrated approach to fighting.
Rather than relying on either infantry, tanks, artillery, or air power alone
to get the job done, the American army discovered it could win battles
only by using all available manpower and material resources in coordinated combined arms operations—the tactics and techniques used by a

1

force composed of two or more of the basic combat arms of infantry, artillery, and armor. A combined arms force may receive support from engineers, close air support (CAS), and a number of other assets. In December 1941, American officers could not have conducted or even described the attack Bayerlein observed at Singling. But within less than three short years, they had learned to use sophisticated combined arms tactics with deadly efficiency. The army's ability to learn on the battlefield and to implement improved methods of combined arms warfare contributed significantly to the American success in World War II.

Military institutions since the time of Alexander the Great have had to cope with wartime change. New enemy tactics require commanders to adjust their fighting methods, and armies must alter their techniques when fighting on difficult or unfamiliar terrain. Technological advances present special challenges as armed forces seek the best way to employ new weaponry. But military institutions' record for anticipating and adapting to change is uneven. The eminent British military historian Michael Howard once argued that an army's peacetime military doctrine is usually wrong because military leaders, unlike other professionals, have no sure method of testing or verifying their doctrines and practices short of combat, but it is not important whether or not an army has its doctrine and tactics perfected at the beginning of a war as long as they are not fundamentally flawed. What is crucial is an army's ability to perfect its doctrine and tactics as quickly as possible after the shooting starts. Victory belongs to the army that can learn from its mistakes and adapt to a new and unfamiliar environment. The U.S. army's performance in the European Theater of Operations (ETO) during World War II provides a particularly instructive example of how one force was able to adjust on the battlefield in order to overcome its opponent.[2]

Combined arms warfare has been one of the key challenges to military institutions in the twentieth century. The history of modern combined arms operations began in November 1917, when a large force of British tanks and infantry pushed German units back several miles along a sector of the Western Front near Cambrai, France. The attack proved that the concerted action of a combined arms team of infantry, artillery, and tanks could overcome trenches, barbed wire, and machine guns and restore mobility to the static battlefields of World War I. Cambrai positioned the combined arms team at the center stage of twentieth-century warfare and signaled that such teams would dominate conventional battlefields for some time to come. The eminent British military theorist B. H. Liddell Hart called Cambrai "one of the landmarks in the history of warfare, the dawn of a new epoch."[3]

Success in conducting combined arms warfare is an important measure of the effectiveness of an army. Economic strength and industrial output play key roles in determining the outcome of wars, but nations must still mobilize, train, deploy, and fight combined arms forces to achieve tactical and strategic objectives. An analysis of operations during the American army's greatest campaign of the twentieth century, the fighting in the ETO during 1944–1945, sheds considerable light on the strengths and weaknesses of the U.S. military as well as the American approach to fighting wars. The European campaigns of 1944–1945 are the central focus of this study because the U.S. army then reached its highest levels of performance and capabilities as more Americans took on the burden of defeating the German army.

The American army was successful because it proved itself capable of quickly adapting to new and sometimes unexpected circumstances. An unusual variety of challenges faced the U.S. combined arms team. The German army generally fought on the defensive, considered by many military experts as the stronger form of warfare. The enemy enjoyed the advantages of fighting from prepared defenses and strong fortifications, both of which they defended with exceptional skill. Americans often found themselves battling on terrain for which they were not prepared. The French hedgerow country, the narrow streets of Aachen and Brest, the dark recesses of the Huertgen Forest, and the frigid, snow-covered hills of the Ardennes all presented unique challenges. The combined arms team also had to overcome problems in its own training, equipment, and organization. Flawed prewar doctrine for the employment of certain combat formations and weapons systems was identified and corrected. The American army proved unusually adroit in modifying its composition and practices with new tactical techniques, technological innovations, and organizational changes. Only by adapting under combat conditions was the army able to overcome the enemy.

The European campaign of 1944–1945 was one of mixed successes and hard fighting. The notion that the American army achieved victory in World War II only because of its employment of overwhelming numbers of lavishly supplied troops against an exhausted Wehrmacht is untrue. American combat power had definite limits imposed by constraints on resources and time. The decision to limit the size of the army to ninety divisions, the soldier replacement system, and the organization of some combat formations reduced the army's effectiveness. Inexperience blunted the fighting ability of many units, and some commands had much more difficulty than others in making the transition from novice to veteran. Senior American commanders were adept at operational maneuver and in concentrating firepower, but inadequate numbers of combat formations and occasional manpower and logistical shortages hampered operations. American air power came of age in the ETO and was a potent force in air-ground operations. Despite the army's espousal of the offensive, Americans were better defensive fighters and blunted the German army's most vigorous attacks. A major lesson of the campaign was that competent, aggressive leadership was an absolute prerequisite for success. However, leadership had to be exercised in ways not envisioned by the peacetime army.

Implementing change in the midst of war is a complex process that is related to almost every function a military institution performs. In order for an army to adapt effectively on the battlefield, it must consider its own doctrine, organization, training, tactics, weapons, and soldiers. The need for change may come from an army's realization that it must correct various shortcomings and inefficiencies or from outright defeat. Altering an entire army's approach to war requires major revisions in doctrine, but units in the combat zone can implement minor changes in doctrine and fighting techniques. New ideas may originate from major headquarters or from soldiers on the front lines, but regardless of the style, armies must ensure the dissemination of new concepts and techniques among units. Novel battle tactics, newly formed or reorganized units, and technical improvements in weapons and equipment are some of the more common categories of wartime transformation. Combat zone training programs convert new ideas into actual practice as soldiers learn a wide variety of skills that improve their protection and endurance during extended combat operations. The determination, capabilities, and skills of the opponent, the amount of time available, the weather and terrain of the region, and the amount of matériel and equipment on hand all have a bearing on the extent of adaptations. The most effective changes are usually conceived in a timely manner and are properly implemented by combat units, but the success of adaptations ultimately depends on how much they contribute to the final victory.

The army's campaign from the Normandy beaches to central Germany illustrates almost all of the characteristics of a major field force initiating and implementing significant organizational change. American commanders discovered prewar doctrine was largely correct and not in need of major revisions. However, they came to realize that doctrine had limited use during wartime operations. Commanders learned to apply doctrine flexibly or to ignore it altogether, as they sought ways to defeat a tenacious enemy defending from inhospitable terrain and employing unique tactics. Combat revealed a number of shortcomings in organization and capabilities. Americans implemented an unusual variety of tactical and technical innovations, and commanders altered both branch-specific combat techniques and combined arms tactics to overcome different types of enemy defenses under varying conditions of weather and terrain. Soldiers learned a wide variety of methods that improved their performance and chances for survival. Ideas for tactical and technical innovations sprang from all units and ranks and spread throughout the commands in the theater. Units then trained and drilled soldiers in the new practices. Unlike armies who have had the opportunity to adapt during lulls between campaigns, the nonstop tempo of operations in the ETO often precluded the development of army-wide solutions to problems and left little time for training between battles. Circumstances forced the U.S. army to adjust its combat techniques under fire in the midst of a relentless, offensive campaign. As a measure of success, the large number of adaptations in the ETO permitted Americans to close with and destroy the enemy more quickly and effectively while minimizing their own casualties and inflicting maximum damage on the Germans. Finally, the fighting of 1944–1945 validates the assertion that successful armies must have the ability to change quickly and to adapt their combat techniques in order to win.

Warfare in the industrial age is rich with other examples of armies adapting in combat. During the American Civil War the rifled musket radically altered open order battle tactics and helped generate the static siege lines at Vicksburg and Petersburg. During World War I, the combination of trenches, barbed wire, and machine guns created the ghastly deadlock on the Western Front. Desperate to find a way to overcome the stalemate, the German army instituted a number of innovations that resulted in new infiltration tactics in which storm troopers evaded enemy defenses. During World War II, the Soviet Army arose from the ashes of its catastrophic defeat in 1941 to execute a new operational form of warfare that used deep attacks against Hitler's armies.

If armies are a reflection of society, the approach a military organization uses to effect change in wartime should reflect the major characteristics, attitudes, and values of society at large. Every army goes to war with its own unique set of political, social, and economic values. Armies from authoritarian societies with centralized control will have different command and leadership styles than armies from democratic societies that espouse free speech. Social values determine soldiers' attitudes on the utility of war and the value of human life. Whether an army is manned by militiamen and conscripts or volunteer professionals will largely determine manpower and training policies. The business practices and degree of economic development of a nation greatly influence the armed forces, and the economic practices and management styles found in the workplace accompany soldiers to the battlefield.

The practices the German, Soviet, and American armies used to implement change reveal the heavy influence of societal values on battlefield adaptation. The Germans in World War I and the Soviets in the Great Patriotic War used centralized, formal techniques and channels of communication to facilitate adaptation. The Americans in the ETO during World

War II used a more informal approach that eschewed centralized control. The Europeans preferred directed changes from above, while U.S. forces encouraged an entrepreneurial spirit that sought ideas from any credible source. The monarchical and authoritarian traditions of the German and Soviet armies made them more prudent and cautious about implementing change. On the other hand, American soldiers coming from a democratic society that promoted competitiveness and progress were more bold and confident in their ability to generate and implement new combat techniques. A comparison of the processes the German, Soviet, and American armies used to implement change provides valuable insights into the uniquely American approach to waging war and solving problems.

Writings in military history often put forth conflicting arguments about events and developments. In general, a popular argument in recent years is that the German army was the ultimate paradigm of operational and tactical success in World War II, while its American opponents muddled through to victory by the application of overwhelming resources and awesome firepower. A key work that has influenced recent interpretations of the U.S. army's World War II performance is Professor Russell Weigley's *Eisenhower's Lieutenants*. Weigley argues that the army was neither intellectually nor physically prepared for the war in Europe. One of his key premises is that the army, steeped in the traditions of the Indian wars and overseas constabulary duty, was fashioned for a war of mobility and was incapable of generating sustained combat power. According to Weigley, the army went to Europe with a strategic concept that called for the application of sheer power against the enemy, but that it was not organized to generate the brute force its strategic concepts required. From a force structure perspective, the army was too mobile and improperly organized for such demanding actions as attacking the coastal defenses in Normandy, grinding through the hedgerow country, or punching through the Siegfried Line. Weigley is also very critical of American generalship, arguing that it was unimaginative, addicted to playing it safe, and lacked a clear conception of warfare. He concludes that the American army "rumbled to victory" because of a preponderance of matériel resources and that the war dragged on longer than it should have "because American military skills were not as formidable as they could have been."[4]

Another important interpretive work is Martin van Creveld's *Fighting Power*, which presents a comparative analysis of the fighting abilities of the German and American armies in World War II. Creveld exalts the fighting prowess of the German army and identifies the reasons it excelled in war. First, the German army established a single-minded focus on fighting and geared its doctrine, organization, command techniques, and administrative procedures toward winning. Second, the German army insisted on procuring and maintaining quality manpower for its fighting units and geared its entire system toward meeting the social and psychological needs of the individual fighting man. Creveld argues that the American army regarded war not as a struggle between opposing forces but rather as a contest in which machines and firepower would largely determine the outcome. He maintains that the U.S. army viewed soldiers as little more than adjuncts of machines, overlooked their most elementary psychological needs, and placed primary emphasis on bureaucratic efficiency rather than on troop morale or unit cohesion. To Creveld, American combat leadership was mediocre at best, and the U.S. personnel replacement system, with its tendency to treat soldiers like spare parts, was the single greatest reason for the army's problems.

An older, classic work that still influences understandings of the American performance in World War II is S. L. A. Marshall's *Men against Fire*, which probes the human dimension of warfare and analyzes various aspects of individual behavior and the group dynamics of men in battle. Marshall argues that isolation and confusion are the battlefield's primary characteristics, and that what keeps most soldiers fighting is the near presence of their comrades. Based on his work as a combat historian, Marshall concluded that engagements were lost or won because of the actions of a small number of soldiers, and that, on average, only 15–25 percent of soldiers fired their weapons. Marshall also identified other shortcomings in infantry units, such as the tendency to bunch together under fire and the lack of high volumes of small arms firepower.

This book builds on these previous works by providing new insights into how the American army won World War II. Findings based on extensive research in previously unexploited primary source materials place important qualifiers on some earlier assertions regarding the army's performance, validate others, and refute just as many more. A close study of the fighting in the ETO reveals that army divisions were more effective instruments of national policy than is generally believed. A series of key tactical and technical adaptations took place during 1944–1945 that transformed ground units into powerful, cohesive combined arms formations capable of generating awesome firepower and effective ground maneuver. A learning process occurred in each battlefield environment the military encountered, enabling soldiers and airmen to break tactical deadlocks and to close with the enemy. American generals determined that campaigns required both hard fighting and maneuver. Instead of fighting with overwhelming resources, generals often had to cope with personnel and matériel shortages that hampered their efforts. The army emphasized the mechanical aspects of combat, but not to the extent that it disregarded all of the needs of its soldiers. In fact, knowledgeable employment of weapons and machines was a strength that greatly contributed to victory. Manpower problems plagued the army, and leaders implemented new procedures to maximize the use of available troops, albeit with mixed results. Although some small unit leaders may have been weak and incompetent, many others performed with considerable skill and got maximum results from available resources. Confusion and fear dominated the battlefield, causing problems in many small units, and forced soldiers to adapt to changing conditions on the front lines.

An analysis of military operations requires a working knowledge of the key concepts of warfare. Doctrine consists of the fundamental, authoritative principles armies use to guide all of their activities in support of mission accomplishment. From doctrine, an army derives its tactics, procedures, organization, equipment, and training. Strategy is the art and science of employing or threatening the use of military power to secure national policy objectives. Operations is the employment of military forces to attain the goals of military strategy through the design, organization, and actual conduct of campaigns. Tactics refers to the myriad, specific techniques units use in combat. As mentioned earlier, a combined arms force is a fighting organization composed of either two or three of the principal combat arms of infantry, artillery, and armor and can receive support from engineers, air defense artillery, fighter-bombers, and other assets. Combined arms operations refers to the employment and tactics of a combined arms force. On the battlefield, maneuver is the movement of friendly forces in relation to the enemy to secure or retain positional advantage. Firepower is the destructive force produced by direct and indirect fire weapons and other heavy ordnance. CAS assists ground forces by attacking hostile targets in close proximity to friendly troops. Cover is the use of man-made or natural features to provide protection from enemy observation and fire. Concealment provides protection from observation only. Suppression is the use of firepower to neutralize, destroy, or temporarily degrade the effectiveness of enemy weaponry. A field of fire is the area a weapon can cover effectively from a given position, while a field of observation defines the area one can view from a single location. Combat power is a more imprecise expression and represents a subjective evaluation of a unit's capabilities considering numbers, weaponry, and training, as well as the human factors of esprit de corps, leadership, and discipline. Some of the military terminologies used during World War II have found new meanings in present times, but unless otherwise noted, the terms found throughout the text conform to modern usage.[5]

In 1934 the Infantry School at Fort Benning published the military classic *Infantry in Battle*. Fearful that the declining number of active duty veterans from World War I was decreasing the army's readiness, the Infantry School hoped to reintroduce the experience of battle to an untested officer corps with a book describing small unit infantry actions during the

Great War. Col. George C. Marshall, future army chief of staff during World War II, clearly stated the purpose of *Infantry in Battle* in the Introduction:

> There is much evidence to show that officers who have received the best peacetime training available find themselves surprised and confused by the difference between conditions as pictured in map problems and those they encounter in campaign. . . . In our schools we generally assume that organizations are well-trained and at full strength, that subordinates are competent, that supply arrangements function, that communications work, that orders are carried out. In war many or all of these conditions may be absent. The veteran knows that this is normal and his mental processes are not paralyzed by it. . . . This volume is designed to give the peace-trained officer something of the viewpoint of the veteran.[6]

The overall purpose of this study is similar. As the American military shrinks in the aftermath of the Cold War, the number of soldiers who have experienced combat is diminishing. At the same time, threats to national security from regional powers remain. In lieu of actual combat experience, the armed forces must turn to military history to gain insights into the experience of battle. An analysis of combined arms operations in the ETO dramatically illustrates how the American army adapted during wartime to meet unexpected challenges and shows how armies function in battle rather than on peacetime maneuvers or terrain board exercises. If this work stimulates disciplined thinking by strategists and planners on the challenges of future battlefields, and promotes among "peace-trained officer(s) something of the viewpoint of the veteran," then I will have achieved my purpose.

CHAPTER ONE

Lessons Learned in the North African and Mediterranean Campaigns

On reflection, I came to the conclusion that it was fortunate . . . that the U.S. Army first met the enemy on the periphery, in Africa rather than on the beaches of France. In Africa we learned to crawl, then walk—then run. Had the learning process been launched in France, it would surely have . . . resulted in an unthinkable disaster.

—General of the Army Omar N. Bradley

In the early morning hours of 8 November 1942, soldiers of an American joint task force splashed ashore along the coast of North Africa. The widespread seaborne assault, code-named Operation TORCH, was a significant turning point in the United States' participation in World War II. Almost a year after declaring war on the Axis Powers, American ground troops were finally in combat against enemy forces in Europe. The decision to execute TORCH had its origins in America's long-term strategic commitment to defeat Nazi Germany first before turning its maximum effort toward Imperial Japan.

The final operational design for TORCH resulted from months of debate and even quarreling within the British and American high commands. The cornerstone of Allied military strategy for the war in Europe was an Anglo-American assault of the European continent. Although both the British and American Chiefs of Staff agreed on the primacy and purpose of the cross-channel attack, sharp disagreements arose over the timing of the landing. Anxious to get into the war, the U.S. army favored a quick buildup of invasion forces and an immediate attack on the Continent as early as the spring of 1942. Dwight D. Eisenhower, a brigadier general in the War Department's War Plans Division in early 1942, summarized the army's desire to get into the war in Europe as quickly as possible and to get its hands on the enemy: "We've got to go to Europe and fight—and we've got to quit wasting resources all over the world—and still worse—wasting time . . . we've got to begin slugging with air at West Europe; to be followed by a land attack as soon as possible."[1]

Despite American enthusiasm for an early offensive, the British Joint Chiefs of Staff (JCS) were skeptical of American capabilities and believed that any direct strike against Europe in 1942 was beyond the capacity and ability of the U.S. army. Instead, the British favored the employment of American troops in the Mediterranean. The British JCS argued that the best use of the limited numbers of inexperienced American soldiers available in 1942 would be to help in the destruction of Axis forces in North Africa. However, the U.S. military leadership in Washington believed that any Mediterranean venture would be an unnecessary diversion of resources that should be employed in a direct assault against Germany. Unpersuaded by British views, the American JCS stood fast in favor of an early European invasion.

Direct intervention by President Franklin D. Roosevelt settled the arguments over the best use of American forces in favor of Operation TORCH. Although the United States was striking back with success against the Japanese in the Pacific, Roosevelt remained committed to the strategy of defeating Nazi Germany before attempting to overcome Japan. The president realized that the United States had to gain momentum in the European war and directed that American soldiers would be in combat against German formations by the end of 1942. Once American planners received this specific guidance from Roosevelt, they began preparing for the North African landings. For the American army the road to Berlin would begin in the sands of Tunisia.

Operations in the North African and Mediterranean theaters during 1942–1944 were designed to weaken German and Italian forces as the Allies began the slow process of preparing for the invasion of Western Europe. During the fighting in North Africa between November 1942 and May 1943, the U.S. II Corps fought as part of the British 18th Army Group. (See Appendix A for an overview of U.S. army organization and weaponry in World War II.) The defeat at Kasserine Pass in mid-February 1943 was the low point of American participation in North Africa, if not in all of World War II in Europe. But American formations showed great resilience, and under the close watch of emerging senior generals like George S. Patton, Jr., and Omar Bradley, American troops shaped up and bounced back into action. By 13 May Allied forces had cleared all of Tunisia and destroyed the remnants of the once proud Afrika Korps. With the aims of further reducing enemy fighting strength and increasing their own momentum in the Mediterranean, Allied forces landed in southern Sicily on 10 July. With the U.S. Seventh Army under Patton on the left, and Sir Bernard L. Montgomery in command of the British Eighth Army on the right, the Allies overran Sicily in just over thirty-seven days. Already tired of the war, Italy was prompted by the Allied successes to sign a separate armistice with its enemies on 8 September. The Germans immediately assumed responsibility for the defense of the Italian peninsula and did not have to wait long for the next Allied move. On 9 September American and British divisions of the U.S. Fifth Army waded ashore at Salerno.

For the next ten months Allied forces fought a grueling series of battles on the forbidding, mountainous terrain of southern Italy as they attacked northward up the peninsula. Finally, the U.S. Fifth Army seized Rome on 4 June, one of the few high points in the costly campaign. Overall, American participation in the Mediterranean campaigns helped achieve the Allied objectives of weakening the enemy armies and splintering the German-Italian alliance.

As American tanks rolled into Rome, soldiers of the U.S. First Army in southern England were finishing their final preparations for the imminent cross-channel attack against Hitler's Fortress Europe. In addition to the almost simultaneous timing of the two events, another factor linked together the fall of Rome and the Normandy assault. Between the North African landings and the capture of Rome, the American army gained significant combat experience that helped prepare American forces not only for D-Day but for subsequent operations in the European theater. Though the army achieved all of its objectives in the Mediterranean campaigns, uneven battlefield performances justified concerns over the readiness of American units to conduct an invasion of France in 1942. Lessons learned during the fighting in North Africa, Sicily, and Italy taught the army much about the validity of its doctrinal and operational concepts, the worth of its tactics and equipment, and the performance of its soldiers.

For the American army as a war-fighting institution, the most significant outcome of the campaigns in North Africa and the Mediterranean was the conviction that its doctrinal and operational concepts were sound. (See Appendix B for a discussion of prewar U.S. army doctrine and tactics.) From senior generals to junior officers, American commanders believed that the basic doctrinal tenets outlined in Field Manual (FM) 100-5 were valid. Combat experience proved the efficacy of the offensive and that attacking the enemy's flanks was more productive and less costly than frontal assaults. Failures in early battles were credited to the misapplication or lack of judgment and flexibility in following doctrinal tenets, or from attempts to adhere to doctrine too stringently in situations that demanded creative solutions. Convinced of the overall soundness of the army's doctrine, leaders were free to channel their efforts toward solving the specific problems of how to win battles.[2]

One of the most important lessons learned by senior commanders was the need to deny the enemy access to dominating terrain that afforded clear observation over large sectors. By observing American forward battle zones and rear areas, Axis forces could monitor American activities, anticipate their next move, and dominate the entire sector with artillery fire. Taught that commanders usually had a clear choice between seizing ground or destroying enemy forces, American generals learned that such clear alternatives became blurred during prolonged campaigns between large, mechanized armies deployed over widespread areas. Although the annihilation of German and Italian forces remained the ultimate objective of campaigns, the capture of the dominating terrain within a contested area was a prerequisite for defeating the enemy in specific battles and engagements. American generals found that they could not bypass certain pieces of enemy-held terrain, and capturing critical terrain usually demanded a great deal of fighting. For example, during the Tunisian campaign the Germans successfully blocked the U.S. II Corps' advance on Tunis by retaining control of Hill 609. Not until the 34th Infantry Division seized the hill on 30 April 1943 could the offensive toward Tunis resume. Likewise, the U.S. Fifth Army's offensive up the Italian peninsula stalled in the shadow of the abbey of Monte Cassino. Forward progress did not continue until the British Eighth Army occupied the abbey on 18 May 1944.[3]

The most important battlefield lesson learned in the North African and Mediterranean theaters was that the combat arms had to work together as a coordinated combined arms team in order to win. Despite its heavy, prewar emphasis on the need for the coordination of the combat arms, the American army had difficulty conducting combined arms operations. Time and time again experience proved that no single combat arm could prevail, as attacks by infantry or armor alone resulted in heavy losses and a lack of progress. But when operating together in a coordinated effort, the combat arms generated an offensive punch that the enemy had trouble withstanding. For leaders at division level and below, their most important challenge was the development and implementation of combined arms tactics that brought them success. Between the North African landings and the fall of Rome, American leadership spent a great deal of time and effort attempting to correct the deficiencies identified in each of the combat arms in order to prepare a well-coordinated combined arms team.[4]

Shortcomings in each of the combat arms prevented the army from developing its full potential as a potent fighting machine. During infantry operations, commanders discovered that the effective use of fire and maneuver was the most important factor in winning engagements. Yet the greatest challenge facing infantry leadership was to get their units to maneuver under fire. Often in battle for the first time, inexperienced infantry squads had a tendency not to move but to freeze or to seek the nearest protection. Detecting this failure, Axis forces learned to pin down American units with small arms fire and then to punish them further with mortar and artillery shelling. Instead of maneuvering aggressively, infantry attacks all too often merely located and fixed their adversaries. Artillery fire was then called upon to finish the infantry's job of destroying the defenders. Instead of relying on their own means, infantrymen trusted in the big guns of the field artillery to deliver the coup de grace.[5]

By late 1943 infantrymen had learned two techniques that helped reduce casualties. The best way to avoid losses was to keep moving forward and to close rapidly with the enemy. Infantry leaders taught their soldiers that "hitting the dirt" upon enemy contact did not mean freezing in place and that squads had to continue moving forward under fire. Soldiers also discovered that moving out from underneath concentrations of enemy shell fire greatly reduced casualties. Veterans learned to recognize certain hostile shell bursts as an enemy effort to adjust artillery onto their position. Alert leaders became adept at moving their troops to new, safer locations before they were hit by enemy indirect fire.[6] The experience of one battalion of the 180th Infantry in Sicily was typical: "Just about the time we were moving out, a round came in and burst about a hundred yards to the front of us, followed by one about a hundred yards in rear. It was a perfect bracket. We moved forward at the double and escaped the concentration that plastered the area we had been in."[7] Commanders became convinced of the efficacy of both of these techniques, which became common practice during the Italian campaign.

An inability to generate sufficient amounts of small arms firepower was another major problem. Fighting an enemy who was adept at camouflage and used smokeless powder, American riflemen had problems acquiring targets and were reluctant to engage an enemy they could not see. Too many units had problems producing enough firepower to cover the entire area under attack. Patton reported after the Sicilian campaign, "It is the general consensus of opinion of all officers who have actually participated in battle that our men do not shoot enough." Attempting to fight as they had been trained during stateside marksmanship exercises on firing ranges against inanimate paper targets, individual soldiers in combat tried to engage a living, hidden enemy in one-on-one rifle duels. As a collective body, infantry soldiers understood the principle of returning individual fire but failed to realize the importance of an entire unit producing a volume of fire that would cover all known, likely, and suspected enemy positions.[8]

The failure of infantry commanders to employ all of their organic heavy weapons reduced firepower even more and increased the infantry's reliance on artillery support. The purpose of an infantry regiment's mortars and assault guns was to support the rifle platoons. Consequently, these weapons were employed very close to the fighting front and became favorite targets for German artillery, tanks, and other heavy weapons. American mortar, antitank, and assault gun crews often suffered heavy casualties. A tendency developed in which these weapons remained hidden and silent until the salvoes of the supporting artillery landed on the enemy's positions, and only then would they join in the battle. Senior commanders exhorted their subordinates to bring all of their weapons to bear, but the problems infantry units had in generating sufficient firepower continued to plague the army throughout the Italian campaign.[9]

Tank units also discovered several problems that hampered armored operations. Armor leaders believed in the soundness of the fundamental principles of tank employment advocated by the Armored Force School. Fort Knox taught armor officers that tanks should be used in mass, employed in depth on a narrow front, and directed against weak segments of the enemy's line. Once armor units ruptured the enemy's defensive lines, they would rampage throughout the rear areas attacking command posts and support units in an effort to destroy the coherency of the opponent's defense. But the theoretical principles espoused in Kentucky did not align with the realities of combat in North Africa and the Mediterranean. Rugged, mountainous terrain proved unsuitable for the employment of armored forces in mass, and Axis units were seldom weak enough to become easy prey for a sudden, blitzkrieg-style tank attack. Seeing few opportunities to employ armor in its intended role, senior American commanders dispersed their armored assets and used them for infantry support. Tank battalions operating with infantry divisions seldom massed for attacks but remained parceled out to infantry regiments. At the close of the Tunisian campaign, the commanding officer of an armored combat command (CC) complained that "offensive action by American armored troops was marked by a dispersal of effort." Reflecting on his experience as a regimental commander with the 1st Armored Division in North Africa, Col. Peter C. Hains warned the readers of *The Cavalry Journal* that "commanders of tank units must keep an open, flexible mind. Too often the situation demands the employment of armor in a role totally different from the normal school of thought." Denied the opportunity to employ armor in classical ways during the war's early campaigns, American armor leaders entered France hoping to find conditions that would allow them to ride roughshod over their enemies.[10]

One of the army's most significant organizational weaknesses was the apparent failure of having separate, independent tank battalions. General Headquarters (GHQ) tank battalions usually were rotated quickly between different infantry units, not only within a single division but among other divisions as well. During the Italian campaign the commander of the 756th Tank Battalion complained, "My battalion was attached so many times that I almost lost count. In one case the battalion was attached to three different organizations within a period of twelve hours." Such frequent rotation made it impossible to develop the teamwork and esprit required for successful tank-infantry operations. Because of their independent existence, GHQ tank battalions suffered from the

American soldiers showed an early tendency for experimenting with new weapons and equipment. A tank crew prepares for a formal demonstration of a Sherman tank equipped with a flail device and bangalore torpedoes in North Africa, August 1943. (U.S. Army)

lack of crew replacements, supplies, and spare parts. The problem of GHQ tank battalions was a sore one that accompanied the army to the French mainland.[11]

If infantry and armor commanders were troubled over problems in their units, the poor coordination that existed during combined arms attacks was even more disturbing. Combat showed that stateside training lacked emphasis on the planning and execution of tank-infantry attacks. In the aftermath of the Sicilian campaign, a battalion executive officer with the 180th Infantry reported:

> In the U.S. we always trained with what we had, and never had any training in cooperation with tanks. When we got into action over here in Sicily, and were given tanks to support and assist us, we actually didn't know how to use them or work with them. There must be real training for the infantry with actual tanks in realistic combat exercises . . . We were just too unfamiliar with the proper way to use them.[12]

Commanders at all levels realized the need for combined arms training for units that had already been in combat and knew that a better understanding of the capabilities, limits, and tactics of their forces would help ensure the smooth coordination of the combined arms team. In Italy the commander of the U.S. II Corps ordered that problems in the infantry-tank team "should be corrected by intensive combined training. During lulls in combat, rehearsals, command post exercises, and conferences can be utilized to smooth out the operational procedures of these task forces."[13]

Inadequate combined arms training too often resulted in poor performances by tank-infantry teams. Infantry commanders habitually failed to exploit the mobility and firepower of tanks under their control. Conversely, tankers showed a reluctance to advance and take the burden of pressing home the attack away from accompanying riflemen. When tankers did lead the attack, infantrymen had a tendency to lag behind. Tankers often found themselves on their objective, awaiting the arrival of their accompanying infantry while still surrounded by pockets of Germans. On the other hand, riflemen who stayed with tanks during attacks were often killed or wounded by enemy fire directed at the vehicles. Inadequate communications also hampered tank-infantry attacks. Infantry platoons had no way of alerting tankers about antitank traps and heavy weapons, nor could tank crews warn the infantry of enemy positions. After the Sicilian campaign, a staff officer in the 79th Infantry reported that the regiment "had not been trained to work with tanks" and consistently failed to "follow up the tanks properly as they went forward." However, tank and infantry units that trained and fought together for extended periods proved very capable in battle. The 1st Infantry Division noticed a dramatic improvement in its combined arms operations during the Tunisian and Sicilian campaigns. The Big Red One's commander, Maj. Gen. Terry Allen, observed that in Sicily tanks routinely assisted infantry units by conducting short, quick thrusts followed closely by their supporting infantry. Notwithstanding improvements in some divisions, solutions to the perplexing problem of tank-infantry coordination eluded the army in Italy and were still lacking prior to the Normandy battles.[14]

The failure of tank destroyer (TD) units to function in the roles articulated by prewar doctrine indicated that antitank warfare was among the army's most serious problems. The theory for TD employment specified that commanders were to mass their TD assets as a mobile reserve and then use them against the enemy's main armor attack. However, battlefield realities quickly unraveled antitank warfare theories. By 1942 the German army attacked in ways that thwarted TD employment. German tanks no longer struck in massed formations as they had done in 1939–1941 but attacked methodically as a member of a combined arms team.

American TD battalions had no opportunity to destroy concentrations of enemy tanks acting alone and unsupported. Like American tankers, German commanders discovered that the rugged, mountainous terrain of the Mediterranean basin prevented the massed blitzkrieg assaults that American TD battalions were trained to defeat. Battlefield psychology also militated against the doctrinal employment of TDs. Although TD units were supposed to attack enemy tanks that had already ruptured forward defenses, American generals found it almost impossible to hold TD assets in reserve while enemy armor overran forward units. Instead, they followed the impulse to throw TD units into the fight early so as to give frontline troops an immediate antitank capability and to help them hold their own. TD units were also rotated between major commands at a frantic pace and operated without proper personnel and logistical support. Lack of knowledge among junior officers about TD employment and sharp disagreements between American generals on the actual need and purpose of TD battalions did not help the situation.[15]

Aware of the failure of TD battalions to perform according to doctrine, soldiers looked for better ways to employ them. Showing great flexibility and ingenuity, commanders began to use TDs as self-propelled artillery pieces and assault guns. As an artillery piece, the TD proved to be very accurate and had a range 4,000 yards longer than the standard 105-mm cannon. TD units enjoyed even greater success as assault guns. In Italy TD units supported tanks with direct fire that turned back German panzers and demolished enemy pillboxes and other types of prepared defenses. The great accuracy and knockdown power of the TD's three-inch gun proved capable of leveling the sturdiest enemy fortifications. Pleased with their performance in the Mediterranean as self-propelled artillery and assault guns, TD battalions entered the ETO hoping to improve upon their newfound roles.[16]

Unlike the other players on the combined arms team, American field artillery units were effective performers early in the war. The theoretical principles of artillery employment taught by the Field Artillery School at Fort Sill, Oklahoma, worked well under combat conditions. American artillery doctrine called for centralized control with decentralized execution and the use of tremendous concentrations of indirect fire. Artillery commanders agreed that the principles espoused at Fort Sill were correct but still had to be applied with flexibility. In comparison to infantrymen and tankers, artillerymen found the transition from peacetime theory to battlefield conditions less taxing.[17]

A number of procedures that were developed early in the war contributed to the success of artillery operations. Centralized planning and decentralized execution marked artillery operations in Africa and were improved upon in subsequent operations. In Tunisia, division artillery commanders did planning and coordination, while battalion commanders principally concerned themselves with fighting battles. By the fall of Rome, larger operations involving greater numbers of maneuver units and additional artillery battalions resulted in an upward shifting of responsibilities. Artillery commanders and their staffs at army and corps level did centralized planning, while division artillery commanders became active participants in combat. This shifting of responsibilities meant that the artillery firepower within an entire army did not remain parceled out to subordinate elements but could be concentrated and employed in full support of maneuvers at the corps and army level.[18]

The employment of guns in mass, the accurate delivery of concentrated volumes of fire, and the prowess of forward observers (FO) in adjusting shells accounted for artillery units' great success. Instead of relying only on high explosive projectiles, artillerymen learned that combinations of high explosive, delay-fuse, and white phosphorus shells produced the best results. Artillery battalions also excelled in locating enemy gun positions and delivering accurate counterbattery fire. Axis prisoners who had fought against other armies testified to the effectiveness of U.S. artillery fire. Exposed German formations often found themselves subjected to awesome artillery concentrations, and massed artillery firepower often helped stalled infantry and armor attacks regain their momentum. On 15 February 1944, the II Corps artillery delivered a single time-on-target (TOT) volley of 266 rounds onto the summit of Monte Cassino in an effort to destroy entrenched German defenders. And thirty days later, in one eight-hour period, artillery batteries fired 200,000 rounds in support of ground units attacking the city of Cassino. By the summer of 1944, the field artillery had proven itself the most brilliant performer in the American combined arms team.[19]

Infantry-artillery attacks were more coordinated than other combined arms operations for several reasons. Artillery and infantry battalions enjoyed long-standing relationships within their own divisions. Infantrymen and artillerymen had worked together during peacetime exercises, knew how the other operated, and were better able to develop the specific techniques necessary to cooperate with one another in combat. In general, artillery battalions at corps and army levels also had close kinships with divisional artillery battalions. Unit teamwork and even personal relationships helped further the coordination of army, corps, and divisional artillery units that permitted American cannoneers to rock German defenders with backbreaking concentrations of shell fire.[20]

Infantry units also learned two key lessons that maximized artillery employment. Artillery FOs with infantry battalions often became casualties or were not in a good location to call for fires. To solve these problems, infantry regiments in Sicily and Italy began to train all personnel, down to and including platoon sergeants in FO procedures. At the same time, artillery units began to train all members of FO teams in call for fire techniques. By having more people qualified as FOs in the front lines, infantry regiments helped ensure the availabiliy of constant, responsive fire support. Infantrymen also learned the advantage and necessity of closely following supporting barrages. In North Africa ground units lagged almost 500 yards behind friendly shell fire, allowing the enemy time to recover from the bombardment and man their weapons. Maj. Gen. Manton Eddy, commander of the 9th Infantry Division in 1943, told General Eisenhower that peacetime safety restrictions had prevented infantry units from learning how to follow closely behind artillery barrages. Convinced that soldiers had to learn this skill, Eddy instituted a 9th Division training program in which all troops and officers had to march 200 yards behind a moving curtain of shell fire before joining units at the front. Experience showed that infantrymen could advance from 100 to 200 yards behind supporting barrages, a distance that prevented casualties from friendly fire while denying the enemy time to reconstitute their defenses. By 1944 infantry battalions routinely advanced on the heels of supporting artillery fire.[21]

Another serious problem with combined arms warfare was the lack of cooperation between ground forces and the Army Air Forces' (AAF) fighter-bombers. Prewar doctrine for tactical air power was at cross purposes with ground commanders' insistence that CAS was a vital ingredient in land combat. (See Appendix B for discussions of prewar air doctrine and close air support request channels.) Disagreements over the functions of aviation meant that American air and ground units entered World War II without clear procedures on how to work together. In the North African and Mediterranean theaters, air units fought primarily to gain air superiority and disrupt Axis lines of communications (LOCs), and CAS missions received low priority. One Army Ground Forces (AGF) observer reported from Tunisia that air-ground cooperation as envisioned during prewar maneuvers "appeared to be nonexistent." The lack of a functional CAS system prompted one senior commander to write that the air-ground situation in Tunisia was worse than it had been in World War I, and air-ground operations improved little during the Sicilian campaign.[22]

In the eyes of air commanders two problems hampered CAS integration. The first was target acquisition. Attacking fighter-bombers often flew at treetop level at speeds in excess of 200 m.p.h., making the pilot's task of target identification almost impossible. Too often aviators left their airstrips without updated information on the location of enemy formations. Consequently, pilots had to search for their targets and had difficulty in distinguishing between American and Axis units. Numerous American formations in North Africa and Sicily experienced bombing and strafing by friendly fighter-bombers. During the Italian campaign the army used colored smoke grenades and fluorescent marker panels to indicate friendly troop locations and identified enemy targets with artillery smoke projectiles. The second problem was that aircraft could not talk directly to ground units, so ground commanders and air support parties were unable to provide pilots with timely information on the tactical situation, guide fighter-bombers to their targets, or call off aircraft attacking the wrong target or friendly troops. The absence of a direct communications link was a serious deficiency that made unguided fighter-bombers a dangerous player on the combined arms team.[23]

Two other problems further hampered air-ground operations. Far too many units proved incapable of distinguishing between friendly and enemy aviation and did not hesitate to shoot at any aircraft operating overhead. Inexperienced U.S. troops, terrorized by enemy air attacks or demoralized after being strafed and bombed by their own aircraft, tended to shoot first and ask questions later. Ground commanders in Sicily began to stress fire discipline, ordering troops to withhold fire until they could positively identify aircraft or until they had been attacked by hostile aviation. Air commanders told pilots to avoid flying over friendly troops in ways that might cause ground units to mistake them as enemy. By the summer of 1943 the army had mounted a vigorous training program to teach soldiers how to differentiate between friendly and enemy aircraft. Despite these measures, Eisenhower reported after the Sicilian campaign that the problem of aircraft identification had "not been satisfactorily solved" and that ground troops continued to open fire on friendly aircraft. Ground commanders also believed that aviation failed to provide them with photographic and visual reconnaissance information on enemy troop concentrations and movements. And when aerial reconnaissance intelligence did reach ground commanders, it was usually too dated to be of use.[24]

However, the Italian campaign saw the origin of a technique that significantly improved air-ground operations. During the breakout from the Anzio beachhead in the spring of 1944, the AAF cooperated with ground forces in deploying America's first, modern forward air controller (FAC) system for land operations. Code-named HORSEFLY, the system consisted of FACs in single-engined L-5 Sentinel observation aircraft who had direct radio communications with both air-ground support parties located at the headquarters of major ground units as well as the flight leaders of fighter-bomber formations. When ground units identified targets for fighter-bombers, they relayed the information to air-ground support parties, who then passed the target description to the FACs. Loitering over the battle zone, FACs identified the correct target and then radioed to inbound fighter-bombers the most current information on target description and location and enemy air defenses, even suggesting the proper approach and method of attack. Better techniques that would enable fighter-bomber units to attack German units in close combat with American formations would have to be found during the European campaigns.[25]

The first employment of medium and heavy bombers in direct support of ground operations also took place during the Italian campaign. Stalled in front of the Gustav Line in early 1944, the U.S. Fifth Army decided to crack the enemy defenses by massing overwhelming strength against German positions around Monte Cassino. After considerable debate, Allied commanders decided to seize the town of Cassino and the adjacent Benedictine monastery with a coordinated ground and air assault. Apparently, air officers viewed the attack as an opportunity to demonstrate the potential of the bomber as a powerful CAS weapon. On 15 February almost 250 medium and heavy bombers dumped an estimated 600 tons of high explosives on the abbey of Monte Cassino, reducing the ancient structure to rubble. The following month Allied bomber formations put on an even more spectacular display of firepower in support of operations to seize the town of Cassino. On 15 March 435 medium and heavy bombers pummeled Cassino with more than 2,000 bombs, the equivalent of 1,000 tons of high explosives. The awesome, shattering force of this unprecedented bombardment demolished Cassino, smashing entire buildings, felling walls, and choking the streets with rubble. The attacks were a great psychological boost to ground troops and did obliterate their targets, but the effects against enemy units were less than expected and did not relieve Allied soldiers of the burden of reducing German defensive positions. Although the experimental aerial assaults were largely more dramatic than effective, they nevertheless foreshadowed the similar employment of bomber forces in the ETO.[26]

In addition to finding out a great deal about the strengths and weaknesses of the combined arms team, the army discovered new lessons about the nature of combat and the challenges of leading men in battle. Before World War II the army put great emphasis on the importance of small unit leadership in wartime. Combat confirmed the need for competent, inspirational leaders and showed that the outcome of engagements often hinged on the actions of a few influential leaders. Drawing from its leadership experiences in battle, the army identified three essential qualities necessary for successful leadership: initiative, responsibility, and resourcefulness.[27]

While preaching these characteristics of successful leadership, the army learned several effective leadership methods. Commanders discovered that the stress and fatigue of battle made troops docile and careless when not under fire. Relieved to be out of harm's way, the average soldier had a tendency to relax and do little before reentering combat. Leaders learned that they had to make a determined effort to overcome this tendency by making sure soldiers performed basic security and maintenance tasks.[28] A successful infantry regimental commander in Italy informed a stateside visitor of this leadership challenge and encouraged him to "tell your people when you return home, that the hardest job they will have is getting things done. My men know their weapons and tactics thoroughly. My effort is simply to require them to do the things they know must be done. . . . You have to check all the time."[29]

Exercising command from near the front lines rather than from rear command posts was an important lesson learned by regimental, battalion, and company commanders. The need to observe the terrain and the movements of enemy and friendly troops was paramount. The small unit commander's proper location in battle was at a vantage point from which he could see the fight, not in a command post attempting to make decisions based on dated information and the study of a map. However, army literature advised commanders leading from the front to avoid unnecessary exposure to danger. The best frontline commanders were aggressive and took chances but conscientiously avoided unneeded risks to themselves and their soldiers. "Dead heroes are of little further use to their units" and "bravery must be supplemented by brainwork" were constant themes in leadership training. Heavy casualties among the chain of command made commanders train and prepare their subordinates to take charge in the event the commander was killed. In Italy one division commander reported that he lost two regimental commanders, nine battalion commanders, and forty-three company commanders all in one twenty-day span, which illustrated the "need for second and third string replacements to step promptly into the job and carry on." Training subordinates so that they could take the place of fallen commanders was a significant challenge to most units.[30]

American soldiers also discovered many things about combat that they had not anticipated. During peacetime exercises, units tried to outmaneuver one another with quick, lightning thrusts conducted by commanders who believed that in war spirited attacks would help them retain the initiative. However, the notion of high-speed combat was one of the army's first conceptual casualties, as commanders learned that movement on the battlefield was relatively slow and deliberate. In peacetime, commanders only worried about maneuvering and controlling their units and put little emphasis on supply and the specific problems of actually coming to grips with the enemy. Caring for the wounded, handling enemy prisoners, rearming and refueling, gathering and analyzing tactical intelligence, and coordinating a myriad of other requirements ignored in peacetime created demands that retarded the tempo of combat. Locating enemy positions, the effects of fatigue and fear, enemy firepower, and the problems of soldiers huddling together and failing to maneuver under fire were other factors that slowed the American fighting machine. In 1944 a division commander in Italy wrote that the peacetime army had been guilty of rewarding officers for "grandstand moves" that were impossible on the battlefield and gave a "false impression" of what could be accomplished in combat.[31]

However, the army began to institute a variety of techniques to ensure combat would not degenerate into a costly, plodding ordeal. American generals began to differentiate between the concepts of "haste" and "speed." In North Africa some American units conducted rapid attacks just as they had done in peacetime, with little regard for reconnaissance and planning. Axis defenders firing from concealed positions easily brought such uncoordinated attacks to a quick halt. American commanders who too eagerly pushed their troops forward hoping to overwhelm the enemy with the pace of their onslaught were accused of acting with "haste." The army began to emphasize the need for planning at the small unit level but insisted that units could recover time lost to planning through "speed." Soldiers carried out attacks with "speed" by moving quickly from one reconnoitered position to the next and rapidly executing reaction drills practiced in training and rehearsals. Commanders added to the "speed" of their units with rapid decision-making, contingency planning for surprise enemy moves, and forethought on how to handle anticipated problems.[32]

While companies and battalions learned that spirited but ill-prepared attacks produced heavy casualties, higher headquarters soon realized that meticulous preparation and coordination were required for success. Thorough and complete planning was the only way to ensure that all resources were brought to bear in a coordinated fashion. Regimental, division, and corps headquarters had to take the time to conduct detailed analyses of the terrain and enemy situation, to plan supporting fires, to ensure proper medical and maintenance support, to issue thorough orders, and to effect coordination with the commands on their flanks.[33] The commander of the 2d Armored Division best articulated the newfound conviction that detailed planning, rather than élan, won battles:

The mark of a well-trained and superior outfit is the deliberate and assured way it goes into battle, checking on every detail, seeing that everything is set, making provisions for what will probably happen in the immediate future. The mark of a Boy Scout division is its great industry, its hurry and bluster and lack of appreciation for and attention to intimate details that go to make up coordination and assured effort.[34]

By the summer of 1944 division and regimental commanders in Italy were convinced that no operation should be undertaken unless all the "proper and necessary means are made available" to conduct offensives with a reasonable assurance of success.[35]

Like so many soldiers in previous wars, Americans entered battle believing that combat would only strengthen them and improve their performance. Although actual campaigning did transform most units into hardened, veteran outfits, the stress of battle caused others to flounder or fall apart. The degree to which units benefited from battle was a function of the competency of their leadership and the effectiveness of their training and preparation. The campaigns of 1943 proved that new divisions with sound training and competent leaders could perform as well as veteran divisions. However, unprepared divisions with poor leadership could not withstand the stress of battle and were incapable of learning from their mistakes. Furthermore, repeated failures by unready commands shook the confidence of both the individual soldier and the entire unit, making the transition from unblooded novices to experienced veterans even more difficult. General Eisenhower reported that the Sicilian campaign "thoroughly exploded and disproved" the "mistaken notion" that the value of precombat training was minimal because troops could only learn the crafts of soldiering and become effective warriors after having experienced actual combat operations.[36]

Battles in the Mediterranean basin also educated the army to a number of specific procedures that enhanced combat performance. In Tunisia, units were invariably subjected to German artillery fire and counterattacks immediately after seizing their objectives. Commanders soon learned not to consolidate their defenses on the enemy's abandoned positions but to push on beyond the objective area. By continuing to advance, American units avoided enemy artillery fire preregistered on the Germans' own abandoned defensive positions and disrupted the defenders' plans for hasty counterattacks. Senior commanders soon found out that even the best units were capable of only limited, continuous enemy contact and that troops passed their peak efficiency after three days of nonstop combat. When possible, division commanders tried to maintain a reserve that allowed them to rotate tired units out of the line periodically. In the aftermath of the battle of Kasserine Pass, the army began to fear that captured soldiers might have given the Germans valuable information. For almost a year the army de-emphasized the need to provide soldiers with detailed information. However, by the beginning of the Italian campaign, small unit leaders had relearned the principle that all soldiers should be given as much information as possible on the enemy situation and the missions and plans of their unit and adjacent outfits.

Extended campaigning demolished the peacetime notion that a complaining soldier was a happy soldier. Unnecessary, continuous discomfort and stress were not required to convert soldiers into battle-hardened veterans. In fact, American leadership became convinced that subjecting soldiers to avoidable misery sapped the emotional and physical strength needed for battle. Although operations in Sicily and Tunisia had been relatively short or intermittent, continuous combat in Italy precipitated an entirely new problem for the army. Commanders began to notice that troops who had been in the line for extended periods suddenly became apathetic or emotionally unstable. By the late winter of 1943–1944, American forces in Italy had suffered almost 2,000 cases of combat exhaustion. These casualties were a new challenge to American leadership and medical channels, and there was no known cure other than rest. Combat exhaustion was a phenomenon that the army had limited experience in preventing or treating, and it would plague formations during extended operations in the ETO.[37]

While the army tried to assimilate lessons learned, it also worked to correct several significant training deficiencies that left American soldiers unprepared for some situations they faced almost daily on the battlefield. Mine warfare was perhaps the most serious training deficit. The prewar army failed to anticipate or realize the great tactical importance of mines and booby traps and preached that mine warfare was the exclusive realm of the combat engineers. However, the Tunisian campaign taught American generals that all units had to become proficient in mine detection, disarming, and clearing. Also lacking was expertise in infantry units' ability to plan and conduct patrols. Before the war, company grade officers believed that intelligence channels would provide them with detailed information about the enemy, but small unit leaders quickly learned that only they could obtain the particular specifics of enemy locations and activities. Continuous, aggressive patrolling by patrol teams formed and trained in infantry companies was the only means commanders had of gathering detailed, timely intelligence. Inadequate weapons training was another problem. Although troops received thorough training in the handling of their principal firearm, they received almost no instruction in how to operate other rifles or crew-served weapons. Combat convinced the army that soldiers had to be trained to operate all weapons organic to their unit. In addition, soldiers needed vehicle and aircraft recognition training, more knowledge of the capabilities of enemy weapons, and the ability to distinguish between the various sounds of Allied and Axis airplanes, vehicles, and weaponry. Peacetime training did not teach troops enough about how to maintain themselves, their equipment, or their weapons during extended field operations.[38]

As American commanders worked to fix shortcomings in their units, they became increasingly aware of another significant problem well beyond their capacity to solve: the unsatisfactory quality of individual replacements and the caliber of officer replacements. In the fall of 1943 a large majority of veteran division commanders indicated their dissatisfaction with most junior officer replacements, who were "lacking in aggressive leadership, self-reliance, and the ability to meet emergencies." Although training and leadership deficiencies accounted for many junior officer problems, lack of practical field experience hampered their best efforts. Leading their troops into battle, inexperienced junior officers quickly became veterans or casualties. The most troubling aspect of the officer replacement system was cumbersome personnel policies that prohibited the reclassification of officers who failed in combat. For example, commanders could relieve infantry officers who had not performed well, but they had to be reassigned to an infantry position elsewhere instead of being transferred to a new military specialty. Only stateside personnel boards convened by the AGF had the power to reclassify unfit officers.[39]

The quality of enlisted soldier replacements was a point of even greater concern. Most replacements had adequate knowledge of their personal weapon and equipment, but they were unprepared to live and fight on the front lines. Commanders complained that new troops lacked aggressiveness and initiative, and experienced soldiers had to spend an inordinate amount of time shepherding and prodding the new arrivals. Junior officers also believed the average replacement soldier did not hate the enemy enough, lacked the killer instinct, and tended to fraternize with enemy prisoners of war (PW). Because of these problems, new troops needed additional, remedial training before they entered combat.[40]

At least two factors accounted for the mediocre quality of replacement troops. Manpower and mobilization decisions early in the war resulted in much of the nation's most qualified manpower serving in the navy, marines, or AAF. After the Selective Service System went into effect, the army still tended not to send the best draftees to the AGF. These decisions galled senior army leaders in the AGF and in the overseas theaters, who argued that the policies were flawed and that it took as much intelligence to make a good soldier as it did a good sailor or airman. The final outcome was that ground combat units failed to receive their proportionate share of high quality volunteers and draftees.[41]

The second reason for the poor quality of new troops was the excessive transit time within the replacement system. After his basic training, the typical soldier spent from four to five months traveling overseas to his new unit, a sojourn that deteriorated his morale, discipline, training, and physical fitness. While making their way toward the front lines, replacements were often unsupervised and grouped in replacement depots with casualties, battle-fatigue cases, and misfits from combat units, an experience that either frightened or demoralized new soldiers. Once a replacement reached his unit, he usually underwent an intensive refresher course in basic soldiering tasks. Unfortunately, soldiers sent to divisions already in combat and suffering heavy losses did not receive additional training and were put directly onto the firing line where more often than not they became instant casualties. The individual replacement system was barely adequate during the early campaigns, and in the spring of 1944 it was unclear if the system would meet the army's increased needs during the heavy fighting expected in Western Europe.[42]

The American army displayed a number of common traits as it attempted to adapt in combat and to repair shortcomings in tactics, equipment, and organization that became apparent during the early battles in North Africa and the Mediterranean. The army was quick to identify problems with combined arms warfare and to take tentative steps to improve the combined arms team's effectiveness. The process of gathering and evaluating lessons learned and other needs for change was comprehensive. Senior generals and common soldiers alike were quick to articulate new ideas and techniques intended to improve their performance. However, the learning environment was very unstructured, with ideas for adaptations coming from a wide number of sources. Although the process encouraged initiative and ingenuity, there was no centralized system of control. Higher headquarters observed change in subordinate units, but there was no formal means to ensure that positive adaptation was occurring throughout the army. Systems for inspecting and monitoring training and the proper implementation of tactical and technical improvisations did not exist. Still, the fact that the American army was capable of identifying and correcting its deficiencies was even apparent to the enemy. In May 1943 the German high command discerned that American forces had the ability to learn on the battlefield and would develop quickly into worthy opponents. An evaluation of the American performance in North Africa concluded that despite defects in leadership and a lack of experience, the Americans were quick to learn from their mistakes and certainly would improve over time.[43]

Several methods marked the adaptation process. The army displayed a strong ability for disseminating what it had learned on the battlefield. A substantial majority of after-action reports, training pamphlets, other types of literature, and commanders' conferences were dedicated to passing on the lessons learned. For the most part, changes in tactics and the use of weapons took place during combat with short lulls providing opportunities for remedial combined arms training. Interludes between operations in Tunisia, Sicily, and Italy allowed for more thorough training periods. Units were willing to use existing, available resources to fix problems rather than demanding more troops and equipment as an easy solution. Commanders accepted the idea that they would have to fight and win using the troops and equipment already in their units. The army was quick to identify several differences between peacetime training and actual combat. Generals discovered that campaigning required equal amounts of maneuver and hard fighting and that clear choices between capturing terrain or destroying enemy forces usually did not exist. Officers began to recognize the need for new command and leadership styles. Troops learned a wide variety of lessons that helped them successfully live and fight on the front lines for extended periods.

Despite its early weaknesses, the army displayed several broad strengths that had long-term significance. Combat proved that the army's fundamental doctrines on warfare were correct; there was no need to suspend or slow the tempo of operations while the army reevaluated its broad, institutional approach. In only two areas—antitank warfare and air-ground operations—did doctrine need major revisions. Convinced that the army's doctrine was correct, field commanders were free to concentrate all of their efforts on prosecuting the war and addressing more specific, immediate problems. Leadership at all levels displayed the ability to produce practical and sometimes ingenious answers to difficult problems and then to implement the solutions during fighting. Combat in 1942–1944 saw great improvements in air-ground operations, better coordination of the combined arms team, and new tactical methods employed by each of the combat arms. After an inauspicious start, air-ground operations began to show promise with the HORSEFLY control system, and heavy bombers demonstrated some potential as a powerful air-ground weapon. Staffs displayed the ability to concentrate and coordinate vast amounts of firepower, and soldiers had a knack for mechanical mastery of their weapons and for determining the best ways to employ them in battle.

Still, the performance of units in the Mediterranean seemed to justify concerns over the army's ability to mount a successful cross-channel attack in 1942. Although American operations had achieved all of their objectives, U.S. forces had displayed the symptoms of an inexperienced, expanding army trying to come to grips with increasingly difficult missions. Widespread problems in tank-infantry coordination, the absence of an effective CAS system, organizational problems with separate tank and TD battalions, the lack of quality replacements, and a number of other difficulties continued to hamper the army prior to D-Day.

But the time to repair these problems ran out in the last days of May 1944, as the U.S. First Army began to board shipping that would carry it to the beaches of Normandy. In addition to the deficiencies identified in the Mediterranean, bad weather, inhospitable terrain, and a veteran enemy battling from prepared defenses were additional challenges awaiting the American army in Europe. Since 1942 American commanders had anticipated the difficulties they would encounter during offensives aimed at the very heart of the Third Reich as well as the challenge of repairing shortcomings within their own formations. On 6 June 1944, the time finally had arrived to confront and overcome these obstacles.

CHAPTER TWO

Busting the Bocage

What held us up at first was that we originally were organized to assault the beach, suffered a lot of casualties among key men, then hit another kind of warfare for which we were not organized. We had to assemble replacements and reorganize. Now we have had time to reorganize and give this hedgerow warfare some thought. I think we will go next time.

—*Brig. Gen. Norman D. Cota, on the 29th Infantry Division's experience in Normandy*

Although the Allies had scored several victories in the Mediterranean, the senior American and British leadership fully realized that the ultimate purpose of all their efforts was a successful cross-channel attack followed by offensives that would carry their armies into Nazi Germany. On 12 February 1944, the Combined Chiefs of Staff issued a directive to General Eisenhower outlining the broad purpose and general conduct of operations on the Continent. At the very heart of the directive was the Combined Chiefs' mission statement to Eisenhower, a single sentence sublime in its simplicity: "You will enter the continent of Europe and, in conjunction with the other United Nations, undertake operations aimed at the heart of Germany and the destruction of her armed forces."[1] In one breath the Combined Chiefs summarized the purpose of American and British operations for the remainder of the war and outlined the broad blueprint for Allied victory in Europe. Every American division, regiment, and battalion fighting among the cities, forests, and rivers of the ETO could directly relate its efforts to the Combined Chiefs' mission statement to the Supreme Allied Commander.

The first steps toward the ultimate goal of destroying Nazi Germany took shape as the key concepts of Operation OVERLORD. The senior Allied leadership was in wide agreement about the overall strategy for the invasion, which consisted of three phases. The first was the seizure and establishment of secure beachheads large enough to permit the landing of substantial forces and adequate supplies. The second phase called for expanding the coastal enclaves into a substantial lodgment area. In the final phase, the British and American armies would conduct a powerful attack to rupture the German army's defenses and then push beyond the pe-

31

rimeter of the lodgment area. The Allied armies would break out of
Normandy with the British and Canadians under Montgomery on the left
conducting the main attack and moving in a general direction toward
Paris, while Bradley's U.S. First Army on the right conducted supporting
attacks and protected the Allied southern flank.[2]

In contrast to Allied harmony over the operational concepts for OVER-
LORD, heated controversies took place in the German high command over
the best way to repel the enemy invasion. The German commander in
chief in Western Europe, Field Marshal Gerd von Rundstedt, favored a mobile defense. Rundstedt disagreed with his most trusted subordinate, Field
Marshal Erwin Rommel, the "Desert Fox," who commanded Army Group
B and bore direct responsibility for the defense of the northern coastlines
of France. Rommel favored a strong forward defense that would defeat
the Allied invasion on the beaches. Rundstedt and Rommel never fully
settled their dispute, but circumstances after the Allied landings on 6 June
forced them to adapt a third course of action. Rundstedt and Rommel cooperated in concentrating forces against the enemy beachheads and proposed to Hitler that they fight a series of defensive battles while assem-
bling forces for a massive counterattack. However, relentless British
pressure around Caen forced the Germans to commit all of their reserves,
leaving few forces available for large-scale counterattacks.

On 29 June Hitler intervened and announced a new plan for the defense of France. The Fuehrer believed he had to do whatever it took to
keep the Allies penned up in Normandy and to prevent them from conducting mobile operations. To carry out a blitz campaign, the Allies
needed enough favorable terrain on which to deploy and maneuver their
forces. Hitler believed the best way to prevent this was to contain the expansion of the beachheads, so he ordered German forces to conduct a
savage battle of attrition along a strong, static line that would capitalize on
the defensive characteristics of the Normandy hedgerow country. Hitler
knew that his Western Army occupied extremely favorable defensive positions in Normandy, so he ordered it to stay and fight to the last.

The German Seventh Army, under the command of Gen. Paul Hausser,
opposed the U.S. First Army. Seventh Army consisted of three fresh infantry divisions, the remnants of four more infantry divisions that had suffered heavy casualties during the early fighting in Normandy, a parachute
regiment, and three regimental-sized combat teams known in the German
army as *kampfgruppen*. The aggregate strength of the Seventh Army was
35,000 combat troops, supported by a wide assortment of heavy weapons and approximately eighty tanks. In compliance with Hitler's orders,
General Hausser deployed his troops along a fixed front and intended to
make the Americans fight and die for each inch of ground. The Germans
lightly manned their forward defensive line, keeping the bulk of their

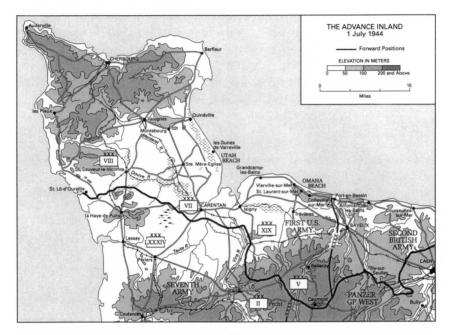

Map 2.1. The Advance Inland, 1 July 1944 (Sherry L. Dowdy)

troops in reserve. The reserves formed into counterattack units and received tanks and assault guns for extra punch. Once the German forward lines had identified the main American assault, counterattacking units were to move through the thickets and snarls of the hedgerow country onto the enemy's flanks and rear. Well aware of the hedgerows that favored their defensive efforts, the Germans called these tactics "bush warfare."

In addition to the dispositions and fighting ability of the German army, the features of the French countryside had a particularly strong influence on American operations. (See Map 2.1.) The terrain in the British sector on the Allied left was an expanse of gently rolling pastures and cultivated fields suited for mechanized warfare, but the ground held by the U.S. First Army did not facilitate mobile operations. First Army was responsible for a frontage of more than fifty miles that stretched westward from the village of Caumont to the port of Cherbourg. The American left, the ground between the boundary line with the British and the Vire River, was broken and uneven, a patchwork of small hills, low ridges, narrow rivers, and steep valleys that hampered long-range observation and impeded cross-country movement. The center of the American sector was low ground containing extensive marshlands of soft, moist soil that made travel by foot difficult and vehicle traffic almost impossible. Heavy rains made the marshlands even less trafficable, restricting movement to the few asphalt roads that traversed the bogs. On the American right the terrain was more favorable. Between the marshes in the center of the sector and the coastline on the extreme right flank, a group of hills rose up to dominate the northern end of the Cotentin Peninsula all the way to Cherbourg.

The compartmentalized nature of the countryside was the most striking feature of the terrain in the First Army sector. The swamplands restricted all cross-country maneuver, making the use and control of the road network a necessity, while the natural, uneven lay of the land in the rest of the sector made command and control of deployed forces extremely difficult. Despite these natural obstacles, the most pervasive and formidable barrier in the American sector was man-made.

For centuries Norman farmers had followed the practice of enclosing the plots of their arable land, pastures as well as orchards, with thick hedgerows known to the French as *bocage*. The hedgerow country in the American sector started about ten miles inland from the Normandy beaches and extended in a wide swath from Caumont on the American left to the western coast of the Cotentin Peninsula. In reality the hedgerows are sturdy embankments, half earth, half hedge. At their base they resemble dirt parapets and vary in thickness from one to four feet with heights that range from three to fifteen feet. Growing out of this earthen wall is a hedge that consists of small trees and tangles of vines and brush. This vegetation has a thickness of between one to three feet and varies in height from three to fifteen feet. Originally intended to serve as fences to mark land boundaries, to keep in livestock, and to prevent the erosion of the land by sea winds, the hedgerows surround each field, breaking the terrain into numerous walled enclosures. Because the fields are small, about 200 by 400 yards in size, and usually irregular in shape, the hedgerows are numerous and set in no logical pattern. Each field has an opening in the hedgerow that permits access for humans, livestock, and farm equipment.

The military features of the bocage are obvious. The hedgerows divide the country into tiny compartments, provide excellent cover and concealment for defenders, and present a formidable obstacle to attackers. Numerous adjoining fields can be organized to form a natural defensive position echeloned in depth. The thick vegetation provides excellent camouflage and limits the deployment of units. The hedgerows also restrict observation, making the effective use of heavy caliber direct fire weapons almost impossible and hampering the adjustment of artillery fire. Anyone occupying a high place that afforded a clear view of the surrounding countryside would have a distinct advantage.

Like terrain, the weather greatly influenced operations. More than anything else, persistent rains during June and July hampered First Army's efforts. The early summer of 1944 was the wettest since 1900.[3] Rainy weather turned marshlands into a bottomless morass and added immeasurably to the daily miseries endured by the foot soldier. Low visibility and cloud ceilings often grounded aircraft, denying commanders the air support they so desperately needed. Additionally, a major channel storm ravaged the invasion beaches during 19–23 June, severely restricting the movement of supplies onto the mainland and creating shortages in several key commodities. Extremely long days and short nights put a premium on the hours of darkness. Nighttime was used to rearm, resupply, rest, and plan for the next day's operations. Short nights limited the time available for these activities, and early dawns often found exhausted American units unprepared to conduct operations.

Landing in France on 6 June, the U.S. First Army quickly consolidated its foothold on the Normandy beaches. Elements of Maj. Gen. J. Lawton Collins's VII Corps seized Utah Beach, while Maj. Gen. Leonard T. Gerow's V Corps assaulted Omaha Beach. Moving to complete the first phase of Allied strategy by securing and expanding their beachheads, the American VII and V Corps began to push inland. By 12 June the Americans had captured Carentan and effected a linkup between the heretofore separate beachheads. Meanwhile, Maj. Gen. Charles H. Corlett's XIX Corps began to arrive in France and reinforce the American effort.[4]

Confident that First Army had sufficient forces on hand to prevent the Germans from eliminating the beachheads, General Bradley moved to implement the second phase of Allied strategy. On 14 June, VII Corps launched an offensive to seize the badly needed port facilities at Cherbourg. Collins's attack enjoyed good success, and Cherbourg fell on 26 June. While VII Corps moved against Cherbourg, the remainder of First Army stood on the defensive, warding off German attacks and preparing for future operations. With the American beachheads and Cherbourg secure, First Army prepared to resume the offensive. Bradley's mission was to continue the expansion of the lodgment area and relieve enemy pressure on the British with a full offensive against the Seventh Army. Scheduled for 1 July, the attack was to push the Germans out of Normandy and open the way for American operations into Brittany.[5]

Bradley had available the equivalent of thirteen divisions organized into four corps. On the American right was Maj. Gen. Troy H. Middleton's VIII Corps, consisting of the 82d Airborne and the 79th and 90th Infantry divisions. The newly arrived 8th Division was also assigned to VIII Corps to replace the 82d Airborne, which was scheduled to return to England for rest and refit. To the left of VIII Corps, in the vicinity of Carentan, was Collins's VII Corps. Three infantry divisions, the 83d, 4th, and 9th, were under VII Corps' control. On Collins's left stood Corlett's XIX Corps, which consisted of the 29th, 30th, and 35th Infantry Divisions and newly arrived elements of the 3d Armored Division. Maj. Gen. Gerow's V Corps held the American left flank and was anchored on the village of Caumont. The V Corps had under its command the 1st and 2d Infantry Divisions and the 2d Armored Division. Of the total number of divisions in Normandy, fewer than half (the 1st, 2d, 4th, and 9th Infantry Divisions, the 82d Airborne, and the 2d Armored) had any combat experience.[6]

However, by early July, First Army was painfully aware of its slow progress, as it fell far behind preinvasion estimates of advance. Within days after the Allied invasion, Americans found themselves facing a stubborn opponent on terrain that favored the defender. Planners within Supreme Headquarters, Allied Expeditionary Force (SHAEF), thought that by 20 June First Army would be far inland occupying the line Lessay–St. Lo–Caumont, but not for another month would Bradley's divisions occupy the sector. Commanders identified the three factors most responsible for their slow progress: the inhospitable hedgerow country, the tenacity and organization of the German defense, and various problems with their own units.[7]

The formidable barriers presented by the hedgerows and the military characteristics of the bocage seem to have taken First Army by complete surprise. Allied planners were aware of the nature of the bocage country, but American commanders had done little to prepare their units for fighting among the hedgerows. Caught up in solving the problems of the D-Day landings, American leaders failed to see beyond the beaches and paid little attention to the potential problems of hedgerow combat. As early as 8 June General Bradley called the bocage the "damndest country I've seen." General Collins of VII Corps was equally surprised by the nature of the hedgerow terrain and told Bradley on 9 June that the bocage was as bad as anything he had encountered on Guadalcanal. Perhaps Brig. Gen. James M. Gavin of the 82d Airborne best summarized the surprise of the senior American leadership: "Although there had been some talk in the U.K. before D-Day about the hedgerows, none of us had really appreciated how difficult they would turn out to be." In a survey conducted after the campaign, not one out of a hundred junior officers questioned stated that he had prior knowledge of the nature of the hedgerows. A summary of these interviews stated that the officers as a whole were "greatly surprised" by the bocage. Capt. Charles D. Folsom, a company commander in the 329th Infantry of the 83d Division, admitted that the hedgerows presented a problem his unit "had never before encountered" and that preinvasion training had "not taken the hedgerows into consideration."[8]

Even though the hedgerows were serious impediments to offensive operations, the primary factor holding up the American advance was the German defense. As First Army fought its way inland it discovered that

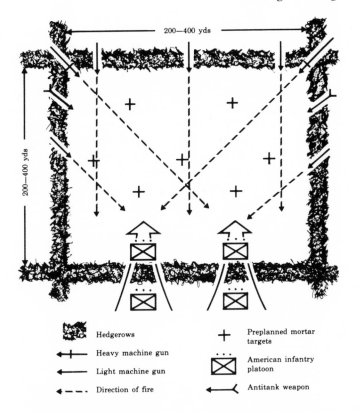

200—400 yds

200—400 yds

	Hedgerows	+	Preplanned mortar targets
	Heavy machine gun		American infantry platoon
	Light machine gun		
	Direction of fire		Antitank weapon

Figure 2.1. German Hedgerow Defense (*Source*: Michael D. Doubler, *Busting the Bocage: American Combined Arms Operations in France, 6 June–31 July 1944* (Fort Leavenworth, Kansas: Combat Studies Institute, U.S. Army Command and General Staff College, 1988), 24.)

the Germans were well prepared and very adept at defending the hedgerow country. The enemy defense was organized in successive belts and designed to destroy the coordination and momentum of American attacks while exploiting the defensive advantages of the hedgerows. The forward defensive line was a series of interconnected, compartmentalized fields. Small detachments defended each field and its surrounding hedgerows. Behind these forward positions the Germans organized a defensive zone consisting of echeloned belts of prepared battle positions. Available tanks and assault guns were distributed throughout the battle zone to blunt American attacks and to support German counterattacks.[9]

The Germans organized each field as a defensive stronghold and confronted the attacking Americans with a deadly mixture of direct and indirect fires. (See Figure 2.1.) Machine guns were the primary weapons of the

German defense. At the opposite corners of each field in positions dug into the earthen embankments of the hedgerows, the Germans emplaced heavy machine guns whose purpose was to pin down attacking infantrymen in the open, making them easy targets for small arms and preplanned indirect fires. Light machine guns and machine pistols supplemented the heavy machine-gun fire and were emplaced in positions to the front and flanks of the attackers. The Germans used their light machine guns to place bands of grazing fire along the bases of hedgerows paralleling the American attack; the purpose of the grazing fire was to inflict casualties on American infantrymen seeking cover and concealment during their advance. Indirect fire support was a key, defensive component. Once pinned down in the open, preplanned artillery and mortar fire punished American units. German mortar fire was particularly effective, causing as much as 75 percent of all U.S. casualties during the Normandy campaign.[10]

Other measures enhanced the hedgerow defenses. The Germans habitually dug slit trenches into the hedgerow embankments for protection against American artillery and mortar barrages. German commanders linked together defensive positions with wire communications that allowed them to coordinate the defense of their sector. Snipers guarded forward positions against infiltration and delivered harassing fire during lulls. Booby traps and mines abounded within the thick vegetation, and tripwire explosives were a German favorite. To combat American armor at close range, German infantry used the *panzerfaust*, a highly effective, hand-held antitank weapon. At longer ranges Germans engaged American armor with tank main guns and self-propelled guns, and used the legendary 88-mm antiaircraft gun in a ground defense mode.[11]

The early fighting in Normandy demonstrated the efficacy of the German defense. American infantry commanders soon realized that conventional methods would not work in the bocage. They initially attempted to use normal fire and maneuver tactics with two rifle platoons abreast followed in turn by the third rifle platoon and the weapons platoon. However, companies could not spread out and maneuver because of the thick vegetation and the compartmentalized terrain. With German defensive fires covering all natural breaks in the hedgerows, platoons were forced to hack their way through the dense vegetation. As the point men of leading platoons emerged from the hedgerows, they found themselves exposed to almost point-blank German machine-gun fire. Pinned down in the open in the middle of a well prepared kill zone, infantrymen were unable to keep moving forward. Squads returned fire with their own rifles and automatic weapons, but it was not enough to overpower the defenders. American commanders quickly discovered that four or five German defensive positions could pin down an entire infantry battalion and hold up an attack for long periods.[12]

Commanders were also powerless to influence the battle with increased firepower. Heavy vegetation and the close proximity of the defenders made it impossible to bring forward and set up heavy machine guns. Company commanders used their organic 60-mm mortars in an attempt to knock out German machine-gun positions. However, the hedgerows and combat at close quarters made the observation and adjustment of mortar and artillery fire almost impossible. Opponents often fought one another at ranges of less than 300 yards. Short distances made calling for artillery fire risky since unadjusted rounds could easily land on friendly troops. Many engagements were fought at such close range that even if friendly rounds landed on German positions, shrapnel and concussion would endanger American lives. Unable to observe the enemy and to call fire on him from a safe distance, infantrymen were deprived of field artillery and mortar support.[13]

The bocage also adversely affected command and control. Companies and battalions did not attack along fixed frontages as prescribed in army doctrine. Instead of attacking along a frontage of 200–500 yards, company-sized attacks were canalized into single fields. Likewise, battalions attacked on fronts as narrow as 300 yards in order to seize a group of adjacent hedgerow fields. Standard control measures and boundary lines between units were almost meaningless in the compartmentalized terrain. Commanders learned to orient their attacks along roads and paths. At company level, maintaining proper orientation proved difficult. Hemmed in on all sides by the hedgerows, platoons lost their sense of direction and without a fixed reference point often became disoriented and could not pinpoint their own location on their maps. These orientation problems aggravated normal difficulties in getting platoons and companies to advance under fire.[14]

Bad terrain and the Germans were not the only factors hampering operations. American commanders observed many shortcomings in the training and effectiveness of their troops. As experience in other theaters had shown, lack of aggressiveness was a major problem in most infantry units. Infantrymen failed to maneuver in order to place more effective direct fire on the enemy. Instead, units maneuvered to locate the Germans and then called for heavy weapons and indirect fire to finish them off. Even after artillery had pounded enemy positions, many infantry units were slow in seizing their objectives. General Bradley acknowledged that the infantry's slowness in following supporting artillery barrages was a major problem.[15]

Like combat in North Africa and the Mediterranean, the fighting in Normandy showed that infantrymen were not convinced of the potency and effectiveness of their own rifle and machine-gun fires. Failure to maintain the proper distribution and volume of small arms fire was a major problem. Infantry doctrine stressed covering the entire objective with small arms fire to keep the enemy from returning fire, but the average rifleman failed to keep up a steady rate of fire. Instead, he tended not to shoot at suspected enemy positions but to wait for a definite target to appear before opening fire. Consequently, many concealed German positions were not fired upon.[16]

Inexperience also dulled the effectiveness of infantry units. In battle for the first time, infantrymen had to rely on their training and their leaders to get them through the initial trauma of combat. Many learned how to survive through their own experiences or from the misfortunes of others. Green troops of all ranks had a tendency not to move under fire, preferring the protection of the closest cover or simply hugging the open ground. German snipers were a particular source of fear.[17] The experience of a platoon leader in the 9th Division illustrates how green troops can react under fire: "One of the fatal mistakes made by infantry replacements is to hit the ground and freeze when fired upon. Once I ordered a squad to advance from one hedgerow to another. During the movement one man was shot by a sniper firing one round. The entire squad hit the ground and froze. They were picked off, one by one, by the same sniper."[18] For the average infantryman, becoming "battle wise" was a terrible, if not fatal, experience.

Tank crews discovered that the vegetation and the compartmentalized terrain of the hedgerow country negated their best assets, mobility and firepower. The hedgerows were physical barriers that restricted maneuver, while thick vegetation and limited visibility prevented the long-range use of main guns and machine guns. At first, tank commanders were reluctant to operate within the confined spaces and tangles of the hedgerows and kept their vehicles road-bound, but staying on main roads and paths made tanks easy targets. The Germans sited their panzers and 88s to take advantage of long fields of fire along highways and trails, and preplanned their indirect fires to strike American armor moving down roads, over bridges, and through intersections. Early in the campaign tankers attempted to execute massed attacks in column down highways, but such blitz actions were usually ineffective and took heavy losses. Armor leaders soon realized that tanks had to stay off highways in order to survive. Unable to maneuver cross-country or along the road network, the only alternative left was to operate within the hedgerows' confined spaces. Because they could neither use their mobility to lead attacks through the hedgerows nor support the infantry with the firepower of their main guns and machine guns, tanks assumed a passive role and merely followed the attacking infantry while awaiting suitable opportunities for employment.[19]

It became evident early in the campaign that the poor tank-infantry co-ordination that had affected units in the Mediterranean still persisted within First Army. Many factors accounted for the weakness. The bocage rendered doctrine for the coordinated use of tanks and infantry irrelevant. Having never faced such a situation before, commanders and soldiers were unsure how riflemen and tankers were supposed to operate together in the difficult terrain. Another cause for poor tank-infantry coordination was that many infantry commanders had not worked with tanks before and lacked firsthand experience in how to use armor. The operations officer of Collins's VII Corps best summed up this problem: "More combined training for infantry battalion commanders is needed. They should know how to use all of their tools. . . . We have had to teach this in battle the hard way. The same also applies to regimental commanders." Primarily concerned with the problems of amphibious warfare, infantry divisions had failed to train adequately with their assigned tank units, and all too often supporting tank battalions were not assigned to infantry divisions until a few weeks prior to D-Day. For example, the 745th Tank Battalion was not assigned to the 1st Division until 21 April, and tank companies were not attached to individual regiments until they were already in combat after D-Day. Consequently, the exact details of how tanks and infantry should work together were largely neglected until riflemen and tankers found themselves thrown together among the hedgerows.[20]

As previous campaigns had shown, the best performer in the combined arms team was the field artillery. Infantry commanders understood artillery doctrine and knew how to employ their fire support. Infantry-artillery coordination was consistently good throughout First Army. When conditions permitted, the artillery wreaked havoc. German prisoners consistently stated that American artillery fire was extremely effective, and captured officers with experience in Russia believed that American artillery was more powerful and devastating than Soviet artillery.[21]

By late June most commanders throughout First Army realized the peculiar nature of the fighting taking place in the hedgerows. From a tactical standpoint, hedgerow combat was unlike anything they had encountered ever before, consisting of small unit actions aimed at reducing the German positions in each field rather than sweeping maneuvers to seize major objectives. Veterans with experience in North Africa and the Mediterranean had not encountered anything comparable, and training had not prepared unblooded soldiers for these unique tactical problems. Fighting in the bocage put a higher premium on leadership and initiative at the small unit level. Some commanders compared the hedgerow fighting to combat in jungles or forests; others said it was more akin to Indian fighting.[22]

The First Army leadership realized it had to find ways to smash through the German defenses before a stalemate ensued. Because of the need to keep pushing inland, the Americans could not afford the luxury of suspending operations in order to repair shortcomings within the combined arms team or to determine the best way of busting through the German defenses. Doctrine and standard procedures offered little assistance to commanders trying to develop methods that would overcome the hedgerow barriers, degrade the German defense, and restore the initiative to the attacker. The central challenge was to find ways to rupture the hedgerow defenses and get units moving forward quickly instead of systematically grinding through prepared defenses. Since the hedgerows and the confined spaces within the beachhead precluded outflanking maneuvers, the only available alternative was the one least desirable: frontal assaults straight into the enemy's kill zones. Compounding First Army's tactical dilemma was the fact that solutions would have to be found and implemented during offensive operations.

Unable to outflank or bypass enemy positions, American soldiers had to find ways to restore tactical mobility and to bring more heavy-caliber weapons to bear. The most obvious solution was for commanders to maximize the advantages of the tools most readily available to them—the mobility and firepower of the combined arms team. The key challenge was to find a way to unite the efforts of the separate components of the combined arms team into a concerted attack. As early as 9 June, First Army headquarters began to grapple with the problems of how to get through the hedgerows. In a conversation with an armor officer on his staff, General Bradley wondered whether tanks could blow their way through the hedgerows with their main guns and machine guns. All throughout First Army during June and July, officers, NCOs, and enlisted men contemplated methods to overcome the German defense.[23]

Infantry commanders realized that before their units could maneuver, they had to find a way to place heavy, direct firepower on the Germans. The most obvious solution was to better integrate the large caliber weapons of supporting tanks into the attack. Instead of advancing in separate echelons as prescribed in prewar manuals, infantry and armor had to attack simultaneously while mutually supporting one another. If tanks and infantry worked closely together, riflemen could advance while tanks delivered heavy direct-fire support with their machine guns and cannons.[24]

However, before infantrymen and tankers could operate together, they had to overcome several technical obstacles. The most pressing and difficult problem was to find ways for First Army's M4 Shermans to overcome the physical barrier presented by the hedgerows: earthen embankments and heavy vegetation that were almost impassable obstacles. Another impediment to tank-infantry coordination was inadequate communications.

If Shermans could bash through the hedgerows and communicate with their supporting infantry, the combined arms team might prove capable of breaking the stalemate.

The search for a solution to the armored mobility problem typifies the problem-solving processes that took place throughout First Army. Tank units discovered that a Sherman could drive over the top of small hedgerows, but negotiating larger hedgerows was a hazardous if not impossible task and exposed a tank's thin underbelly to antitank fire. The first attempts at penetrating the hedgerows involved the use of specially equipped dozer tanks, a relatively new invention in 1944 that consisted of an M4 Sherman equipped with a blade similar to those on commercial bulldozers. Dozer tanks normally removed obstacles or improved defensive positions, and they had the horsepower to push their way through the most formidable hedgerow. However, there were too few of them in First Army to support large-scale operations on wide frontages. A tank battalion assigned to an infantry division had only four dozer tanks, not enough to support division operations in which each infantry regiment might encounter dozens of hedgerows. In July 1944 First Army made frantic efforts to increase the number of its dozer tanks by requisitioning 278 additional dozer blades. However, units could not sit by idly and wait for supply channels to produce the badly needed devices. Weeks might pass before enough dozer tanks became available to allow widespread armor operations through the hedgerows.[25]

The urgency of the situation resulted in several improvisations that allowed tanks to maneuver through the bocage. The first expedient solution came from the 747th Tank Battalion assigned to Maj. Gen. Charles H. Gerhardt's 29th Infantry Division. The 747th was not equipped with dozer tanks, so instead of trying to drive directly over the hedgerows, someone suggested using demolitions to blow gaps in them. After experimentation, the tankers discovered that two 24-pound explosive charges blew a sizable hole in a hedgerow. On 24 June, engineer squads from the 29th Division's 121st Engineer Combat Battalion emplaced demolition charges on hedgerows during a limited attack by elements of the 747th Tank Battalion and the 115th Infantry. The attackers discovered, however, that the 24-pound charges did not always create a hole large enough for the Shermans, so after the attack, the engineers decided to increase the size from 24 to 50 pounds.[26]

Several problems resulted from increasing the size and weight of the explosive charges. The commander of the 121st Engineer Combat Battalion, Lt. Col. Robert R. Ploger, conducted an informal study of the logistics involved in supporting a tank attack with 50-pound explosive charges. Ploger assumed that in a typical attack a tank company moving a distance of a mile and a half through the bocage would encounter thirty-four separate hedgerows. As a result, each tank company needed 17 tons of explosives. Demolitions were not readily available in such quantities, and the problems involved in the transport and emplacement of enough explosives seemed insurmountable. Other techniques were needed.[27]

The engineers then suggested that explosives be buried within the hedgerow embankments, which would greatly increase their efficiency, allow the use of smaller charges, and alleviate problems associated with availability, transport, and emplacement. Unfortunately, other conditions prevented the burying of charges. Digging holes large enough and deep enough in earthen embankments covered with vines and filled with roots proved to be a laborious if not impossible task and during an attack would simply take too long. An attack could proceed only as fast as charges were emplaced and detonated, and slow-moving American attacks would give the Germans too much time to react. Engineers and infantrymen also would be dangerously exposed to mortar fire while planting demolitions.[28]

Tankers and engineers finally developed the most effective technique for using explosives. In a conference between officers of the 747th Tank Battalion and Lt. Col. Ploger, someone suggested equipping tanks with a mechanical device to gouge hollows in the hedgerows for the explosives. After some experimentation, the tankers finally equipped an M4 Sherman with two pieces of commercial pipe, each 4 feet long and 6½ inches in diameter. The tankers welded the pipes onto the Sherman's front slope and reinforced the weld with angle irons. Shermans so equipped simply rammed into a hedgerow embankment and then backed away, leaving two sizable holes for the explosives. Ploger's engineers also learned to pack the demolitions into expended 105-mm artillery shell casings, thereby greatly increasing the efficiency of the charges and making transport and handling much easier. The method proved so successful that the 747th outfitted numerous tanks with the pipe devices.[29]

Several factors soon led to an even better method of breaching the hedgerows. Tankers discovered that demolitions took away the element of surprise. An explosion alerted the Germans that an attack was under way, clearly marked where the Sherman would appear, and formed an aiming point for defensive fires. During experiments to test the feasibility of the pipe devices, the tankers of the 747th discovered that a Sherman equipped with pipes could sometimes plow its own way through smaller hedgerows, so 1st Lt. Charles B. Green decided to construct a stronger bumper device for that purpose. Made from salvaged railroad tracks, the improvised tank bumper proved incredibly strong and permitted any Sherman to bull its way through the thickest hedgerows. After proving successful in combat, maintenance teams welded the bumper onto many of the 747th's Shermans.[30]

A great number of technical innovations helped turn the tide in Normandy. A Sherman tank is equipped with a hedgerow cutter constructed of materials from German beach obstacles. (U.S. Army Military History Institute)

By late June many units throughout First Army had developed similar means to breach the hedgerows. The 83d Infantry Division in VII Corps used two 25-pound explosive charges. Engineers packed the explosives in a sandbag, buried them by hand two feet into the hedgerow embankment, and then tamped the hole full of dirt to increase the effectiveness of the charge. Other units copied the techniques developed in the 29th Division. The 703d Tank Battalion, attached to the 4th Infantry Division in VII Corps, adopted the 747th's hedgerow busting techniques and found them "highly successful." In VIII Corps, the 79th Infantry Division also developed another type of hedgerow cutter for use on its Sherman tanks.[31]

Soldiers of the 2d Armored Division's 102d Cavalry Reconnaissance Squadron invented the hedgerow device that gained the widest publicity. During a discussion between some of the 102d's officers and enlisted men, someone suggested putting saw teeth on their tanks to cut through the hedgerows. Many of the troops laughed at the suggestion, but Sgt. Curtis G. Culin took the idea to heart, designing and supervising the construction of a hedgerow cutting device made from scrap iron pulled from a German roadblock. Testing showed that the device allowed a Sherman to cut easily through the hedgerows. Because the blades made a tank resemble a large pachyderm with tusks, troops called the device a "rhinoceros," and Shermans equipped with Culin's invention became known as rhino tanks. Although the most famous of the hedgerow reducing devices, Culin's rhinoceros was only one of many such methods invented and employed throughout First Army.[32]

Culin's device soon got the attention of the chain of command within First Army. On 14 July, General Bradley attended a demonstration of Culin's hedgerow cutter and watched as Shermans plowed through the hedgerows "as though they were pasteboard, throwing the bushes and brush into the air." Very impressed by the demonstration, Bradley ordered the construction and installation of as many of the hedgerow cutters as possible. The First Army Ordnance Section assembled all available welders and welding equipment to complete the project and used scrap metal from German beach obstacles to construct most of the hedgerow cutters. In a prodigious effort between 14–25 July, First Army welding teams produced over 500 hedgerow cutters and distributed them to subordinate commands for installation. By late July, 60 percent of First Army's Shermans were mounted with the device.[33]

Battle in the early stages of the campaign showed that inadequate communications prevented close coordination between tankers and infantrymen. The din of battle and roar of tank engines drowned out voice communications between tank commanders and troops on the ground, and infantrymen could not get the attention of tankers busy inside their vehicles. The most significant problem was that the majority of tank and infantry radios operated on different wavelengths. Of the seven radios authorized in an infantry company, only the company commander's transmitted and received with tank radios. Conversely, in a tank platoon only the platoon leader and the platoon sergeant had radios that netted with an infantry company commander's radio.[34]

Soldiers were quick to improvise several solutions to communication problems. One technique involved the use of two infantry field telephones. Infantrymen strapped one phone onto the rear of a Sherman's back deck and then connected it by wire to a second phone located inside the tank turret. By using the back deck telephone, soldiers could direct tankers against concealed German positions. However, infantrymen were forced to expose themselves to enemy fire while talking on the back deck telephone. Some units tried to solve the problem by letting a long strand of communications wire trail behind the tank. Infantrymen then connected a field telephone to the end of the trailing wire and talked with the tank crew from a safer position. However, dangling wires often accidentally broke, pulled loose from the tank, or got entangled in the tank's treads. Infantrymen and tank crews discovered the best way to communicate was through a tank interphone box connected directly into the tank's intercom system and mounted on a Sherman's back deck in an empty ammunition container. To talk with tankers, infantrymen simply plugged a radio handset into the interphone box. The handset's long cord permitted soldiers to lie down behind or underneath the tank and protect themselves while talking to the tank crew. By mid-July, many divisions in First Army used field expedient methods for tank-infantry communications.[35]

Units also found ways to facilitate better radio communications. Tank and infantry outfits tried to increase the span of control by procuring additional radios. Tank platoon leaders in some units acquired extra manpack armor radios for use by the infantry. Other tank units tried to install infantry radios in their vehicles, but with poor results. A popular method of increasing command and control was for infantry commanders to ride in the command vehicle of the attached armor unit, using a manpack infantry radio to control the movements of his platoons and attached tanks simultaneously.[36]

Troops developed a wide variety of visual signals and standing operating procedures to coordinate their actions. Because tankers and infantrymen used different standard hand and arm signals, soldiers had to develop new signals for various functions. Tank-infantry teams invented signals for "commence fire," "cease fire," and to indicate the location of enemy positions. Leaders also used smoke grenades and flares to control their subordinates. Many infantry squad and platoon leaders carried rifles that fired tracer bullets for use in marking targets. Infantry commanders learned to assign the same squads to work with supporting tanks and found that familiarity between tank crews and infantry squads greatly increased soldiers' confidence and proficiency.[37]

Inadequate observation of artillery targets was another problem that adversely affected combined arms operations. Operating in the flat hedgerow thickets, artillery FOs could not see well enough to adjust fire onto German positions or targets in the rear. A shortage of FOs also hampered operations. Artillery battalions normally assigned one FO to each rifle platoon in an infantry company, while tank companies received only one FO for use by the company commander. Because tank companies rarely operated as a single unit, tank platoons did not have their own means of calling for fire, and unfortunately, tank platoon leaders often were incapable of sending correct calls for fire or could not adjust rounds properly.[38]

Aerial FOs provided the best means for observing enemy targets. In First Army each division had ten light aircraft assigned for liaison missions, and each corps headquarters had from fifty to seventy aircraft. The airplanes were either L-4 Piper Cubs or the larger L-5 Stinson Sentinels. Aircraft carried a pilot and a skilled FO equipped with radios linked to the supporting artillery fire direction center. Loitering over a designated sector, FOs called fire on forward enemy positions and lucrative targets in the German rear and adjusted barrages in support of American ground attacks. They also adjusted artillery fire to neutralize German gun positions firing on American fighter-bombers engaged in CAS missions. In Normandy, aerial FOs conducted the majority of observed target fire missions with "universally excellent" results.[39]

However, technical innovations in mobility, communications, and artillery observation were not enough to ensure a coordinated combined arms effort. With the problems of armored mobility and tactical communications largely solved, leaders had to develop new small unit tactics that would allow artillerymen, riflemen, and tankers to work closely together against the German hedgerow defense. It was not enough that technical adaptations permitted tankers and infantrymen to move together on the battlefield. A new set of combined arms tactics was needed that would fully integrate the capabilities of infantry and armor, exploit the advantages of each, and compensate for any weaknesses caused by the hedgerow terrain. Commanders at all levels soon began to experiment with methods that permitted infantry and tanks to work closely together. Units began to train and conduct rehearsals in rear areas before trying new tactics in combat. The result was the implementation of several different methods that allowed the combined arms team to overcome the German defense.

Events within the 29th Infantry Division best illustrate the development and implementation of new hedgerow tactics. In an attempt to expand the Normandy beachhead, First Army ordered Corlett's XIX Corps to attack on 16 June and seize prominent terrain north and east of St. Lo. XIX Corps ordered Gerhardt's 29th Division to conduct the main attack and to seize key terrain near the villages of St. Andre-de-l'Epine and Villiers-Fossard. The attack jumped off early on the morning of 16 June and failed to make any substantial progress. By late afternoon it was obvious that the 29th Division's regiments would not reach their initial objectives before nightfall. Corlett ordered the lead elements to dig in for the night and to resume the attack the next day. The 29th Division continued to attack for two more days, but with few results. By nightfall on 18 June, the division was exhausted, bloodied, and unable to continue. The German hedgerow defense had successfully stopped the best American efforts to smash through the bocage.[40]

Other operations in the 29th Division's sector highlighted shortcomings in tank-infantry coordination. An attack on 20 June by the 175th Infantry and Company B, 747th Tank Battalion, against German positions near Villiers-Fossard demonstrated the problems of operating among the hedgerows. Using standard tank-infantry tactics, the tankers led the attack and the infantry followed. Tankers and infantrymen failed to support one another and soon became separated as the tankers blew the hedgerows with explosives and plunged forward alone. German machine guns pinned down the infantry, while unescorted American tanks soon fell prey to German antitank fires. Company B lost four tanks in the attack, and finally both tankers and infantrymen had to withdraw to their initial positions.[41]

Frustrated by their failures, leaders within the 29th Division were determined to find ways to succeed. General Gerhardt directed the assistant division commander, Brig. Gen. Norman D. Cota, to supervise the development and implementation of novel hedgerow tactics. The tactics developed by the 29th Division were a departure from normal doctrine in that neither the tanks nor the infantry led the attack but fought closely together and protected one another while closing with the enemy.[42]

The 29th Division's solution relied on the firepower and maneuver of small, closely coordinated combat teams. Each team consisted of a single tank, an engineer team, and a squad of infantry reinforced by a light machine gun and a 60-mm mortar. Before the attack, the infantry and engineers occupied the hedgerow that served as the jump-off position for the assault. (See Figure 2.2.) The attack began when a Sherman equipped with pipe devices nosed into the hedgerow and opened fire with main gun and machine guns. The Sherman first fired a white phosphorous round into the corners of the opposite hedgerow to eliminate German heavy machine-gun positions. The tankers then systematically put machine-gun fire along the entire base of the enemy hedgerow. The 60-mm mortar supported the attack by lobbing shells into the fields directly behind the German positions. The infantry attacked when the Sherman opened fire with its machine guns. The squad moved through the hedgerow deployed on line and advanced across the open field using standard methods of fire and movement. The infantry stayed away from the hedgerows on their flanks in order to avoid enemy grazing fire. The Sherman continued to support the attack until the infantry's advance masked the tank's machine-gun fire. As they closed on the German positions, American infantrymen threw hand grenades over the hedgerow to kill or confuse German defenders on the opposite side. Simultaneously, the Sherman backed away from its firing position, and the engineers emplaced demolitions in the holes left by the Sherman's pipe devices. After the explosives blew a hole in the hedgerow, the Sherman moved forward to provide close support to the infantry squad. The tankers and infantrymen then flushed the hedgerow of any remaining defenders and prepared to continue the attack. The engineer team and machine-gun and mortar crews then displaced forward to support the next assault.[43]

On 24 June elements of the 29th Division conducted a full rehearsal in

Phase I

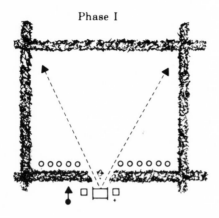

Tank lays down suppressive fire as
infantry moves through hedgerow.

Phase II

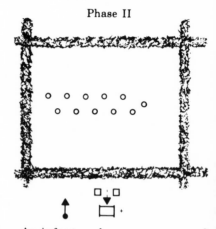

As infantry close on enemy and
mask tank's fire, tank backs away
and engineers emplace charges.

Phase III

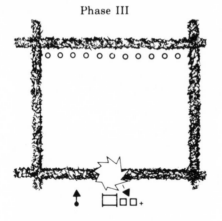

Demolitions gap hedgerow as
infantry assaults the objective.

Phase IV

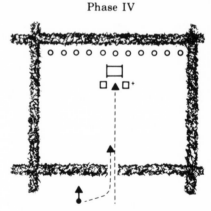

Tank advances to help infantry
clear objectives. Other elements
displace forward and prepare to
continue the attack.

⬚ Sherman tank

↑ 60-mm mortar
●

◻ Engineer team

o o Infantrymen

+ Mortar observer

Figure 2.2. 29th Infantry Division Hedgerow Tactics (*Source*: Michael D. Dou-
bler, *Busting the Bocage: American Combined Arms Operations in France, 6
June–31 July 1944* (Fort Leavenworth, Kansas: Combat Studies Institute, U.S.
Army Command and General Staff College, 1988), 41.)

the division rear area to test the validity of the new close-assault tactics. An infantry platoon, a tank platoon, and three engineer teams rehearsed the new tactics during several simulated attacks. Lessons learned during the exercise helped improve the effectiveness of the hedgerow tactics. The infantry discovered that they could not move a light machine gun quickly enough to keep up with their advance. Instead, the infantry preferred to use Browning automatic rifles (BAR) to provide suppressive fire. Infantrymen learned to coordinate their attack with tankers by using rear deck telephones mounted on the backs of the Shermans. Mortar observers discovered that by standing on a Sherman's rear deck they could see the next hedgerow and adjust rounds onto the German positions. Mortar crews also learned that they could help protect the infantry by obscuring German observation with smoke shells. Tankers found out that they had to dismount and cut away vegetation to clear adequate fields of fire and observation. And the rehearsals made tank commanders realize that they had to control their machine-gun fire closely to avoid hitting friendly infantrymen.[44]

After the rehearsal on 24 June, the 29th Division's operations staff prepared diagrams and explanatory notes outlining the new hedgerow tactics in detail. The operations section then distributed the information as a training memorandum to all regiments within the division. Units practiced and rehearsed the new tactics in preparation for their next bout with the Germans, but the 29th Division did not have to wait long for a chance to use its new combined arms tactics.[45]

On 11 July XIX Corps attacked southward toward St. Lo as part of an American offensive to push the German Seventh Army out of Normandy. XIX Corps ordered the 29th Division to attack and seize key terrain east of St. Lo. As part of the division's attack plan, General Gerhardt ordered the 116th Infantry to conduct the main attack and capture St. Andre-de-l'Epine, then swing westward and attack along a major ridgeline to occupy the village of Martinville. (See Map 2.2.) The regimental commander ordered the 2d Battalion, 116th Infantry, to lead the attack with the other battalions following in column. Company B of the 121st Engineer Combat Battalion and Company A of the 747th Tank Battalion supported the 2d Battalion. The lead battalion planned to execute the attack with two rifle companies that had been trained and organized to execute the 29th Division's new hedgerow tactics.[46]

The attack started at 0600 hours on 11 July after a furious twenty-minute preparatory bombardment by five battalions of artillery. Initial progress was slow and discouraging. The 2d Battalion advanced with two companies abreast and encountered determined resistance from enemy positions in the first hedgerows. The tank-infantry-engineer teams continued to push forward, and by 1100 hours they finally broke through the

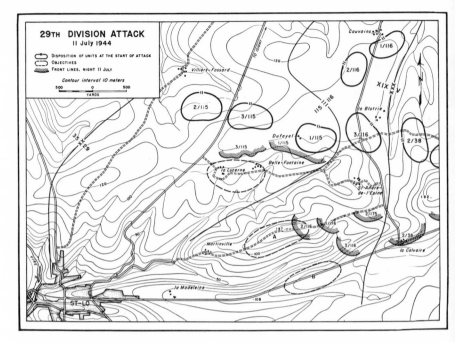

Map 2.2. 29th Infantry Division attack on St. Lo (*Source*: *St. Lo*, American Forces in Action Series (Washington, D.C.: War Department, Historical Division, 1946; reprint ed., Washington, D.C.: U.S. Army Center of Military History, 1984), 55.)

organized German defense. Enemy resistance eased and then collapsed. The 2d Battalion finally made rapid progress, seized the ridge line to its front, wheeled to the right, and continued to move. Before nightfall it had advanced another mile toward Martinville and was in an excellent position to continue the attack toward St. Lo.[47]

The 116th Infantry's attack showed the effectiveness of the 29th Division's hedgerow tactics. Compared to other operations in the bocage, the 2d Battalion made spectacular progress. It achieved a major penetration of the enemy line and completely ruptured the German main line of resistance (MLR). General Gerhardt attributed the success to tank-infantry-engineer teamwork. Mortars delivered fire on the German positions, tanks provided direct fire, engineers breached hedgerows, and infantry attacked while protecting the Shermans against antitank fires. Infantry casualties were relatively light during the attack, and not one Sherman was lost.[48]

Maj. Gen. Walter M. Robertson's 2d Infantry Division in V Corps had a similar experience with hedgerow combat. During 12–16 June, the 2d Division battered itself against Hill 192, the highest terrain feature in the St. Lo area, which allowed the Germans to observe all major activities within the entire V and XIX Corps' sectors. Hill 192 was also one of the most heavily defended German strongpoints in the entire First Army sector. After repeated assaults over a four-day period, the division failed to take Hill 192 and suffered 1,253 casualties.[49]

In the aftermath of the June attacks, the 2d Division began to look for successful ways to attack through the hedgerows. The tactics they developed and employed varied slightly from the procedures used in the 29th Division. Engineer teams accompanied each Sherman tank as well as each infantry squad. Once the infantry squad attacked and secured an enemy hedgerow, the accompanying engineers immediately began to prepare the hedgerow for demolition. Engineers with the Sherman gapped the hedgerow holding up the tank, and then swept a path for the tank through the open field with mine detectors. Two infantrymen provided constant local security for the Sherman. Follow-on infantry platoons actively probed the hedgerows to look for concealed Germans and to eliminate snipers.[50]

As part of the major offensive of 11 July, First Army ordered V Corps to attack and seize the dominating terrain east of St. Lo. General Gerow ordered the 2d Division to once again attack and seize Hill 192. The objective was just to the left of the 29th Division's sector of operations, so the two divisions were to move in concert during the offensive. (See Map 2.2.) General Robertson ordered the 38th Infantry to conduct the 2d Division's main attack. The regimental commander decided to conduct a powerful frontal assault with two battalions abreast.[51]

The 2d Division's attack started at 0630 hours on 11 July after a devastating twenty-minute artillery bombardment. The 1st and 2d Battalions led the attack supported by two tank companies from the 741st Tank Battalion and an engineer company from the 2d Engineer Combat Battalion. The Germans put up stiff resistance from the very beginning. One tank company lost six Shermans to German panzerfausts. Fanatical Germans defending one position refused to surrender and were run over and buried alive by one of the 741st's dozer tanks. However, the 38th Infantry began to make good progress by using its new hedgerow tactics. Devastating artillery fire supported the infantry advance by maintaining heavy barrages in front of the attacking units. Around noon the 38th Infantry finally reached the top of Hill 192, as the Germans disengaged and withdrew to the south. By nightfall the 38th Infantry had cleared Hill 192 and was well entrenched in positions on the hill's southern slopes.[52]

Like the 29th Division's attack against the Martinville ridge, the 2d Division's attack was an outstanding success, and the principal reason was the proper use of the tank-infantry-engineer teams. The infantry found that the tanks' rear deck telephones helped greatly in coordinating the attack.

One battalion commander reported that because of the new hedgerow tactics he lost no troops to sniper fire, although in previous operations, snipers had caused over 50 percent of all casualties. A second reason for success on 11 July was the awesome firepower of American artillery. The 2d Division's own artillery units fired twenty thousand rounds in support of the attack. Altogether American artillery battalions dumped 45 tons of high explosives on the Germans defending Hill 192.[53]

Armored divisions also studied how best to attack through the bocage. The lead elements of the 3d Armored Division arrived in Normandy in late June and were assigned to XIX Corps. By 29 June, 3d Armored Division's Combat Command A (CCA), commanded by Brig. Gen. Doyle O. Hickey and consisting of the 32d Armored and the 36th Armored Infantry regiments, was ready for combat. As troops arrived in France, Hickey's staff and some of his unit commanders talked to Corlett's XIX Corps staff about operations in the bocage. Based on the previous combat experiences of XIX Corps units, the tankers decided to develop their own special tactics for hedgerow combat.[54]

The 3d Armored Division devised hedgerow tactics that emphasized coordinated combined arms efforts by tanks and infantry. Again, mobility and firepower were the key elements in the tactical formula. Like other units in First Army, 3d Armored Division discovered that dozer tanks and engineer teams with demolitions could breach the most formidable hedgerows. Tank platoons operating with infantry squads and supported by artillery and mortar fire were expected to deliver enough direct firepower to root out the most determined defenders.[55]

Unlike infantry divisions that developed hedgerow tactics for single tanks and infantry squads, 3d Armored Division devised a method of assault based on the coordinated action of a tank company and an infantry company. (See Figure 2.3.) Units attacked on a front usually three fields wide and always assaulted the center field last. The attack began as engineer teams or dozer tanks gapped the first hedgerow while indirect fire fell on and behind the forward German positions. An entire tank platoon then attacked, with one section moving forward along each hedgerow paralleling the axis of advance. The Shermans put main gun fire into the hedgerow to their front and sprayed the side hedgerows with heavy machine-gun fire. During the early phase of the assault, the tanks moved slowly enough so that supporting infantry could move with them and provide local security. The tanks also tried to protect themselves against German close infantry assaults by always staying at least twenty yards away from the nearest hedgerow. After reaching the main German defensive position, the tanks turned inward and worked their way toward the center of the field, covering the hedgerows with heavy machine-gun fire.

Phase I

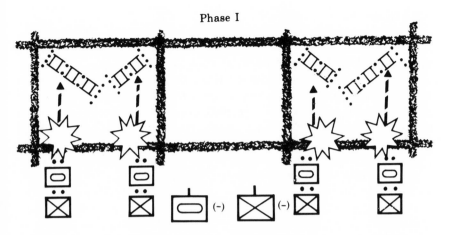

Phase I—Dozer tanks or engineer teams gap hedgerows as indirect fire falls on German positions. Tank and infantry teams attack along outer edges of fields, then sweep across the objective.

Phase II

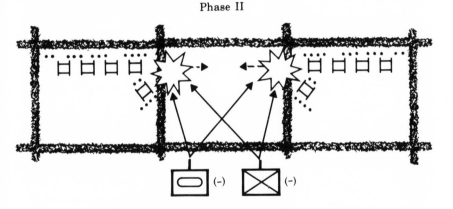

Phase II—Parent companies move forward and provide suppressive fire as friendly forces gap hedgerows of center field. Tank and infantry teams assault German position from the flanks.

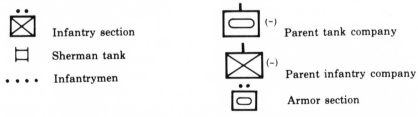

Figure 2.3. 3d Armored Division Hedgerow Tactics (*Source:* Michael D. Doubler, *Busting the Bocage: American Combined Arms Operations in France, 6 June–31 July 1944* (Fort Leavenworth, Kansas: Combat Studies Institute, U.S. Army Command and General Staff College, 1988), 52.)

Together the tanks and infantry cleared the German position and then prepared to continue the attack.[56]

The second phase of the assault began when engineers or dozer tanks gapped the hedgerows bordering the center field. Assault teams of infantry and tanks from each of the original attacking platoons then attacked the flanks of the center German position. Follow-on forces moved forward to occupy the hedgerow delineating the original line of departure (LD) and provided suppressive fire with tank cannons and machine guns. The attacking sections moved toward the center of the German position, spraying the hedgerow with machine-gun fire and rooting out any remaining defenders. Once the final objective was secure, the companies reorganized and prepared to continue the attack by repeating the same sequence of events. The 3d Armored Division's hedgerow tactics had several merits. By not directly attacking each field with frontal assaults, the tankers hoped to secure a maximum amount of terrain while minimizing exposure to enemy fire. Commanders also believed that by initially attacking and securing the outside fields, the Germans defending the center would withdraw in order to maintain the overall continuity of their defenses.[57]

On 29 June CCA, 3d Armored Division, entered battle in support of the 29th Infantry Division. General Hickey's mission was to reduce a German salient that protruded into the American lines near the hamlet of Villiers-Fossard. The position was heavily defended and at its furthest point jutted 2,000 yards into American lines. XIX Corps ordered CCA to move forward through the 29th Division to attack and reduce the salient. The attack began at 0900 hours on 29 June after a punishing fifty-minute preparatory bombardment by fighter-bombers of the IX Tactical Air Command (TAC) and seventeen battalions of artillery. The tankers initially met fierce resistance, but coordinated tank-infantry-engineer teams successfully pushed the Germans back. Twelve dozer tanks played a major role in breaching the hedgerows. By the evening of 30 June, CCA had successfully reduced the salient and was relieved by the 29th Division.[58]

CCA's attack proved that coordinated combined arms actions could overcome the German hedgerow defense but also showed that the Germans were a determined and resourceful enemy. Lead infantry elements noticed that extensive wire communications ran between all German positions, enabling FOs in trees to bring down accurate mortar and artillery fire. In the two-day attack, German indirect fire caused 351 out of a total of 401 American casualties. Not one Sherman was lost while moving through the hedgerows with infantry protection. However, an uncoordinated armor assault in the last phase of the operation again showed the necessity for combined arms action. In an unsupported blitz attack across the open spaces of an abandoned airfield south of Villiers-Fossard, CCA lost twenty-seven Shermans. Long-range antitank fires hit thirteen tanks, while German panzerfausts destroyed fourteen others. Even with the loss of 27 of its 116 tanks, effective combined arms tactics permitted CCA to reduce the Villiers-Fossard salient with a relatively low cost in men and equipment.[59]

American efforts around St. Lo reached a climax on 18 July, when the 29th Division finally managed to push troops into the city center. By the following evening, XIX Corps had firm control of St. Lo, and the Germans abandoned any hope of holding onto the vital road junction. With St. Lo in hand, First Army was more confident in its ability to control events along the front. Other battles west of St. Lo had placed American divisions on higher, firm ground from which they could launch a large, coordinated offensive. General Bradley had just such an attack in mind and put together a campaign plan that would rupture the defenses of the German Seventh Army and precipitate a major breakout into the Brittany Peninsula and the interior of France. Operation COBRA called for a massed aerial bombardment of German lines followed by a breakthrough and exploitation by mobile columns. The offensive began on 25 July and achieved its desired results. On 1 August Patton's Third Army became operational and began to overrun Brittany while supporting First Army attacks further inland. With the COBRA offensive and Third Army's entry into the battle, the Americans began the war of movement and firepower that the Germans had fought so long and hard to prevent.

For the American army, its first major fight in the ETO was one of its hardest. Not until the Huertgen Forest or the Ardennes offensive would American units again be so hard-pressed in battle. In Normandy First Army gained institutional experience on how to conduct large-scale maneuvers, and inexperienced troops became either casualties or seasoned veterans. A central aspect of the campaign is that the American army showed itself capable of adapting to a new and hostile environment. Great changes occurred as commanders and soldiers came to grips with the problems of confronting an experienced enemy on terrain that distinctly favored the defender. Troops showed a remarkable capacity to learn from their mistakes and experiences as they devised new tactics and procedures to meet the unanticipated challenges in the bocage. At the small unit level, junior officers, sergeants, and enlisted men invented ways to solve tactical problems and learned under fire how best to use their organic weapons and equipment. Not only did the army adapt, but it did so very quickly and in a great number of ways. Forces that crossed the Normandy beaches in June had evolved a great deal by late July. The greatest changes took place in combat units, where tankers, infantrymen, engineers, and artillery FOs became close-knit partners in a coordinated effort. In the preinvasion period, tankers probably could not have visualized the hedge cutters and back deck telephones that were on most of their tanks by the opening of the COBRA offensive. Nor could commanders have imagined the tactical combinations they had to develop in the bocage. By the end of July, First Army used on a routine basis a large number of combat techniques and procedures unheard of in the preinvasion period.

In its search for solutions to the difficulties of hedgerow combat, the American army encouraged the free flow of ideas and the entrepreneurial spirit. Coming from a wide variety of sources, ideas generally flowed upward from the men actually engaged in battle and were then either approved or rejected by higher commanders. Within the bottom ranks of the army, individual soldiers suggested ways that enabled their units to move against the enemy. Sgt. Culin's hedgerow cutter is the best example of a single soldier's idea that influenced all of First Army. At the opposite end of the spectrum, general officers also produced ideas on how to defeat the Germans, such as General Cota's supervision of the development of hedgerow tactics in the 29th Division.

Another characteristic of the adaptation process was the absence of centralized control. First Army staff made no distinct attempt to devise solutions for the whole command to use in overcoming the German defenses, although it did publish and distribute to all units a series of "Battle Experiences," reports that contained information and lessons learned in battle. The bulletins were not directive in nature, but subordinate commanders were expected to use the information to assist them in finding ways to beat the enemy. In fact, in only one area did First Army headquarters take an active role in dealing with tactical problems: the production and distribution of Sgt. Culin's hedgerow cutter.

What explains First Army's decentralized, collective method of tactical problem solving? First, it was not in a position to analyze systematically the German defense and produce one best solution for attacking through the hedgerows. First Army simply did not have the luxury of halting operations while seeking a uniform, coordinated solution to the hedgerow defenses; it had to push inland and expand the beachhead as a prelude to larger operations. Second, the American army as a whole insisted that the coordination of the tactics and techniques of the combined arms team was a command function, not a staff responsibility. Senior leaders expected their subordinates to develop and execute solutions for overcoming the German defense instead of waiting for the staffs of higher headquarters to devise the very best answer to a tactical problem. Corps and division commanders received orders and were expected to execute them as quickly as possible while overcoming all difficulties.

The hedgerow battles reveal a disadvantage of the decentralized problem-solving process. Successful adaptation often hinged on the competence and experience of the leaders and soldiers within a unit. If leaders were not knowledgeable or lacked experience, units could expend precious time and lives in an uncertain search for answers to tactical problems. In Normandy, commanders were held responsible for developing and implementing solutions to tactical problems and were often given wide latitude in finding answers. Commanders within each division listened to ideas from their units, learned from the experiences of other divisions, and then developed their own tactics. While commanders throughout First Army sought to capitalize on the firepower and mobility of the combined arms team, the specific tactics developed within each division were somewhat different, reflecting the individual commanders' ideas and experiences on how to best attack through the hedgerows. Commanders who did not perform well were relieved; several division commanders lost their posts during the campaign.

The new tactical methods proved their effectiveness by playing a significant role in the defeat of the Germans. Although perhaps not alone decisive, new tactical and technical innovations allowed American units to move forward while suffering significantly fewer casualties. The attacks against the Villiers-Fossard salient, the Martinville ridge, and Hill 192 by the 3d Armored, 29th, and 2d Infantry Divisions respectively, are the best examples of combined arms attacks that made good progress with few casualties. Without the development and use of special hedgerow tactics, the army might have become bogged down in a brutal war of attrition with the Germans, a situation that would have morally and materially disrupted the Allied war effort.

The battlefield changes that took place in Normandy illustrate how the element of time affects the ways armies adapt during both peace and war. In peace, armies usually have more than enough time to change doctrine and tactics or to field new weapons. The major limiting factors are usually lack of funding or other resources. During wartime, the exact opposite is usually true. Armies normally have adequate monetary and matériel resources as they expand, modernize, and change to meet the challenges of war, but time to perform the tasks is at a premium. Units in Normandy had the manpower and weapons required to implement needed changes, but everyone was working against the clock to push the Germans back and to move inland. Often field forces have the greater part of a war or the span of several campaigns to make major changes, and armies can also adapt during breathers between intense but intermittent battles. U.S. airborne forces in Europe and American marines in the Pacific in World War II both had opportunities between major battles to evaluate their performance, absorb lessons learned, and make required changes. The army in the ETO, however, did not have the luxury of changing slowly over several campaigns nor were their long breaks in the fighting. Adaptations occurred during a protracted, bloody campaign that did not give the combatants any meaningful respite until the end of the war.

The Normandy campaign illustrates the importance of precombat training in preparing soldiers for battle. Effective cooperation between the combat arms was the most serious training deficiency. A First Army report warned that the "development of operational procedures and techniques between the infantry and close support tanks must not be left until arrival in the combat zone."[60] Yet this is exactly what happened. After two years of combat in other theaters, it is surprising that the army did not put more emphasis on tank-infantry training. Undoubtedly, the lack of an organic tank battalion within each infantry division prevented armor and infantry units from training together on a regular basis. Furthermore, infantry formations preparing for the D-Day amphibious assault found little time for combined arms training with tank units. Adding to the difficulty was the fact that each of the combat arms had its own training weaknesses, and the peculiar nature of the bocage particularly exacerbated already existing training deficiencies.

Deprived of combined arms training opportunities prior to D-Day, training conducted just behind the front lines played a key role in the American success. Tankers and infantrymen familiarized themselves with each other's capabilities and methods and conducted remedial training on how to work together under fire. Soldiers had to be trained and drilled on how to use new mechanical devices and execute novel hedgerow tactics. Training conducted in rear areas by the 29th and 2d Infantry Divisions and the 3d Armored Division typifies the combat zone training experiences that took place throughout First Army.

Casualties on both sides reached staggering proportions. The hedgerow battles were an early indicator of the tremendous manpower challenges that the American army would face in sustaining the combat power of its leading battle units. By 17 July the Germans had suffered almost 100,000 casualties. First Army fared little better, and by 31 July it too had suffered 100,000 casualties, with 85 percent of the losses occurring in infantry units. Before D-Day, SHAEF planners had expected only 70 percent of casualties to be among infantrymen. The 29th Division, which was in continuous combat longer than any other division in First Army, alone suffered 9,939 casualties. Rifle companies often numbered about one hundred men, or less than half strength. Casualties among junior officers were particularly high because hedgerow combat placed a premium on the role of the small unit leader. In one infantry regiment that entered combat on D-Day, all of the company grade officers except four lieutenants were either killed or wounded by the third week in July. By that time all four lieutenants commanded companies. Infantry losses became so serious by mid-July that First Army put in an immediate request for an additional 25,000 infantry replacements.[61]

A surprisingly high number of troops suffered from combat exhaustion. As many as 30,000 soldiers experienced some form of mental disorder. For the average infantryman, the compartmentalized bocage compounded fears of being alone on the battlefield and isolated from comrades. The physical barrier of the high, thick hedgerows separated squads and platoons, making them unaware of the efforts of adjacent units. Soldiers began to believe their group alone was battling the entire German army. Thick vegetation restricted the visual and voice communication among comrades that play such a vital role in diminishing fear. The dim depths and enclosures compounded the mental anxiety that accompanied combat exhaustion, and fatigue and lack of sleep further aggravated the problem. Every division in Normandy took steps to deal with combat exhaustion, and by late July First Army operated two 1,000-bed combat exhaustion treatment centers.[62]

The American tendency to rely upon the lavish use of firepower is another striking feature of the campaign. To expend munitions rather than human lives is certainly a sound practice, but combat in the bocage proved that firepower alone cannot defeat the enemy. Despite awesome preparatory bombardments, the Germans still stood and fought and had to be killed or captured by American infantrymen and tankers. An important battlefield lesson was that firepower and aggressive maneuver had to work hand in hand in order to defeat a well prepared defender.

One of the greatest deficiencies on the American side was the total lack of knowledge about the characteristics of the bocage and the hostile nature of the hedgerow country. Despite accurate, detailed analyses by SHAEF and First Army staffs, the chain of command at the highest levels did nothing to prepare for hedgerow combat. Concerned about preparing for the amphibious landings, generals failed to see beyond the beaches and to plan and prepare for the battles in the Normandy countryside. With some training, units might have been better prepared for combat in the bocage. After the war a senior American general admitted that information on the hedgerow country was "more than adequate" and that ground units were forced "to get into the country and be bruised by it before we could really take a measure of it." The negligence of the senior Allied leadership in not acting upon available information constitutes one of the greatest intelligence failures in the ETO.[63]

Still, the paramount lesson from the Normandy campaign is that successful armies must have the ability to adapt to unforeseen circumstances. First Army devised and implemented technical and tactical solutions to the problems of hedgerow combat while fighting a grueling and costly campaign. The infantrymen, tankers, artillerymen, and engineers of the combined arms team experienced several modifications to their equipment, tactics, and organization that played a key role in the success. Because of its ability to adapt under fire, First Army performed well in Normandy and laid the foundation for operations that would carry American armies across France and toward Germany. However, significant challenges lay ahead in Alsace-Lorraine, the Ardennes, and along the riverbanks of the Moselle that would tax the resourcefulness and ability of the American combined arms team.

CHAPTER THREE

The Air-Ground Battle Team

We could not possibly have gotten as far as we did, as fast as we did, and with as few casualties, without the wonderful air support that we have consistently had.

—*Maj. Gen. J. Lawton Collins, commander,*
U.S. VII Corps

Long before the Allied armies landed in Normandy, British and American air power had mounted major aerial offensives aimed at Germany's centers of population and industry. In the spring of 1944, in addition to continuing the strategic bombing campaigns, Allied air power conducted air interdiction operations to destroy the French transportation system and isolate Normandy as a prelude to the D-Day invasion. Despite successes in strategic bombing and the systematic destruction of France's transportation network, American air power in the summer of 1944 was not yet prepared to support ground forces. Although some improvements in CAS had occurred in Italy, functional air support systems still eluded the American military. Both the theory and practice of conducting air-ground operations were inadequate to support the initial, large-scale offensives on the Continent.

However, by the spring of 1945 American tactical air power had become a key player in ground combat. During fighting in France and along Germany's western borders in 1944, senior air and ground commanders came to realize that air power was a key ingredient in achieving victory in ground operations. Unaided by air doctrine that put little emphasis on the conduct of CAS missions, they hammered out the specifics of an effective air-ground operations system. American pilots, the air control system, and both air and ground commanders learned new techniques and procedures for the full integration of CAS. Air formations adapted quickly as they sought the best ways to bring their combat power to bear in ever-changing environments. By the end of the war, air and ground units had gone far beyond doctrinal tenets for the employment of tactical air power. As a result, fighter-bombers and heavy bombers had become powerful members of the combined arms team.

American air power doctrine reached a new level of maturity in July

1943 with the publication of FM 100-20, "Command and Employment of Air Power." Drawing heavily from British experience in North Africa, and incorporating the lessons of American air efforts in the Mediterranean, the manual further defined the characteristics of air power and the command relationship between air and ground units. The first paragraph of FM 100-20 trumpeted in boldface type the AAF's arguments in favor of autonomy: "LAND POWER AND AIR POWER ARE CO-EQUAL AND INTERDEPENDENT FORCES; NEITHER IS AN AUXILIARY OF THE OTHER." Flexibility was identified as the "greatest asset" of air power because the "whole weight" of air units could be concentrated against selected targets in turn. The theater commander was to hold command authority over air units, while operational command over AAF units was to rest with the senior air commander. FM 100-20 emphatically stated that AAF units should never be assigned to AGF units except under the most unique circumstances.[1]

For overseas units more interested in beating the enemy than in intra-service rivalry between the AAF and the AGF, FM 100-20 advanced air-ground operations by prescribing the priority of missions for tactical air units. The number one priority was to "obtain and maintain" air superiority. After achieving command of the air, tactical aviation was to isolate the battlefield by disrupting enemy LOCs. The third priority mission was the destruction of enemy units in direct contact with friendly forces. Despite the acknowledgment that CAS was a valid mission, FM 100-20 pointed out that air attacks against enemy units were "profitable" only at "critical times." CAS missions were considered "most difficult to control, are most expensive, and are, in general, least effective," while ground targets were described as usually "small, well-dispersed, and difficult to locate." FM 100-20 also stipulated that in particularly opportune or critical situations strategic bombardment could be brought to bear in support of ground operations. In essence, the new doctrine reflected the popular notion that air power should not be squandered as "flying artillery" against enemy units but best employed to interdict enemy LOCs and gain air superiority.[2]

Air and ground commanders overseas viewed the new air doctrine from varied perspectives. They agreed that flexibility was indeed air power's most important characteristic, but unlike doctrine writers in the United States, they had witnessed firsthand the destructive effects of air attacks and had realized that the other key trait of combat aviation was its tremendous firepower. Air leaders acknowledged FM 100-20's call for the attack of enemy ground units as a valid AAF mission, though they believed it was not the best use of resources. Ground commanders sharply disagreed with FM 100-20's doctrine on CAS and believed the fighter-bomber should become a powerful participant in the combined arms team. They argued that the Luftwaffe had proved the efficacy of CAS missions by consistently blooding U.S. units in North Africa and Sicily. Although great improvements in air-ground operations had been made in Italy, doctrine and the legacy of prewar bickering over the best use of tactical aviation prevented the fighter-bomber from becoming a full-fledged partner in land combat.[3]

In addition to disagreements over doctrine, technical and training factors retarded the development of close coordination. Although the HORSE-FLY air control system employed in Italy in the spring of 1944 showed great promise, communications problems hampered air-ground operations. Fighter-bombers and ground formations still had no way of communicating by radio because the very high frequency (VHF) radios used in aircraft did not net with the sets used in infantry and armor units. Target identification by pilots in low-flying, fast-moving aircraft remained a serious problem. The military had to find better ways of marking enemy targets and friendly troops in close proximity to one another. Training problems also prevented closer cooperation. Prior to D-Day, fighter-bomber units were actively engaged in destroying the French transportation system or escorting bombers over Germany and were unavailable to train with ground troops. As the invasion neared, air commanders were more willing to train with ground units, but army divisions were too deeply involved with rehearsals for the D-Day assault to train with the aviators. General Bradley admitted: "As a result of our inability to get together with air in England, we went into France almost totally untrained in air-ground cooperation."[4]

The principal challenge facing air and ground commanders in the ETO was to find the best ways to integrate tactical aviation into the ground war. There was no doubt about American air power's ability to sweep the Luftwaffe from the sky and to interdict German LOCs. There was also no doubt that the AAF would fly in direct support of ground operations, but how well air units could perform CAS and the specific procedures for conducting the missions remained uncertain. Prior to OVERLORD, airmen and soldiers still did not know exactly how they were to work together during CAS missions.

The lack of a viable air-ground operations system did not prevent the AAF from preparing for operations in the ETO. On 16 October 1943, the Ninth Air Force became operational with the mission of supporting the D-Day landings and then flying in support of the ground armies. By 6 June 1944, the major combat formations of the Ninth Air Force included the IX Bomber Command and the IX and XIX TACs. Direct support of ground operations fell to the two TACs. For the Normandy campaign, IX TAC was in direct support of First Army and retained operational control of XIX TAC's fighter-bomber groups. On the eve of OVERLORD the two TACs comprised five wings of eighteen fighter-bomber groups that included approximately 36,000 airmen and 1,500 aircraft. Like their counterparts in ground units, the aviators lacked significant combat experience. Most pi-lots had flown heavy bomber escort missions with the Eighth Air Force, but firsthand knowledge of how to conduct CAS missions was at a pre-mium among IX and XIX TAC aviators.[5]

Fighter-bomber operations in the ETO best exhibit the ability of air and ground units to adapt together under fire while finding better ways to de-feat the enemy. Operations just after D-Day reflected the lack of training and the persistent doctrinal and technical problems with air support. In-stead of acting in concert with ground units by attacking specific enemy positions, fighter-bombers ranged behind German lines to attack targets of opportunity. IX TAC operations on 7 June were typical: in response to a V Corps request for "continuous fighter-bomber support" against enemy artillery positions shelling Omaha Beach, pilots instead flew wide-ranging armed reconnaissance missions south of the beachhead. That day IX TAC flew 467 sorties, attacking German vehicles and troop formations caught in the open rather than the artillery batteries firing on American units. Tar-get identification problems continued to plague operations, and fighter-bombers too often attacked American ground units by mistake. An irate staff officer in the 1st Infantry Division summed up the attitudes of ground troops. Angry over the attack of one of the division's artillery bat-talions by American aircraft, the officer complained that if all the fighter-bombers could do was shoot up friendly troops, "we don't want them over here." Within a few weeks, however, aircraft overhead were a boost to ground units and a constant threat to the Germans.[6]

The development of successful air-ground operations was largely due to the personal efforts of Maj. Gen. Elwood R. "Pete" Quesada, the com-mander of IX TAC. Prior to D-Day, Quesada too held the popular belief that air assets should never engage enemy targets within range of Ameri-can artillery. However, the intensity and severity of the bocage fighting soon changed his mind. Heavy casualties and slow progress convinced him that fighter-bombers had to become active participants in the battle. More than any other single factor, Quesada's own willingness and deter-mination to assist ground troops resulted in the development of new air-ground operations procedures and techniques. General Bradley wrote: "Unlike most airmen who viewed ground support as a bothersome diver-sion to war in the sky, Quesada approached it as a vast new frontier wait-ing to be explored."[7]

In addition to Quesada's personal commitment, coordination and plan-ning by liaison officers were other key factors. In compliance with AAF doctrine, IX TAC and First Army exchanged liaison officers at higher com-mand levels. General Quesada set the standard for cooperation by collo-cating his headquarters with General Bradley's. IX TAC staff personnel permanently manned an Air-Ground Operations Center that worked closely with First Army headquarters. Each First Army division had an AAF air support party and every corps had an air control element. Thirty ground liaison officers from First Army's G-3 Air staff worked on a permanent basis with every wing, group, and squadron within IX TAC. They advised commanders and facilitated the flow of information and coordination required to integrate air power into ground units' battle plans.[8]

The normal CAS mission involved a squadron of twelve P-47s. All were armed for strafing missions, and eight of the aircraft carried two 500-pound bombs. During ground attacks, the bomb-carrying aircraft engaged targets while the other P-47s watched for German fighters or attacked enemy positions firing on the bombing aircraft. After completing their mission, all twelve aircraft then conducted strafing and armed reconnaissance behind German lines. Six aircraft usually sufficed during missions against smaller targets. For larger operations, several squadrons attacked numerous German targets spread over a wide sector. Because of the confined spaces in the beachhead, airfields were very close to the fighting front, and pilots commonly found themselves over enemy lines just after takeoff. A typical sortie usually lasted only fifteen minutes, with pilots flying as many as five sorties each day.[9]

The difficulties aviators had in differentiating enemy targets from friendly forces was the first coordination problem solved in Normandy. At first, American ground units displayed cerise fluorescent panels to show their location. The idea was for only forward combat units to display panels, thus marking the trace of the front lines. However, fearful of attack by friendly aircraft, ground units of all types displayed their panels, and pilots, seeing fluorescent panels throughout the beachhead, became confused about the exact location of the front lines. American troops also used colored smoke to mark their location. However, units in close contact with the Germans discovered smoke grenades gave away their position and warned the enemy of impending air attacks. Soldiers determined that the best way to mark CAS targets was with artillery smoke shells. When submitting requests for CAS, commanders requested smoke to mark targets, and supporting artillery then delivered shells at the exact moment specified as TOT for aircraft. Early combat experience showed that fighter-bombers could not always appear over the target area in time to observe the smoke missions. Direct VHF radio communications between fighter-bombers and artillery units solved the problem. Once airborne, flight leaders contacted the artillery unit responsible for marking their targets and either confirmed or adjusted the TOT for the smoke mission. By coordinating their actual TOT with the delivery of smoke shells, pilots usually identified their targets.[10]

In the early stages of the campaign, poor coordination resulted in serious tactical errors, but as airmen and soldiers gained more experience they learned better ways to coordinate their attacks. Before air strikes, ground units normally withdrew about 1,000 yards to create a bomb safety zone between themselves and the enemy, a precautionary measure against the effects of high explosives and inaccurate bombing. Sometimes infantrymen withdrew only to discover that the air strike had been canceled. In the interim, the Germans moved forward and occupied the bomb safety zone, forcing infantry units to fight again for the terrain they had just abandoned. Infantry units were also too slow in attacking positions that had been hit by fighter-bombers, giving the Germans time to reorganize and man their weapons. Commanders soon learned to use artillery barrages to augment fighter-bomber strikes. Prior to air strikes, they placed heavy artillery fire on the target and suspected flak positions. When fighter-bombers came on station, artillery units finished their barrage by marking the target with colored smoke. After the air strike, artillery units once again pounded the enemy position until infantrymen had crossed the bomb safety zone and were within 400 yards of their objective. As ground units became more confident in the abilities of fighter-bombers, and pilots more proficient in spotting and hitting targets, bomb safety zones decreased dramatically. By late July, aircraft engaged German positions as close as 300 yards in front of American troops.[11]

In Normandy the most common use of CAS was as preparatory bombardments for ground attacks, as commanders learned to combine the firepower of artillery battalions and fighter-bomber squadrons. Preparatory fires usually consisted of an initial artillery bombardment, followed by a series of air strikes, and then more artillery fire. By early July the use of CAS as an integral part of preparatory fires was a standard practice throughout First Army. As the initial phase of the preparatory bombardment for CCA 3d Armored Division's attack against Villiers-Fossard on 29 June, IX TAC aircraft bombed and strafed German positions for twenty-five minutes. For the attack on Hill 192 on 11 July, the 2d Infantry Division planned preparatory fires that included over 280 sorties by IX TAC fighter-bombers, but ground haze and limited visibility forced the cancellation of the missions. Poor weather during June and July greatly hampered fighter-bomber operations, and approximately 50 percent of all planned missions were not flown.[12]

Fighter-bombers were also effective against German targets of opportunity, and aircraft played a major role in the defeat of the strongest German counterattack of the hedgerow fighting. On 11 July the Panzer Lehr division launched a major attack against XIX Corps, but by nightfall American air and ground units had prevailed. IX TAC alone claimed a total of twenty-two German tanks destroyed. Fighter-bomber pilots attacked German armor from the rear so that machine-gun bullets entered a tank's hull through exhaust portals and damaged its engine. Ground units found disabled German tanks with little external damage, but with a dead crew and extensive interior damage. Investigation revealed that machine gun bullets had entered the tanks through open hatches, then ricocheted around inside, destroying equipment and mutilating crewmen.[13]

High performance aircraft carried out other tasks as well. Like aerial forward observers in light aircraft, fighter-bomber pilots learned to use specially prepared aerial photographs of the Normandy countryside with superimposed artillery control graphics to call for and adjust rounds. IX TAC allocated as many as ten sorties per day for the sole purpose of artillery adjustment. Aircraft also performed photographic and visual reconnaissance missions that provided ground commanders with the most current information on enemy activity.[14]

The most important development in air-ground operations in Normandy was the creation of new types of FAC parties, and the concept for the effective use of FACs with frontline units was General Quesada's own brainchild. He realized that the problems of target identification and coordination of air strikes would not be solved until ground units were able to talk to their supporting fighter-bombers with VHF radios. With a direct communications link between maneuver units and supporting aircraft, air strikes would be better integrated into the plan of attack. Quesada also believed that experienced fighter-bomber pilots, not specially trained ground officers, were needed to perform FAC duties. Only an experienced aviator could convey to another pilot in familiar terms the kinds of information needed to guide fighter-bombers to their targets and to complete their missions.[15]

In a planning session for the COBRA offensive, Quesada told Bradley he could maintain continuous fighter-bomber cover over every exploiting armored column to protect them from German air attack and to destroy ground targets. The initial plan was to provide each armored column with a VHF radio and an experienced FAC. Eventually, Bradley agreed to provide Quesada's IX TAC with Sherman tanks that would carry FAC parties among the lead elements of armored columns. Communications personnel installed VHF radios in the tanks so FACs could talk directly to fighter-bombers. FAC teams also trained with the ground units that they were to support during the breakout. On 19 July a tank-mounted FAC team from IX TAC arrived at the headquarters of CCA, 2d Armored Division, and trained with the staff and commanders of that armored unit until the COBRA offensive began.[16]

On 20 July IX TAC Headquarters issued Operations Order No. 20 that contained instructions on the conduct of the new air-ground operations system:

Each of the rapidly advancing columns will be covered at all times by a four ship flight . . . [which] will maintain a close armed recce [reconnaissance] in advance of the . . . column. They may attack any target which is identified as enemy, directing attention to the terrain immediately in front of the advancing column. The combat command commander may monitor [radio] channel 'C' to receive any information transmitted by the flight of fighter-bombers which is covering him. [He] may also request this flight to attack targets immediately in front of him. Targets which require more strength than the four ship flight will be passed back through ASP [air support party] channels, and the mission will be accomplished by fighter-bombers on ground alert.[17]

Because of the type of air-ground support envisioned in the IX TAC order, the new technique for CAS became known as "armored column cover" (ACC). The 20 July directive contained the basic fundamentals for ACC missions that remained unchanged for the duration of the ETO campaigns.[18]

On the first day of the COBRA offensive, IX TAC fighter-bombers, guided by FAC teams riding in tanks at the head of armored columns, conducted air-ground operations to an extent never before attempted by American forces. Usually, flights of eight P-47s conducted ACC missions. They operated on a rotating basis, thereby assuring continuous cover over armored units. ACC aircraft stayed over lead armor elements and attacked any targets that pilots identified as enemy or any target requested by the controlling FAC. ACC fighter-bombers also patrolled ahead of American columns as far as 30 miles along the route of march in search of enemy units and defenses. Pilots sent back reports on the enemy situation to their FAC, who then forwarded the information to armor commanders.[19]

ACC missions flown during 25–31 July reflect the effectiveness of the new air support techniques and the growing rapport between the combatants, as commanders and pilots coordinated their efforts by talking directly with one another. In one case a tank unit commander asked a circling P-47 pilot, "Is the road safe for us to proceed?" The response "Stand by and we'll find out" came over the radio as supporting fighter-bombers performed a closer inspection of the road ahead. Spotting a number of German vehicles, the aircraft attacked with bombs and machine guns that disabled the targets. A report of "All clear. Proceed at will." from the P-47s let the ground commander know that it was safe to resume his advance. Tank units learned to mark targets for aircraft with main gun rounds or machine-gun tracers, while pilots became adept at conducting reconnaissance by fire in order to locate German positions. Demoralized crew members and passengers of enemy vehicles were quick to surrender to American ground units after having experienced bombing and strafing.[20]

Because of its rugged construction, heavy firepower, and ability to haul large bombloads, the P-47 Thunderbolt was ideally suited for close air support missions. (U.S. Army Military History Institute)

Fighter-bomber strikes coordinated with ground attacks began to exhibit the hallmarks of American air power: flexibility and firepower. The best example of CAS took place on 29 July when a fleeing column of German tanks and vehicles three miles long became trapped between elements of the 2d and 3d Armored Divisions. American tanks, artillery, and fighter-bombers inflicted heavy losses for several hours, and two days later ground units confirmed that 66 tanks, 204 vehicles, and 11 artillery pieces had been destroyed and another 111 vehicles damaged. For the week, IX TAC flew 9,840 sorties of all types, including 400 ACC missions, while dropping more than 2,000 tons of bombs. By the end of July, air-ground operations in First Army began to resemble the effective air support system American forces had sought since the beginning of the war. The hard-earned improvements and lessons learned in Normandy put the air-ground component of the combined arms team on solid ground for the remainder of the war.[21]

After the U.S. Third Army became operational in August 1944, Maj. Gen. Otto P. Weyland's XIX TAC flew in direct support of Patton's troops. Air-ground operations between Third Army and XIX TAC after the Normandy breakout illustrate the flexibility and firepower of tactical aviation, the newfound teamwork enjoyed by air and ground units, and the ability of American forces to adapt in combat. Leaving behind the confines of the bocage, Patton's armored columns advanced westward into Brittany and by the end of the month were moving east in pursuit of German forces retreating across France. The new, mobile war of exploitation placed unusual demands on Weyland's fighter-bomber formations. Although most air-ground operations in Normandy had been preplanned CAS missions, the majority of XIX TAC's sorties were on-call CAS and ACC missions. Patton assigned XIX TAC five different missions: to protect the southern exposed flank of Third Army along the Loire River; to retain air superiority; to conduct armed reconnaissance deep behind German lines; to assist advancing columns with ACC; and to support ground units in the capture of the Brittany ports of Brest, Lorient, and St. Malo.[22]

Third Army fighter-bomber missions during August reflect the increased maturity of air-ground operations. As Patton's armored units swept across Brittany, they received constant support from XIX TAC P-47s. In a series of ACC missions between 1–5 August, fighter-bombers in direct radio contact with ground units assisted in the elimination of seventeen German defensive positions. Immediate air support requests often required XIX TAC to vector fighter-bombers onto unplanned targets. One CAS mission called for an immediate attack on a group of fifteen German tanks deployed among heavy trees. Ground controllers dispatched an entire P-47 squadron to the target, where they dropped sixteen 500-pound bombs in a tight pattern that broke up the armored formation. After completing their CAS missions, fighter-bombers flew forward of American columns to collect intelligence and to strike deep against the enemy, ranging as far as 30 miles ahead of leading tank units. Fighter-bombers also helped Third Army Headquarters maintain positive control over its subordinate commands by providing timely, accurate information on the location and activities of far-flung American columns. As soldiers and aviators worked together, they increased their knowledge of how to conduct CAS missions, better understood the limits and capabilities of one another's weapons systems, and achieved greater confidence in their abilities. By late August Patton's troops were eager to have fighter-bombers overhead, and Weyland's pilots began to feel a newfound pride in their ground support roles. General Patton characterized the relationship between XIX TAC and Third Army as "love at first sight."[23]

As summer passed into early fall, air and ground units faced a new type of war. No longer pursuing a beaten foe, they began to encounter a reconstituted enemy determined to defend the western frontiers of Germany. By late September American ground forces comprised four separate armies stretching from Maastricht, Holland, in the north to the Vosges Mountains in the south. Tactical aviation continued to provide CAS to all of the armies, and IX TAC and XIX TAC continued to support First and Third armies. On 14 September Ninth Air Force activated the XXIX TAC to fly in support of Ninth Army, while on the American right flank XXII TAC conducted CAS missions with Seventh Army.[24]

Several factors altered air-ground operations during the autumn of 1944. The tactical situation no longer required the summer's ACC missions. The German army was intent on defending the heavy forests, rivers, and fortresses blocking the approaches to Germany. Air power had to work more closely with ground units in the systematic attack of strong enemy defenses. Bad flying weather and shortening daylight hours kept fighter-bomber units from getting at the enemy. As rates of advance slowed, artillery battalions were more capable of providing the continuous fire support that fighter-bombers had provided during the pursuit across France. The TACs also began to expend more effort against enemy LOCs in the hope of choking off supplies and reinforcements to German divisions defending west of the Rhine River.[25]

Air units adapted well and discovered the best ways to bring their combat power to bear against prepared defenses. In the attack of villages that the Germans had converted into defensive strongholds, fighter-bombers altered their bomb loads to employ a mix of high explosive, fragmentation, and napalm ordnance. P-47s first dropped high explosive bombs that damaged German units and disrupted their defense by toppling buildings and walls. Fragmentation bombs then hit to kill anyone not under cover. Finally, napalm was used to burn out or demoralize the Germans and to ignite combustible materials uncovered by previous bombing and shelling. XIX TAC enjoyed great success using new combinations of ordnance during Third Army operations around Metz in October.[26]

Fighter-bomber attacks achieved the best results when attacking targets that were very close to friendly troops. Infantry commanders preferred to use big 8-inch guns or 240-mm howitzers to support attacks against prepared defenses, but employing such heavy artillery was hazardous when friendly forces were within 500 yards of the positions. Improved air-ground coordination allowed fighter-bombers to strike very close to American units, sometimes within 300 yards. A well-placed 500-pound bomb had much greater knockdown power than artillery shelling, and ground commanders began to feel that the destructive power from air strikes was worth more than any artillery preparation, especially when ground assaults immediately followed air attacks.[27]

Artillery battalions, fighter-bomber pilots, and FACs learned ways to reduce the effectiveness of increased German antiaircraft fire. The stabilized front permitted the enemy to mass and coordinate flak batteries that were a considerable threat to fighter-bombers. Artillery units became adept at destroying German antiaircraft positions around CAS targets that had been spotted by FOs, FACs, or pilots. XIX TAC believed that such co-ordination inflicted great damage on German antiaircraft units and significantly reduced aircraft losses from ground fire. Artillerymen and pilots produced the best results during the Battle of the Bulge, when the Germans massed the largest number of mobile flak units ever assembled on the Western Front.[28]

Improvements in the HORSEFLY system of forward air control first used in Italy were another outcome of the autumn campaigns. Increased resources and the full use of the expanded air-ground liaison teams that worked between the armies and the TACs produced a functional system of airborne FACs. Each TAC dedicated several L-5 Sentinel aircraft to HORSEFLY operations. Aircrews consisted of a pilot who had experience in air-ground operations, a veteran FAC, and an officer from the supported corps or division G-3 Air staff who was familiar with the intended targets and the terrain in the sector. The typical HORSEFLY airplane carried an extensive set of VHF radios that allowed the FAC to talk simultaneously with a fighter-bomber formation, the corps or division G-3 Air staff, and the ground units directly below. For preplanned missions, the HORSEFLY crew received thorough briefings on the target, the surrounding terrain, and enemy activity. Once airborne, the HORSEFLY established visual and radio contact with Thunderbolts at a predesignated point, led the flight to the target area, and then pointed out the target to the fighter-bombers. If further identification was necessary, the FAC could contact an artillery unit with instructions to mark the target with colored smoke. While fighter-bombers attacked the target the HORSEFLY observed from afar, making decisions about whether additional aircraft were needed to complete the mission and reporting the final results. For on-call missions, G-3 Air sections dispatched HORSEFLY planes to the target area from forward air strips or vectored FACs already in the air. While HORSEFLY gathered information on the target and the tactical situation, fighter-bomber flights scrambled from strip alert or ground controllers diverted in-flight missions toward the new target. G-3 Air sections then radioed HORSEFLY with the location of the coordination point, the call sign, the radio frequency, and the expected time of arrival of the fighter-bomber flight. After establishing contact, HORSEFLY and the fighter-bombers attacked the target using the same procedures employed in preplanned missions.[29]

Airborne FACs learned several ways to improve air-ground operations. They began carrying colored smoke grenades for marking targets when communications with artillerymen failed or when artillery units could not fire smoke missions. FACs painted white identification stripes or other bright, distinctive markings on their upper wing surfaces so that fighter-bomber pilots could more easily make visual contact. HORSEFLY pilots learned that they were not invulnerable and were careful to stay beyond the range of flak and to remain alert against the occasional threat of German fighters. The TACs also experimented with using high performance aircraft as HORSEFLY controllers. P-47s or P-51s controlling air-ground operations could range across the battlefront faster and do a better job of escorting fighter-bomber missions than slow-moving L-5s. They could also use their machine guns to mark targets, strafe antiaircraft positions, or join in the attack of ground targets. However, their faster speeds prevented the detailed observation and intelligence-gathering before and after air strikes that helped make the HORSEFLY system successful. By war's end aviators agreed that using high performance aircraft as air controllers was practical, but that smaller, slower planes were best suited for HORSEFLY operations.[30]

The improved HORSEFLY system solved almost all of the communications and target identification problems American forces had experienced since North Africa. The excellent radio network enabled FACs to coordinate air strikes by talking simultaneously to ground units, fighter-bombers, higher headquarters, and supporting artillery battalions. The positive control HORSEFLY exercised over fighter-bombers ensured positive target identification while minimizing the chances of a mistaken attack against friendly troops. Airborne FACs had excellent opportunities to gather immediate information on intended targets and the activities and location of German and American units. Pilots and observers in HORSEFLY aircraft had the same perspective of the battle zone as fighter-bomber pilots and were better able to describe the actual target and to suggest the safest air approach and method of attack than FACs on the ground. HORSEFLY operations enjoyed wide success throughout the ETO and were a standard practice by the time U.S. divisions were advancing east of the Rhine.[31]

Statistics on the operations of the IX, XIX, and XXIX TACs in support of 12th Army Group illustrate the extent of the fighter-bomber's role. Between 6 June 1944 and 8 May 1945, fighter-bomber units flew a total of 212,731 sorties while performing their air superiority, battlefield interdiction, and close support roles. CAS missions in direct support of 12th Army Group equaled 69,326 sorties, or just over 32 percent of the total tactical air effort. Ammunition expenditure data attest to the tremendous firepower of the fighter-bomber. IX TAC dropped 35,000 tons of bombs and fired 24 million rounds of .50-caliber machine-gun ammunition at the German army between D-Day and the end of the war. XIX TAC fighter-bombers fired approximately 500 rounds of .50-caliber ammunition per sortie and dropped an average of 120 bombs per 100 sorties in support of Third Army.[32]

Ground commanders had criticized the AAF for failing to provide tactical intelligence during the Mediterranean campaigns, but improvements in the collection and dissemination of aerial visual and photographic reconnaissance produced better battlefield intelligence in the ETO. Ninth Air Force and the major army commands established an extensive network of air-ground liaison and intelligence teams to handle the flow of information. Eventually each TAC had an aerial reconnaissance group of two squadrons assigned for intelligence-gathering operations. One squadron specialized in photo reconnaissance and flew front-line coverage, broad area, and pinpoint photographic missions. During planning for deliberate attacks, photo reconnaissance provided detailed information on terrain features and enemy dispositions. The other squadron flew visual reconnaissance missions and specialized in deep area searches, route reconnaissance, and detailed observation of specific locations. Visual reconnaissance worked best on fluid battlefields where ground commanders needed immediate intelligence. Pilots became experts in observing enemy troop movements, tracking elusive targets, and gathering information on command posts and supply depots. Because information from visual reconnaissance had to be disseminated as quickly as possible, pilots radioed in-flight reports directly to TAC headquarters; often corps and divisions monitored these same frequencies to listen in on timely pilot observations.[33]

Enhanced reconnaissance provided additional intelligence, but not all commanders were satisfied with their aerial reconnaissance support. Problems included photographs that did not get to ground units in a timely manner and in sufficient quantities to be of use, dissatisfaction with cumbersome air photo request procedures, visual reports from pilots that sometimes did not reach units until after attacks, and aerial reconnaissance that was too vague and lacked specifics. Frustrated by their lack of adequate aerial reconnaissance, many divisions put observers aloft in their own organic light aircraft. Ground commanders had stopped arguing for control of fighter-bomber units, but problems with aerial reconnaissance prompted them to continue calling for the AAF to assign reconnaissance squadrons to army corps. Although aerial reconnaissance did improve in the ETO, a fully functional air-ground reconnaissance team failed to materialize.[34]

On several key occasions, senior air and ground commanders tried to bring the weight of heavy bomber formations to bear in support of ground operations. By diverting these aircraft from strategic targets in Germany or against enemy LOCs in France, the army hoped to employ the bombers' extraordinary firepower to alter dramatically the battlefield situation. On certain special occasions senior commanders sought to devastate large segments of the Germans' forward defensive lines and to strike deep against reserves, command posts, and support troops in order to create conditions for a major breakthrough. Much like fighter-bomber operations with ground units, the methods and techniques for employing bombers went through many changes that resulted in more effective air support.

Senior air and ground commanders for the most part were keenly interested in finding ways to use strategic air power against the German army. Many senior AAF bomber generals were against the diversion of heavy bombers from their strategic targets, but other airmen were more interested in demonstrating that heavy bombers could perform as a CAS weapon. General Eisenhower and a great number of senior ground commanders wanted to muster every available resource against the enemy and viewed the use of bombers as a powerful augmentation of their own direct and indirect fire weapons. The bombing of Monte Cassino during the Italian campaign had produced mixed results, but the attack was dramatic proof that bombers could act in concert with ground formations. However, neither the AGF nor the AAF had directed any effort toward developing ways of integrating bombers into land warfare. Army and air doctrine contained casual references to the tactical use of bombers, but no major ground or air headquarters was prepared to coordinate or control bomber forces. Nevertheless, in the spring of 1944 there was little doubt that bomber formations would help destroy the German Army in Western Europe.[35]

Heavy bomber employment in Normandy was a key development in air-ground operations and highlighted the problems and limits of using the big aircraft in a close support role. To help guarantee the success of the initial amphibious landings, First Army targeted Eighth Air Force heavy bombers against German defenses on Omaha Beach. Weather predictions calling for overcast forced the heavy bombers to anticipate the use of instrument bombing techniques. If bad weather precluded direct observation of targets, AAF commanders authorized bombardiers to delay the discharge of their bomb loads by thirty seconds beyond the release point to ensure that bomb loads would not land among the assault waves. All briefings to crews stressed the dangers of short bombings. To enhance target acquisition, bomber formations would fly down an air corridor perpendicular to the coastline. However, the best means of controlling the attack was absent: just like early fighter-bomber operations in the ETO, there was no direct radio link between the bombers and First Army headquarters.[36]

Despite intensive planning, the heavy bomber preparatory fires on D-Day produced few results. Minutes after sunrise on 6 June, 1,083 B-17 Flying Fortresses and B-24 Liberators from Eighth Air Force struck the Omaha Beach sector. Thick overcast covered the landing site and the fear of hitting friendly troops prompted bombardiers to delay the release of their bomb loads. Consequently, 2,944 tons of bombs missed their intended targets and fell from a few hundred yards to as many as several miles inland. The attack did detonate some enemy minefields and disrupt communications, but the German coastal defenses were left unscathed. For the landing troops the miscarried bomber attack was a bitter disappointment and foreshadowed the other painful misfortunes that would take place that day on "Bloody Omaha." After D-Day, Maj. Gen. Clarence R. Huebner, the commanding general of the 1st Infantry Division and overall commander of the Omaha landing force, commented that a successful bomber attack was "sorely needed" and that "the lack of this success was keenly felt during the Normandy assault."[37]

The most dramatic and well-known use of heavy bombers occurred a few weeks later during the opening phase of First Army's COBRA offensive. Frustrated over the slow, meat grinder war in the bocage, General Bradley hoped to wrest the initiative from the Germans by massing overwhelming combat power against a narrow sector of the enemy's defensive lines west of St. Lo. The COBRA offensive was to begin with an avalanche of firepower delivered in time-phased combinations by bombers, fighter-bombers, and massed artillery and designed to wipe out German units occupying terrain that was designated as the initial objective of American battalions ordered to breach the enemy's forward lines. The plan called for the saturation bombing of a rectangular area three-and-one-half miles wide and one-and-a-half miles deep, south of the St. Lo–Periers highway. After the massive bombardment and first ground attacks, VII Corps units would attack to rupture the coherence of the Seventh Army's defenses and to push deep into enemy territory.[38]

Concerns about employing heavy bombers in the close proximity of ground units resulted in intense planning, and First Army put primary importance on measures to prevent the accidental bombing of American troops. By late July ground units were familiar with the techniques used in working with fighter-bombers—display of fluorescent panels, withdrawal to create a bomb safety zone, and marking targets with artillery smoke—and prepared to use the same methods in the hope of keeping heavy bomber payloads from falling on their positions. Bradley wanted the bomber formations to traverse the length of the rectangular target area by flying beyond and parallel to the St. Lo–Periers highway, a terrain feature easy to recognize from the air that also traced the forward positions of U.S. units. Such an approach would keep bombers from flying over friendly troops, and any bombs falling outside the target area would impact in German rather than American territory.[39]

Air generals balked at Bradley's proposed avenue of approach, and argued that flying parallel to the St. Lo–Periers highway would maximize the bombers' exposure to flak, presented a much narrower target to bombardiers than flying across the width of the bomb zone, and might result in congestion and confusion as the air armada flew along the restricted corridor. According to Bradley, concerns over the bombing of friendly troops prevailed, and air generals agreed to fly the bombing runs parallel to the road. First Army also agreed to withdraw VII Corps units behind a bomb safety zone 1,500 yards north of the road. In order to prevent excessive cratering that might impede VII Corps units from exploiting the shock effects of the bombardment, the airmen consented to using bombs of 100 pounds or less instead of larger, standard ordnance. With all preparations complete, it was still unclear whether the control measures used to coordinate fighter-bomber strikes were adequate enough to integrate heavy bombers into ground operations.[40]

Continuous bad weather postponed the aerial offensive until 24 July. In preparation for the bombardment, VII Corps units withdrew to create a bomb safety zone. Unfortunately, heavy cloud cover canceled the attack, but inadequate radio communications prevented some bomber formations from receiving the abort order. More than 300 bombers arrived over the target area and dropped their ordnance. Owing to the mix-up of orders, bad weather, and human error, many bombs fell behind American lines, killing 25 and wounding 131 soldiers in the 30th Division. Bad weather and the short bombing prompted Bradley to cancel the ground portion of the offensive and to reschedule the entire attack for the next day.[41]

The bombing accident on 24 July resulted in serious recriminations among the senior American leadership. While investigating the causes of the short bombing, Bradley was "shocked and angered" to discover that the Eighth Air Force had attacked along an air corridor running perpendicular, not parallel, to the St. Lo–Periers road. Airmen told Bradley that the parallel approach was too restrictive and made it impossible to get all of the bombers over the target area in the allocated time. Furthermore, air commanders informed First Army on the evening of 24 July that they would use the perpendicular approach again during the full-scale COBRA bombardment, and that any changes to the air attack plan might result in the postponement of the offensive for several more days. The news from Eighth Air Force angered Bradley, who accused the airmen of a "serious breach of good faith" in overflying ground units and in presenting him with a fait accompli on the air attack scheduled for the next morning. Weighing the risks of another short bombing against the costs of further delay, Bradley decided to proceed with the attack.[42]

On the morning of 25 July, the COBRA offensive began with a massive aerial assault of unprecedented proportions, as more than 1,500 heavy bombers dropped 3,300 tons of bombs. Instead of orienting its efforts on the attack of specific ground targets, the Eighth Air Force concentrated on plastering the entire target area with saturation bombing. More than 380 medium bombers continued the attack and dropped 650 tons of high explosives and fragmentation bombs, while 550 fighter-bombers dropped in excess of 200 tons of high explosives and napalm on specific targets. The Norman countryside shook beneath the brunt of the aerial onslaught.[43]

Inadequate command, control, and communications reduced the bombardment's overall effectiveness. Artillery smoke shells marking the boundary of the target area proved worthless, since the bombers could not see the marking smoke because of cloud cover or wind dispersion. Both smoke shells and fluorescent panels tended to blend in with exploding ordnance and the muzzle flashes of German and American artillery pieces. Great clouds of dust and smoke from the initial bombings made terrain features unidentifiable to pilots and bombardiers in all but the first group of bombers. Unable to aim and eager to avoid hitting American troops, some bombardiers released their loads late, with much of the ordnance falling outside the target area. The Eighth Air Force did take two special measures to prevent short bombings. A weather reconnaissance sortie flew over the target area ahead of the bombers to confirm adequate visibility, and air commanders lowered bomb release altitudes to as low as 12,000 feet in the hopes of improving target acquisition.[44]

Unfortunately, human error resulted in a repeat of the short bombings of the previous day. The bomb loads of seventy-seven aircraft fell within American lines, killing 111 and wounding 490. The bombing's most conspicuous friendly casualty was Lt. Gen. Lesley J. McNair, commander of the AGF. McNair had gone to France to observe firsthand the results of stateside training programs; a bomb landed in his foxhole, killing him instantly. Initially, the short bombing dismayed and dejected American ground commanders. The incident outraged the Supreme Allied Commander, who was on hand at First Army headquarters to observe the launching of the offensive, and Eisenhower resolved never again to use heavy bombers in a close support role. Bradley feared that the short bombing might require the cancellation of the ground offensive, but as messages flowed into First Army headquarters reporting units' readiness to begin the ground attack, initial pessimism faded. The COBRA offensive went forward as scheduled at 1100 hours on 25 July.[45]

Unlike the preparatory bombardment against Omaha Beach, the COBRA air attack wreaked havoc on the Germans. Although casualty figures are sketchy at best, as many as one thousand perished, and the bombing killed or wounded almost a third of the total combat troops in the target area. Only a handful of vehicles remained in operation, and German command posts and communications facilities were heavily damaged or totally obliterated. The bombardment transformed the pastoral French countryside into a lunar landscape with a pall of death and destruction. After VII Corps' advance through the target area, General Collins reported that the bombardment had been "extremely effective" against German forward defenses, had "disrupted completely" enemy communications, and had proved "shattering" against enemy morale.[46]

For all of its positive effects, the difficulties with the COBRA bombing increased the need for better coordination between ground and bomber headquarters and improved techniques for heavy bomber employment. Grafting the procedures used to control fighter-bombers onto heavy bomber operations proved inadequate and resulted in over 750 American casualties. Using smoke shells to mark the target area and fluorescent panels to identify friendly troops was ineffective. As in early fighter-bomber operations, there was no direct communications link between troop units and supporting bombers. A functional command network of VHF radios might have prevented the short bombing of 24 July and better coordinated the main bombardment the next day. One lesson learned was that cloud cover easily thwarted heavy bomber employment while fighter-bombers could operate in much worse weather. Air leaders recognized that instrumentation and radar would greatly assist in guiding bombers to the target area and in aiming bomb loads, and that better methods were needed to mark targets. In a gross understatement, First Army's after-action report on the COBRA bombing admitted that "certain features" of heavy bomber employment in ground operations would "require further study."[47]

The second large-scale use of strategic air assets in a ground battle took place in November 1944. After the pursuit across France, the First and Ninth armies undertook a series of bloody battles to secure objectives on the German frontier north of the Ardennes. Breaching the Siegfried Line and capturing Aachen were costly, laborious tasks, and not until early November were the two armies ready to resume the offensive toward the Rhine. The 12th Army Group plan called for a coordinated attack by both armies in the direction of Julich and Duren that would cross the Roer River and continue westward toward the Rhine. Aware of the need to get the armies moving westward again after the hard fighting on the German frontier, Bradley decided to commit heavy bomber forces in support of the offensive.[48]

The air plan, code-named Operation QUEEN, called for a combined bomber attack by the Royal Air Force (RAF) and the Eighth Air Force in concert with all units of the Ninth Air Force. Unlike the COBRA bombing, no effort was made to saturate the entire target area. Instead, the air effort focused on smaller, specific targets. The bomber formations planned to strike defensive strong points throughout the sector, enemy troop concentrations, and German communications centers. Ninth Air Force's medium bombers and fighter-bombers would attack German forward defenses and support First and Ninth armies with ACC and CAS missions.

The actual date of the attack depended on clear skies but was set for not later than 16 November.⁴⁹

A series of adaptations by the Eighth Air Force raised hopes for the attack's success and reduced fears of a repeat of the COBRA short bombings. Electronic devices to improve bombing accuracy included a vertical beacon on the ground that indicated to pilots and bombardiers the exact position of their aircraft in relation to friendly troops and the bomb release point. Two additional marker beacons kept the bomber stream on course as it approached the target area. A major adaptation was the establishment of a ground control station at IX TAC Headquarters that had direct radio communication with the bomber formations. Eighth Air Force mission briefings again emphasized the dangers of short bombings. To prevent accidental bombings due to faulty bomb release mechanisms, aircraft were to open their bomb bay doors over the English Channel.⁵⁰

Ground forces also improvised several measures to mark the target area and friendly troop locations. Two large, white panels, each measuring 150 by 50 feet were placed outside of Aachen and Liege to visually mark the bombers' air approach corridor. Ground units identified their locations by laying down a long line of cerise and orange panels just behind their positions. These panels, each measuring 36 by 7 feet, were placed at a density of four panels per mile for the entire width of the American sector. Fifteen silver barrage balloons were put aloft 4,000 yards behind American lines at an altitude of 2,000 feet to identify the bomber passage point over troop units. Antiaircraft batteries prepared to fire a series of red smoke shell airbursts at high altitude that would direct bomber pilots toward the target area, and artillery battalions planned to place fire on sixty-four flak positions. In one of the best examples of air-ground staff coordination in the war, IX TAC had direct telephone and radio communications with both antiaircraft and field artillery units to ensure the maximum integration of supporting fires with the bomber attack.⁵¹

On the morning of 16 November, RAF Bomber Command and Eighth Air Force bomber groups lifted off from their airfields in England with the hope of dealing the German army a mortal blow. Approximately 2,200 heavy bombers, 250 medium bombers, and 300 fighter-bombers took part in the bombardment, which lasted almost two hours. The heavy bombers unleashed a tidal wave of almost 10,000 tons of ordnance, while the RAF virtually demolished Duren and Julich. American bombers had few difficulties in attacking their assigned targets. The massed efforts of First and Ninth Army's artillery battalions—a total of 1,246 guns—chimed in with an hour-long preparatory bombardment of over 50,000 rounds. The German frontier quaked under the combined weight of the bomber and artillery attacks.⁵²

From the perspective of minimizing friendly fire casualties, the QUEEN bombing was a notable success. The improvised target marking measures worked, and radio beacons were an invaluable aid in marking the front lines and in keeping bombers within their established air corridors. Bombers easily identified the high altitude smoke shell bursts and used them to orient on the target area. Huge marker panels on the ground were less effective than they might have been because of scattered cloud cover. Radio communications between IX TAC and Eighth Air Force worked well. The barrage balloons tracing the American front lines proved almost useless; German ground fire destroyed nearly all of them during the bomber attack. A few scattered incidents of short bombings that caused minimal casualties did occur, but they were attributable to human error or mechanical failure. In contrast to the COBRA bombings, Operation QUEEN proved that heavy bombers could strike tactical targets without threatening friendly troops. A Ninth Army after-action report on QUEEN concluded that with the "newly developed safety aids," heavy bombers could strike within 2,000 yards of friendly troops without fears of short bombings.[53]

Unfortunately, the overall effects of QUEEN were disappointing, and the ground attack did not achieve breakthrough proportions. Deep dugouts reduced German casualties and the shock effects of the bombing, so that enemy soldiers were able to man their defenses immediately after the bombardment. In retrospect, American commanders regretted that they had not attempted to bring the bomber strike closer to friendly lines and right on top of the most forward German positions. A 4,000-yard bomb safety zone had kept the heavy bombers from striking enemy positions directly opposing American units, but they were very successful in striking targets deep in the enemy's zone. Communications centers were hit hard and out of action for extended periods. Bomber strikes against secondary defenses were effective but did not help American ground units to advance.[54]

Even though tactical air power had an inauspicious start in the Mediterranean, the situation improved dramatically in the ETO. The ultimate success of air-ground operations occurred because airmen and soldiers succeeded in finding the best ways to integrate air power into the ground war while simultaneously battling the German army. Ground troops and aviators adapted to varying conditions and displayed flexibility in changing old procedures or inventing ways of making CAS more effective. Innovations took place in an unstructured fashion and sought to take best advantage of air power's inherent flexibility and firepower. American airmen and soldiers displayed a knack for the mechanical mastery of their weapons and equipment. Because of the adaptations, air power became a fully integrated member of the combined arms team, inflicted massive damage on the enemy, and helped ground units advance faster with fewer casualties.

Two broad categories of air-ground adaptations took place in the ETO. The first series of innovations was largely technical and produced a workable system of air control. AAF air controllers operating on the front lines and having direct radio communications with supporting fighter-bombers were the key to successful air-ground operations. Air support parties riding in tanks at the head of armored columns and controlling ACC missions were the most effective air control system developed. A desire to improve further air-ground operations also produced an enhanced HORSEFLY system. The tragedy of the COBRA short bombings resulted in communications networks that allowed air controllers to maintain positive control over heavy bomber formations. An extensive infrastructure of air-ground liaison officers coordinated air missions at all command levels and made competent CAS a reality. Without doubt, neither air nor ground commanders in the prewar period could have imagined the mature, integrated air control systems that emerged during the battles of 1944.

With functional air control systems in place, other innovations in target acquisition and tactical employment soon followed. Ground units developed several different methods for identifying themselves to supporting aviators and then fought without the fear of attack from friendly aircraft. Infantrymen learned to seize their objectives immediately after air strikes, while artillery batteries discovered ways to mark targets for air strikes and to attack flak positions firing on fighter-bombers. Bombing and strafing by aircraft that were part of an integrated air-land combined arms battle plan inflicted great damage and materially assisted ground units in seizing their objectives. CAS was best employed during mobile operations when leading armored columns were beyond the range of supporting artillery. Sustained air support also tended to buoy the spirits of GIs while demoralizing their enemies. Tactical intelligence from pilots helped ground commanders locate the enemy.

A key aspect of air-ground adaptations was that they took place in almost a doctrinal vacuum. The broad, USAAF concepts in FM 100-20 for the employment of tactical aviation proved largely correct, but no other literature provided specifics and the fast pace of wartime operations prevented a comprehensive, detailed approach to the development of CAS procedures. The burden for developing most of the theory and all of the practice for air-ground operations fell to units in the combat zone. Caught up in battle and unaided by doctrinal tenets, airmen and soldiers improvised the best ways of cooperating together on the battlefield. The largest adaptation tasks went to the air leaders in the Ninth Air Force, and more specifically, to the commanders of the TACs supporting the field armies. An authoritative, postwar report on air-ground operations complained that because of the doctrinal void "no publication could be used as a guide or reference during active operations in this theater." It concluded that the "splendid cooperation" between the TACs and ground forces "was developed during operations."[55]

As air leaders rejected their long-held belief that aircraft should not be employed as "flying artillery," they abandoned their prewar bias against CAS in favor of participation in air-ground operations. Once the AAF realized that it could inflict great damage on the Germans and help ground troops advance, aircraft became a vital player in the combined arms team. A willingness to participate in the ground war was the catalyst that precipitated functional air control systems. General Quesada's enthusiasm for better air-ground cooperation resulted in air support parties that worked directly with ground units, and new-found attitudes permitted the employment of heavy bombers in major attempts to shatter the coherence of large portions of the enemy's defensive zones.

Flexibility was one of the hallmark characteristics of air-ground operations. The TACs were able to reallocate fighter-bomber assets to air superiority, battlefield interdiction, or CAS missions depending on weather and the tactical situation. XIX TAC's operations in August—flying ACC missions for Third Army, providing air support against Brest, and protecting Patton's exposed southern flank—best illustrate the flexibility of air power. The TACs also exercised a flexible application of combat power by massing their efforts at critical times in support of ground operations such as the COBRA offensive and Operation QUEEN. Heavy bomber forces displayed agility by shifting their efforts from strategic targets in Germany to the support of ground troops.

Air power also generated awesome amounts of firepower. From the OVERLORD preparatory bombardments to the AAF's final operations in the spring of 1945, air units threw mountains of ordnance at the German army. A key factor in attriting the enemy, the concentration of firepower reached its zenith during heavy bomber attacks augmented by medium bombers, fighter-bombers, and massed artillery. The COBRA and QUEEN bombings were natural manifestations of the U.S. army's propensity to use overwhelming firepower. However, a key lesson of air-ground operations was that awesome amounts of firepower alone were not decisive; ground units still had to attack and root out the enemy.

The employment of heavy bombers to support ground operations was the most unorthodox use of air power in the ETO. Little was written on the practice before the war, and airmen and soldiers improvised all of the techniques used in bomber strikes. The willingness of ground commanders to use heavy bombers early in the ETO fighting was a strange contradiction. Fighter-bomber operations in Normandy showed the inadequacy of the air control system, so it is difficult to see why General Bradley expected heavy bomber coordination to occur without significant problems. Before D-Day, bomber commanders were aware of the problems of target acquisition, bombing accuracy, and the possibility of short bombings while using their big aircraft in a close support role, yet solutions were not found until Operation QUEEN. However, by November enough thought and planning had occurred so that bombers could participate in the ground war without threatening friendly troops. Homing beacons, radio communications, and marking aids prevented short bombings and helped bombers find their targets. The QUEEN bombing shows that airmen and soldiers had the ability to adapt, but quicker changes would have made bomber strikes effective sooner and possibly saved American lives.

Heavy bomber operations had distinct advantages and disadvantages that made bomber employment controversial. In general, bombing was effective against hasty defenses, communications centers, and command posts and had a great shock effect on enemy troops. Heavy bombers could concentrate their efforts to strike deep against specific targets or saturate entire areas with firepower. Their tremendous bomb weight resulted in damage and demoralization to German forces that far exceeded anything that artillery battalions or tactical aviation could muster. Extended operating ranges permitted heavy bombers to fly from permanent airfields in England and to mass against any tactical target on the Continent. On the other hand, bomber strikes were difficult to plan and coordinate, the accuracy of bombing was less than desired, and German heavy fortifications seemed impervious to bomb loads. Some ground commanders believed that bomber strikes failed to meet expectations and did little to help armor and infantry units seize their objectives. Despite adaptations to prevent short bombings, friendly bomber attacks remained a cause of concern. Air generals continued to argue that heavy bomber attacks were not the best use of strategic air assets, but General Eisenhower still ordered several heavy bomber strikes. In 1944 the Eighth Air Force flew approximately 8 percent of all its heavy bomber sorties in support of army operations. Of the entire tonnage dropped by the Eighth Air Force in 1944–1945, over 12 percent was delivered in support of ground troops.[56]

The question of whether or not air units could properly support ground forces was answered during the Normandy campaign. However, the specifics of how aircraft would work in close concert with ground units in the assault of the German frontier remained unclear. Broader uncertainties existed about how army units themselves would perform under varying conditions of terrain and enemy defenses. As the American air-ground battle team blitzed across France, the challenges of assaulting cities, villages, heavy fortifications, rivers, and forests loomed on the horizon.

CHAPTER FOUR

Battles of Buildings and Cobblestones

The general plan evolved was to use artillery and mortar fire across our front to isolate the sector, thus preventing Germans from entering . . . the area under attack; then to use direct fire from tanks, tank destroyers, and machine guns to pin down the defenders and chase them into cellars; and then to move in with bayonets and hand grenades to destroy or capture the defenders.

—*Lt. Col. Derrill M. Daniel, commander of 2/26th Infantry, on the battle for Aachen*

Exhilaration rushed through the ranks of the American army in August 1944 as ground forces broke free from the nightmarish confines of the bocage country. First and Third Army columns, supported by Ninth Air Force fighter-bombers, swept across the open spaces of Brittany and southern France in pursuit of a beaten enemy. The thrill of the chase generated false expectations as many soldiers believed the Normandy breakout and the battles at Mortain and Falaise-Argentan had annihilated the entire German army in the West. Talk swept through the ranks that the war might be over by Christmas. However, the events of the fall of 1944 dashed all hopes for an early victory. Hard fighting brought Americans back to reality and hammered home the fact that the road to final victory would be long and painful.

The advances after Normandy carried American armies into eastern France and to Germany's frontiers. There a new type of war confronted the American soldier as German units defended the approaches to their homeland by fighting from prepared defenses in the streets of major cities and small villages. Although American doctrine contained broad principles for urban warfare, units had to change their methods and discover new ways to bring all of their combat power to bear. The specifics of how a combined arms force should work together in urban warfare emerged during operations, as once again, the key to success was the American army's ability to adapt in battle.

Enemy dispositions and terrain had a great influence on the campaigns of late 1944. The German army had taken a severe beating in Normandy, but by late summer slackening Allied pressure, shortened LOCs, and the passage of time gave the Germans opportunities to reconstitute units and prepare defenses west of the Rhine. They hoped to defend natural barriers like the Moselle River and the rugged, forested terrain in eastern France, Belgium, and along Germany's western borders. The Maginot and Siegfried Line fortifications and the ancient, walled cities in the regions were also linchpins of German defensive plans. German units and forced laborers worked frantically to construct and improve defenses before the next phase of Allied operations began.

In the aftermath of OVERLORD, General Eisenhower decided in favor of a "broad front" strategic approach that called for the Allied armies to close on the Rhine River while destroying as much of the German army as possible. At the same time, logisticians were to work feverishly on improving the Allied supply situation. In the spring of 1945, the Allied armies would jump the Rhine and push further into central Germany. Montgomery and Patton argued long and hard that a single thrust into Germany, aggressively executed and supported with all available supplies, might end the war sooner. But Eisenhower's concerns over constrained logistical support, stiffening enemy resistance, and the risks associated with an advance along a single axis overrode his subordinates' arguments.

American army groups implemented the Supreme Commander's decision with sweeping schemes of maneuver. (See Map 4.1.) The intent of Bradley's 12th Army Group was to close on the Rhine River by early winter while destroying German forces west of it. The terrain in the American center—the Eifel Mountains and the rugged Ardennes and Huertgen Forests—dictated that the main efforts would take place on either side of these obstacles. In the north, First and Ninth armies would attack eastward toward the Rhine River along the axis Mastricht-Aachen-Cologne. The West Wall fortifications, Aachen, and the northern fringes of the Huertgen Forest were major obstacles in their path. To the south, Third Army would attack across the Moselle into Lorraine, seize or bypass Nancy and Metz, and then advance toward the Saar. On 15 August Lt. Gen. Jacob L. Devers's 6th Army Group, consisting of the U.S. Seventh and French First armies, landed in southern France and began an offensive up the Rhone River valley. Devers's mission was to link up with Third Army and to clear Alsace and the Vosges Mountains while pushing for the left bank of the upper Rhine. In a related action designed to relieve logistical problems, Bradley ordered American forces to seize the port city of Brest on the tip of the Brittany peninsula. During August and into the autumn, U.S. forces would be fighting in three different directions.

The German army prepared to blunt American advances with the tenacious defense of urban centers and small villages. Americans had little practical experience in street fighting and drew most of their know-how from publications and training. The army's writings on urban warfare

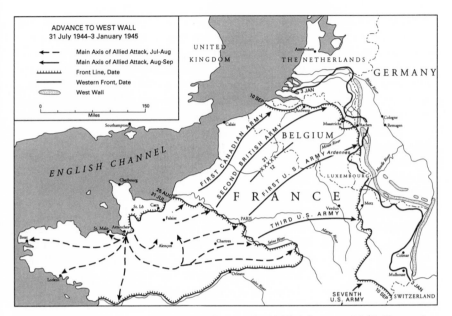

Map 4.1. The Advance to the West Wall, 31 July 1944–3 January 1945 (Sherry L. Dowdy)

were broad in scope and perhaps the most mature portion of its doctrine. The 1941 edition of FM 100-5 prescribed the general characteristics of city combat: reduced fields of fire and observation, difficulties with command and control, and increased emphasis on close combat. FM 100-5 also stipulated that mechanized forces were of "little value" in street fighting and that their use might result in "excessive casualties, both in personnel and vehicles." In 1943 the War Department published FM 31-50, "Attack on a Fortified Position and Combat in Towns," that further expanded on FM 100-5's principles for urban fighting. FM 31-50 was noteworthy for its great number of specific details on the tactics and techniques of city combat.[1]

Doctrine portrayed urban combat as a rigorous, costly form of warfare that should be avoided, and offensive operations were fraught with difficulties. Urban areas restricted the use of maneuver and firepower, artillery could provide little support to infantry units battling the enemy at close quarters, and tanks were to avoid street fighting. Limited observation and fields of fire made finding and fixing the enemy more difficult. Streets and buildings tended to fragment and decentralize operations, hindering the ability of commanders to maintain positive control over their units. Buildings, streets, basements, and sewers provided the defender with a great number of fighting positions and routes for counterattacks. Attackers had to occupy and clear every structure, and urban terrain aggravated problems with using support weapons and resupply.[2]

Although doctrine conveyed an accurate picture of the urban combat environment, significant challenges still faced American units. Commanders had to apply prescribed tactical methods while trying to span the gap between urban warfare doctrine and battlefield realities. They also had to be alert for flaws in doctrine and tactics and then work to repair the shortcomings. Troops at all levels had to learn new lessons in street fighting and to find ways to surmount unexpected challenges. Just as important, Americans had to determine the enemy's defensive schemes and then find the best ways to find, fix, and defeat him.

The army's first broad experience with urban combat occurred during the capture of Brest. OVERLORD planners had originally targeted the city for inclusion in the Allied logistical network, and the supply situation in late August demanded that the Allies capture additional ports. A fortress city of 80,000 people located on the tip of the Brittany peninsula, Brest had an excellent deep water harbor. The mission of capturing Brest fell to Maj. Gen. Troy H. Middleton's VIII Corps, which consisted of three infantry divisions—the 2d, 8th, and 29th—and with all supporting troops reached a peak strength of 50,000 soldiers. Middleton's plan was to isolate Brest by occupying the dominating hilltops north of the city. If the Germans refused to surrender after VIII Corps had encircled the city, Middleton planned to use his divisions in a series of alternating offensives to put increasing pressure on the garrison.[3]

The commander of Brest was Generalleutnant Herman B. Ramcke, a tough parachute commander who gained notoriety during the German airborne assault on Crete in 1941. Hitler ordered Ramcke to defend Brest to the last man, and he intended to do just that. Ramcke knew he could not defeat the U.S. VIII Corps, so he planned to bleed his enemy as much as possible and to make the Americans expend ammunition and supplies intended for use against the German homeland. He also planned to destroy entirely the city's harbor facilities, thus denying the Allies immediate use of the port. The German 2d Parachute Division and the 343d (Static) Division, with a combined strength of approximately 30,000 effectives, were the backbone of the city's defense. Ramcke anchored his defense on an extensive network of concrete pillboxes, gun emplacements, minefields, and other obstacles located on the hills north of Brest. If dislodged from these positions, he planned to fight a delaying action back into the city where he would embroil VIII Corps in bloody, house-to-house fighting.[4]

German urban warfare doctrine guided the actions of soldiers defending built-up areas throughout Western Europe. German forward units blunted enemy attacks by defending a series of well-prepared, mutually supporting positions. Once the front lines had identified and contained the enemy's main effort, reserves would counterattack. They exercised great care in preparing the MLR for defense. First, they placed reserves of drinking water, rations, ammunition, and medical supplies in protected caches. Then they shut off all utilities and disconnected telephone lines, denying the enemy access to water, communications, and electricity. They established the MLR in an irregular pattern so that its exact location would be hard to determine. Large stone and concrete buildings became natural strongholds. The Germans fought from buildings on the outer edge of city blocks and never defended structures that attackers could easily surround or bypass. Heavy machine guns dominated avenues from dug-in positions at the corners of streets and buildings, and open spaces such as large intersections, traffic circles, city parks, cemeteries, and railroad yards were converted into defensive kill zones. Tank ditches and barriers blocked the way for armored vehicles, and sewers served as covered and concealed routes for resupply, infiltration, and relief operations.[5]

According to doctrine, German commanders were to retain the initiative in urban fighting by using their reserves to counterattack the flank and rear of enemy advances. But battlefield realities unhinged such theories. The Germans often lacked sufficient manpower to contain American attacks while simultaneously holding out strong reserves. Open streets covered by American machine guns were impossible to cross without heavy casualties or took too long to traverse. Buildings were barriers that further reduced and canalized counterattacks. Unable to counterpunch, German urban combat degenerated into a stubborn, close quarters slugging match along a static line of defense. Although the combination of forward defense with counterattacks worked well for the Germans on other battlefields, urban terrain denied them the use of one of their most effective defensive methods.[6]

Middleton began the Brest campaign on 21 August with limited objective attacks that secured key terrain around the city. The main effort began four days later after a strong preparatory bombardment by heavy and medium bombers and VIII Corps artillery. The 29th Division operated on the right flank and the 2d Division on the left, while the 8th Division conducted the main attack in the center. For several days VIII Corps fought hard to dislodge Ramcke's soldiers from positions outside the city. By 8 September, the 2d and 8th Divisions had pushed the Germans back into the city, where the campaign entered its last and most bitter phase.[7]

For the next ten days Americans received their baptism of fire with street fighting in the ETO. The earliest and most important lesson learned was the need for combined arms action. Infantry units bore the brunt of the fighting but required vital assistance from the other combat arms. Engineers detected and cleared mines and booby traps, removed obstacles, cleared streets of rubble, and repaired cratered avenues to make them usable as supply lines. Demolition teams emplaced and detonated explosive charges in support of infantry attacks. Aircraft strafed and bombed German units and performed aerial reconnaissance. Combat at close quarters usually precluded artillery support, so infantry commanders made maximum use of their organic mortars. In a great departure from urban warfare doctrine, commanders learned to use armored vehicles in street fighting. In the absence of artillery support, infantry units came to rely on the direct firepower of main guns on tanks and TDs to blast enemy positions at point-blank range. Armored vehicles could blow passageways through walls and buildings and bull their way over obstacles and through small structures. VIII Corps' tank battalions had been reassigned to Third Army for the pursuit across France, so TD units stepped in to provide armor support. Another departure from prewar antitank doctrine, infantry support in city combat, added a new function to the unexpected roles that TD units had performed in the Mediterranean.[8]

Urban combat's enclosed, compartmentalized environment presented commanders with serious command and control problems. Observation over the whole battle area was impossible, and radios failed to function among city buildings. Platoons and squads found themselves isolated as they fought to seize and clear buildings and single rooms. Surrounded by walls or buildings on all sides, map coordinates and graphic control measures did little to help troops keep moving in the right direction, and the broken and fragmented terrain negated normal planning factors. Instead of attacking along a standard frontage of 200–500 yards, rifle companies moved against city blocks or single buildings. In contrast to mobile warfare, the tempo of urban combat was slow and torturous. Close combat put great demands on leaders at the lowest level, and commanders began to refer to city combat as "a corporal's war."[9]

Answers to command and control problems quickly emerged. Battalion commanders learned not to designate company-sized objectives but instead oriented rifle companies along attack zones usually two city blocks in width. Battalions attacked with two companies forward and the third company in reserve. Because buildings effectively protected a unit's flanks from German counterattacks, commanders learned to plow ahead through the urban maze without maintaining contact with adjacent units. Instead of using normal control graphics and military maps, units drew detailed sketch maps of their own zones of operation and identified their objectives and coordination points using letters and numbers. Infantrymen discarded their radios, relying instead on wire communications. Commanders learned that boundaries between units should never run along avenues and that one outfit should have full responsibility for a street. Company commanders ordered platoons to secure specific build-ings and streets, while squads cleared individual rooms, basements, and hallways. Infantry commanders discovered that hurried operations re-sulted in heavy casualties and confusion caused by the intermingling of bypassed Germans with friendly troops. Detailed planning and methodi-cal execution made for slower operations, but resulted in steady forward progress with fewer casualties. Rotating units off the front lines to rest and refit proved too difficult and confusing in darkness, so most battalions re-lieved companies during evening twilight. Units also preferred to feed, evacuate casualties, and bring supplies forward during daylight rather than stumble about at night.[10]

Infantry units devised a whole host of new assault tactics and tech-niques. Soldiers learned quickly that the worst place to be during street fighting was on fire-swept boulevards, and they adapted a unique ap-proach to street fighting not contained in doctrine. Instead of maneuver-ing down city streets, infantrymen moved from building to building by blasting holes in the walls of adjacent structures. After soldiers secured a room adjacent to another building, engineer demolition teams placed the charges against the wall. All troops then pulled back through several rooms to create a safety zone. The explosion blew a hole large enough for infantrymen to dash through and clear the next room. The explosion took the Germans by surprise and usually incapacitated anyone on the other side of the wall. Although laborious and time-consuming, the wall-busting tactics proved effective and reduced casualties.[11]

Infantry platoons and squads changed their basic configuration to cre-ate more effective formations for city combat. Platoon leaders rejected standard, open-order tactics with squads abreast in favor of tight, colum-nar formations. Squads lost their identity as platoons reorganized into two large sections; one conducted assaults while the other followed in close support. The assault section contained at least two BAR teams and a ba-zooka team. Assault sections moved rapidly and aggressively, clearing each building in order: ground floor, upper floors, and finally basements and cellars. Special demolition and flamethrower teams often joined the attackers. Support sections covered assault groups with fire support, as-sisted the assault section as needed, and remained alert for counterat-tacks. Some units reconfigured single squads into searching and covering parties, both under the control of the squad leader, who moved close be-hind to maintain positive control. Searching parties consisted of four rifle-men organized into pairs using the "buddy system" for maximum team-work. The covering party consisted of a second assault team under the assistant squad leader and a BAR team of three soldiers that served as the squad's base of fire.[12]

Operations by Company F, 2d Battalion, 23d Infantry illustrates many

The American army adapted a number of tactical methods that helped soldiers win urban battles. Infantrymen of the 2d Division advance on the outskirts of Brest, France, September 1944. (U.S. Army Military History Institute)

of the lessons units learned in Brest. The company, commanded by Capt. George H. Duckworth, was at the forefront of a major offensive by the 2d Division to capture the city's center. Company F, consisting of about 170 enlisted men and 7 officers, had entered the ETO across Omaha Beach on June 7. Captain Duckworth was the only officer who had survived the fighting from Normandy to Brittany and only one-third of the original enlisted men were still present for duty; the other 70 percent were replacements who had seen considerable combat in Normandy and around Brest. Duckworth was confident in his men's abilities and believed his unit's morale, discipline, and esprit de corps "were excellent."[13]

From 10–13 September, Company F engaged in a macabre firefight to gain control over a city cemetery defended by elements of the German 2d Parachute Division. The Germans hoped to use the cemetery's relatively open spaces and surrounding buildings to generate enough massed firepower to slow the 2d Division's advance. They anchored their defense on large, marble burial vaults and mausoleums on the cemetery's western edge that they had converted into heavy machine-gun positions. Automatic weapons covered every foot of open ground, all entrances to the walled cemetery, and the surrounding streets, so that anyone trying to move through the area was subjected to heavy crossfires and grazing fire.[14]

Company F was at the forefront of the 2d Battalion's main attack when it first made contact with the cemetery's defenders around 1800 hours on 10 September. The rifle platoons pushed forward into the cemetery, but heavy machine-gun fire from what seemed like all directions stopped the advance. Withdrawing to safe positions, Captain Duckworth decided to stop and use nightfall to conduct a thorough reconnaissance and to prepare for the next day. The fight resumed the following morning at 0900 hours. Before the attack, Duckworth skillfully used his mortars to place preparatory fires on the Germans, but the mausoleums were unaffected. Both assault platoons made small initial gains, but movement in the cemetery was impossible. Ricochets off headstones and flying splinters from granite grave markers aggravated the effects of enemy fire. German mortars joined the fight, toppling tombstones and unearthing coffins. Pinned down in the open and suffering heavy casualties, the assault platoons withdrew. Squads fighting to secure buildings adjacent to the cemetery made little progress, and enemy machine-gun fire made the streets impassable. Both sides exchanged heavy fire for the remainder of the day, but Company F's attack was stalled.[15]

That night, the battalion commander and all of the company commanders huddled at the 2d Battalion command post to develop a new attack plan. The next day Company F would once again make the main effort reinforced by a rifle platoon from Company G. Knowing that further frontal assaults would fail, the battalion commander decided to outflank the Germans with a novel approach: Company F would envelop the cemetery's defenses by using the wall-busting techniques that other units had discovered. The new plan called for Duckworth's 1st and 2d platoons to blast their way through the walls of the buildings on either side of the cemetery, while the 3d Platoon and the Weapons Platoon pinned down the Germans in the cemetery with supporting fire. The platoon from Company G would join the fight on order. The best news came when Captain Duckworth learned that a TD section would join his attack sometime the next day. During the night, work details moved a large supply of TNT forward to F Company's positions while the unit's leadership completed their attack plans.[16]

At 0900 hours on 12 September, F Company's mortars opened the assault with concentrated fire into the cemetery. German resistance was again strong, but blasting holes through the interior walls of buildings on either side of the cemetery worked with remarkable success as the shock effects from the explosions and the unorthodox tactics took the enemy by surprise. Immediately after the explosion, assault teams rushed through the breach to clear and seize the adjacent room. The platoons then repeated the procedure and continued their advance into the next building. The method was slow, but it resulted in steady progress with minimal casualties.[17]

Several hours later rifle squads were in a position to shoot down onto the Germans from the higher stories and roofs of buildings on either side of the cemetery. The promised TDs finally rumbled up to F Company's position and added tremendous firepower to the attack. Their main guns blasted German machine-gun positions near the cemetery at point-blank range, slammed rounds into buildings sheltering snipers, and destroyed machine-gun nests putting fire on F Company from positions several blocks behind the cemetery. The cobblestone streets and masonry buildings shuddered under the attack of American infantry, mortars, engineers, and TDs. By nightfall the Germans had suffered heavy casualties and maintained only a toehold on the cemetery.[18]

At mid-morning on 13 September Company F swept through the cemetery against slight resistance. With all of his rifle platoons now abreast, Captain Duckworth attacked toward the city's center. Hours later the 2d Battalion had advanced far beyond the cemetery and was exerting strong pressure when the Germans brought everything to a standstill by setting fire to buildings that blocked the American advance. Although this last-ditch effort stopped the attack, the Germans had been unable to prevent Company F and the 2d Battalion from reducing the cemetery stronghold. New wall-busting tactics, a unique outflanking maneuver, and the effective use of all available weapons in a combined arms effort had eliminated one of the strongest German defensive positions in Brest.[19]

The army's other great test of strength in city combat took place in Aachen. In early autumn, First Army, now under the command of Lt. Gen. Courtney H. Hodges, began a series of offensives designed to carry American units from Holland to the Rhine. The army commander's initial plan was to breach the German West Wall north and south of Aachen, then encircle and contain the city's defenders while the bulk of First Army pushed eastward. Hodges's attack plan contained the hallmark characteristics of blitzkrieg warfare: an initial assault that ruptured the enemy's MLR, the bypassing of a major city considered an obstacle rather than an objective, and an exploitation deep into the enemy's rear area that focused on destroying enemy forces rather than capturing terrain. Sound in theory, the plan became unglued in its execution. Stiff German resistance along the West Wall and around Aachen weakened American divisions. Hodges became convinced that he lacked the combat power both to contain German units in Aachen and to continue the larger offensive toward the Rhine. Modifying his original plan, he decided to reduce Aachen while the rest of First Army maintained a strong shield against German efforts to relieve the city.[20]

In and of itself, Aachen was not of great military significance. The city of 165,000 people was neither a key transportation hub nor a strong fortress, and it did not occupy key terrain. However, Aachen was the first city in Germany threatened by the Allies, and the Germans found it impossible to surrender it without a fight. The city's defense rested in the hands of Col. Gerhard Wilck, the commander of the 246th Volks Grenadier Division. Altogether, Wilck had available 5,000 soldiers and a small assortment of tanks, assault guns, and artillery pieces. Although he lacked adequate resources to defend the city, Wilck had no shortage of guidance about what was expected from him and the 246th Division, as Hitler took a personal interest in the battle and ordered a fanatical, house-to-house "last stand." Evacuation was out of the question, and the German high command told Wilck that he was to hold the city ". . . to the last man, and . . . , if necessary, allow himself to be buried under its ruins."[21]

After the Germans ignored a surrender ultimatum on 10 October, the VII Corps commander gave the final order for Huebner's Big Red One to go in and wrest Aachen from German control. Already having suffered heavy casualties east of Aachen and fighting along an extended front, the 1st Infantry Division found it almost impossible to mass adequate forces against the city. Only one regiment, the 26th Infantry, was available and it was short one of its three battalions, but the regimental commander decided to put all of his combat power forward and not hold back any reserves. The 26th Infantry would attack through the city from east to west with both battalions abreast. The 2d Battalion on the left would conduct the main attack through Aachen's urban center, while the 3d Battalion on the right would sweep through industrial parks and seize higher ground on the city's north side.[22]

Lt. Col. Derrill M. Daniel commanded the 2d Battalion and led his soldiers in one of the classic small unit actions in the ETO. Learning several days before the attack that his battalion would conduct the main effort into Aachen, Daniel's detailed planning reflected the growing belief that sweat expended during preparations saved blood in combat and won battles. Daniel decided to fight his battalion as a group of combined arms company teams, and each rifle company received three Shermans or TDs and two towed antitank guns, as well as two bazookas, one flamethrower, and two heavy machine-gun teams. Daniel specified a zone of action for each unit, and company commanders assigned single streets to each platoon. The battalion's attack zone was extremely wide, about 2,000 yards on average. In order to cover the entire front, Daniel decided to put every platoon forward and to fight without a reserve. He established a series of checkpoints and phase lines based on streets and prominent buildings so that the rifle companies could coordinate their actions and report progress. To provide the large amounts of ammunition required for city combat, the battalion established an ammunition dump that could be moved forward behind the rifle companies. Aachen's 20,000 remaining civilians posed an acute problem. Realizing that differentiating noncombatants from enemy soldiers in the urban maze would be extremely difficult, Daniel decided to minimize civilian casualties and speed the attack by evacuating everyone, soldiers and civilians alike, as the battalion advanced through the city.[23]

Daniel developed an effective method for orchestrating his combat power. Artillery and mortar fire would strike deep across the battalion front to isolate the battle area, pin down enemy reserves, hammer their defenses, and prevent easy withdrawals. Tanks, TDs, and infantry would move down side streets while mutually supporting each other. Machine guns would dominate main streets and intersections to prevent enemy lateral movement, and soldiers planned on searching every room, closet, and cellar to make sure they did not bypass a single defender. Leaders continually impressed upon their soldiers the need for maintaining a heavy volume of fire with all available weapons. Concentrated fire would not only kill and suppress the enemy, but also might bring walls and structures crashing down on top of the Germans. The battalion adopted an aggressive motto—"Knock'em all down"—that captured both the spirit and the method soldiers would use in the battle for Aachen.[24]

The preparatory bombardment for the 1st Division's attack reflected the army's growing sophistication in applying firepower. On 11 and 12 October, IX TAC fighter-bombers combined with VII Corps and 1st Division artillery battalions in a fierce bombardment intended to stun the city's defenders. Aircraft attacked specific targets marked with red artillery smoke and conducted area bombardment missions. Altogether IX TAC dropped more than 160 tons of bombs during the two-day period, while twelve battalions of corps and division artillery rocked the city with 10,000 rounds. Under the deafening roar of the bombardment on 12 October, the 2d Battalion moved into jump-off positions for the main assault scheduled to commence the next day.[25]

The 2d Battalion's experience on 13 October introduced the Big Red One to the rigors of city combat. The battalion devised a unique tactic to destroy suspected German positions just on the other side of a high railroad embankment that marked the jump-off line for the attack. At 0930 hours, every rifleman in the battalion heaved a hand grenade over the embankment, and explosives from a tidal wave of over 1,000 grenades signaled the opening of the attack. Soldiers clambered over the embankment, scrambling for the nearest cover, and were soon joined by tanks

Armored vehicles joined the fight in villages and cities to give vital assistance to the infantry. A tank-infantry team of the 1st Infantry Division clears downtown Aachen, October 1944. (U.S. Army Military History Institute)

and TDs. Initial resistance was light. By noon E and F Companies were heavily engaged and plowing forward through a maze of rubble and damaged buildings. Tanks and TDs found they could blast or bulldoze their way through smaller buildings holding up their advance. Soldiers in the 1st Division also discovered a key lesson VIII Corps infantrymen had learned in Brest: survival in city combat meant staying out of the streets. Fighting in the late afternoon saw soldiers moving from building to building by blowing holes in walls with dynamite and bazookas. By nightfall Daniel had pivoted his battalion to the left to occupy a line perpendicular to his original jump-off position. With all three companies deployed on line and no reserves available, the battalion prepared to push westward toward the city's center.[26]

For the next eight days Daniel's battalion fought a desperate, combined arms battle as it drove the 246th Division further back into Aachen. Heavy caliber fire from tanks and TDs helped break up the continuity of the German defense and assisted infantrymen during close assaults. On one of the few occasions in the ETO, American artillery was able to fire parallel to the fighting front and drop shells extremely close to troops, sometimes within the same city block, without danger from short rounds. Stone masonry buildings protected soldiers from close artillery support that might otherwise have been lethal. Artillery FOs learned to use delayed fuses so that shells penetrated several floors and exploded right among the enemy instead of detonating on rooftops. Flamethrowers also proved extremely effective. Soldiers learned the importance of searching every hiding place, as the 246th Division used Aachen's sewer system to mount local counterattacks and to move patrols behind American lines, forcing the 2d Battalion to locate and block every manhole and underground passageway to prevent further infiltration. Without a reserve, Daniel fought off counterattacks by shifting troops across his extended front. Companies fought in daylight and used nighttime to rest, reorganize, and resupply.[27]

Several engagements illustrate the army's willingness to use overwhelming, destructive firepower. On 13 October the 3d Battalion commander observed that larger buildings housing German defenders could easily absorb tank and TD cannon fire, so he called for a self-propelled 155-mm artillery piece that proved capable of blowing apart any structure. Impressed with the gun's use, the regimental commander sent one to support Colonel Daniel's attack. On 16 October a strong German defensive position centered on the city's main theater building held up G Company's advance; artillery, mortar, and armored vehicle firepower proved ineffective against it. In a scene more akin to the infantry-artillery tactics of the American Civil War than the open-order tactics of modern warfare, Daniel pushed the big gun forward to operate among his infantry squads. Downtown Aachen's buildings and cobblestone streets shuddered under the thunderous onslaught from the 155-mm, as it slammed more than a dozen shells into the position, tore the theater's outer facade from the face of the building, and broke the back of local German resistance. On similar occasions the 2d Battalion also employed the artillery piece to smash German defenses, and Daniel reported the gun's effects as "quite spectacular and satisfying." After his capture, Colonel Wilck protested the use of direct fire artillery at such close range, calling it "barbarous" and claiming it should be outlawed, but his appeals fell on the deaf ears of VII Corps soldiers whose sensibilities had been dulled by the heavy fighting since D-Day.[28]

By the afternoon of 21 October Daniel's soldiers had secured all of the downtown area and were pushing westward when they received word that the Aachen garrison had surrendered. During the next few hours over 1,000 Germans surrendered, bringing the 1st Division's total prisoner count for the battle to 5,600. The reduction of Aachen cost the 1st Division 498 casualties among the assault battalions. The Germans admitted to only 5,100 casualties, but losses were probably heavier. About 80 percent of all buildings had been destroyed or badly damaged; Aachen ended the war a burned out hulk of its former self.[29]

In retrospect, Colonel Daniel credited his battalion's success to several factors. The slow, thorough search of every area and the use of all available firepower permitted the battalion to take its objective with fewer casualties, convincing Daniel's soldiers that in city combat thoroughness was more important than speed. Daylight operations facilitated command and control and the maximum employment of weaponry. Soldiers had to avoid streets as much as possible and maneuver within buildings, blasting their way between structures when necessary. The close integration of infantry, armor, artillery, and engineers generated combat power the Germans could not withstand. A reserve could have assisted in the clearing of positions and helped maintain contact with units on the flanks, but reserves were a luxury Daniel could not afford. The commander of the 26th Infantry also drew conclusions on the battle: "We employed common sense, normal tactical principles, and maximum firepower."[30]

The attack of heavily defended villages across open terrain in eastern France and along the German border was another significant challenge of urban combat that taxed the ability of the American combined arms team. The confined spaces of the bocage and of city streets kept tankers and infantrymen close together and helped facilitate better coordination. But the attack of villages required maneuvering over open ground and made combined arms coordination more challenging. Nevertheless, commanders experimented and improvised in order to develop new tactics for capturing villages.

American commanders could find little in army doctrine about combined arms tactics against village strongholds, and in 1944 official doctrine still called for infantry and armor to attack in separate echelons and not as an integrated team. In July the War Department published a revision to its basic manual on tank-infantry cooperation, FM 17-36, "Employment of Tanks with Infantry," while the Armor School at Fort Knox issued a separate supplement to FM 17-36 in an effort to provide overseas commanders with new ideas on combined arms tactics. Unfortunately, neither manual went far enough in advocating combined arms action. Doctrine still called for separate infantry and tank units to maneuver and provide fire support for one another and failed to describe coordinated fire and maneuver by tank-infantry teams. Fire support planning was simple and unimaginative, and there was no mention of air support. Events in Europe were simply outpacing doctrine, and units in combat had to meet demands for coordinated, combined arms action faster than stateside staffs could revise or recommend new tank-infantry tactics. Commanders filled the void by using sound tactical principles, their own experience

and judgment, and the optimum use of men and weapons to develop sophisticated tactics for attacking village defenses.[31]

In contrast to American doctrine, German theories were mature and
complex, drawing heavily from broad wartime experience on the Eastern
Front to produce guidelines for defending villages. German doctrine contended that villages became focal points during combat across the open
countryside, since villages dominated road networks, provided cover and
concealment, and were natural strongholds. If defended stubbornly, small
towns became breakwaters that could slow the advance of numerically
superior attackers. Commanders were never to locate the MLR at the village's edge. Instead, the main effort was to take place on the best terrain
surrounding the town or from buildings within a village's interior. Posi-
tioning troops on the edge of town was discouraged; the location gave no
great advantage and exposed soldiers to the enemy's direct firepower. Inside a village the MLR ran through areas best suited to stop armored attacks, and German infantry platoons fought using the defensive techniques of city combat. Streets were blocked with hasty obstacles,
barricades, and barbed wire, and the largest buildings became strongholds. German doctrine stipulated that the main line of resistance was
"the defender's shield, the reserves are his sword," so the best units were
put into reserve and from assembly areas in the middle of town they were
to counterattack enemy penetrations.[32]

Operations by the 2d Armored Division to capture German villages east
of Aachen reflect the increased complexity of combined arms tactics. As
the "Hell on Wheels" division fought its way toward the Roer River in November and December, units devised elaborate fire and maneuver tactics.
Tank-infantry teams supported each other by fire and movement during
the approach and final assault of the objective. Artillery and mortars
shelled the objective, while preplanned and on-call CAS hit hard with
bombing and strafing. TDs sat on the flanks in support, and engineers
moved with assault troops to clear obstacles. The new tactics played a key
role in the division's capture of the major crossroads village of Alsdorf
along with several surrounding objectives.[33]

The 2d Armored's approach to fighting put great emphasis in preparations before battle. The division commander, Maj. Gen. Ernest N. Harmon, emphasized that the secret to a successful attack was in the "close
coordination of all means at the right time and place." Units developed
detailed plans, took time for thorough coordination, and made sure
everyone understood their part in the battle. Working communications
were essential, and infantry commanders rode in command tanks to facilitate radio control over tank-infantry teams. FOs and FACs went into battle
riding vehicles from which they could observe the battle area and maintain radio contact with supporting artillery and fighter-bombers. As a rule,

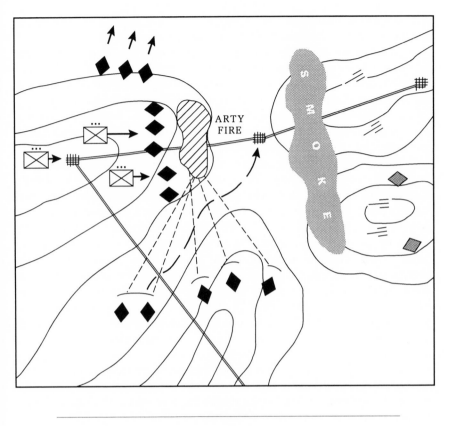

LEGEND

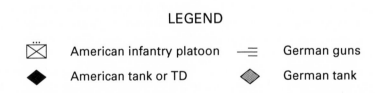

Figure 4.1. 2d Armored Division Fire and Maneuver Tactics (Sherry L. Dowdy)

commanders maximized the firepower and shock effect of tanks and TDs by using platoon-sized formations, since breaking up armored platoons into smaller sections greatly dissipated their strength. To avoid disrupting the tempo of the battle, units made specific plans for rotating platoons out of combat to rearm and refuel.[34]

The typical 2d Armored Division attack against village strongholds called for the complete orchestration of the combat arms. (See Figure 4.1.) While company teams of infantry and tanks moved into forward attack positions, the artillery dumped heavy concentrations on villages and surrounding positions. Indirect fire sealed off the objective area by striking deep against enemy positions, hilltops, and crossroads. Artillery and mortars also delivered a heavy smoke screen behind the village that blinded Germans in supporting positions and silhouetted the village to the attackers. Tanks and TDs in hull defilade firing positions on the flanks of the attack further isolated the objective area by repelling counterattacks. Armored vehicle firepower could also put fire on the objective or prevent reinforcements from reaching the village.[35]

Two separate groups conducted the attack; one assaulted the village while the other provided fire support. Tank platoons usually supported by fire, while assault teams consisted of both tank and infantry platoons. The support platoon assumed hull-down positions close enough to the village to permit the use of both main guns and machine guns. The best positions put the tanks' line of fire perpendicular to the attacker's axis of advance so that assaulting troops never masked their own direct fire support. The platoons in support could put maximum firepower on the Germans while the attackers moved across open ground and closed on the village. As the attackers moved through the village, tanks continued to provide close support by conducting reconnaissance by fire against suspected enemy positions or pinned down Germans units trying to maneuver in defense of the village. Once their mission was over, the support tanks moved forward and joined the fight, taking up defensive positions beyond the village from which they could best repel German counterattacks. If required, the supporting tank platoon could maneuver around behind the village to attack German defenses from the rear.[36]

The key principle in the new combined arms tactics was the simultaneous use of maximum firepower and maneuver by tank-infantry teams. Sweeping aside the prewar practice of separate waves of tanks and infantry attacking in echelon, company- and battalion-sized units of both tanks and infantry now moved as one. Commanders linked firepower and maneuver together by having one tank-infantry team rush toward the objective while the other supported by fire. General Harmon considered the fire and movement principle "fundamental" to small unit success, and 2d Armored Division soldiers coined an original term for their method of having a firing element to protect and support assault troops. For the first time American soldiers used the word "overwatch," an expression that came to dominate American tactical thinking. On 13–14 December the 2d Armored Division hosted a conference of XIX Corps unit commanders, and General Harmon briefed them on the techniques of fire and maneuver and the concept of "overwatch"; in the afternoon the participants viewed demonstrations on the new tactics.[37]

The 30th Infantry Division, under Maj. Gen. Leland S. Hobbs, also gained considerable experience in attacking villages during operations on the Cologne Plain in November. Like many other commands in the ETO, the "Old Hickory" Division learned that fire and maneuver by tank-infantry teams aided by direct and indirect fire support was the only way to capture villages. When attacking a group of villages arrayed along a line parallel to the fighting front, it was best to first capture a village on the flank, then attack the others in order. Direct fire weapons could converge more firepower on a flank village, and assault troops were less exposed to defensive fires. The captured village then served as a good base from which to launch the next assault against the adjacent town. Villages on reverse slopes denied assault troops effective direct and indirect fire support, so the 30th Division used the stealth and surprise of night attacks to grab the towns. A direction of attack perpendicular to a village's long axis facilitated rapid capture and prevented the Germans from fighting a defense in depth. An integral part of attack plans was a scheme for repelling counterattacks. Assault elements had to include antitank teams trained to eliminate German panzers at close quarters. Commanders used aerial photos and sketch maps drawn by patrols to brief their troops. Platoons attacked sections of towns while squads concentrated on clearing single buildings.[38]

The 30th Division's leadership put great emphasis on units taking the time and effort required for coordination. The actual capture of a village took only about an hour, but commanders needed several hours to coordinate artillery, mortar, tank, TD, and infantry fire support and to brief their troops. Regiments learned to reduce the time between attacks by rotating the main assault mission among their battalions. While one battalion fought to capture a village, another prepared for the next assault. The speed of a coordinated attack often caught the Germans by surprise. The leaders of the Old Hickory Division concluded that orchestrated, aggressive attacks gained objectives quicker, inflicted more casualties, and resulted in fewer losses than did rushed, clumsy efforts that relied on firepower and adrenaline to overwhelm the enemy. Giving units adequate time to prepare for village assaults made better sense than putting units "under pressure to inch forward, showing some progress hourly."[39]

After a series of battles in November against village strongholds north of Aachen, the 30th Division went to great lengths to record and disseminate the lessons it had learned. On 13–14 December General Hobbs hosted a training session for the division's leaders that taught the techniques and methods of attacking villages. The officers ended the two-day session with a demonstration of the techniques used in one of the division's most successful village attacks followed by a terrain walk of the actual battlefield.[40]

The attack of villages across the entire American front produced other important lessons. Commanders had to base their plans on the results of personal reconnaissance and detailed information on the enemy. Successful operations included coordinated, combined arms attack over suitable terrain using maximum firepower and maneuver. Units learned to isolate and dominate villages by capturing the surrounding key terrain. Village attacks also impressed upon soldiers the difference between "haste" and "speed" and the need for planning and coordination. Attacks conducted with few preparations and little knowledge of the terrain or enemy situation resulted in failure and heavy casualties. As the fighting in Europe progressed, village attacks included more preparation and coordination, and with aggressive action units regained time lost to planning. Troops moved methodically but quickly against known enemy positions in planned attacks that achieved their purpose with fewer losses, and by late 1944 many units had learned the benefits of these coordinated attacks.[41]

Troops learned many new tactical lessons while capturing village strongholds. Whenever possible, initial attacks against a village's outer perimeter focused on enemy escape routes because German troops tended to surrender early if their getaway path was blocked. The most effective way to gather intelligence was for night patrols to sneak into villages and detect the sights and sounds of German defensive preparations. Tankers learned to avoid bridges and road intersections near villages because they were usually mined. Infantry rode on tanks during assaults but dismounted just outside of villages. Tank-infantry teams discovered that the best way to attack through villages was moving abreast down parallel streets. In armored divisions infantry rode their halftracks as far forward as possible before dismounting. During assaults, halftracks drove close behind tanks to shield themselves from enemy fire. Shock and firepower worked wonders against lightly defended villages, and some infantry units found that during assaults they could ride on the back decks of tanks with all guns blazing and then dismount after the tanks were inside the town.[42]

As the army advanced across Western Europe, it learned a great number of lessons in urban warfare and made significant changes in its combat techniques. The first, most critical lesson was the need for combined arms action; infantry alone could not bear all of the burdens of city combat. The greatest challenge units faced was to develop and put into practice a wide variety of new tactical and technical means. Attacking through city blocks by blowing holes in the walls of adjacent buildings was one of the most significant tactical innovations employed, the use of armored vehicles was another. When it was more important to reduce rather than bypass cities, commanders committed tanks and TDs into urban centers to help the infantry. The most advanced tactical innovation was the development of sophisticated combined arms tactics for capturing village strongholds. Commanders discovered that their greatest challenge was maintaining positive command and control during close quarters combat. They relied on wire communications instead of radios and crafted plans from detailed, hand-drawn sketches rather than military maps. And commanders accepted the notion that they had to plow straight ahead through the urban maze, fighting without reserves and with little regard for flank and rear security. New techniques were devised for employing weapons and explosives at close range, and junior leaders reorganized their troops into assault and support teams that worked well in capturing and clearing structures. Soldiers learned to avoid streets filled with enemy fire and quickly discovered the best ways to search buildings, to use the weapons and special tools most appropriate for urban combat, and to organize work teams for resupply and rearming during darkness.

The implementation of tactical and technical adaptations for urban combat reveals significant aspects of the army's process for managing change. Fighting in a huge theater of operations with hundreds of miles between units, centralized control of the process of change by higher headquarters was all but impossible. Units engaged in Brest, Aachen, and hundreds of other locations in France and Germany took the initiative in finding solutions to urban warfare difficulties. Leaders' actions reflected the American belief that military doctrine was a guide for action, not absolute dogma, and they modified or ignored doctrine while creating new tactics. Urban warfare adaptations support the idea that terrain alone can be the single determining cause for major adjustments in an army's fighting methods, and changes occurred in almost every aspect of small unit operations: command and control, tactics, organization, weaponry, and logistics. The army used both formal and informal information channels to disseminate new ideas and lessons learned, and a large number of unit after-action reports, information bulletins, and field demonstrations addressed urban warfare problems and solutions. The final effect was to help U.S. units achieve better proficiency against the expertise that the German army had gained on the Eastern Front and in other theaters.

The army's experience in city and village fighting validated much of its doctrine on urban combat, and although largely correct, urban warfare theories did require some modifications. For example, artillery played a more significant role than prescribed in doctrine. Although it could not give direct aid to units, artillery helped win battles by attacking German LOCs, command posts, and reserves. Prewar doctrine warned against employing armor in the close confines of urban terrain, but the need to provide infantry units with direct fire support prevailed. TD units found themselves drifting further away from their original antiarmor roles, yet they performed yeoman's service as assault guns in street fighting and as direct fire support weapons in village combat.

Infantry and armor commanders drew on the general guidelines of fire and maneuver doctrine to develop a more sophisticated style of combined arms tactics for village fighting. Writings before the war discussed how commanders should combine maneuver, firepower, and the best use of terrain to gain enemy positions, but the drawback was in the army's belief that tanks and infantry attacked as separate echelons. Going beyond prewar tactical thinking, commanders put together tank-infantry-artillery teams that simultaneously maximized shock and firepower. Armored and infantry divisions improvised to produce the genesis of the modern, combined arms fire and maneuver tactics that Americans would use into the 1990s.

The technical and tactical adaptations devised by units during urban battles raise a broader question about U.S. matériel superiority during the campaigns in the ETO. A popular argument is that American units overwhelmed the Germans with superior numbers and resources. If this were true, why then did American units emerge victorious only after a continuous process of learning and change? It is clear that American soldiers were not so numerous or lavishly equipped that they could easily overpower their opponents. To the contrary, it was only after the learning and adaptation processes that units were able to cope with unfamiliar challenges. It was not overwhelming numbers of American soldiers that defeated the Germans, but the variety of unique, innovative tactics and methods that they employed—wall-busting techniques, reorganization of units into clearing and support teams, close support from engineers, tanks, and TDs, and new fire and maneuver tactics against village strongholds.

German units effectively followed urban warfare doctrine in defending cities and villages, but broader circumstances often doomed their efforts. The German high command tied the hands of its field commanders with strict orders to defend to the last, and Hitler himself insisted on the "do or die" defense of Brest and Aachen. American commanders were especially good at encircling and isolating German defenses before the final attack. Middleton insured the German defeat at Brest by surrounding the city before VIII Corps began its main effort. Likewise, Hodges's corps sealed off the approaches to Aachen before the 1st Division entered the city. At the small unit level, regimental and battalion commanders used maneuver and firepower to isolate villages. With units unable to withdraw or receive reinforcements, German urban battles were a lost cause from the start. The Germans often lacked the strength to both defend forward and husband reserves, and conditions kept them from mounting counterattacks. Without the threat of counterattacks against their flanks and rear, American units relentlessly pushed ahead through urban centers. All of these factors combined to commit the German army to a vicious war of attrition it had no chance of winning.

City and village combat helped disprove the American prewar notion that the tempo of combat was rapid and that recklessness won battles. Actual experience taught commanders that they needed time for adequate planning and that in combat the going was slow. Attacking units required detailed, specific plans based on the best available intelligence, and platoons needed time to reorganize from regular squad organizations into clearing and support teams. Clearing buildings was a labor-intensive, time-consuming exercise that units could not avoid. To refuel and resupply among devastated buildings and rubble-choked streets took time, as did the evacuation of noncombatants and PWs. Commanders discovered that coordinated attacks pressed with speed and vigor saved lives and recouped time expended during planning and preparations.

Urban combat illustrates a key aspect of American combined arms tactics: the willingness to use heavy caliber weapons and an abundance of explosives at close quarters. In Normandy, explosives gapped hedgerows and tanks used their main guns to knock out enemy machine-gun nests at short ranges. Urban battles saw the practice carried to new extremes, as demolitions not only blew paths through buildings for assault troops, but also traumatized and incapacitated the enemy. Point-blank cannon fire from tanks and TDs obliterated German positions and knocked down walls. The tendency to use close quarters firepower reached a zenith when Colonel Daniel used a 155-mm howitzer to demolish German defenses in Aachen's main theater building. Americans were not disturbed by their uninhibited use of firepower at close range and usually expressed great pleasure with its results. As U.S. troops moved toward Germany, they exhibited a tendency to use any means that would inflict maximum damage on the enemy while minimizing their own casualties.

The attack of cities and villages was not the only test of urban warfare the army faced. While some divisions came to grips with the problems of fighting on urban terrain, others confronted the problems of reducing heavy fortifications. As the American armies advanced to the German frontier, they braced for even harder battles against steel and concrete defenses. If city and village fighting had challenged the American soldier's ability to adapt and innovate under fire, battles against man-made defenses seemed sure to carry those challenges to even greater heights.

CHAPTER FIVE

Struggles against Steel and Concrete

The Fort Benning method of attacking pillboxes using flame throwers and pole charges was not effective
—*After-action report of 1st Battalion, 119th Infantry,*
on the assault on the Siegfried Line

The early autumn battles of 1944 convinced Allied soldiers of all ranks that the war in Europe was entering a new, more difficult phase. With the summer pursuit over, the campaign took on a character more akin to the battles of 1914–1918 than to mobile, mechanized warfare. Several circumstances prevented the Allies from pushing on into Germany and forced a near stalemate along the entire front. Logistics was the prime limiting factor: the supply system could not expand quickly enough to keep pace with advancing formations, and inadequate port facilities restricted the flow of supplies onto the Continent. Shortages of fuel and ammunition had a direct influence on the battles that took place along the approaches into Germany. There were not enough divisions available to contain centers of enemy resistance while simultaneously conducting exploitations deep into rear areas. Commanders found it difficult to maintain the strength of attacking units and often had to fight without any reserves. Mounting casualties began to dull the cutting edge of many divisions, and replacements were either unavailable or not of good enough quality to sustain units embroiled in nonstop fighting.

As Allied predominance on the battlefield began to wane, German fighting power started to recoup from the disastrous retreat across France. Remnants of units began to rally along the German frontier as the German high command put increased priority on shifting resources to the Western Front. Troop units and talented commanders moved in from Italy, Scandinavia, and the Eastern Front. Although the defense of cities and villages in certain sectors helped German commanders slow the Allied onslaught, they hoped to halt the Allies with the defense of heavy fortifications. The German army manned the pillboxes of the West Wall and the large bastions found around most French cities with the aim of stopping the Allies while buying time to better prepare for the defense of the German homeland.

The task of defeating a determined enemy fighting from sturdy fortifications taxed the resolve and resourcefulness of U.S. forces since they had almost no practical experience in battling heavy fortifications. Although doctrine contained broad principles for reducing fortified positions, it was left up to fighting units to devise the tactics and techniques required. Success resulted because soldiers adapted and innovated under fire and quickly learned that only a fully synchronized combined arms effort could defeat heavy fortifications. An article in the *Infantry Journal* made the best argument in favor of combined arms action, declaring that unsupported infantry assaults against strongly fortified positions were doomed and warning that "a man with bayonet and grenades does not 'fight' walls of concrete and steel." But in the early autumn of 1944 American combat units were unsure as to just how they would overcome heavy defenses.[1]

FM 100-5 provided commanders with a conceptual framework for attacking fortified positions. According to doctrine, lead units were to bypass enemy fortifications and let follow-on forces capture them at leisure. If fortifications were impossible to avoid, units were to reduce them by direct attack. FM 100-5 warned that frontal assaults had "little prospect of success" unless the attackers had a "high degree of technical training" and enjoyed "great superiority" in combat power. The attack of a fortified locality occurred in four phases: the elimination of the outpost system and movement toward the main defenses, the breaching of the fortifications at their weakest point, the holding open of the breach against enemy counterattacks, and the passing through of mobile reserves that would isolate and encircle remaining fortifications and attack deep into the enemy's rear. After bombardments by heavy artillery and bombers, engineers and "other special troops" were to attack the openings of fortifications with explosives. After the charges exploded, assault troops were to "rush the position and overpower hostile personnel remaining active." Doctrine cautioned that compared with normal breakthrough operations, breaching fortifications required greater superiority in combat power, the use of specially trained and equipped assault troops, and absolute secrecy and thoroughness in preparations.[2]

Commanders wanting to know more about attacking fortifications could turn to FM 31-50. Published in 1944, the manual reflects the Allies' wartime experience in the attack of fortified positions and American concerns over the eventual assault of Germany's West Wall. Fortified positions fell into one of three categories—localities, lines, and zones—depending upon their extent and depth. FM 31-50 warned that the American infantry division might not have enough combat power to reduce fortifications on its own, so divisions were to operate as part of a larger force and receive augmentation from the other combat arms. Engineers supported attacking troops by breaching minefields and obstacles. Artillery was to fire longer and more intensive bombardments, knock out pillboxes, gap obstacles, and provide cover to assault troops by cratering the ground. Air power was to maintain air supremacy, conduct area bombing, and attack enemy reserves and LOCs. FM 31-50 maintained that the use of tanks was "inadvisable," and that armor's best employment was in exploiting breakthroughs. The reputation of TDs as excellent assault guns in the Mediterranean surfaced in FM 31-50; it recommended TDs as "among the best weapons" for the attack of fortifications. FM 31-50 informed commanders that attack frontages would be greatly reduced, that operations would be slow and tedious, and that only elite assault formations using special weapons and tactics could succeed against heavy fortifications.[3]

One of the army's greatest shortfalls was its neglect in developing doctrine and equipment to support mobile operations against heavy fortifications. The U.S. peacetime maneuvers of 1940–1941 and British operations in North Africa confirmed the need for additional resources to support infantry attacks against prepared positions. As late as 1941, FM 100-5 made no mention of the use of mechanical methods to clear obstacles, reduce forts, or provide assault troops with armored protection. Units had to breach obstacles and assault fortifications with hand-placed explosives while only indirect fire and smoke protected them from enemy fire. The Mediterranean campaigns revealed that mine warfare was one of the U.S. army's worst Achilles' heels, and that troops lacked the proper training and equipment to detect and clear minefields. The American Chief of Engineers worked frantically to develop explosives and mechanical means troops could use against minefields and pillboxes, but with little success. Because it had begun too late in addressing mobility support problems, army units deploying to Europe were not adequately equipped or trained to breach obstacles and reduce fortifications.[4]

Commanders in the ETO faced several significant challenges in the attack of fortified positions, because although doctrine was generally correct, many concepts were either overstated or invalid. Enveloping fortifications and taking them from the rear made for ideal doctrine, but the realities of battle often required frontal assaults. Compared to writings on other types of combat operations, training literature lacked details on how units were to prepare for and conduct attacks. Troops in the field had to improvise to compensate for the absence of heavy equipment for mobility support. Doctrine discussed the need for special assault troops using unique weapons and tactics, but gave commanders little specific information. Commanders had to determine the best ways to carry out coordinated, combined arms attacks using available manpower and resources, and they also had to train and rehearse their soldiers in new assault tactics and techniques.

An analysis of attacks against fortified localities, lines, and zones shows the types of challenges the American combined arms team overcame. The best example of the reduction of a single, fortified locality occurred during VIII Corps' battle for Brest. Although the 8th and 2d divisions closed in on the city from the north and east, the 29th Infantry Division attacked from the west. The Germans had manned and reinforced several large fortresses astride "The Blue and the Gray" Division's axis of advance. One of these was Fort Montbarey, perhaps the most formidable bastion within Brest's outer defensive network, which consisted of concrete inner works surrounded by four massive walls of earth-filled masonry forty feet thick and forty feet high. On its north and west sides a dry moat twenty feet wide and fifteen feet deep served as an antitank ditch, and the Germans laid thick minefields on both sides of the moat. Montbarey contained no heavy guns, and the 100-man garrison defended it with only small arms and machine guns. Several concrete pillboxes, heavy antiaircraft guns, and open gun pits nearby commanded the approaches to Montbarey and added significant firepower to its defense.[5]

From 14–16 September the 29th Division's 1st Battalion, 116th Infantry, fought to reduce Montbarey. The purpose of the first attack phase was to isolate the fortress and to get troops up close to the large walls. During the night of 13–14 September the 1st Battalion moved into attack positions. Before dawn, teams from the division's 121st Engineers moved forward to clear two paths through the minefields. At the same time, the battalion began to capture or destroy Montbarey's outlying defenses. At sunrise, Company C attacked to capture all of the German positions west of the fort. In a hard day of fighting at close quarters with hand grenades and bayonets, the company managed to seize all of Montbarey's western outer defenses. Heavy, accurate artillery fire reduced, but did not eliminate, fires coming from Montbarey's eastern defenses. By late afternoon the 1st Battalion had all but isolated the fortress from its supporting positions.[6]

Getting troops into assault positions near the large walls proved much tougher than isolating the fort. On the afternoon of 14 September, while Company C and the 29th Division's artillery worked over the fort's surrounding defenses, the rest of the battalion launched a combined arms attack to tighten the noose around Montbarey. Three TDs from the 644th Tank Destroyer Battalion moved into positions from which they could fire on the fortress. To the delight of American troops, special flamethrower tanks from the British Royal Armoured Corps joined in the attack. (Before the Brest campaign VIII Corps had anticipated the problems of battling fortifications and requested armored vehicles from the British that would enhance mobile operations against fortifications. Four Churchill tanks from B Squadron, 141st Tank Regiment, equipped with special flame-throwing devices, joined VIII Corps at the beginning of the campaign and played a significant role in reducing strongholds.) At 1300 hours, mortars, flamethrower tanks, TDs, and engineers went to work on the fort's outer defenses. Mortar crews laid down a thick smoke screen to block German observation. TDs and tanks opened fire against the fort's defenses while engineers continued to clear the minefields; by 1630 hours they had opened two large gaps through the mines.[7]

A tank-infantry assault at 1700 hours completed the preliminary operations. Three Churchills led the attack, moving in column along a cleared path in the minefield. The first tank made it through, but the second struck a mine and was disabled. With the path blocked, the third tank could not advance. The lead Churchill found itself alone and isolated on the enemy side of the obstacle. The tank commander, Lt. Herbert A. Ward, realized his precarious situation and knew his only chance for survival was to attack. Looking like a twentieth-century version of a mythological fire-breathing dragon, the Churchill lashed out at the north and east sides of the fort with long plumes of flame. Soldiers of the 1st Battalion watched in awe as Ward's Churchill spewed flame, shells, and bullets at the Germans. The 1st Battalion commander called the action "as bold an act as I have ever seen." Covered by Ward's heavy fire, riflemen from Company B crossed the minefield and captured German positions just outside the fort. They reported that Germans who had not been wounded or driven off by the Churchill's attack were "completely terrified and incapable of action." Ward's Churchill soon ran out of fuel for the flamethrower, but he continued to cover the infantry advance with main gun and machine-gun fire until he expended all of his ammunition. As darkness fell, Company B was securely in position just outside of Montbarey's walls. American soldiers spent the following day improving gaps in the minefield, creating a passage through the moat for armored vehicles by partially filling in the antitank ditch, and making other preparations for the final assault.[8]

On 16 September Montbarey's besiegers literally hammered, burned, and blasted the fortress into submission. The Churchills delivered the opening blows by circling the fortress while scorching it with plumes of flame. Montbarey's walls had proved impervious to direct and indirect fire, so the battalion commander decided to smash his way inside through the main gate. A TD rolled forward and fired fifty rounds at point-blank range in an attempt to open the entrance. However, the Germans had reinforced the gate with scrap metal, rocks, and heavy debris, and it refused to budge. The TD's unsuccessful efforts prompted the battalion commander to send for a 105-mm howitzer, and in a scene similar to the siege operations of eighteenth-century warfare, soldiers brought the gun forward and placed its muzzle twenty yards from the main gate. The cannon hammered the gate partially open with more than fifteen rounds and then sent numerous high explosive and white phosphorous shells slamming into the inner courtyard.[9]

A lull in the fighting occurred when infantrymen found another way into Montbarey. While clearing German positions on the north side, they discovered an underground passageway blocked by a heavy door at the juncture with the fort's north wall. Wanting to achieve surprise and minimize casualties, the battalion commander decided to breach the north wall with explosives. Engineers and riflemen lugged boxes of TNT into the passageway until they had emplaced 1,500 pounds of explosives against the fort's wall. Meanwhile, the battalion commander sent in a surrender ultimatum that the fort commander, an SS officer, flatly rejected. The rebuffed American commander shot back with a terse rejoinder: "I intend to blow you to hell." The negotiations over, engineers and infantrymen withdrew 300 yards to escape the blast's effects. When all was ready, the officer overseeing the demolitions effort made a final check with the battalion commander. Angered by his confrontation with Montbarey's commanding officer, the 1st Battalion commander's order to attack was graphic and short: "F——— 'em! Blow 'em all up!" With a tremendous roar the north wall erupted in a geyser of earth and stone, with much of the debris sliding into the moat. Infantry platoons with tanks in close support moved in fast, climbed over the shattered wall that had settled into the moat, and stormed into Montbarey's interior. The subterranean explosion and follow-on assault completely stunned the garrison, who surrendered without firing a shot. By nightfall, the infantry had cleared the fort and rounded up seventy-five prisoners. With Montbarey in American hands, the way was now clear for the 29th Division to push into Brest.[10]

The capture of Fort Montbarey illustrates many of the characteristics of U.S. operations against fortified positions. Preliminary moves validated one main point of doctrine: attackers had to isolate a stronghold from its surrounding, supporting defenses. The use of Churchill flamethrower tanks emphasized two weaknesses in American theory and practice. Contrary to doctrine, armored vehicles had a key, direct combat role in attacking strongholds. Second, the army lacked the right types of armored vehicles and heavy equipment to support mobile operations against fortifications. The 1st Battalion's methods also show the American tendency to use overwhelming firepower during close combat. Using a cannon at point-blank range to batter down Montbarey's main gate and an abundance of explosives to rip away part of the outer wall are just two examples of the army's increased willingness to use any means necessary to blow its enemy into submission.

No line of steel and concrete defenses challenged the army like the German West Wall, a fortified belt extending along Germany's western border from the Dutch frontier in the north to near the city of Basel on the Swiss border. In the spring of 1940 the West Wall, known to Americans as the "Siegfried Line," consisted of more than 3,000 concrete pillboxes and bunkers. For much of the war German concerns on other fronts resulted in the line's neglect, but in August 1944 Hitler ordered substantial work done to bolster its defenses. Forced labor and German troops emplaced minefields and obstacles, cleared fields of fire, and dug trenches, foxholes, and antitank ditches that added depth to the line. Although the intensive labor effort did result in many improvements, both the German and American armies discovered that the West Wall's principal strength was in its aged steel and concrete fortifications.[11]

Unlike the French Maginot Line, the West Wall was not a single line of elaborate, individual fortresses but a belt of many small, mutually supporting pillboxes. The pillbox line alone was not intended to defeat an enemy offensive but to blunt and contain the attack until German mobile reserves could arrive and counterattack. On average, pillbox density was ten positions per mile. The typical pillbox measured 20 to 30 feet in width, had a depth of 40 to 50 feet, and was 20 to 25 feet in height; the walls and roofs were usually 3 to 8 feet thick. The structure consisted of poured concrete reinforced by wire mesh, steel rods, or larger steel beams. At least half of the pillbox was buried below ground level. Most had two firing ports or embrasures; one housed a cannon or heavy machine gun pointed toward the enemy, the other allowed protection of the pillbox's rear entrances. Single embrasures had limited fields of fire, but mutually supporting pillboxes provided thorough coverage of the defensive zone. Each pillbox had several ammunition storage rooms and living quarters for its defenders, usually about fifteen soldiers.[12]

The West Wall first challenged American units as they approached the German frontier north of the Ardennes in mid-September. (See Map 5.1.) Below Aachen, VII Corps conducted a hasty attack that broke through a portion of the wall, but General Collins was unable to exploit his success. On 18 September XIX Corps reached the German frontier north of Aachen and took up defensive positions for the first time since leaving Normandy. To the north, Operation MARKET-GARDEN, the huge Allied airborne and ground assault designed to move around the northern end of the West Wall, had miscarried. Further south, American units struggled to cross the Moselle and overcome fortifications in Lorraine. The only place where American forces were in a position to breach the wall and continue the attack toward Germany was in the XIX Corps sector. First Army's assignment for XIX Corps was clear and simple: breach the Siegfried Line, attack eastward toward Cologne, and advance as far as the Roer River. To

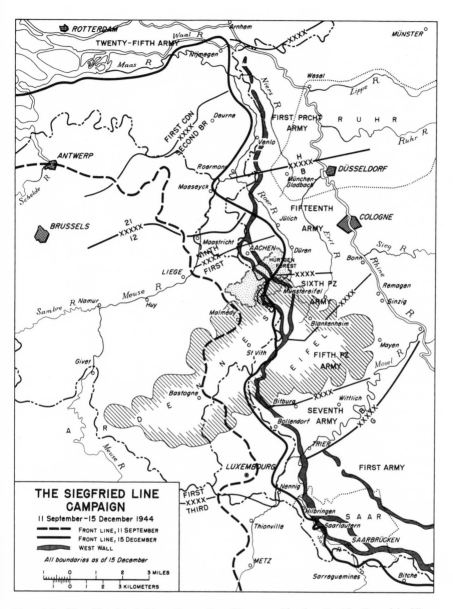

Map 5.1. The Siegfried Line Campaign (*Source*: Charles B. MacDonald, *The Siegfried Line Campaign* (Washington, D.C.: U.S. Army, Office of the Chief of Military History, 1950; reprint ed., Washington, D.C.: U.S. Army Center of Military History, 1984), map 9.)

accomplish his task, General Corlett had four divisions on hand. Because of their battle experience and position in the line, the 30th Infantry and 2d Armored divisions would lead the attack. Major General Hobbs's 30th Division had the mission of breaching the West Wall and establishing a bridgehead beyond the pillbox line. General Harmon's 2d Armored Division would then exploit the breach by attacking eastward toward the Roer. As Harmon's tanks struck east, the 30th Division would push south to effect a linkup with VII Corps, thus opening a wide gap in the line and closing the circle around Aachen.[13]

XIX Corps planners pored over their maps and performed detailed reconnaissance to determine the best point of attack. The corps front stretched over 15 miles, from near Aachen northward beyond the town of Geilenkirchen, and the West Wall presented a continuous obstacle of uniform strength across the entire corps front. The most serious natural obstacle was the Wurm River, averaging 30 feet in width, with steep banks and surrounding marshy, low ground making it a serious tank obstacle. The Germans had constructed the West Wall to maximize the river's defensive potential, and the pillbox zone extended roughly 2 miles in depth behind it. XIX Corps picked an area approximately 10 miles north of Aachen as the *schwerpunkt* of the corps attack because of the sector's good road network and open terrain.[14]

Once it knew the exact point of attack, the 30th Division began detailed preparations. Reflecting the army's increased emphasis on meticulous planning, the intelligence picture for the Siegfried Line assault was almost as complete and accurate as that developed for the Normandy landings. IX TAC flew extensive aerial reconnaissance that resulted in detailed photos of the pillbox line, the British and French provided sketches and photos taken during the West Wall's construction, and patrols crossed the Wurm River to gather specific details on improvements to the defenses. As a result of these efforts, staff officers had correctly identified at least 90 percent of all pillbox locations before the attack. XIX Corps produced special overprinted maps that plotted all known defenses and obstacles; over 450 of these maps went to the 30th Division, and on D-Day every squad leader carried one. Commanders also received blowup aerial photos of their sectors, and brigade and battalion commanders went aloft in Piper Cubs for a bird's-eye view of the assault area. Many units built detailed sand tables of their attack zones. In one battalion, every man participating in the attack—infantrymen, tankers, engineers, TD crews, and artillery FOs—studied the sand table as leaders explained their exact mission and the actions of adjacent units.[15]

The 30th Division carried out intensive, refresher training in pillbox reduction tactics. All three of the Old Hickory Division's regiments—the 117th, 119th, and 120th Infantry—conducted training down to the squad

Combat-zone training programs helped prepare soldiers for the attack of fortifications. GIs of the 30th Infantry Division use a flamethrower on a German pillbox north of Aachen. (U.S. Army Military History Institute)

level. The regiments remained in their forward positions opposite the Siegfried Line but rotated battalions back to training sites in the rear. A battalion commander in the 117th Infantry best summarized why units needed additional training: "All of the training we had back in the States and in England was now useless because all of our assault detachments had been wiped out in previous battles and there was a complete turnover in battalion personnel. We had to start from scratch."[16] Each company conducted at least two days of refresher training on the use of pole and satchel charges, bangalore torpedoes, flamethrowers, and bazookas. Troops learned how to use all of the equipment in their platoon so that if a demolition man or flamethrower operator were wounded, someone else could pick up the weapon and continue. Platoon leaders reorganized their troops into assault and covering sections and conducted reviews of the roles and methods of each. Companies trained on assault tactics and conducted full rehearsals of attacks against simulated pillboxes. Engineers practiced the speedy construction and emplacement of bridging for the Wurm River assault, while armored units rehearsed river crossing and close infantry support techniques.[17]

Training for the Wurm River assault resulted in innovations typical of the American army. Soldiers found a gully with standing water that they used to practice crossing the Wurm, while another battalion used a road to simulate the river. The original attack plan called for troops to use assault boats, but the 30th Division's officers came up with an idea for using special ladders to get across the river. The division's 105th Combat Engineer Battalion went to work with hammers, nails, and saws to build enough ladders for soldiers to train with and to use in the actual crossing. Tankers and engineers came up with their own expedient methods for getting armored vehicles over the Wurm, lashing together logs and metal culverts to use as fill in the streambed. Shermans would pull the materials to the riverbank on special sleds, and then tank dozers would push the culverts into the water so that vehicles could drive over them and reach the opposite bank. Other tankers devised log mats that they could roll across the streambed to use as a base for fords.[18]

As soldiers finished their preparations, the 30th Division's senior leaders put the final touches on their battle plan. General Hobbs decided to commit all three of his regiments and to hold back only one battalion in reserve. The main attack would take place on a narrow front less than a mile wide; the 117th and 119th Infantry were to attack abreast, the 117th on the left. With little room to maneuver and no place to hide, both regimental commanders decided to attack straight ahead with battalions in column; extensive artillery and air support were a vital part of the plan. Beginning on 26 September, division, corps, and army artillery battalions took on four separate missions: destruction of pillboxes; prevention of an enemy buildup in the zone of attack; shelling of German artillery, antiaircraft, and mortar positions; and marking of targets for air strikes. Artillerymen learned an important lesson during the bombardment; normal shelling of pillboxes accomplished little, and only direct fire from 155-mm howitzers had the velocity, weight, and accuracy to damage pillboxes. Soon several big 155s were up on the front lines and successfully destroyed or damaged as many as forty-three pillboxes with direct fire. XIX Corps planned to support the 30th Division's assault with a vigorous, preparatory bombardment by medium bombers and fighter-bombers. The objectives of the air attack were to effect a saturation bombing of the breakthrough area, to disrupt German counterattack forces, and to knock out the pillbox line in the zone of attack. Ninth Air Force assigned nine groups of medium bombers and two groups of fighter-bombers to deliver the first punches in the corps attack.[19]

With all preparations completed, XIX Corps set 1100 hours on 2 October as H-hour for the ground attack. Fifteen minutes prior to the air bombardment that began around 0900 hours, artillery units hit over one hundred suspected flak locations with counter-antiaircraft fire. The "blackout" firing was highly successful and airplanes encountered little ground fire. The air attack was almost a total failure, as scattered clouds and problems with target identification caused the medium bombers to go astray. Bombs fell neither on friendly troops nor on their intended targets, and fighter-bombers had better luck hitting targets marked with artillery smoke. As bomber formations droned away from the target area, twenty-four battalions of massed artillery lashed out at the pillbox line and likely enemy locations. The shelling's greatest effects were to strip away camouflage from pillboxes, rip up wire obstacles, and force Germans in supporting positions to take cover. Cannoneers dug deep into their ammunition reserves to compensate for the air bombardment's poor results. Between 0600 and 1800 hours on 2 October, 372 artillery tubes fired 18,696 rounds in support of the ground attack. The 30th Division's mortars provided a rolling barrage just in front of attacking troops that cut barbed wire and suppressed the pillboxes.[20]

At 1100 hours the 117th and 119th Infantry charged across the Wurm and toward the pillbox line in columns of battalions. In the north, the 117th crossed the river on improvised foot bridges in the face of considerable enemy small arms, mortar, and artillery fire. By nightfall the two lead battalions had reduced eleven pillboxes and seized their objectives on the far side of the Wurm. Thick woods and steep ground made the 119th's going difficult. Not until around noon the next day did the battalions finally push forward and begin reducing the pillbox line. Overnight on 2 October engineers put heavy bridging over the Wurm that permitted the 2d Armored Division to get into the fight. Marshy ground canalized armored employment on the next day, but as the infantry expanded the bridgehead, tank units began to maneuver.[21]

Several lessons emerged as XIX Corps soldiers grappled with the pillbox line. Although units adhered to broad doctrinal principles for attacking fortifications, they learned that the emphasis placed by doctrine and peacetime training on the frontal assault of pillbox embrasures was misguided. A corps after-action report emphasized that the "elaborate, concrete stronghold reduction techniques" advocated by the Engineer School at Fort Belvoir and the Infantry School at Fort Benning were "neither used nor applicable." Assault troops had to deal not only with pillboxes, but with the numerous German positions placed to provide additional strength and depth to the pillbox line. A clear majority of German troops and weapons manned the secondary positions, and in fact, seizing those positions became the key to capturing the line. Once American troops isolated the pillbox line by eliminating the supporting defenses, German resistance usually collapsed.[22]

The pillbox reduction tactics created by the 30th Division relied on simplicity and combined arms fire and maneuver. (See Figure 5.1.) Each infantry company formed three assault teams of approximately twenty men each. In addition to their personal weapons, each assault team carried a bazooka or flamethrower, six satchel charges, two additional BARs, and fragmentation and colored smoke grenades. Attacks began with artillery and mortar fire to suppress secondary defenses, force German gunners to close pillbox embrasures, and tear away camouflage. Under the cover of indirect fire, teams of engineers, infantry, and tanks or TDs

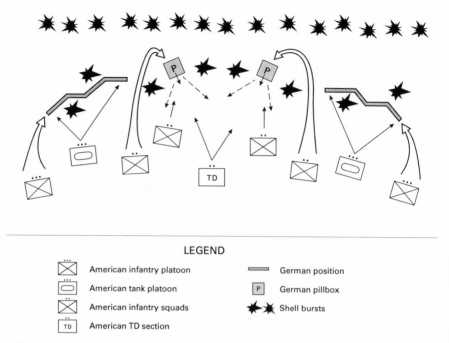

Figure 5.1. 30th Infantry Division Pillbox Reducing Tactics (Sherry L. Dowdy)

moved into final attack positions. As artillery fire shifted beyond the objective, direct fire from armored vehicles against the pillboxes prevented German gunners from manning their heavy weapons. Infantry platoons with three- or four-man engineer demolition teams maneuvered their way behind the pillboxes under the cover of armored vehicle firepower while other infantry outfits attacked German supporting positions. Assault troops attacked the rear doors of pillboxes with satchel charges, bangalore torpedoes, and bazookas. As a general rule, Germans surrendered after assault troops blew down the rear entrance, and entering to capture and clear pillboxes was usually unnecessary. Grenades thrown inside through firing slits or doorways torn open by explosives forced even the most stouthearted pillbox crews to surrender. Troops needed an average of thirty minutes to capture a single pillbox.[23]

Experience yielded a number of valuable lessons. As troops moved in on a pillbox, indirect fire to the front and flanks smothered German defenses beyond the objective area. With threats from supporting defenses eliminated, troops could concentrate all their efforts on the pillbox. Commanders learned that they had to push beyond captured pillboxes to avoid a downpour of German artillery and mortar fire. Preparing for counterattacks was a must. Operations usually halted an hour before sundown so that units would be ready for German ripostes that came right after dark. Flamethrowers were put to good use, but infantrymen preferred to use bazookas against pillbox doors and embrasures. Team leaders effectively used smoke grenades to lift and shift tank and artillery fire. Reconnaissance by fire assisted troops in finding well camouflaged pillboxes, and infantrymen and tankers used machine guns firing armor-piercing ammunition to spray areas thought to contain pillboxes. When the bullets struck concrete, they sparked and ricocheted wildly. Mortar shells then tore away the camouflage to expose the position.[24]

The performance of Company B, 1st Battalion, 117th Infantry, shows the validity of the 30th Division's pillbox reducing tactics and the benefits of precombat training. After crossing the Wurm River on the morning of 2 October, Company B's platoons pushed ahead while mortars and machine guns kept the Germans' heads down. Support squads took up positions from which to fire on pillbox embrasures, while specially organized assault teams armed with demolitions, flamethrowers, and bazookas moved in. Training ensured that soldiers knew their job, and they went to work with grim determination. Satchel charges, bazookas, and grenades battered down pillbox entrances, while riflemen kept pillbox embrasures closed. A flamethrower team's liberal use of hot gas prompted one pillbox to surrender without a fight, and in another instance a jet of flame squirted through a firing slit detonated ammunition inside the pillbox. Most prisoners appeared shaken by the artillery bombardment. The 117th Regiment's commander attributed the company's success to their thoroughness in prebattle training, speed of execution, and high degree of coordination. In XIX Corps' first penetration of the Siegfried Line, Company B seized eight pillboxes in less than two hours.[25]

Defeating German counterattacks trying to restore the pillbox line challenged XIX Corps. In heavy fighting on 4–6 October, German units hammered at the American encroachment. Counterattacks varied in strength from company to battalion size with support from four to six tanks and generally occurred right before dark or just prior to daylight. During the battles U.S. commanders began to realize and appreciate improvements in combined arms operations. On 5 October the 117th Infantry's fight against German counterpunches was an "excellent example" of cooperation between infantry, tanks, and TDs. The next day the 119th Infantry grappled with two German infantry battalions supported by tanks and heavy artillery. All morning long American fighter-bombers and artillery supported tank-infantry teams. The regimental commander reported that deadly artillery fire and two "beautiful" air strikes helped turn the tide. A platoon leader in the 117th Infantry gave a vivid account of the combined arms coordination he had experienced: "We had real tank-infantry cooperation. . . . The tanks just machine gunned the Jerries in their holes and when the doughs came up it was mass murder." Americans stood fast under the counterblows, then lunged forward even further. By 7 October the 30th Division was through the pillbox line. As General Hobbs began to push south for a juncture with VII Corps, Harmon's tanks in the north battled their way eastward toward the Roer River. By the evening of 16 October, the 30th Infantry and 2d Armored Divisions had blown a gap in the West Wall fourteen miles wide, penetrated six miles beyond the pillbox line, and established contact with VII Corps.[26]

Adaptations in combined arms tactics, thorough training, and detailed planning made XIX Corps' deliberate attack of the Siegfried Line a notable success. Companies used gullies, ditches, and roads to simulate the Wurm River while training for the opening phase of the attack. Infantrymen and engineers built duckboard ladders to get across the river. In the absence of mobile assault bridges, tankers lashed together fascines that they strapped on their vehicles to help them cross the Wurm. The greatest adaptations took place when commanders changed their tactics and formations to reduce the pillbox line. They rejected the army's established method of attacking pillboxes—frontal assaults by troops using hand-placed explosives—and preferred to move around behind and attack positions from the flank or rear. Commanders also developed tactical combinations that enabled troops to attack pillboxes and their supporting defensive positions concurrently. Infantry units reorganized into assault and support detachments and integrated tanks, TDs, engineers, and artillery support into their formations.

Prebattle training was also instrumental in the success. The 30th Division's training program in the days just before the assault had three significant results. First, the Old Hickory Division had suffered major losses in the battles for France, and units needed time to rebuild cohesion threatened by the rapid turnover of personnel and to give remedial training to replacements. Second, previous combat experience had taught commanders that troops needed thorough cross-training in all weapons. Soldiers had to know how to use their personal weapon as well as special equipment like satchel charges, bangalore torpedoes, and flamethrowers. During the fighting along the pillbox line, units were largely successful because they were able to keep their special weapons functioning despite casualties among the original operators. Last, prebattle training insured that the combined arms team acted in concert, as infantrymen, tankers, TD crews, engineers, and artillery FOs practiced together the specific techniques they would use against the pillboxes. Because of the training, units were able to cooperate closely while reducing a single pillbox or during sustained attacks from one position to the next. After the campaign the XIX Corps leadership concluded that the "best technique" to reduce a fortified line was to employ a combined arms team of thoroughly prepared soldiers. Staff Sgt. Howard King of Company A, 117th Infantry, saw the benefits of unit training firsthand. "Even when we got a new pillbox to take," he remarked after the fight, "we just pushed out our support and assault detachments mechanically."[27]

A detailed intelligence picture greatly assisted in the reduction of the pillbox line. Aerial and photo reconnaissance as well as plans and pictures of the fortifications under construction provided valuable information, while infantry and engineer foot patrols gained the most accurate and detailed intelligence. XIX Corps did an unusually good job of disseminating the collective intelligence picture to assault units, which received photos and overprinted maps of their objectives; many constructed detailed sand tables to prepare for the offensive. Timely and accurate intelligence gave troops several marked advantages. Leaders were able to develop detailed plans down to the lowest level, so that soldiers knew the exact locations and capabilities of nearly all pillboxes and supporting defenses, while staff officers drew up fire support plans that included the attack of every known pillbox.

Although firepower provided by artillery and bomber units proved effective in most battles, it failed to achieve significant results against the Siegfried Line. The artillery's most important role was in hammering German counterattacks, and although not accurate enough to destroy individual pillboxes, artillery fire was effective in isolating the battle area, attacking secondary defensive positions, destroying minefields and wire obstacles, and making shell craters that gave infantrymen cover. Medium bombers accomplished almost nothing in the 2 October bombardment, prompting XIX Corps to report that air-ground support techniques were "obviously unable" to coordinate medium bombers with ground forces; not until Operation QUEEN in the following month would American forces demonstrate this ability. However, the attack did show that fighter-bombers had become a strong partner in the combined arms team. From 2 to 25 October, IX TAC flew forty-one missions in the 30th Division zone, striking enemy counterattacks and sometimes hitting targets within 200 yards of American GIs. XIX Corps characterized fighter-bomber support throughout the campaign as "extremely flexible, sensitive to rapidly changing conditions, and outstandingly effective."[28]

The reduction of the great fortress city of Metz and its surrounding defenses best illustrates how U.S. troops conducted the attack of a fortified zone. Between 5 September and 21 November 1944, Patton's Third Army tried a number of different schemes to bypass or reduce the Metz fortifications. The campaign shows the adaptability of commanders and soldiers in meeting tactical challenges, the ways in which the combined arms team worked together to overcome a fortified zone, and the distinct limits the army had in generating combat power.

During the month of August, Patton and Third Army conducted a dazzling pursuit to the German border, the rapid advances suiting the psychology and temperament of Patton the cavalryman. The pursuit reached its high-water mark on 31 August, when Third Army tanks crossed the Meuse River at Verdun. By evening on the next day, small cavalry patrols had probed as far east as the Moselle River, and Patton could take great pride in the fact that at the end of August his troops were 150 miles beyond the Seine River, a barrier SHAEF planners believed that American troops would not reach until 3 September.[29]

However, in the aftermath of the summer pursuit, a number of conditions began to prevail that warned of the stalemate and bloody battles that soon followed. In dashing across France, Third Army had outrun its logistical network, and severe gasoline, ammunition, and supply shortages began to crop up in the last days of August. On the morning of 2 September, forward columns flooded army headquarters with reports that their fuel tanks were bone-dry. Third Army was frozen in its tracks. All but drunk with the success of the autumn pursuit, overoptimism was rampant among the army's senior leadership. Patton and his corps commanders knew little of the enemy's efforts to rally on the German border and knew even less about the fortifications around Metz and along the Maginot and Siegfried lines. Because of bad weather, ground units would sorely miss the outstanding air support they had enjoyed during the late summer. Vehicles were in dire need of repair and routine maintenance, and soldiers had grown weary from the frantic pace of the long pursuit. Casualties in the battles around Metz and Nancy would stretch the individual replacement system to the breaking point. With priority of supply movement going to food, fuel, and ammunition, clothing for cold and wet weather remained stacked in supply dumps far to the rear. Unprepared for the cold, rainy weather of Lorraine, Third Army soldiers were to suffer greatly from trench foot, exposure, and combat exhaustion.

On 4 September SHAEF gave the green light for the resumption of Third Army's offensive through Lorraine. Patton's mission was to attack eastward, "occupy the sector of the Siegfried Line covering the Saar and then to seize Frankfurt" while taking advantage of "any opportunity of destroying enemy forces withdrawing from southwest and south France." Determined to overcome all obstacles, Patton lost no time in getting his army moving again. A few days respite had allowed the fuel situation to improve somewhat, and on 5 September he issued orders for the immediate resumption of the offensive. Third Army contained two corps during most of the Lorraine campaign. Maj. Gen. Manton S. Eddy's XII Corps would undertake operations in the army's southern sector around

Nancy, while the XX Corps, under Maj. Gen. Walton H. Walker, focused its efforts on an attack through the Metz fortified zone and toward the Siegfried Line. XX Corps consisted of the 7th Armored Division and the 5th and 90th Infantry divisions. Patton instructed Walker to secure crossings over the Moselle, then push relentlessly toward the Rhine. Neither Patton and his staff nor the XX Corps senior leadership, showed much regard for the enemy opposition that they might encounter along the Moselle or around Metz.

While Third Army tried to cope with the supply crisis, the Germans worked mightily to piece together a coherent strategy and enough troops to defend Lorraine. Hitler's personal influence shaped the operational concept for the battles around Metz. Contrary to all Allied intelligence estimates that envisioned German troops rallying on the West Wall, Hitler ordered his units to defend as far forward as possible. The Germans declared Metz a "fortress city" that would serve as their bulwark in defending northern Lorraine, tying down as many American units as possible and serving as a secure base for counterattacks. In his decision to defend Lorraine, Hitler displayed some method in his warrior-king madness. A forward defense bought valuable time for units to prepare better for the defense of the West Wall. Of even more significance, Hitler believed the stubborn defense of Lorraine was the only way he could gain enough time to plan and muster forces for a decisive Sunday punch against the Allied armies during the early winter.[30]

The German high command made a herculean effort to organize resistance at the scene of the crisis in Lorraine. Reinforcements rushed in from as far away as northern Italy and Denmark, and local commanders worked miracles in reconstituting units that had been cut to pieces in Normandy and during the retreat across France. Responsibility for the Metz sector fell to Generalleutnant der Waffen-SS Herman Preiss and his XIII SS Corps. By 5 September Preiss had an equivalent of four-and-a-half divisions available to defend the Metz area. (See Map 5.2.) To the north around Thionville, the 48th Division prepared to defend the line of the Moselle. To the left of the 48th Division, the 559th Volksgrenadier Division established defensive positions as far south as Maizieres-les-Metz. On the extreme German left, the veteran 17th SS Panzer Grenadier Division made ready to defend the Moselle around Arnaville. The actual defense of the Metz fortifications fell on the 14,000 soldiers of Division Number 462, a composite unit of fortress troops and students, staff, and faculty members of the numerous military schools located in Metz. Many of these soldiers were among the best the German army had to offer, having been selected for additional schooling based on their exemplary performance on the battlefield. The division defended west of Metz along an arc that stretched from Maizieres-les-Metz south to Dornot. In reality, the XIII SS

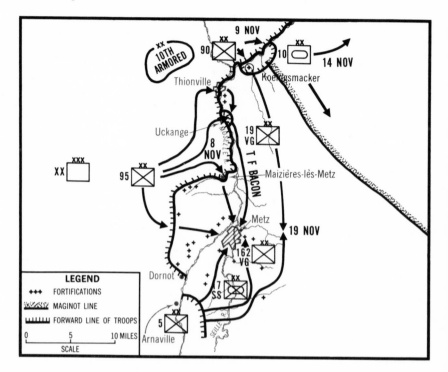

Map 5.2. XX Corps' Capture of Metz, 8–21 November 1944 (*Source*: Christopher R. Gable, *The Lorraine Campaign: An Overview, September–December 1944* (Fort Leavenworth, Kansas: Combat Studies Institute, U.S. Army Command and General Staff College, 1985), 27.)

Corps was a patchwork of new, old, and reconstituted battalions that differed widely in experience and weaponry and whose fighting ability ranged from very good to poor.[31]

The actual fortifications around Metz were extensive but varied greatly in quality. The first set of modern fortifications had been built under the direction and supervision of the celebrated French engineer Vauban, whose fifteen forts around the city composed an inner ring of defenses that functioned primarily as infantry strongholds. After the Franco-Prussian War, the Germans constructed a second, outer belt of twenty-eight forts and fortified groups west of Metz that occupied high ground six miles from the city along an arc stretching from Maizieres south to Dornot. The outer forts were essentially hardened artillery positions consisting of a main bastion with several smaller supporting positions. The fortress superstructures were generally below ground with their large-caliber guns firing from rounded, revolving turrets that protruded slightly from the fort's concrete surface. In the fall of 1944 some forts were in good condition, while others lacked functioning guns, ammunition, and fire control equipment. Substantial garrisons manned the main fortresses, skeleton forces defended others, and some positions stood empty.[32]

In contrast to the Germans' extensive knowledge of the terrain and defensive works around Metz, Third Army possessed almost no information about the locations, characteristics, and capabilities of the city's fortresses. Working in an information void, intelligence estimates on the threat posed by the Metz defenses were little more than guesswork. Walker's XX Corps staff believed that the defenses were outmoded and that if the Germans did stand and fight, they could be easily defeated.[33]

On 7 September XX Corps renewed its offensive toward Germany that Patton and Walker hoped would culminate in the capture of crossing sites over the Rhine. The 5th Infantry Division, commanded by Maj. Gen. S. LeRoy Irwin, attacked the outer ring of the Metz fortresses on the west bank of the Moselle and ran into trouble. Fighting over rough ground against fortresses defended by the experienced Division Number 462, Irwin's soldiers made little progress. The "Red Diamond" Division made two attempts to get over the Moselle. The first crossing at Dornot was uncoordinated, ill-supported, and resulted in a disaster. A successful river crossing took place at Arnaville on 10 September, but breaking out of the bridgehead proved impossible. Then, on 25 September, Patton's greatest fears materialized. With the Allied supply situation showing no sign of improvement, Eisenhower gave full priority of supplies to Montgomery in the Lowlands and ordered Third Army to hold its positions. Unwilling to let the Germans seize the initiative, Patton ordered his corps to go on the defensive but to maintain aggressive patrolling and reconnaissance. "Old Blood and Guts" received permission to conduct several limited operations that would put Third Army in a good posture for resuming its offensive. Walker believed the best approach to Metz was from the south, but before XX Corps could mount such an offensive, it would have to punch a hole through the outer ring of Metz's heavy fortifications by reducing one of the large, key forts. The attack resulted in a major reverse for XX Corps and one of the army's most bitter experiences in reducing fortifications.[34]

The XX Corps staff identified Fort Driant as the key bastion southwest of Metz. Set on dominating heights on the west bank of the Moselle two miles north of Dornot, Driant's tactical significance was unquestionable. Its heavy guns dominated the Moselle River valley and added considerable firepower to the defenses west of Metz. Any attack north along the Moselle had little chance of succeeding unless American forces captured or neutralized Driant. Squatting at the top of a bare, rounded hill that rose 360 yards above the Moselle River, the fort looked roughly like a rectangle, more than half a mile in length and varying in width from 500 to 800 yards. Fort Driant faced toward the southwest but had all-around offensive and defensive capabilities. Its main defenses consisted of four casements that each mounted a three-piece battery of either 100- or 150-mm guns protected by reinforced concrete walls seven feet thick. The casement roofs were built flush to the outer surface of the fort, and only the armored gun mounts protruded from the large concrete plateau along with a few reinforced observation posts, pillboxes, and troop bunkers. From the outside, Fort Driant appeared much like one large slab of concrete that covered 355 acres of ground. A moat 60 feet wide and almost 30 feet deep protected the front of the fortress, and a thick band of barbed wire 60 feet in depth encircled the entire work. A network of underground tunnels provided the Germans easy passage between all batteries and fighting positions. Fort Driant was built to house a garrison of almost 2,000 soldiers, and enough Germans manned the defenses to make them fully functional. In all, Fort Driant was probably the most formidable and well-prepared heavy fortification that the American army attempted to reduce in all of World War II.[35]

The first attempt to take Fort Driant was hastily conceived, improperly supported, and failed miserably. The 5th Division's 11th Infantry received the mission of capturing the fort. Driant's guns had inflicted heavy casualties on the 11th Infantry during the Dornot river crossing, and some believed the regiment merely wanted revenge against the fort's defenders. Estimating that the fort was lightly garrisoned and believing that one heavily reinforced infantry battalion could take Driant, the 11th Infantry had little information to use in planning the initial attack, and troops went into battle with only a vague idea of the fort's works and the surrounding terrain. On 27 September the 2d Battalion, 11th Infantry, reinforced by elements of the 735th Tank and 818th TD battalions and an engineer company, made the first attempt to capture Driant. XIX TAC fighter-bombers and supporting artillery hit the fort with bombs, napalm, and shells throughout the morning and early afternoon but did little damage. Around 1400 hours, the 2d Battalion moved forward against Driant's south face, but the attack ground to a halt on the edge of the fort's moat when troops failed to get through an extensive barbed wire entanglement. German machine guns and mortars hacked away at the attackers, and fire came from several pillboxes and supporting defenses that the Americans did not know existed. Tanks and TDs moved forward to blast away at the Germans, but their guns only chipped and scarred the thick concrete. The assault troops hung on in shallow foxholes until early evening when General Irwin ordered a withdrawal. Generals Walker and Irwin argued long and hard over the reasons for the failure, but regardless of the exact cause, the first effort to reduce Driant had been a total fi-asco.[36]

Two days later Walker ordered the 5th Division to go after Driant again. The Red Diamond Division's leadership believed that with better intelligence, detailed planning, and more resources Driant would fall, and the next few days saw intensive preparations. As fate would have it, the 5th Division acquired detailed drawings of Fort Driant on 28 September, the day after the first assault. Aggressive patrolling helped complete the intelligence picture of Driant's outer defenses, and a better grasp of the enemy situation resulted in a revised, expanded plan of attack. The 11th Regiment's 2d Battalion, reinforced by Company B, 1st Battalion, would conduct a dual assault. Company B had the mission of bashing its way into the fort from the south while Company E, 2d Battalion, conducted a supporting attack against the opposite end of the fort. The 2d Battalion's key objectives were the four barracks and casements in Driant's southern half. Again, a tank and an engineer company were in support, their assets split between the assault units.[37]

The 5th Division mustered all available combat power for the attack. Air support parties drafted plans for air strikes, and XX Corps artillery displaced to new firing positions so that all guns could reach Driant. Tankers planned to employ dozer tanks to assist infantrymen through obstacles. Engineer units gathered large stocks of satchel and pole charges, bangalore torpedoes, and flamethrowers, and tankers and engineers worked together to coordinate the use of a new explosive device known as a "snake." It consisted of a pipe 60 feet long and 3 inches in diameter filled with explosives. Soldiers were to push the snake into wire obstacles and across minefields and then detonate it to clear a wide lane through the obstacle.[38]

General Irwin was confident in the division's preparations and set the assault for mid-morning on 3 October. D-Day dawned with overcast skies that grounded aircraft, and it was clear to all that the attack would have to proceed without air support. Anxious to get things started, Irwin ordered his infantry forward. Under the pall of a heavy artillery and mortar smoke screen, the assault companies headed toward Driant's walls at 1145 hours. Bad luck plagued the attack from the start. The dozer tanks broke down, and none of the snakes made it into position because of mud and a series of accidents. Company E's supporting attack in the north had some initial success. Soldiers somehow managed to blow a breach through the barbed wire obstacle, but as they rushed through the gap the Germans opened up with a tremendous volume of small arms and indirect fire. The company took heavy losses and soon withdrew back through the barbed wire. By late afternoon Company E was frozen in its tracks. Without armored vehicle and heavy engineer support, the infantrymen were powerless, remain-

GIs experimented with new methods for using weapons and equipment. Officers of the 5th Infantry Division supervise work on improvised "snake" explosive devices used in the attack on Fort Driant, October 1944. (U.S. Army)

ing in position for four days and finally withdrawing without setting foot in the fort. Company E paid heavily for its attack on Driant—of the original 140 attackers, only 85 men survived.[39]

The main effort by Company B against Driant's southern half had better success. When it was apparent that the dozer tanks and snakes were out of action, Shermans attached to Company B moved forward and blew a hole in the wire barrier that allowed the infantry to rush forward and reach the fort. The company commander, Capt. Harry Anderson, was a one-man army in the initial action, leading from the front, dropping hand grenades into German bunkers, and inspiring his soldiers to follow him into Driant. Tanks moved close behind the assault squads, blasting away at German positions at point-blank range, and before long Company B had established a toehold inside the fort. The Germans soon recovered from the initial assault and turned every available gun on the attackers. By midafternoon it looked as if Company B's attack would also fail when one soldier's actions made the difference. One squad had managed to climb up onto the roof of the southernmost barracks and had discovered a ventilator shaft. Braving enemy fire, Pvt. Robert Holmlund opened the shaft's cover and pushed several bangalore torpedoes down the opening. The explosions forced the Germans to evacuate the barracks, which Company B soon occupied, and before long the Americans had captured the next barracks building. (For his key part in the assault, Private Holmlund received the Distinguished Service Cross but was never able to wear it; a German shell later killed him as he was checking his squad's positions.) At 1730 hours the reserve unit, Company G, moved atop Driant to reinforce the attack's success, and darkness found Companies B and G firmly established on Driant's southernmost corner.[40]

Over the next few days the fighting settled into a torturous pattern, as two separate battles raged for control of Driant. The first was a close-quarters, seesaw fight in the underground tunnels that connected the barracks and gun positions. The Americans entered the tunnel system through the southern barracks and attempted to shoot and blast their way through the interconnecting passageways. Iron doors and other obstacles blocked the tunnels at regular intervals, and soldiers used explosives and welding equipment to clear a path. The close-quarters battle in the underground passageways became a dark death trap that accomplished little and caused heavy casualties. Atop the fort, the battle fared not much better. Attacking companies tried to inch forward, but intense enemy fire stopped them cold. American tanks, TDs, and artillery tried to silence the casements and pillboxes, but the concrete defenses were just too strong. The all-steel revolving turrets were impervious to explosive charges, and neither burning gasoline nor thermite grenades hurt the defenders secure in their underground protection. German machine guns and artillery barrages pummeled American troops who had little cover or concealment. The garrison launched day and night counterpunches by emerging from Driant's tunnel system, attacking the Americans' flank and rear, and then disappearing back into the fort.[41] Late on 5 October the commander of Company G sent back a sobering, grim assessment of the battle atop the fort:

> The situation is critical, a couple more barrages and another counterattack and we are sunk. We have no men, our equipment is shot and we just can't go. . . . The few leaders are trying to keep what is left intact and that's all they can do. The troops are just not sufficiently trained and what is more they have no training in even basic infantry . . . if we want this damned fort let's get the stuff required to take it and then go. Right now you haven't got it.[42]

By the evening of the third day, movement across Driant's surface was impossible, and the original assault companies were unable to move forward or to withdraw. The attackers had become the besieged.

Recognizing the gravity of the situation, General Irwin organized a special combined arms task force whose mission was to put renewed energy into the attack by launching new efforts across Driant's surface and through the tunnel system. Between 7–9 October, the task force attempted to salvage the operation but failed to achieve any real results. By 9 October the 5th Division had experienced enough of Driant's defenses, and Walker, Irwin, and Patton's chief of staff decided to call off the attack. Units extricated themselves slowly, protected by artillery fire and explosive charges, and sunrise on 13 October saw the last American troops leave Driant. The fort extracted a heavy price from the 5th Division: 64 killed, 547 wounded, and 187 missing. Almost half of the assault force became casualties, while many more suffered temporary effects from exhaustion and near suffocation in the tunnels. The attack achieved none of its intended results, and further sapped the 5th Division's strength and fighting spirit.[43]

The Driant debacle produced two major conclusions that had a profound influence on the remainder of the Metz campaign. First, Third Army realized that its formations needed additional training in the attack of heavy defenses. After being relieved on 16 October by the fresh 95th Infantry Division around Fort Driant and Arnaville, the 5th Division withdrew to rear areas to rest, refit, and conduct ten days of refresher training in the attack of fortifications based on the lessons learned at Driant. Units used old pillboxes and bunkers of the Maginot Line to practice tactics and the use of explosives. Engineer troops worked with infantry platoons on the use of flamethrowers, satchel charges, and bangalore torpedoes and trained with tankers on the emplacement and detonation of snakes to make sure that the errors at Driant would not happen again. To the north, the 90th Infantry Division withdrew from the front lines to undergo a similar week-long training period, practicing the methods and teamwork needed to reduce fortified positions. Other units conducted courses on the use of explosives, the attack of fortresses, and house-to-house fighting. Poor performances by replacements also convinced commanders to implement remedial training for new soldiers. Rotating small units on and off the front lines allowed replacements to experience combat before they were thrown into the large battles brewing for control of the Metz fortified region.[44]

Second, all commanders agreed it was better to encircle and isolate the Metz fortified zone rather than undertaking direct and bloody efforts to reduce the defenses, and the desire to avoid a head-on confrontation shaped plans for the fortified zone's capture. On 3 November XX Corps headquarters issued orders outlining the broad scheme of maneuver. Previously XX Corps had wanted to surround and reduce the Metz fortresses, but the final order clearly stated that the "primary mission of all troops" was the "destruction or capture of the Metz garrison, without the investiture or siege of the Metz Forts." Walker's battle plan called for four divisions to attack in as many directions along the corps' 30-mile front. The 90th Division would cross the Moselle near Koenigsmacher and attack south, while the 5th Division would break out from the Arnaville bridgehead and attack to the northeast. These divisions would join hands east of Metz to isolate the city and prevent the escape or reinforcement of the garrison. The 95th Division's initial mission was to tie down German troops west of the Moselle. As the 90th and 5th divisions closed the ring about Metz, the 95th Division would cross the Moselle and capture the city itself. The 10th Armored Division's mission was to follow and support the 90th Division's attack, while pushing columns toward potential crossing sites over the Sarre River. In essence, Walker planned to encircle and capture Metz as a prelude to the major push toward Germany.[45]

Although heavy rains turned the countryside into a sea of mud and grounded all aircraft, Patton ordered Walker's troops to attack on 9 November. Despite incredible downpours and stiff resistance, the 90th and 5th Divisions made good progress, while the 95th Division advanced westward and established several bridgeheads over the Moselle. The 95th Division decided to mount the main effort against Metz using a combined arms task force consisting of the troops within the bridgeheads at Uckange and Thionville. Col. Robert L. Bacon took command of part of the task force—2d Battalion, 378th Infantry—at the Thionville bridgehead at mid-morning on 15 November with orders to attack south toward Metz, clearing the east bank of the Moselle as he went. After attacking south and joining with the 1st Battalion, 377th Infantry, at Uckange, Bacon began preparations for the advance on Metz. He intended to attack on a narrow front, avoid strong enemy defenses, and rely on surprise, mobility, and firepower to accomplish his mission. In addition to two infantry battalions, Task Force (TF) Bacon consisted of a tank company, two companies of TDs, a cavalry troop, and an engineer platoon organized into two columns that would advance on parallel and mutually supporting axes. If the Germans held up one column, the other would maneuver to attack the enemy's flank and rear.[46]

TF Bacon burst out of the Uckange bridgehead at 0700 hours on 16 November in two separate columns heading straight for the city. Tanks and TDs headed the advance, while the infantry and engineers followed in trucks or on foot. Bacon did a splendid job of using his twin columns in alternating jabs and punches that had the Germans reeling back, unable to stop the advance. Armored firepower hit the enemy first, then the infantry moved in to mop up or mount a concerted attack depending on the degree of resistance. The rapid advance caught many German units by surprise and prevented them from slowing Bacon's attack. Later in the day

Bacon felt that he needed more punch as he moved toward the inner ring of the Metz defenses, and he requested additional direct fire support. The 95th Division sent two self-propelled 155-mm howitzers that Bacon placed at the head of his columns. The big guns blew to bits several German positions blocking the road to the city. By the evening of 17 November, TF Bacon had covered over twenty miles and was fast approaching the outskirts of Metz.[47]

On 18 November Colonel Bacon confronted the last major hurdle between his columns and downtown Metz: Fort St. Julien, one of the strongest of Metz's inner defenses. Sitting on dominating terrain less than 4,000 yards from the city center, it commanded the two main roads leading into Metz from the north. The fort was actually a reinforced infantry stronghold with high thick walls, surrounded by a moat some forty feet deep and forty feet wide. Lacking artillery, the fort's defenses consisted primarily of infantry firing positions manned by a garrison of 362 Germans. The only way into Fort St. Julien was over a covered causeway that spanned the moat on the fort's rear, or west, side.[48]

Colonel Bacon assigned 2d Battalion, 378th Infantry, the mission of reducing St. Julien. The plan was for the battalion to swing around west of the fort through the town of St. Julien-les-Metz and attack the fort's rear wall. The assault started at 0700 hours on 18 November through a dense fog that enshrouded the battlefield. While trying to get through St. Julien-les-Metz, the Americans collided with a German infantry battalion that had been sent to bolster Fort St. Julien's defenses. Heavy fighting erupted as the 2d Battalion pushed its way forward. The Germans conducted a fighting withdrawal back toward the fort, and by noon the Americans had taken up positions just outside its walls. Tanks, TDs, and the task force's 155-mm guns, as well as the big 240-mm guns of the XX Corps artillery, pounded the fort for an hour while the infantry prepared for a final assault.[49]

Under the protective fire of tanks and TDs, the infantry planned to reduce Fort St. Julien with a direct assault against the rear wall over the moat's causeway. The first attack jumped off in early afternoon but made little progress against withering small arms fire. A large iron door at the far end of the causeway also blocked any direct access to the fort's interior. Two Shermans moved forward to protect the infantry and spray enemy positions with machine-gun fire. Then a TD drove up and tried to batter down the iron door with its 90-mm gun. The crew fired several rounds at a range of less than 50 yards, but the barrier refused to budge. Clearly, the Americans needed a bigger hammer to knock down the fort's door, and it soon appeared in the form of one of the self-propelled 155-mm howitzers. With loud claps of flame and thunder the gun slammed ten rounds into the door, but it still refused to move. The artillerymen decided that if the door was indestructible, its stone facing was not. The 155-mm smashed twenty more rounds into the fort's rear wall and totally demolished the door's mounts. Finally, Fort St. Julien's main door collapsed inward with a mighty crash. The infantry were close at hand and stormed over the causeway with fixed bayonets. The direct firepower had taken the fight out of most of the garrison, who quickly capitulated.[50]

On the morning of 19 November, TF Bacon moved into Metz and began clearing the northern portion of the city. A few hours later the 5th and 95th divisions made contact east of Metz and put a firm clamp on German escape routes. The next day American units went to work in earnest to clear the city, and on the afternoon of 22 November, XX Corps headquarters reported that Metz was all clear. However, six major bastions in the fortified zone remained defiant. General Walker forbade any attempts to reduce the fortresses by direct assault, and they were left to wither on the vine. On 26 November the first fort capitulated, and by the end of December dwindling rations and plummeting morale forced the surrender of the others. In one of the great ironies of the ETO campaigns, Fort Driant finally surrendered to the 5th Division; the Red Diamonds had suffered terribly at Driant, but at 1545 hours on 8 December the German commander surrendered the fort without a shot.[51]

The two different approaches that XX Corps used to reduce the Metz fortified zone stand out in stark contrast. Rather than seeking enemy weaknesses, XX Corps and the 5th Division first decided to attack Fort Driant, one of the strongest points in the entire fortified zone, and the mistakes were legion. Commanders had a blurred and incomplete intelligence picture and failed to provide the resources to give the attack any chance of success. There was no time for detailed planning or to give troops refresher training. Driant's ability to absorb blows from air strikes and artillery took away the American advantage in firepower. Units did not have the right types of armored engineer vehicles to support attacks against pillboxes and casements, and tanks and TDs tried to fill the void but with no result. Walker's decision to spread his divisions wide and encircle Metz while bypassing heavy fortifications reflected the desire to avoid further bloody repulses. TF Bacon's drive toward Metz illustrates the American preference for mobile operations. With speed and surprise, the task force's twin columns used fire and maneuver to overcome Germans fighting in the open rather than from fortifications. In the reduction of Fort St. Julien, TF Bacon displayed typical attack methods, as the Americans isolated the fortress and then battered down the works with the biggest club they could find. The capture of Metz by converging columns and the subsequent bloodless capitulation of the outer fortresses more than justified Walker's indirect approach in reducing the fortified zone.

Americans displayed a flair for improvising new tactical methods while battling fortifications and heavy defenses. Commanders used common sense and judgment to selectively apply or ignore doctrine and to incorporate lessons learned during training. Field forces all but rejected the army's "school solutions" for reducing fortifications. Instead of conducting frontal assaults using hand-emplaced explosive charges against embrasures, they found ways to attack defenses from the flank or rear. Small unit initiative and aggressiveness played a much larger role in reducing heavy fortifications than did firepower. Infantry commanders excelled in determining the best ways to use their riflemen and to distribute and employ tank, TD, and fire support assets. Small units were especially adept at using maneuver or indirect fire to isolate and suppress enemy positions. Commanders did not hesitate to use weapons in unorthodox ways and were quick to blast and batter their way into strongholds using flames, explosives, tanks, TDs, and direct fire artillery.

In the absence of suitable equipment to support mobile operations, GIs developed a number of technical expedients. The attack on Montbarey demonstrated the efficacy of flame weapons, but it was technology borrowed from the British. American flamethrower tanks finally made it to the ETO but saw little action. Although man-portable flamethrowers saw wide use, most soldiers considered them too heavy and mechanically unreliable. Without an armored engineer vehicle to help clear obstacles, units tried a variety of other methods. Tank dozers played the lead role in filling craters and bulling through wire barriers. The use of explosive snakes to clear wire obstacles at Driant showed promise but failed miserably. On some occasions, flail tanks beat paths through minefields, but the inability of Americans to detect and clear minefields remained a serious shortcoming.

The lack of mechanical means and special equipment for reducing fortifications points to a major disadvantage in the American adaptation process. The technical problems of battling heavy defenses were difficult enough to require the energies and resources of the entire army. Instead of fighting units struggling with these problems, the army should have engaged its technical and logistical bureaucracy in developing special vehicles, weapons, and equipment. The preference for problem solving at the lowest levels precluded the development of army-wide solutions, and adaptations in the field using limited resources were generally modest and had mixed success in achieving objectives and preventing casualties. Troops would have had greater success and suffered fewer losses if the army had developed armored special equipment for clearing obstacles under fire and assaulting fortifications.

Divisions fighting in the ETO found that doctrine on the attack of fortified positions was largely correct but needed several revisions. Doctrine described situations in which units prepared for the attack but spent much longer actually reducing fortifications and exploiting their success. In combat, the exact opposite was true, and units spent days preparing for battles that they expected would not last very long. Intelligence collection and dissemination and training in the techniques of attacking heavy defenses were the most crucial aspects of preparations. XIX Corps spent more than two weeks preparing for the Siegfried Line assault, while the actual operation took only seven days. XX Corps invested five weeks in preparing for the last phase of the Metz campaign, with most of the fortified zone falling within two weeks after the opening of the offensive. In 1945 the Infantry School at Fort Benning concluded that of all the time allocated to reducing a fortified position, units should spend half the available time preparing for the attack. The actual assault was to take only 5 percent of the time available, with the breakthrough and exploitation phases consuming the remaining 45 percent.[52]

Doctrine wrongly prescribed the use and effects of many weapons systems, and FM 100-5 overestimated the roles of artillery and air power. Artillery did good work in isolating the battle area and destroying obstacles, but indirect fire was too inaccurate to strike fortifications and inflict any significant damage. The best use of artillery was not even mentioned in FM 100-5: units had great success using self-propelled artillery pieces as modern-day battering rams. The 29th Division at Fort Montbarey and TF Bacon on the road to Metz both used direct fire artillery to bash their way into strongholds. Air strikes had almost no effect on reinforced positions. Heavy bombers were too inaccurate to strike pinpoint targets, and fighter-bombers could hit fortifications, but their ordnance was not powerful enough to be effective. Doctrine maintained that armor commanders should avoid fortifications and husband their armored formations for breakthroughs and exploitations. Although armored forces did conduct breakthroughs, they also played a key role in attacking fortifications. In fact, the mobility and firepower of tanks and TDs greatly assisted infantry units in almost every assault, and several armored divisions demonstrated the ability of tank and mechanized units to reduce pillboxes.

FM 100-5 put repeated emphasis on the requirement for "special units" with unique equipment and training to attack fortifications. Commanders in First and Third Army may have looked for these special units, but they were nowhere to be found. The army faced the West Wall and the Metz defenses with standard units of regular infantrymen, tankers, TD crews, and engineers, whose employment hammered home a vital lesson to commanders. In a long, costly campaign, the use of "special units" was unrealistic; leaders had to conduct different types of operations with the troops that filled their own squads, platoons, and companies.

Just as in the hedgerow battles, units discovered that remedial training readied them for the special techniques needed to attack fortifications. In its preparations for the Siegfried Line attack, the 30th Division provided a textbook example of how a unit can conduct prebattle training in a combat zone. Commanders formed small combined arms teams that practiced pillbox reduction techniques, and by training together as a single unit, soldiers in each of the combat arms learned one another's capabilities and limits. Training also gave units time to recover from the rigors of battle and to assimilate lessons learned. After the 5th Division's debacle at Fort Driant, the Red Diamonds rebounded and conducted extensive training based on lessons learned during the assault. Training throughout XX Corps during the October lull laid the foundations for the successes of November.

What did the Germans derive from their defense of heavy fortifications? They certainly achieved the goal of stemming the Allied advance. Battling against the Siefgried Line between September and December, First Army pushed only 22 miles into Germany while suffering 47,039 battle casualties. It took Third Army three times as long to reduce the Metz fortified area than it took Patton's columns to dash from the Normandy hedgerows to the banks of the Moselle. Considering the desperate situation in the fall of 1944, fighting from heavy fortifications seemed the best way to redeem the war in the west, and the defenses around Aachen and Metz bought the German army the time needed to muster forces for the Ardennes offensive. Yet, without mobile reserves to back up the fortifications, a static defense could not hope to succeed. The elimination of the garrisons of the Metz fortresses and the West Wall robbed the German army of precious manpower it could not replace; in defending the northern portion of the West Wall opposite the U.S. First and Ninth armies, the Germans lost 95,000 troops. Although fighting from static positions gave the Germans several advantages, it engaged them in a war of attrition they were bound to lose.[53]

Urban defenses and fortified positions were not the only obstacles barring the way toward Germany. Units could take great satisfaction in the fact that they had discovered ways to overcome man-made defenses, but yet another type of barrier lay ahead. Rivers were natural obstacles just as formidable as any pillbox or village stronghold and provided the Germans with wonderful opportunities to slow and bleed the American armies. As they closed on the German frontier, American soldiers at all levels had to muster their ingenuity and fighting skills in a series of attacks that moved them closer to Berlin—one river at a time.

CHAPTER SIX

In Spite of Hell and High Water

What it all came down to, I realized, was the success of our infantry, tanks, and tactical air in pushing the Germans far back from the crossing. . . . The faster we built our bridge, the more troops, tanks, and artillery pieces our generals would be able to send into the attack that would ultimately provide the best security for the bridge. In my mind that afternoon, everything—everything—depended on us.

*—Lt. Col. David E. Pergrin, commander, 291st
Engineer Combat Battalion, at the Remagen
Bridgehead, 9 March 1945*

The first great task American troops faced in the ETO was to cross a major water obstacle and land on a hostile shore. But getting across the English Channel and onto the Normandy beaches was not the last time U.S. soldiers had to overcome a major water barrier against enemy resistance. The Seine, Meuse, Moselle, Roer, Sarre, and Rhine rivers and their tributaries ran squarely across the invasion routes leading from Normandy to Germany. American divisions moving toward the Reich discovered that rivers were natural obstacles just as formidable and deadly as any man-made defenses of steel, concrete, and brick. To win the war, American forces had to master the skills required to cross rivers in the face of enemy fire, often under the most trying weather conditions.

River crossings included a large number of advantages and disadvantages for the opposing forces. For American units advancing toward Germany, major rivers were unavoidable obstacles. Operation MARKET-GARDEN showed the limits of airborne assaults against water barriers, and the rest of the American army had to ford, paddle, or use bridges to cross rivers. Assaulting rivers was a labor-intensive endeavor that required extensive planning and coordinations, and strong enemy resistance added to the difficulties. Assault troops were dangerously exposed and canalized during the actual crossing, and the restricted space within most bridgeheads made it difficult to employ maneuver and firepower. Once on the far bank, the entire command was at risk until it could establish a secure bridgehead. The Germans used the many defensive advantages rivers afforded as they tried to prevent any crossing by U.S. forces. From defensive positions on dominating terrain, the Germans sought to disrupt bridging and assault efforts by fire, and then counterattacked to push American troops back into the water. In contrast to American crossings that usually took place at different locations, the Germans were able to concentrate all their power against a single crossing site.

The doctrine and tactics of river crossings were well developed and known throughout the American army. The tactical objective was to establish one or more bridgeheads that would protect the crossing of follow-on forces. In situations where heavy resistance was expected, infantry divisions forced crossings "on a wide front with several determined attacks at separated localities." When little opposition was present, units were to cross immediately and hold a shallow bridgehead until the remainder of the division arrived. The selection of crossing sites depended on tactical and technical considerations. Ideal were crossing points that provided good covered and concealed approaches to bridging sites, offered clear observation of the far bank, and possessed good attack routes from bridge exits to prominent terrain or roads on the far shore. Technical considerations included moderate river currents, low banks, lack of obstacles, and suitable approaches and exits around the bridges.[1]

FM 100-5 stipulated that river crossings took place in three successive phases. First, attackers crossed on assault boats, foot bridges, or small ferries to occupy ground that prevented enemy forces from placing direct small arms fire on the crossing site. In the second phase, troops expanded the bridgehead to eliminate any observation of the bridge site. With the threat from observed artillery fire eliminated, engineers could emplace pontoon bridges to pass heavier vehicles and equipment into the bridgehead. Last, friendly forces pushed out the bridgehead perimeter further to facilitate uninterrupted crossing operations and to create enough space for additional forces to mass and maneuver within the bridgehead. Units conducted hasty crossings against light resistance using their own resources and when there was little time for planning. Deliberate attacks required more preparation time so commanders could bring to bear additional assets against prepared defenses. FM 100-5, however, prescribed the same procedures and tactics for all river crossings, whether hasty or deliberate.[2]

The army enjoyed a wide mix of river crossing capabilities. To transport infantry, the engineers employed the standard M2 assault boat that could carry a crew of three engineers and a twelve-man rifle squad complete with weapons and equipment. An entire rifle company could cross at one time in seventeen boats. Before engineers emplaced bridges, they used infantry support rafts to cross supplies, antitank guns, and light vehicles and artillery and evacuated casualties on return trips. Infantry support rafts consisted of six M2 assault boats lashed together beneath plywood treadways, all powered by an outboard motor and capable of ferrying the equivalent of a 2½-ton truck fully loaded. Engineers were armed with a

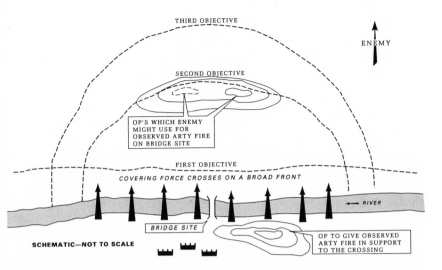

Figure 6.1. U.S. River Crossing Doctrine, 1943 (*Source*: U.S. War Department, Field Manual 5-6, *Operations of Engineer Field Units* (Washington, D.C.: U.S. Government Printing Office, 1944), 87.)

variety of tactical bridges. The smallest was the infantry footbridge, consisting of a single walkway supported by a series of light pontoons and capable of spanning rivers up to 400 feet wide. The M-2 treadway bridge was the workhorse that engineers used in river-crossings. It consisted of two parallel tracks of steel gridway flooring mounted atop large pneumatic floats and had an overall capacity of 40 tons. Army standards called for engineer units to construct a 362-foot treadway bridge in five hours during daylight or in seven and one-half hours at night.[3]

Combat engineers played the most important support role in river crossings. Using assault boats and pneumatic floats, each infantry division had an engineer battalion with only limited capabilities for ferrying troops and light equipment. The bulk of the army's river-crossing capabilities were in separate engineer battalions and special bridging companies found at army and theater level. These units were pooled into Engineer Combat Groups and were allocated to corps or held under army control depending on the tactical situation. During most river crossing operations, army headquarters attached Engineer Combat Groups with extra bridging capabilities to the assault divisions, where they worked under the control of the division's engineer officer.[4]

The army combined FM 100-5's broad guidance for river crossing operations with engineering capabilities to develop the tactics and techniques for attacking rivers. (See Figure 6.1.) The crossing of the initial assault waves took place in four phases, all under the cover of darkness. First, infantrymen occupied assembly areas to complete preparations, then moved to attack positions close to the river. There, engineer guides met the infantry and led them to the riverbank, where assault boats waited. The engineers then ferried the infantry across in successive waves. The attack frontage for an infantry battalion was from 600 to 2,400 yards, with single rifle companies operating in a zone half as wide. The last phase of the assault called for the infantry to capture terrain that controlled the crossing sites. When crossing sites were free from enemy small arms fire, engineers built footbridges and put infantry support rafts to work to speed more troops and equipment into the bridgehead. Until heavy weapons and equipment reached the far bank, the infantry had to fend off enemy counterattacks with artillery fire, antitank guns, and hasty obstacles. After the riflemen had taken a second line of objectives that prevented enemy observation of the crossing area, engineers floated treadway bridges. When more troops and heavy equipment were across the river, infantry divisions attacked to gain a third set of objectives that permitted complete protection of the bridging sites and made the entire bridgehead secure.[5]

In the ETO the army learned that its basic river crossing doctrine was correct, but commanders were faced with a number of unexpected difficulties because doctrine inadequately addressed combined arms operations. Although FM 100-5 put primary emphasis on deliberate river crossings by the infantry, corps and division commanders had to experiment with the best ways to employ infantry and armored divisions simultaneously. In the early stages of most crossings, bridgeheads received hard counterblows from German armor, so commanders had to find ways to place early antitank capability on the far shore. Often the sequence of seizing objectives and emplacing bridges prescribed in doctrine was impossible, forcing engineer units to build bridges under heavy fire. Doctrine implied that there was a correlation between the expansion of the bridgehead and the commitment of follow-on forces, when in reality heavy German resistance on the far bank often prompted commanders to put bridges across rivers early and to throw everything they had into the fight, regardless of the size of the bridgehead. FM 100-5 called for divisions to conduct crossings over a wide front, but commanders found it almost impossible to mount multiple efforts of adequate strength. Against strong enemy resistance, division and corps commanders tended to concentrate all their power into only one or two crossing sites. Doctrine also assumed that key terrain controlling the crossing sites lay far back from the river, but what were units to do when high ground on the opposite shore dominated the entire area? Doctrine never discussed the problem of forcing a crossing against direct, heavy resistance, yet commanders faced such circumstances repeatedly. And assault crossings were to occur in darkness, but this was often impossible.

Almost every American corps and division in the ETO performed some type of river crossing operation. But Third Army's efforts to cross the Moselle River during the Lorraine campaign best illustrate the wide variety of problems, setbacks, and successes that American troops experienced. From early September to mid-November, Patton's divisions crossed the Moselle at several different points while battling both determined enemy resistance and atrocious weather. Third Army mounted a prodigious, sustained effort that had no parallel in U.S. military history since the armies of Ulysses S. Grant had struggled to cross the mighty Mississippi and lay siege to Vicksburg in 1863.

Patton's first effort to cross the Moselle occurred at the very outset of the fighting in Lorraine, as General Eddy's XII Corps sought to encircle and capture Nancy. The corps consisted of three divisions—35th and 80th Infantry and the 4th Armored—and operated in the southern portion of Third Army's sector during the dash across France. On 31 August the 4th Armored Division crossed the Meuse River, and the corps commander ordered the division to keep moving west and to jump the Moselle before the Germans could organize a defense. But Third Army's supply crisis of early September brought XII Corps to a grinding halt. During the pause, Maj. Gen. John S. "P" Wood, the 4th Armored commander, and Maj. Gen. Horace L. McBride of the 80th Infantry Division convinced Eddy to alter plans for crossing the Moselle. The division commanders pointed out that the Moselle was a formidable barrier, that the enemy situation was unclear, and that the corps' armor should not be risked in a hasty crossing but used to exploit a bridgehead already established by the infantry. Convinced by their arguments, Eddy revised his original plan. The 80th Division would now attempt to cross the Moselle at several points north and west of Nancy with CCA, 4th Armored, following close behind. The corps' main effort would take place in the vicinity of Pont-a-Mousson, a village on the Moselle about 15 miles northwest of Nancy. There General McBride ordered his infantry to establish a bridgehead so CCA could cross the Moselle, bypass Nancy, and block German escape routes to the east. With their gas tanks partially replenished and the infantry moving by foot, the 80th Infantry and 4th Armored Divisions headed for the Moselle in the early morning hours of 4 September. None of the troops had yet seen the river and the surrounding terrain or had any idea of the enemy situation, yet their confidence and morale were high.[6]

A good look at the situation around Pont-a-Mousson would have dampened the Americans' ardor, as the Moselle presented a formidable barrier. (See Map 6.1.) Throughout the sector it averaged 150 feet in width, with a current of about 6 miles per hour. Depth at possible crossing sites mea-

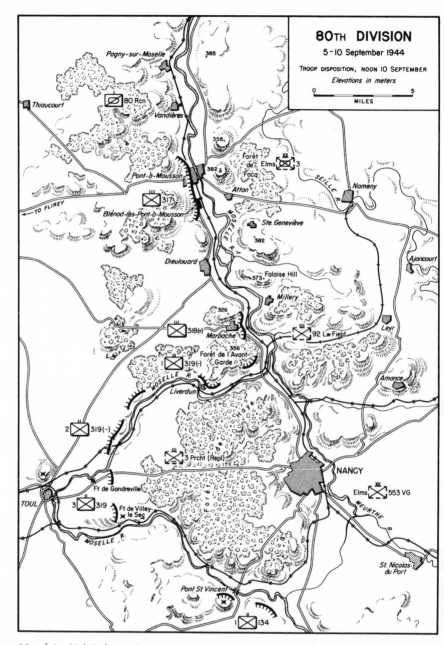

Map 6.1. 80th Infantry Division Attempts to Cross the Moselle River, 5–10 September 1944 (*Source*: Hugh M. Cole, *The Lorraine Campaign, U.S. Army in World War II* (Washington, D.C.: U.S. Army, Office of the Chief of Military History, 1950; reprint ed., Washington, D.C.: U.S. Army Center of Military History, 1984), map 2.)

sured 6 to 8 feet, but as the Americans would discover, a soft, muddy bottom made fording impossible. The small Marne-Rhine Canal and a railroad line running from Nancy to Metz paralleled the river's course along the western bank. All of these obstacles lay within the Moselle's flat flood plain that varied in width from 400 to 1,000 yards, and its open expanse guaranteed that any crossing attempt would be fully exposed to enemy observation and fire from a series of high hills on the eastern bank. The 3d Panzer Grenadier Division occupied that bank in a zone that extended from Pagny-sur-Moselle southward to Millery. The division had been transferred to Lorraine from Italy and was almost up to full strength, though its engineer and tank battalions had not yet reached the Moselle. The Germans used the respite brought on by the American supply crisis to dig in and to consolidate positions overlooking the river. By 4 September the 3d Panzer Grenadier Division was ready for a fight, and tensions heightened that afternoon when observation posts (OPs) spotted columns of American infantry approaching from the west.[7]

The 80th Division's 317th Infantry had no idea the Germans were watching as they moved into assembly areas among the wooded hills west of Pont-a-Mousson. While soldiers made ready to cross the Moselle, the regimental commander, Col. A. D. Cameron, developed his plan. The primary consideration was speed, and the Americans hoped to retain the initiative by jumping the river with few preparations. Patrols inspected the river under the cover of darkness and reported suitable crossing sites near Pagny-sur-Moselle, Vandieres, and Dieulouard. Although a night crossing was preferable, the late hour and lack of intelligence prompted Colonel Cameron to postpone the attack until daylight. His attack plan was almost a direct lift from the pages of FM 100-5, as he decided to cross the Moselle the next morning on a five-mile front with two battalions abreast in order to capture the dominating heights on the far bank. The 1st Battalion was to cross in assault boats near Blenod-les-Pont-a-Mousson, and then maneuver to capture Hill 382 across from Pont-a-Mousson. Meanwhile, the 2d Battalion would ford the river near Pagny-sur-Moselle, grab Hill 385, and then continue to attack southward to secure Hill 358. The 3d Battalion was in reserve and was ordered to follow the 1st Battalion to help expand the bridgehead. Cameron assured his battalion commanders that air and artillery support would be available, and the 305th Engineer Combat Battalion would ferry the 1st and 3d Battalions across in rubber assault boats.[8]

The next day dawned bright and clear as units headed for their crossing sites. For the 317th Infantry, the next twenty-four hours became a living hell, as the 2d Battalion's attack encountered almost every imaginable setback. At 0900 hours the battalion moved forward with companies in column, but company commanders grew apprehensive when their artillery support did not materialize. As the companies deployed onto the flood plain and began to look for a way to get over the Rhine-Marne Canal, all hell broke loose. German mortar and artillery fire erupted among the units, and everyone scattered and took cover. Under murderous shelling, the Company E commander crawled forward to the canal only to discover that without bridging or boat support a crossing was impossible. By noon the 2d Battalion was pinned down in the open without any artillery support whatsoever. Commanders feared that a withdrawal under the intense shelling might result in excessive casualties, so for the rest of the day soldiers remained huddled in shallow foxholes and exposed to a continuous artillery and mortar bombardment. By nightfall the 2d Battalion had suffered 8 percent casualties without setting one boot on the far shore, and a "jittery feeling"—an early symptom of combat exhaustion—existed throughout the companies.[9]

Under the cover of darkness units withdrew from the flood plain and regrouped for a second attempt at crossing. Engineers reported finding a fording site one mile to the south at Vandieres, and before midnight the 2d Battalion was on the move. Company F found an abandoned barge it manhandled into position lengthwise across the canal for use as an expedient footbridge. By 0300 hours on 6 September, the battalion was busy crossing the canal. Company E went first, advancing cautiously across the half-mile of flood plain, and began to look for the fording site. Around 0400 hours fire from six German machine guns on the opposite bank ripped into E Company. Soon the entire battalion was completely disorganized and pinned down without artillery support, an unfordable river to the front and a canal to the rear. The battalion commander knew his companies were in an exposed position, so he issued orders for them to withdraw back to the canal. Fear and confusion reigned as troops moved helter-skelter to the rear. Companies became intermingled, and dawn found the riflemen taking cover as leaders tried to impose order on the chaos. But first light also gave the Germans a chance to see their enemies, and soon a torrent of artillery and mortar shells began to fall. The whole ordeal pushed several soldiers beyond the breaking point. They panicked and tried to run to the rear; the shelling killed some, while others drowned trying to get across the canal. Around 0630 hours the battalion commander issued orders for a withdrawal, but the 2d Battalion was not able to reach safety on the west bank until late afternoon. The battalion had suffered 15 percent casualties among the enlisted men and lost six officers. The executive officer reported that morale was "very low" because the soldiers felt they had been given an almost impossible mission and had been "needlessly exposed" to prolonged German shelling.[10]

The other battalions of the 317th experienced similar defeats. On the morning of 5 September, the 1st Battalion reached Blenod, crossed the canal on a civilian footbridge, and had moved 200 yards across the flood plain when German machine guns opened fire. Soldiers tried to keep moving forward, but mortar fire brought the advance to a stop. The shelling inflicted many casualties and destroyed most of the rubber boats intended for crossing the Moselle. By 1500 hours the 1st Battalion had withdrawn and taken cover in Blenod. Seeing the 1st and 2d Battalions' failed attempts, General McBride ordered the 3d Battalion to force a crossing at Pont-a-Mousson. However, the battalion had no engineer support and was unable to find a fording site.[11]

The 317th Infantry then attempted night crossings. The 1st Battalion advanced from Blenod, but halfway across the flood plain the Germans opened up with tremendous firepower. Suffering heavy casualties and badly shaken, the 1st Battalion staggered back to the protection of Blenod. The 3d Battalion's night crossing at first enjoyed success, and the 305th Engineer Combat Battalion managed to ferry across four infantry platoons from Companies I and L that established a shallow bridgehead on the far bank and started digging in. At daybreak intense German fire began to punish the platoons. The Americans attempted to strengthen the bridgehead, but disaster struck before reinforcements could arrive, as the 3d Panzer Grenadier Division launched a series of vicious counterattacks. The 3d Battalion watched enraged and helpless from the west bank as the Germans wiped out the bridgehead. By 1100 hours the four platoons no longer existed; 140 Americans were killed or wounded and another 20 taken prisoner. Finally, General Eddy canceled any further crossing attempts, and the 317th Infantry slowly went into defensive positions on the western bank.[12]

Although the 317th Infantry's attack failed, the attempted crossings did conform with doctrine in several important ways. The regiment attacked at multiple points across a broad front, planning to exploit the most successful crossing site, and the plan also called for the capture of the high ground controlling the crossing sites. However, proper procedures alone could not overcome serious misjudgments, a lack of planning and coordination, and German firepower. The Americans were surprised to encounter stiff enemy resistance and were completely unprepared to handle it. Poor reconnaissance and intelligence gathering plagued the operation from beginning to end. Darkness kept commanders from viewing the area before the attack, so soldiers had no firsthand knowledge of crossing sites. Infantry and engineer patrols reported fords that did not exist, and the combined arms team failed to function. CAS did not materialize, the artillery was unable to provide any support, and not one tank or TD joined the fight. Alone and unsupported, the infantry had no chance of getting over the river. Finally, the Germans enjoyed all the advantages of defending from high ground and were able to dominate the crossing sites with firepower orchestrated from their positions overlooking the Moselle.

During the next several days, units recovered while the 80th Division developed another scheme for getting over the Moselle. The new plan was a complete reverse of the original action and contradicted river crossing doctrine. Considering the stiff resistance encountered on the far bank, General McBride decided against multiple crossing sites. Instead, the 80th Division would concentrate all its combat power at a single point to establish a solid bridgehead and blow a breach in the German lines. The first attempt had been a hasty attack during daylight; the new plan called for a deliberate crossing at nighttime. The 80th Division selected another crossing site near Dieulouard, a small hamlet about four miles below Pont-a-Mousson. The 317th Infantry would cross first and establish a bridgehead by securing the high ground on the far bank, then the 318th Infantry would cross and occupy high ground in the northern portion of the bridgehead. Staff officers prepared extensive fire support plans. The 305th Engineer Combat Battalion would support the initial crossings while the 117th Engineer Combat Group made ready to emplace heavy bridging. CCA, 4th Armored Division, was to follow the 80th Division into the bridgehead. After crossing the Moselle, CCA was to blitz almost 30 miles eastward to occupy terrain around Arracourt and sever German LOCs and escape routes from Nancy.[13]

Intensive preparations followed. Patrols and unit commanders scouted the river but kept activity to a minimum around Dieulouard so as not to alert the Germans about the location of the next assault. Artillery battalions fired on German targets, while counterbattery fire searched for enemy guns. The 305th Engineers planned to put bridging across the canal and to position assault boats on the west bank under the cover of darkness, while the 1117th Engineers prepared to emplace heavy bridges the day after the assault. On 10 September Ninth Air Force medium bombers attacked roads and bridges between Nancy and the Dieulouard sector to make the Germans' rapid reinforcement of the bridgehead more difficult. The next day fighter-bombers bombed the high ground opposite Dieulouard and Pont-a-Mousson. The 317th Infantry massed its .50-caliber machine guns near Dieulouard to provide direct fire support. The 80th Division also decided to use its air defense assets in a ground support role, and halftracks of the 633d Antiaircraft Artillery Battalion, armed with quadruple-mounted .50-caliber machine guns, rolled into positions near Dieulouard and made ready to smother the Germans with lead.[14]

By 11 September other Third Army units had gained toeholds across the Moselle, and General Eddy ordered the 80th Division to cross at Dieulouard the next morning. After midnight the 2d and 3d Battalions, 317th Infantry, began moving toward the crossing sites as nine battalions

Engineer teams performed valuable service in manning small assault boats during river crossing operations. Soldiers of the 44th Infantry Division cross a river in Germany near the end of the war. (U.S. Army)

of artillery began shelling the 3d Panzer Grenadier Division. Tracer bullets from over fifty .50-caliber machine guns arched through the night sky, giving protection to assault troops crossing the Moselle on footbridges and paddling across in rubber and plywood assault boats. German resistance was spotty. By sunrise the 3d Battalion had secured high ground near Falaise Hill, and at 0800 hours the 2d Battalion occupied defensive positions on the heights around Ste. Genevieve. The 1st Battalion soon followed and moved onto Hill 382. By noon the 317th Infantry had consolidated positions along a 3,000-yard front. The 318th Infantry lost no time in crossing over into the tentative bridgehead and establishing battle positions to support the 317th's forward defenses. The original plan called for the engineers to begin emplacement of heavy bridging in the late afternoon after the infantry had cleared the enemy off the opposing heights, but the speed of the advance and absence of German activity prompted General McBride to order the engineers to start work early. As evening settled on 12 September, the infantry continued to consolidate while the 1117th Engineer Combat Group began to push heavy pontoons into the Moselle. The Americans remained puzzled and a bit worried about the lack of enemy resistance.[15]

Luckily, the 80th Division had crossed where the Germans had temporarily stripped their lines to provide troops for emergencies elsewhere. But while the Americans worked during 12 September to strengthen their bridgehead, the Germans rushed troops back to Dieulouard and prepared to pour everything they had into a powerful, nighttime counterattack. After dark, German mortar and artillery fire quickened, as gunners got the range on the bridging sites, and at 0100 hours the storm broke. Attacking from positions in the Foret de Focq, three battalions of German infantry supported by fifteen tanks and ten assault guns attempted to roll up the American left flank and destroy the bridge. The fighting was intense and confused. The Germans pushed the 317th Infantry out of Ste. Genevieve, as American troops fought a delaying action back toward the crossing site. Sunrise fully exposed the extent of the crisis faced by General McBride. American infantry had rallied at various places, but enemy attacks surged around them and came within one hundred yards of the treadway bridge. Engineers threw down their special tools and equipment, grabbed their M-1 rifles and machine guns, and fought to defend their bridge. By 0600 hours the counterattack had reached high tide. An impasse settled over the battlefield; Americans had stood fast in their positions, and the Germans were too tired and blooded to keep pushing forward. The 80th Division retained its toehold on the far bank, and the treadway bridge was unharmed, but the overall situation in the bridgehead was tenuous.[16]

Suddenly, armored vehicles from the 4th Armored Division appeared on the treadway bridge and quickly deployed into the bridgehead. The armor's fortuitous appearance was a combination of luck and the willingness on the part of American commanders to close with the enemy. Because of the light resistance to the 80th Division's original crossing, General Wood ordered his CCA, commanded by Col. Bruce C. Clarke, to cross over into the bridgehead. Around 0400 hours on 13 September, Clarke's units—37th Tank and 53d Armored Infantry battalions with the attached 1st Battalion, 318th Infantry—began moving toward Dieulouard. The news and noise of the German counterattack reached the column, and Clarke took several steps in anticipation of entering the fight. He told his units to move as far forward as possible, pull off the road, and wait for further orders. Clarke then worked his way up the column, picked up the commander of the 37th Tank Battalion, Lt. Col. Creighton Abrams, and headed toward the bridge. Clarke and Abrams reached the crossing site around 0700 hours and came upon General McBride. Soon Generals Eddy and Wood arrived, and an impromptu council of war ensued. The generals discussed the hazards of crossing CCA during a pitched battle on the far bank and the problems of maneuvering tank units in the confined bridgehead. Finally, the generals asked Clarke and Abrams for their opinion. Clarke said he could not "fight the Germans on this side of the river." Abrams gave the best answer. Pointing to the high ground on the far side of the river, he bluntly told his superiors that capturing the hills was "the shortest way home." Impressed with the colonels' arguments and aggressive spirit, the generals ordered CCA over the Moselle.[17]

Abrams's tanks began crossing about 0800 hours. They rumbled over the bridge and rapidly deployed into battle formations. Soldiers of the 80th Division watched with relief and elation as M4 Shermans drove the Germans before them. The hills reverberated with the crack and boom of tank cannons and the throaty, staccato bursts of .50-caliber machine guns. The 37th Tank Battalion, with close support from the 53d Armored Infantry, mounted a violent attack northward toward Ste. Genevieve. The blow struck the Germans when they were weakest, and the gray-clad infantry began a hasty retreat. Before long Abrams's soldiers had recaptured Ste. Genevieve and Hill 382. CCA's actions allowed the 80th Division to catch its breath, and at 0930 hours the American infantry launched a counterattack to regain positions lost to the Germans. With the 80th Division on the rebound, the 4th Armored Division launched a second attack to break out of the bridgehead. At 1000 hours CCA moved northward to take up positions along a main highway heading to the east. Free from the fighting around the bridgehead, and with a good road and beautiful weather, CCA shot eastward down the road like a compressed spring suddenly released. Clarke's soldiers began a daring exploitation across the German rear area that led to the vicious tank battles around Arracourt. Meanwhile, the 80th Division's counterattack had resulted in the restoration of the original perimeter by late afternoon.[18]

Although the Americans believed the crisis had passed, the Germans were mustering forces with which they hoped to wipe out the entire bridgehead. On the afternoon of 13 September, as many as six German battalions were on the road to Dieulouard. Between 14–16 September some of the most bitter fighting in the ETO took place as the Germans tried to push the 80th Division back into the Moselle. Most counterattacks took place at night or under the cover of early morning fog. Moving over the broken terrain, German small units infiltrated into American lines causing great confusion, then other units attacked the 80th Division's forward positions. The largest counterattack took place at dawn on 15 September as five battalions of infantry and a tank battalion tried to wipe out the northern half of the bridgehead. Ste. Genevieve and Hill 382 exchanged hands several times, and the intense fighting took its toll on both sides as casualties mounted. The 3d Battalion, 319th Infantry, was cut off and surrounded, and the 80th Division artillery commander, Brig. Gen. E. W. Searby, was killed in hand-to-hand combat. The final German efforts to smash the bridgehead took place on 16 September, but attacks against both flanks failed in the face of aggressive maneuvering by infantry and armor units and artillery and air support. Having failed to push the Americans back into the Moselle, the Germans began to withdraw toward the east. This last effort marked the end of the Dieulouard bridgehead battles, a series of engagements in which the American combined arms team showed its defensive abilities against the enemy's best efforts.[19]

Although the Germans contested almost all river crossings in the ETO, there were times when the American soldier battled an equally formidable enemy—the weather. No river crossing better illustrates the problems of fighting both the enemy and severe weather than the 90th Infantry Division's struggle in the Koenigsmacher bridgehead. As part of XX Corps' broad offensive to encircle and capture Metz in early November, General Walker ordered Brig. Gen. James A. Van Fleet's 90th Division to cross the Moselle above Metz and form the northern arm of the American pincer movement against the city. After an extensive reconnaissance of the division's zone, Walker and Van Fleet decided to assault the river in the vicinity of Koenigsmacher.[20]

Preparations and planning by the "Tough Hombres" of the 90th Division in the two weeks prior to the attack were the main reasons for the assault's initial success. Engineers and infantry worked closely together to ensure that things would go right on D-Day. XX Corps assigned the 1139th Engineer Combat Group to support Van Fleet's attack, now set for 9 November. The 1139th's missions were to cross the infantry in assault boats, to ferry supplies and evacuate the wounded on infantry support rafts, and finally to span the Moselle with two treadway bridges. Between 4–7 November engineer teams joined all of the 90th Division's regiments and conducted classes and rehearsals in the carrying, loading, unloading, and paddling of M2 assault boats. Commanders reorganized their units into boat teams and did detailed planning for the crossing and the battles on the far shore. Since the 90th Division had little experience in using assault boats due to an almost unbelievable turnover in riflemen since landing in France, the precombat training paid great dividends.[21]

Van Fleet developed a battle plan that called for a predawn river crossing to secure high ground on the far bank. The Tough Hombres would attack with two regiments abreast. The 358th Infantry on the right would cross at Cattenom and capture the high ground on the far bank, while the 359th would cross at Malling and secure the bridgehead's left flank by occupying another set of heights. The 357th Infantry was initially in division reserve and was to cross the Moselle behind the regiment that had the most success. It would then attack to establish a defensive position in the center of the bridgehead between the positions established by the other two regiments. Van Fleet's intent was for his regiments to occupy by the end of the first day the key terrain controlling all of the crossing sites so that the engineers could begin installing bridges. His plan was a page right out of army doctrine, but the enemy, mud, rain, and cold combined to convert a straightforward river crossing into one of the most miserable and difficult operations in the ETO.[22]

The last days before the attack saw the 90th Division and all its attached units moving into final positions. Four miles west of the Moselle the Cattenom Forest provided the covered and concealed positions that units wanted close to their crossing sites. The forest was on the forward slope of a long ridge and within sight of German outposts, so the Americans moved into positions under the cover of darkness and bad weather. On two successive nights twenty battalions of corps and division artillery displaced into firing positions on the rear slopes behind the Cattenom Forest. XX Corps' 3d Cavalry Group did a splendid job of patrolling the river and reporting on the physical characteristics of the crossing sites. On the night of 7 November, all other units slipped into the forest, the sound of their movement covered by the 3d Cavalry's gunfire and a persistent rainfall that turned the countryside into a sea of mud and caused the Moselle to run over its banks. The rains soaked troops to the bone, transformed foxholes into pits filled with icy water, and made roads impassable. By the morning of 8 November, Van Fleet had concentrated the entire 90th Division, six battalions of supporting artillery, three battalions of tanks and TDs, three engineer battalions, and three heavy bridging companies into positions overlooking the Moselle. Commanders briefed all their troops on final attack plans, while artillery battalions registered their guns. That night, miserable and saturated, the infantry waited in their foxholes for H-hour.[23]

As darkness fell on 8 November, the engineers moved forward and organized the assault boat staging areas. The engineers had watched the Moselle with increased anxiety, and a close look confirmed their greatest fears. The river averaged about 350 feet wide in the attack zone, but the incessant rains had caused it to rise rapidly, and in some places it was now 600 feet wide with the current moving fast and picking up speed. Commanders on the spot knew that high water alone could not keep them from getting at the Germans; at 0300 hours the first wave of the Tough Hombres slid their assault boats into the Moselle's muddy, thrashing waters. After reaching the far bank, the boat crews began the hazardous return trip to pick up the next rifle companies, but the empty boats were too difficult to handle in the raging waters and the swift current swept most of them 1,000 yards downstream. The infantry on the near bank grew apprehensive and impatient as they waited for the boat crews to return. German shells began to fall among the riflemen, and unit commanders decided to use the boats held in reserve to cross the second wave. By 0500 hours both lead battalions were on the far bank and moving toward their objectives. All evidence suggested that the crossing caught the Germans by surprise, but sunrise saw an increase in enemy activity.[24]

Throughout 9 November the 90th Division focused all of its efforts in getting men and equipment into the bridgehead. The rising river forced infantry units to load into their assault boats in waist-deep water. Engineer boat crews performed herculean labors in getting their craft across the river, discharging their cargo of men and guns, and then returning to the west bank only to repeat the adventure again. Losses in assault boats were heavy, and the engineers had to press into service boats husbanded for ferrying and bridging operations. The engineers tried to get infantry support rafts into action, but the Moselle was too turbulent. At Malling the very first infantry support raft trying to cross capsized, spilling men and equipment overboard. A larger raft went to work later in the day carrying ammunition and rations across and returning with the wounded. The 1139th Engineers attempted to emplace a footbridge, but the raging Moselle snapped an anchor cable and the entire bridge was swept downstream and lost. By noon the river was 800 yards wide. The 90th Division's unit history best describes the Moselle: "The river, never mild at its best, sounded in an angry roar, foamed and swirled and eddied and flung itself against its shores." Despite the water's fury and the strengthening German resistance, American engineers and infantry made progress. By sundown eight infantry battalions were on the far bank holding a bridgehead six miles wide and two miles deep.[25]

The real danger came during the next few days as the Germans regained their balance. The infantry were clamped in the vise of a determined enemy to their front and a churning river at their back. With the Moselle all but impassable, the 90th Division could not get heavy guns, vehicles, or supplies into the bridgehead. The infantry—hungry, tired, soaked, and numbed to the bone—fought the Germans with rifles, hand grenades, and sheer guts. Twenty battalions of artillery did a magnificent job of supporting the infantry, but the troops on the far shore desperately needed fresh supplies and armor support. It soon became clear that if the Tough Hombres were to hold their bridgehead, the engineers would somehow have to get a treadway bridge across the Moselle.[26]

Combat engineers struggled mightily to overcome the forces of nature. The rising river inundated the roads leading to bridge sites with five feet of water, making any immediate crossing impossible. At Malling, soldiers of the 991st Engineer Treadway Bridge Company labored in chest-deep water and managed to install a bridge by sundown on 10 November, but the swift current made the treadway buck wildly, and no vehicles were able to cross until the afternoon of the next day. Around sunrise on 12 November, a group of TDs were inching their way across the bouncing bridge when disaster struck. The concussion from a number of German shells that landed very close to the bridge and the weight of the TDs caused the bridge to snap. Soldiers watched horrified as a huge section of the treadway broke loose, the large pontoons tumbling and turning as the current swept them away. Luckily, two TDs made it across and were instrumental in turning back one of the largest German counterattacks against the bridgehead. Undeterred by the accident, the 991st's engineers improvised on the spot and used parts of the remaining bridge to lash together a large, sturdy raft powered by motorboats and capable of carrying tanks. Working under enemy shell fire, the engineers managed to ferry across a company of tanks and TDs by nightfall on 12 November. For their ingenuity and valor under fire, the 991st Engineer Treadway Bridge Company earned the Distinguished Unit Citation.[27]

Similar efforts took place at the second crossing site at Cattenom. High water prevented bridging operations, so the 179th Engineer Combat Battalion ran a pontoon ferry during 9–11 November. Work on the treadway began in earnest on the afternoon of 12 November, and a smoke generator company screened the bridging site as the 179th's engineers pushed their pontoons into the river. The fast current and churning water at midstream made joining the pontoons a hazardous and difficult chore. By the next morning the engineers had almost completed the bridge, laboring under the cover of the smoke screen to anchor the 645-foot treadway section into place. Suddenly, a vehicle on the east bank struck a mine, and the engineers realized that they had emplaced the far end of the bridge in a German minefield that had been covered by the now-receding floodwaters. For the next five hours the engineers went through the nerve-racking ordeal of clearing the underwater mines. By 1645 hours the bridge was ready, and under a smoke screen's protective blanket, the 90th Division's heavy equipment began to pour into the bridgehead.[28]

By dawn on 14 November most of the 90th Division was on the far bank. For the first time in six days the hard-pressed riflemen enjoyed hot food, overcoats, blankets, and dry socks. The assistance had come none too soon; by 14 November six of the nine infantry battalions were below 50 percent strength. With the treadway at Cattenom anchored in place, the Tough Hombres considered the Koenigsmacher bridgehead secure. After visiting the Cattenom bridge site on 14 November, General Patton declared the 90th Division's passage of the Moselle "an epic river crossing done under terrific difficulties."[29]

Other river crossing operations during the autumn and winter of 1944–1945 yielded a number of valuable tactical lessons. Commanders discovered that crossing assault waves in the vicinity of planned bridge construction sites enabled the engineers to start bridging operations sooner.

Most units learned that artillery shelling, direct heavy weapons fire, and bad weather muffled the sounds of engineers and assault troops moving to the river and crossing the first attack wave. Tank, TD, and especially antiaircraft battalions excelled in providing direct fire support into bridgeheads from firing positions on the near bank. Recognizing that antitank capabilities had to get into bridgeheads quickly, infantry units began to carry extra antitank mines and bazookas. Commanders realized the importance of rehearsals in speeding assault boat crossings. Infantry battalions increased command and control at the crossing site by posting the commander or a senior staff officer, who helped sort out confusion on the friendly shore and maintained liaison with the commanders of succeeding attack waves. The army learned not to overlook the need for engineer support on the far bank, since engineer troops were needed to clear or emplace obstacles in the bridgehead and too often engineer assets became totally engaged in crossing operations. Throughout the ETO a standard practice developed where division engineer battalions supported the bridgehead fighting, while attached engineer groups handled assault boat and bridging duties.[30]

The most important technical lesson learned was the use of smoke generators to mask and protect crossing sites with thick billows of white smoke. The army had originally created smoke units to screen rear areas and command posts against observation and attack by enemy air power. At Arnaville, France, on 10 September 1944, the army improvised the employment of smoke generators to provide support to frontline units for the very first time. Smoke generators of the 84th Chemical Company successfully produced an effective smoke screen that covered units of the 5th Division crossing the Moselle. For several days smoke generators blanketed crossing and bridging sites with a white haze that kept American casualties down and forced German direct and indirect fire to shoot indiscriminately into the bank of white smoke. News of the successful smoke operation at Arnaville spread throughout the armies and soon became a standard practice during river crossings.[31]

Units discovered many other technical lessons as well. Engineers learned not to emplace bridges near civilian bridges or in the vicinity of prominent terrain features, since the Germans always seemed to have their guns registered on the latter and easily could shift fires onto construction sites. Establishing medical aid stations and warming houses near the river to treat soldiers injured or soaked during crossings saved lives and put soldiers back into the battle sooner. For the first time the army took safety precautions to save lives; soldiers began to wear life preservers during crossings, and engineers operated powerboats downstream from crossing sites to pick up riflemen thrown into the water by enemy fire or accidents. The need to preserve assault boats was paramount, since losses from accidents, enemy fire, and river conditions could be staggering. During XII Corps' crossing of the Our and Sauer Rivers on 7–11 February 1945, the engineers began with 304 assault boats and 5 powerboats; by the close of the operation, bad water conditions and German fire had destroyed 161 craft and 2 powerboats. Engineer and infantry units stressed proper loading to avoid capsizing in rough water and to facilitate steering, and riflemen learned that shifting weight when the boat came under fire or when casualties occurred could overturn it. Engineers stressed to infantrymen that assault boats were their only lifeline until bridges were emplaced; if it was impossible to return boats to the near bank, they were to pull the craft up on the bank or tie them up rather than abandon them. Engineer commanders emphasized to boat crews that if swift currents swept them below the crossing site they were to pull, push, or drag the boat back to the embarkation point in order to get it back into the crossing operation.[32]

The army's most dramatic river crossing of World War II occurred in the closing weeks of the war, when the 9th Armored Division captured a bridge over the Rhine River at Remagen. The exploits there are usually held up as examples of the initiative of individual soldiers and of the army's rapid and successful exploitation of an unexpected fortune. Ironically, the army's most famous river crossing in the ETO was in almost all respects a complete reverse of the practices and procedures recommended in river crossing doctrine. The Remagen bridgehead is an excellent example of how the army applied standard doctrine and methods with flexibility.

After the battles in the Ardennes, the American armies conducted a series of large offensives that propelled units toward the Rhine. By early March First Army was approaching that last major water barrier on a front extending from Cologne southward to Koblenz. Almost everyone discussed the possibility of seizing a bridge over the Rhine, but hopes for capturing an intact bridge grew thin as the Germans successfully destroyed several bridges in the face of approaching Allied columns. First Army's offensive was not intended to cross the Rhine. Instead, General Hodges was to close on the river, effect a linkup to the south with Third Army along the Ahr River, and mop up pockets of German resistance on the west bank.[33]

The U.S. III Corps, commanded by Maj. Gen. John Millikin, operated on First Army's right flank and had the mission of establishing contact with Third Army. Millikin ordered the 9th Armored Division to clear the west bank of the Rhine and to seize crossings over the Ahr River to the south. On the morning of 7 March the 9th Armored Division was moving in two parallel columns toward the confluence of the Ahr and Rhine rivers. CCA, on the right, was to seize two crossing sites over the Ahr River and establish contact with Third Army. On the left, Combat Command B (CCB) was to clear Remagen and Kripp, and then capture another crossing site over the Ahr further to the south. In December 1918, III Corps had crossed the Rhine at Remagen as part of the Allied occupation forces at the close of World War I. Now, a war later, troops from III Corps were destined to repeat history and cross the Rhine once again at Remagen.[34]

As CCB moved toward the Rhine, an artillery spotter plane flew ahead of the armored columns looking for targets of opportunity. Around 1030 hours, Lt. Harold Larsen of the 9th Armored Division artillery received a shock. As his cub plane approached Remagen, Larsen looked down and saw the black superstructure of the Ludendorff railroad bridge standing out in stark contrast to the fog and mists that lingered in the river valley. German engineers had built the bridge in 1916 to facilitate lateral communications between the eastern and western fronts. Named after the World War I hero Eric von Ludendorff, the bridge measured 1,069 feet long and was buttressed by four stone piers. The roadway supported two railroad tracks, and along both sides of the bridge ran planked footpaths. Two large towers, built of dark brown stone and resembling the turrets of medieval castles, sternly stood guard over the approaches at each end of the bridge. Larsen was the first American to see that the Ludendorff bridge still stood, and he wasted no time in radioing the incredible news to CCB Headquarters. Brig. Gen. William M. Hoge, the CCB commander, immediately ordered his units nearest to Remagen to take the bridge.[35]

Very few places along the Rhine were less suited for a large-scale river crossing. (See Map 6.2.) Doctrine recommended that crossing sites have good approach and exit routes as well as terrain easy to capture on the far bank, but Remagen lacked all of these. Only one main road entered Remagen from the west, and it ran perpendicular, not parallel, to American supply lines. On the far bank two roads ran east away from the bridge. Both wound through wooded, hilly ground, and the Germans could easily block the roads. The terrain on the far bank was a defender's dream. Near the east end of the bridge the Erpeler Ley, a towering height of 500 feet that rose precipitously from the river, dominated the entire Rhine River Valley. The ground on the east bank rose steeply away from the bridge for about 5,000 yards through a series of rough, wooded hills. The Germans would have ideal defensive positions in country best suited for dismounted infantry, not the tanks and halftracks of the 9th Armored Division.[36]

The actual capture of the Remagen bridge fell to a task force commanded by Lt. Col. Leonard Engeman and consisting of the 27th Armored Infantry and 14th Tank battalions. TF Engeman moved toward the Rhine on the morning of 7 March unaware that the Ludendorff bridge still stood, and before noon had occupied a large woods west of Remagen.

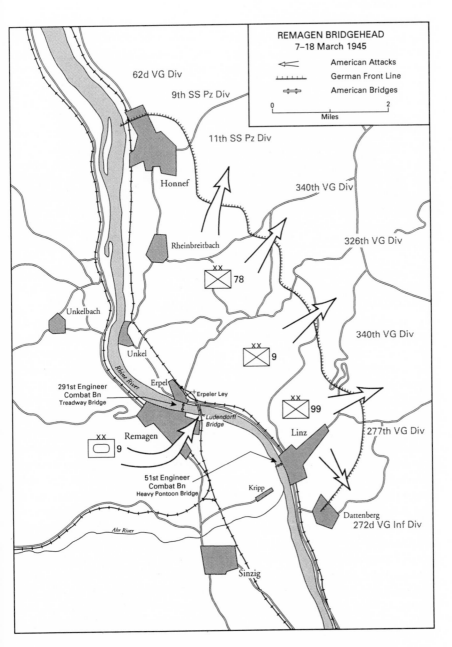

Map 6.2. The Remagen Bridgehead, 7–18 March 1945 (Sherry L. Dowdy)

The Bridge at Remagen, March 1945. The capture of the Ludendorff Bridge and fighting in the Remagen bridgehead reflect the competency and complexity of U.S. combined arms operations. (U.S. Army Military History Institute)

Discovering around 1300 hours that the Germans had failed to destroy the bridge, Engeman issued orders for his troops to clear Remagen and capture the west end of the bridge. The fighting began with a coordinated combined arms attack against Remagen. At 1350 hours 1st Lt. Karl H. Timmerman's Company A, 27th Armored Infantry, attacked on foot from the high ground west of Remagen, and a platoon of new M26 Pershing tanks from Company A, 14th Tank Battalion, covered their move. Mortars and artillery shelled the east bank and attempted to lay down a smoke screen to prevent German troops from observing the attack. Timmerman's riflemen met light resistance. Around 1420 hours the Pershing tanks roared ahead, joined Company A, and together began moving along the main street through Remagen and toward the Ludendorff bridge. By 1500 hours Timmerman's troops, the tank platoon, and one platoon from Company C, 27th Armored Infantry, were at the west end of the bridge.[37]

As the infantry cleared Remagen, General Hoge arrived on the scene and ordered Colonel Engeman to capture the bridge immediately. Timmerman received the order to attack and hurried to get his forces organized. Company A would cross the Ludendorff bridge first on foot supported by the tank platoon and an infantry platoon from C Company. A team of three engineers joined the group with the mission of cutting demolition wires and removing explosives from the bridge. Suddenly a huge explosion shook Remagen as a volcano of stone and earth erupted near the west end of the bridge. The Germans had detonated a huge cratering charge that gouged a deep hole in the earthen causeway joining the main road and the bridge platform, making it impossible for vehicles to approach the bridge. Timmerman's lead platoon was about ready to attack when a second explosion went off. The infantrymen watched in awe as the bridge's superstructure jumped, steel and lumber members flew through the air, and a giant cloud of dust and black smoke rose. The Germans had attempted to destroy the bridge, but not all of the charges had detonated. As the smoke and dust clouds cleared, everyone gaped with disbelief that the bridge still stood. Timmerman saw that the explosions had torn big holes in the roadway but that the footpaths were still intact. Shouting "Get goin', you guys, get goin'!" Timmerman and the lead platoon stepped onto the Ludendorff bridge.[38]

Tanks, TDs, mortars, artillery, and engineers worked together to support the infantry attack, and indirect fire peppered the far bank. Tanks and TDs placed fire on German positions, silencing enemy guns in the bridge's stone towers and in a barge floating on the Rhine, while the infantrymen pushed forward, ducking and dashing from one steel girder to the next. The engineer team moved right with the infantrymen, cutting every demolition wire they could find, tearing explosive charges off steel girders, and tossing them into the Rhine below. As Company A neared the end of the 1,000-foot span, several men entered the stone towers to flush out some Germans, while others continued ahead. The first Allied soldier to set foot across the Rhine was an assistant squad leader, Sgt. Alex Drabik. Moments later, around 1550 hours, Lieutenant Timmerman and a group of soldiers joined Drabik on the far bank. Company A turned downstream and began to sweep through Erpel, and companies B and C soon followed. By nightfall American troops were on high ground around the east end of the bridge and blocking all roads with obstacles or mines.[39]

A mad rush ensued as everyone tried to strengthen the toehold on the far bank. While the 9th Armored Division and III Corps worked to get units moving toward Remagen, TF Engeman's engineers repaired the Ludendorff bridge's main floorway. By midnight they had covered over the gaping holes caused by the afternoon's explosions, and the 14th Tank Battalion crossed the Rhine. However, an accident on the bridge soon blocked all movement, and a colossal traffic jam ensued that stretched for miles west of Remagen. Just before dawn the Ludendorff bridge again opened for traffic, and two battalions of infantry deployed into the bridgehead. The corps commander tried to bring order out of chaos by establishing a series of objectives on the far bank. In a move consistent with doctrine, General Millikin established three successive lines of objectives whose capture would prevent the Germans from placing fire on the bridge. Within twenty-four hours of the bridge's capture, more than 8,000 Americans were on the far bank—mostly infantry and armor battalions of the 9th Armored and 9th Infantry Divisions—confined in a bridgehead barely two miles wide and one mile deep. As 8 March wore on, German shock at the loss of the bridge dissipated, and they began to mount an organized defense along with efforts to destroy the bridge.[40]

Over the next several days American activities centered on four main tasks: the protection of the Ludendorff bridge; the construction of additional bridges; reinforcement of troops on the far bank; and expansion of the bridgehead. Both sides instinctively knew that American success depended on keeping an open lifeline into the bridgehead. For the Germans this meant destroying the Ludendorff bridge; for the Americans it meant keeping the battered span intact while throwing additional bridging over the Rhine.

The Luftwaffe took to the skies in one of its last demonstrations of strength and valor. Braving bad weather, American antiaircraft fire, and the hills around Remagen, German aviators flung their aircraft down the Rhine valley in attempts to destroy the Ludendorff bridge. The first air strikes took place on the morning of 8 March and then trailed off until ending eight days later. Between 8–16 March the Luftwaffe flew an estimated 367 sorties over Remagen. Bad weather in Belgium and France kept American aircraft grounded most of the time, so the Germans enjoyed local air superiority. American commanders sought to protect the bridge by rushing antiaircraft battalions to Remagen. The 16th Antiaircraft Artillery Group assumed responsibility for defending the bridge and coordinating the efforts of its own air defense units as well as battalions from III and V Corps. By 10 March batteries of quadruple mounted .50-caliber machine guns as well as 90-mm and 40-mm guns pointed their barrels skyward, as the Americans generated a staggering volume of fire in a defensive umbrella over the bridge.[41] One observer of an air strike remembered, "There was so much firing that the ground shuddered; it was awesome. The entire valley around Remagen became cloaked in smoke and dust before the Germans left—only three minutes after they first appeared."[42] Within a few days time the Americans had massed a total of thirteen battalions of antiaircraft artillery of all types, probably the greatest concentration of air defense assets in the ETO.[43]

American ingenuity played a large role in protecting the Ludendorff bridge. Barrage balloons soon flew over the bridge to obstruct the Luftwaffe's approaches. Engineers constructed a series of log and net booms upstream to intercept German explosives carried to the bridge by the current. Hundreds of depth charges were dropped into the river to deter frogmen and underwater craft, and radar joined in the search for submerged threats. At night powerful searchlights mounted on tanks searched for any unusual activity on the water, continuous outposts along the west bank kept a lookout, and on the bridge itself soldiers stood guard with orders to shoot at anything suspicious in the water below. Taken together, all of these steps thwarted German efforts to sabotage the bridge.[44]

Senior American commanders realized that just saving the Ludendorff bridge was not enough; they had to throw additional bridges over the Rhine in order to expand the bridgehead. On 9 March two combat engineer battalions converged on Remagen and began the daunting task of spanning the Rhine under heavy German fire. In 55 B.C. engineers of the Roman army built a bridge over the Rhine at Andernach so that Caesar could carry out a punitive raid against the Germanic tribes. The construction of that bridge had become a paradigm for how ancient armies were to conduct river crossings. Now, two thousand years later and only twelve miles downstream from Caesar's original crossing site, American engineers would show other modern armies how to cross a major river in the face of enemy fire.

The job of building a treadway bridge fell to the 291st Engineer Combat Battalion, commanded by Lt. Col. David E. Pergrin. The site selected lay just 200 yards downstream from the Ludendorff bridge. Colonel Pergrin studied the situation and realized that his men would be sitting ducks for German small arms fire, artillery, and air strikes; nevertheless, construction began in earnest about 1030 hours on 9 March. The exposed nose of the bridge, where engineers anchored sections of floats and treadways onto the part of the bridge already assembled, soon became known as "Suicide Point"; around 1300 hours a German shell scored a direct hit, killing one engineer and wounding at least five others. By sundown the treadway extended about 200 yards into the Rhine, and it appeared as though the engineers would finish the bridge overnight. But intermittent, accurate shelling as well as occasional fire from German tanks on the far bank kept overnight gains to a minimum. Throughout the next day Pergrin's engineers on Suicide Point worked with grim resolve during heavy shelling and air strikes. An enemy round landed on or near the treadway bridge every five minutes almost all day long. Finally, around 1700 hours on 10 March, the engineers anchored the treadway onto the eastern shore. Total casualties for the operation were one man killed and twenty-four wounded. During its first two days of operation, 3,105 vehicles crossed the treadway. The 291st had laid the first tactical bridge over the Rhine since the Napoleonic wars, and at 1,032 feet, the longest treadway bridge yet constructed in the ETO under combat conditions.[45]

Two miles upstream from the Ludendorff bridge the 51st Combat Engineer Battalion defied German fire to install a heavy pontoon bridge near Linz. Postponing construction until American riflemen cleared the far bank, the 51st began work on the second bridge over the Rhine at 1600 hours on 10 March. Like Colonel Pergrin's battalion, the engineers were exposed to murderous fire, and rising water and a swift current added to their problems. But the engineers' perseverance paid off, and just before midnight on 11 March the pontoon bridge opened for traffic. Because the bridge was exposed and easy to spot from the air, the Luftwaffe tried its best to knock it out. On 13 March German aircraft continuously bombed and strafed the bridge, but protection by American antiaircraft gunners and friendly fighters the next day made further Luftwaffe attacks too costly. With two bridges over the Rhine, engineers closed the Ludendorff bridge for repairs on 12 March.[46]

Ironically, the fortunes of war accomplished what the Germans could not: at 1500 hours on 17 March the Ludendorff bridge collapsed. A series of sharp cracks—the heads of major anchor bolts shearing—were the first indication that something was wrong. The roadway began to vibrate and the superstructure to tremble, as the bridge let out sounds of "screeching, cracking, and splintering as steel rubbed against steel and wood." The huge superstructure swayed and swagged, finally falling into the Rhine with a mighty crash. About 200 engineers were at work on the bridge when the end came, taking the lives of twenty-eight repairmen and injuring another ninety-three. The German effort to destroy the bridge on 7 March had almost severed the upstream truss, and the cumulative loads from the crossing of troops and heavy equipment, bombing, and shelling were just too much for the undamaged portion of the bridge to bear indefinitely. However, the loss of the bridge had little influence on the fighting in the bridgehead because of the prodigious efforts of American engineers in constructing tactical bridges.[47]

With two additional bridges over the Rhine, commanders breathed easier for the bridgehead's security. But the fighting on the far bank was going slowly. Rough terrain favored the defense, and the confined space in the bridgehead restricted the deployment of American units. General Millikin's mission was to cut the Frankfurt-Ruhr autobahn seven miles beyond the Rhine, consolidate his gains, and then break out of the bridgehead. But General Hodges grew dissatisfied with Millikin's handling of the battle and relieved him on 17 March. The new III Corps commander was James A. Van Fleet, former commander of the 90th Infantry Division and experienced veteran of the Koenigsmacher bridgehead. By 17 March, elements of Collins's VII Corps were on the far bank, and both corps attacked to expand the bridgehead perimeter to a width of 25 miles along the Rhine and a depth of 10 miles. On 18 March American troops reached the autobahn and two days later occupied final objectives all along the bridgehead's outer perimeter. Though a resounding success, the crossing of the Rhine at Remagen had its price, and III and VII Corps incurred a total of 7,500 casualties. Enemy losses are impossible to tally, but the Americans captured 11,700 prisoners alone.[48]

The capture of the Ludendorff bridge came as a surprise to the Americans, but so did the circumstances of the entire bridgehead battle, which contradicted almost every aspect of prewar river crossing doctrine. FM 100-5 called for infantry divisions to conduct deliberate attacks at nighttime across a broad front at geographically suitable crossing sites to capture accessible terrain on the far bank, but at Remagen none of these conditions existed. Instead, an armored division carried out a hasty daylight attack at a single point. Approaches and exits at the crossing sites were narrow and confining, and the enemy enjoyed local air superiority. The need to get reinforcements into the bridgehead was paramount, so engineers forged ahead with bridge construction under enemy fire. In 1942 the staffs, instructors, and students in the U.S. army's schools system would have looked askance at any officer prophesying the conditions at Remagen. Yet, three years later the army's most famous river crossing of World War II consisted of an armored division conducting a hasty daylight attack at a single point while engineers emplaced additional bridging under heavy enemy fire.

If the method at Remagen was so unexpected, what explains the success? Individual initiative, valor, and competence played significant roles. Commanders at all levels acted quickly to exploit an unexpected opportunity by seizing the bridge and committing follow-on forces without guidance or orders from higher headquarters. Infantrymen and tankers exhibited extraordinary bravery and initiative in taking the bridge and crossing the Rhine, and engineers putting in extra bridges were the personification of courage under fire. Soldiers proved that they knew their jobs and could carry them out during combined arms attacks, improvising the technical means to protect the bridge against enemy threats.

Senior commanders were also able to impose order on chaos by applying river crossing doctrine with flexibility. Although the 9th Armored Division crossed first, the generals realized that infantry was best suited for establishing bridgeheads. General Millikin also knew the far bank was not good tank country, and he acted quickly to rush infantry regiments to Remagen. The corps commander followed doctrine by establishing three successive lines of objectives that would protect the bridging sites and secure the overall bridgehead. A strict adherence to doctrine would have prevented engineers from installing bridges early, but the need to support the troops in the bridgehead prompted senior commanders to order them built immediately and in the face of enemy fire. Finally, General Millikin tried to conduct the bridgehead fighting according to doctrine by securing in succession key terrain features further away from his crossing sites.

German defenses, difficult terrain, and bad weather convinced the army that river crossings required a full combined arms effort. After initial, bloody attempts at crossing the Moselle, American commanders realized infantry regiments alone could not force deliberate river crossings.

Engineers had to provide assault boat and bridging capabilities, while artillery, tank, and TD units added their weight to the fight. CAS played a large role in many bridgehead battles. Chemical troops learned how to cover bridging sites with smoke screens, while antiaircraft battalions defended crossing sites and lent direct fire support to initial assaults. The Remagen bridgehead is the best example of a combined arms river crossing operation. TF Engeman conducted a tank-infantry-artillery attack against Remagen, then carried out a broader combined arms engagement during the actual crossing of the Ludendorff bridge. Fighting on 10 March saw almost every type of combat capability deployed and working together. The diversity and complexity of activities on the Rhine that day might well have confounded the American army that landed in North Africa in 1942, but three years of wartime experience had raised the army's level of performance to new heights.

The problems encountered during river crossings resulted in a great number of tactical and technical improvisations, and American commanders learned three techniques they incorporated into many river crossing plans. Often units risked crossings when water levels were high or currents swift in favor of gaining the element of surprise. Unfavorable conditions often relaxed German alertness, as happened with the 90th Division at Koenigsmacher. At other times, commanders gained surprise by not firing preparatory bombardments and having their soldiers cross quietly under the cover of darkness. Both methods tended to make the going much easier in the first hours of an assault. Doctrine mentioned almost nothing about direct fire support in river crossings, but commanders were quick to employ heavy weapons during initial assaults. Before tanks and TDs deployed into bridgeheads, their main guns and machine guns supported the infantry in the bridgehead from firing positions on the near bank. Antiaircraft units added lavish ground level firepower to many crossings.

Soldiers were especially adept at technical improvisation. The use of smoke generators to cloak river crossings was one of the great technical innovations in the ETO. Altogether, smoke screens covered twenty-three initial crossings and obscured another forty-one bridging sites. Engineer units were quick to experiment with construction methods when bridging unusually long spans or working in bad weather, and individual soldiers devised a number of ways to string bridge anchor cables. When bridging efforts failed, engineers lashed together heavy rafts to ferry weapons and supplies into bridgeheads. The wide range of countermeasures devised to protect the Ludendorff bridge best demonstrates the American capacity for technical innovation.[49]

River crossing operations provide a good example of the way the army adapted in order to implement new tactics and take advantage of enhanced technology. When units in the field are reorganizing or receiving new equipment, doctrine must change to reflect increased capabilities. The army's prewar river crossing doctrine applied to infantry and engineer forces with little modern equipment and no support from armored units. By 1944–1945 soldiers were armed with a large variety of new weapons and equipment, and units in the field used flexibility, ingenuity, and judgment to modify doctrine and alter tactics in ways that took full advantage of their increased capabilities. Senior commanders revised doctrine by attacking rivers at a single point in daylight so as to combine the power of infantry and armored divisions. On the far bank, commanders learned to fight combined arms battles against stiff enemy resistance as a way to expand their bridgeheads, and units of all types altered tactics and techniques to take best advantage of new equipment like treadway bridges, smoke generators, and infantry support rafts powered by outboard motors.

The process of learning lessons and implementing change during river crossing operations illustrates a major difference between centralized and decentralized methods for controlling adaptation. A centralized process is usually slower and more prudent, and soldiers gain a respite from battle while senior commanders and staffs develop solutions to new problems. An ad hoc adaptation method yields immediate, spontaneous results, but soldiers often remain under fire while learning and changing. New river crossing tactics and techniques did facilitate operations and eventually save lives, but casualties during the learning and adapting process often ran high. American commanders ignored doctrinal guidelines and attacked after sunrise to gain all the advantages that daylight afforded. The use of smoke screens and heavy, direct fire weapons eventually yielded the same degree of protection to assault troops that darkness provided during night operations, but a number of river crossings with high losses—like those at Dornot and Pont-a-Mousson—occurred before the army developed new methods for successful, less costly daylight crossings.

The collective experience in attacking the rivers of Western Europe validated most of the army's theory on river crossings. Still, commanders discovered that certain conditions rendered much of doctrine irrelevant. FM 100-5 seemed to expect a passive defense on the far bank, rather than German troops fighting from prepared defenses and using slashing counterattacks, and Americans had to adapt to overcome both unsuitable terrain and stubborn resistance. Commanders discovered that capturing a series of prominent terrain features away from the river was the best way to secure bridgeheads, and regimental and battalion commanders consistently made sound attack plans and displayed a keen eye for identifying key terrain. Rapid, coordinated crossings were the most successful, and quick reinforcement of the bridgehead helped win battles on the far shore.

FM 100-5 said little about how to coordinate the efforts of infantry and armored divisions, so senior commanders experimented to find the best ways to integrate their rifle and tank formations. Infantry regiments were best suited for deliberate crossings, but armor units could not stand idle on the near bank for long. In general, infantry divisions established initial bridgeheads, then armored divisions crossed to assume a portion of the perimeter or to launch exploitations into the German rear. The 2d Armored Division crossed the Wurm River north of Aachen in close support of the 30th Infantry Division, and the 4th Armored Division's breakout from the Dieulouard bridgehead remains a classic armored exploitation. Armored divisions had limited success in attacking rivers, and Remagen is the best example of an armored force leading the way across a major water obstacle. Without the Ludendorff bridge's massive superstructure to carry its tanks, the 9th Armored could have never crossed onto the Rhine's east bank.

Doctrine insisted that units have multiple, initial crossing sites as a way to find the enemy's weak points and to keep him off balance. However, stiff German resistance converted American efforts at multiple crossings into piecemeal defeats, and the debacle at Pont-a-Mousson showed the hazards of dispersed crossings. Corps and division commanders learned that single, coordinated efforts using all available resources were required to rupture enemy defenses, so they tended to mass all of their efforts into one attack to capture the first prominent terrain feature on the far bank. Dieulouard illustrates the learned American practice of concentrating all available combat power into a single crossing operation. Regimental and battalion commanders had a tendency to concentrate their efforts even further. Regiments hardly ever attacked with two or more battalions abreast; instead colonels employed their battalions in a single column. At the small unit level, battalions attacked in columns of companies, while rifle companies attacked in columns of platoons. These tight formations maximized command and control, permitted the massing of organic weapons, and speeded assault boat operations at narrow crossing sites.

Engineer battalions discovered that waiting to build bridges until construction sites were clear of enemy fire was often impossible. The need to support infantrymen on the far shore was paramount, and the construction of bridges in the face of direct and indirect enemy fire convinced everyone of the competence and courage of engineer troops.

River crossings again taught the army the crucial difference between haste and speed on the battlefield. The actions at Pont-a-Mousson showed that rash crossings attempted without sufficient preparations or adequate knowledge of terrain and the enemy led to disaster, while Dieulouard and

Arnaville proved that a coordinated attack pressed with vigor was the only way to force crossings against prepared defenses. Commanders learned the importance of intelligence gathering and security measures before crossings, as cavalrymen reported on the physical characteristics of the river and the surrounding countryside and engineer and infantry patrols provided specifics about fording, crossing, and bridging sites.

Combat zone training in river crossing methods and rehearsals beforehand buoyed soldiers' confidence, made assaults go smoother and faster, and saved lives. Training in the handling of assault boats paid great dividends. By the autumn of 1944 many infantry divisions had considerable numbers of replacements who had little or no experience in river crossings. Assault rehearsals familiarized replacements with infantry-engineer teamwork while integrating them into units. The 90th Division's training program just before the Koenigsmacher bridgehead is the best example of how precombat training helped to ensure initial success in river crossings.

While Patton's divisions struggled to get over the Moselle and attack Metz, First Army had become absorbed in breaching the Siegfried Line and reducing Aachen. Courtney Hodges still hoped to renew a broader offensive eastward across the Aachen Plain that would carry First Army all the way to the Rhine; little did he know that a crossing of the Rhine River was still six months away. The principal reason for the delay centered around the terrain on First Army's southern flank: the Huertgen Forest and the Ardennes. As autumn turned into winter, the Americans became embroiled in two titanic struggles among the hills, gorges, and tree masses of these forests. The Huertgen Forest campaign would break the back of many good divisions and produce few results, while the Germans' Ardennes offensive would culminate in one of the American army's greatest victories and largely determine the final outcome in the ETO. Both battles took place during ferocious weather among green tangles of heavy forests—an environment for which the army was neither physically nor psychologically prepared.

CHAPTER SEVEN

Confusion and Slaughter among the Firs

In the [Huertgen] forest proper, our gains came inch by inch and foot by foot, delivered by men with rifles—bayonets on one end and grim, resolute courage on the other. There was no battle on the continent of Europe more devastating, frustrating, or gory.

—*Maj. Gen. William G. Weaver, commanding*
general, 8th Infantry Division

The American army firmly believed that the quality of men and equipment had much to do with the outcome of battles. However, divisions operating in the ETO learned that terrain largely determined the tempo and characteristics of combat. As American forces closed along Germany's western border, from the lower Rhine to the Swiss border, they found themselves fighting in one of the most difficult and inhospitable environments in the entire theater—large, dark forests of tall fir trees. Most Americans knew the German fairy tale in which Hansel and Gretel dropped bread crumbs to mark their path through the dim woods. But in late 1944 a swath of killed and wounded marked the advance of American units trying to push their way closer toward Germany.

The army was unprepared for forest combat. Prewar doctrine discussed it in general terms but said little of real substance. FM 100-5 recommended that units bypass forests, but when this was not possible they were to carry out frontal assaults. Doctrine identified limited observation and command and control problems as particular difficulties. Thick stands of large trees greatly reduced artillery employment and allowed only very short and narrow fields of fire for heavy weapons. In thick forests units were to attack in column in order to concentrate their combat power and facilitate command and control. There was almost no discussion of combined arms operations; FM 100-5 addressed the role of armor only in passing and made no mention of CAS or engineers. Doctrine and training literature gave few hints as to how commanders were to overcome the unique problems posed by forest combat, and doctrine seemed to be merely a listing of ways the physical environment would affect normal battle tactics rather than a comprehensive approach to the problem. However, one sentence in FM 100-5 accurately described one of the key characteristics of forest combat: "Numerical superiority is of little advantage in the close combat which usually develops."[1]

Several years of combat experience on the Eastern Front had given the German army a much clearer picture of how to operate in forests. The Germans always established a forward outpost line to delay the enemy and to determine the location of his main effort. Primary defensive positions were well dug in with overhead cover and had support from mortars, artillery, tanks, and assault guns. The aim of the defense was to control all roads and trails while maintaining a uniform front. The German army preferred to conduct a fighting withdrawal back through a series of in-depth defenses rather than let the enemy get in too close to their positions. Counterattacks were not considered as crucial to winning as they were in combat on other types of terrain, probably reflecting the German army's own experience with the difficulties of attacking through thick woods.[2]

German units adapted a whole series of methods to gain every possible advantage. They kept heavy weapons and mortars forward to minimize the problems of moving large equipment about. Antitank weapons targeted trails, roads, and any open areas or breaks in the woods. Tanks fought as assault guns with the infantry to protect the MLR or to add punch to counterattacks. Companies stockpiled caches of ammunition and medical supplies well forward to avoid resupply difficulties. A favorite technique was the extensive use of snipers perched in treetops, and artillery and mortar observers also worked among the tree limbs. Each company designated several soldiers who were to keep track of direction using compasses and to maintain contact with neighboring units. Runners were the preferred method of communication between units. The infantry procured ladders, axes, large knives, and sharp spades to further their work among the trees.[3]

American units attacking into heavily forested areas for the first time discovered the many perils of combat in the woods. Large formations could not find the room needed to deploy their subordinate units. Tree trunks and the overhead canopy restricted observation and fields of fire and often denied the infantry artillery and air support. Maneuvering tanks through thick woods was a difficult if not impossible task that greatly exposed vehicles and crewmen. Maintaining a sense of location and direction was difficult even for those expert with a map and compass. Foliage and dim light made German positions hard to locate, and the forest floor was a haven for mines and booby traps. Thick forests fragmented and compartmentalized small unit actions. For the individual soldier, heavy woods were a cold, dark, damp place that imposed horrendous living and fighting conditions and isolated him from other units as well as the outside world. Many American soldiers had difficulty withstanding the mental stresses forest combat inflicted.

The army's greatest test in forest combat came during the protracted campaign to clear the Huertgen Forest. From mid-September to mid-December, the fight involved parts of seven divisions. Weather, terrain, and a resolute enemy combined to produce some of the most gruesome fighting in the European campaigns. The bocage country had introduced the army to bitter close-quarters combat; the Huertgen hammered home many of those same lessons. The forest exacted a tremendous physical and psychological toll on the army at a time when manpower levels were already ebbing, and the magnitude of the Huertgen fighting was not lost on the participants. For some, the large battles among the tall, thick trees conjured up parallels to the titanic struggles between the North and the South at Chancellorsville, the Wilderness, and Spotsylvania. American veterans of World War I made comparisons with the Argonne Forest. Ernest Hemingway viewed the Huertgen Forest campaign and called it America's "Passchendaele with tree bursts."[4]

The Huertgen Forest, encompassing roughly 50 square miles of densely wooded, rugged terrain along the German-Belgian border, falls within a triangle outlined by Aachen, Monschau, and Duren. To the north lies the flat Aachen Plain, to the south the Ardennes. The region is actually a cluster of smaller forests, but for both Americans and Germans the name became synonymous with the whole area and the entire campaign. A series of ridges running from southwest to northeast divides the forest into compartments, as do the deep gorges of several streams and rivers. Americans and Germans fought savagely to dominate the road network in the heart of the forest. Schmidt, Vossenack, and Huertgen, once sleepy pastoral villages, took on strategic significance as the opponents battled for their control. The dark green forest firs stood close together and towered 75 to 100 feet tall. The dense tree limbs formed an overhead canopy that obscured the sky and let in little sunlight, making the forest floor dark, damp, and devoid of underbrush.[5]

The environment exerted a strong influence in the Huertgen Forest. With the approach of winter, the elements began to pose a threat to soldiers as real as enemy bullets. Rain turned the ground into a sea of mud that made any type of movement difficult. Bad weather grounded air support and restricted observed artillery fire missions. The infantry, forced to live for extended periods in foxholes filled with water, began to experience huge losses due to exposure and trench foot, and damp, cold air caused the cases of respiratory disease to soar. Winter brought cold temperatures and snow that inflicted frostbite and exposure casualties. The horrid living conditions further compounded the misery and stress of frontline troops.

If the fighting conditions were so unfavorable, why did the American army attack into the Huertgen? First Army's goal in the early autumn was to continue a large offensive eastward from Aachen toward Cologne and to close on the Rhine by winter. After First Army had breached the West Wall and captured Aachen, "Lightning Joe" Collins's VII Corps was to lead the main effort across the Aachen Plain. First Army feared the Germans would use the Huertgen Forest as a protected sanctuary from which to launch large counterattacks against the right flank and rear of the American offensive. The original purpose of attacks into the Huertgen was to secure the right flank of VII Corps' attack toward Cologne. Clearing the forest had other positive aspects. An attack through the forest would allow units to capture a large segment of the Siegfried Line from the rear and would put American divisions in a position to support the last stages of the main effort toward the Rhine. In a broader sense, attacks into the Huertgen were consistent with a key goal of all autumn battles: to destroy as much of the German army as possible west of the Rhine.[6]

The army's first experience in the Huertgen indicated that the forest might not be the best place to engage the Germans. Collins ordered Maj. Gen. Louis A. Craig's 9th Infantry Division in the middle of September to clear the western half of the forest in support of First Army operations on the Aachen Plain. VII Corps gave General Craig ambitious objectives that forced the 9th Division to fight dispersed across a far-flung front. German resistance was initially light but congealed as each day passed. The 9th Division became ensnarled in a series of costly, plodding attacks on close terrain that gave few opportunities to exercise American superiority in tanks, artillery, and air support. By the end of the month the division was depleted and far short of its original objectives. It then suspended operations and began preparations for round two in the Huertgen.[7]

While units rested and refitted, the generals developed a second, more systematic battle plan. Hodges still wanted to clear the Huertgen in order to secure the right flank of his offensive toward the Rhine. A close study of the map revealed that the key terrain lay along the line Schmidt-Vossenack-Huertgen. (See Map 7.1.) Capturing the area would give First Army control of the road network, facilitate attacks northward out of the forest, and deny the Germans access to the majority of the Huertgen. First Army would anchor its right flank on the high ground around Schmidt and then pivot in a broad sweep toward the Rhine. The mission of capturing Schmidt, the linchpin of the First Army offensive, fell to the 9th Division.[8]

Orders in hand, General Craig began to formulate a plan for the first large battle in the Huertgen. His main challenge was to concentrate enough force to sustain a drive through the dense woods toward Schmidt. The division was deployed along an extended nine-mile front. One regiment was unavailable, so the 9th Division had only two regiments—the

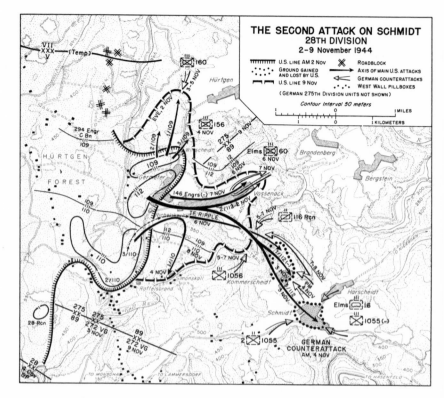

Map 7.1. The Second Attack on Schmidt, 28th Infantry Division (*Source*: Charles B. MacDonald, *The Siegfried Line Campaign* (Washington, D.C.: U.S. Army, Office of the Chief of Military History, 1950; reprint ed., Washington, D.C.: U.S. Army Center of Military History, 1984), 344.)

39th and 60th Infantry—for the main effort. The 39th Infantry would conduct the main attack by moving through Germeter and Vossenack and then hook southward to capture Schmidt. The 60th Infantry would carry out a supporting attack in the southern half of the division's sector to tie down German troops and to protect the 39th Infantry's right flank. Both regiments planned to attack with battalions abreast. The plan had several unavoidable weaknesses. First, there were not enough troops available for the main effort. Attacking with an entire regiment missing was bad enough, but the difficult terrain greatly reduced the 9th Division's chances of only two regiments slugging their way forward to the final objective. Doctrine advised commanders to retain a regiment in reserve, but General Craig was forced to put all but one of his battalions into the fight. Finally, as the division moved east through the Huertgen, it would create a long, exposed northern flank that invited German counterattacks.[9]

The 9th Division was battle tested, having fought in the desert and mountains of North Africa, the rugged mountains of Sicily, the hedgerows in Normandy, and the rolling countryside of France and Belgium. In anticipation of its first fight among dense woods, commanders began to adopt a variety of new, unorthodox formations. The most common tactical adaptation was the forming of special assault, support, and reserve groups in rifle battalions and companies. The typical rifle company had two assault and two support teams. The assault teams fought with M1 rifles, BARs, and grenades, while support groups manned machine guns and mortars and followed the assault groups to provide continuous fire support and flank protection. Reserve platoons, when available, followed to exploit success or to repel German counterattacks.[10]

As the 9th Division prepared for the first attack on Schmidt, the Germans put the final touches on their forest defenses. The 275th Division, commanded by Generalleutnant Hans Schmidt, was to repulse the Americans and deny them access to the dominating terrain on the northern edge of the forest. General Schmidt believed his most immediate task was to keep the Americans off the main highway that headed north out of Germeter, through the upper half of the Monschau corridor, and onto the Aachen Plain at Duren. To defend the road, he had approximately 5,000 effectives organized into three regiments. Schmidt organized his MLR about a mile west of the road he intended to defend. Along the eastern wall of a small gorge containing the Weisser Weh Creek, the Germans quickly constructed a defensive line of log bunkers, foxholes, wire entanglements, minefields, and roadblocks.[11]

The 9th Division began its attack on 6 October. An air-artillery bombardment opened the offensive and buoyed American spirits. Around 1000 hours the artillery marked several targets with red smoke as two groups of P-47s came swooping in over the treetops. Eighty-four aircraft hit a variety of targets along the 9th Division's axis of advance. As the fighter-bombers cleared the target area, seven battalions of artillery began a short but furious bombardment. By 1130 hours the 9th Division's infantry battalions were on their feet and moving toward the enemy.[12]

The fighting during the following days established the pattern for the entire grueling war of attrition that became synonymous with the Huertgen Forest campaign. One good trail in each regimental sector ran parallel to the axis of advance, but the Germans had choked them with felled trees, mines, and other obstacles. Soldiers detected mines by the hundreds, and the going was slow and painful. One battalion of the 60th Infantry ran into a German bunker along the Weisser Weh, and several days passed before they destroyed it. One company ended the first day with only two officers and sixty troops, barely enough to constitute a reinforced platoon. Another battalion saw no direct contact on 6 October but still lost over one hundred soldiers to German shelling. On 7 October a company of the 39th Infantry slipped through a gap in German positions along the Weisser Weh. Moving east, the riflemen soon gained the trees overlooking Germeter, but German fire from the village put the brakes on their advance. The battalion commander decided he could not attack Germeter until tanks and antitank guns were in support and not before he had an established resupply line. The 60th Infantry experienced the same dilemma. On 7 October the 2d Battalion slipped around German positions and by nightfall had occupied positions overlooking the road junction at Richelskaul. The battalion commander decided not to attack across the open without heavy weapons support. The next day engineers worked feverishly to clear a path for vehicles, and by nightfall tanks and TDs were with the infantry. With armored support on hand and a good supply line established, the 60th Infantry successfully captured the road junction on 9 October.[13]

Several lessons in combined arms warfare began to emerge during the first days of the battle. American firepower was powerless to influence the action. American troops were locked in close-quarters combat on the forest floor, making direct artillery and air support impractical. On the other hand, German troops secure in their bunkers and pillboxes did not hesitate to call for fire on their own positions when American riflemen got too close. The umbrella of fir trees made it impossible for pilots to spot targets they could otherwise strike with ease. Prevented from joining the main fight, artillery and air struck deep against German supply lines and suspected troop positions. Without fire support to help the infantry advance, the fighting amid the thick trees degenerated into a series of small, local, "meat grinder" engagements.[14]

The Huertgen taught a number of lessons in tank-infantry coordination. The 746th Tank Battalion had joined the 9th Division in Normandy on 12 June and supported it all across France. Their familiarity made for a smooth-functioning, cohesive team. The 746th entered the forest with one company assigned to each infantry regiment; single tank platoons supported each infantry battalion. Units solved command and control problems encountered in the dense forest by reviving techniques used in the bocage. Infantry commanders rode on command tanks while controlling their platoons by radio. Riflemen strapped field phones onto the Shermans' back decks to establish communication with tank crews. The wooded terrain forced the employment of small tank-infantry teams. Infantrymen provided local security while tanks contributed the firepower and mobility required to keep tank-infantry attacks moving forward. When obstacles stopped the tanks, infantrymen were reluctant to continue alone. An attack on 9 October by 1st Battalion, 60th Infantry, and its supporting tank platoon proved that the tank-infantry team could operate together in the dense woods. After a ferocious ten-minute artillery bombardment against German positions around the open road junction at Richelskaul, tanks and infantry swept across the area together with all guns blazing. Shock and firepower broke the tired defenders; the Americans killed fifty Germans and captured another twenty-five.[15]

The 746th Tank Battalion was the first armor unit to learn hard lessons in the Huertgen. Though the terrain dictated the piecemeal employment of armor, tanks were to act only in pairs. Armor officers believed that their greatest contribution was psychological—tanks encouraged friendly infantry while terrifying the Germans. In almost every instance, riflemen advanced more readily when tank support was available. Tankers felt engineer support was inadequate, and poor tank-engineer teamwork plagued the army throughout the campaign. Tank crews found it difficult to perform necessary maintenance. The infantry liked to have a constant tank presence on the front lines, but tankers could not work on their vehicles while in forward positions. As a result, mechanical failure put many tanks out of action.[16]

Soldiers had to learn a great deal in order to fight and live in the dark, wet forest. Commanders tried to bypass German strongholds but discovered that going around the enemy created another problem. Infiltrating assault teams lacked the punch required to attack final objectives or to cross open areas. Regular planning factors for time-distance coordination were meaningless in the heavy woods. Resupply and medical evacuation had to take place along established roads and trails, not along routes of infiltration. Shells exploding among the treetops not only spewed fiery shrapnel, but also shredded tree trunks, snapped limbs, and blasted wood splinters just as deadly as chunks of metal down onto infantrymen below. Foxholes had to have overhead cover, and infantrymen in the open learned to stand up or crouch behind the protection of a tree trunk to avoid shrapnel and wood splinters from air bursts. Rain and dropping temperatures caused trench foot and frostbite to run rampant. Movement at night was almost suicidal. Any sound brought enemy fire, and many GIs tended to shoot first and ask questions later. Aiming and firing at identifiable targets was impossible at night, and infantrymen were reluctant to throw grenades for fear they would bounce off trees and roll back into their positions. Nighttime's inky blackness made soldiers reluctant to leave their foxholes for fear of not being able to find their way back, so riflemen relieved themselves in their foxholes.[17]

After just a few days, the 9th Division's attack had run its painful course. Only the first objectives around Germeter and Raffelsbrand were in American hands, and the final objective of Schmidt seemed as far distant as the moon. At nightfall on 11 October, no battalion in either of the two regiments had more than 300 men available, and commanders at all echelons had already committed their reserves. A large German counterattack against the division's left flank caused a serious crisis on 12 October. The Americans finally contained the German blow, but by 16 October the 9th Division was dead in the water and had suffered terribly. The advance of about 3,000 yards caused losses of around 4,500 soldiers. Casualty reports showed that since 1 September the 60th Infantry had experienced an almost 100 percent turnover in combat troops. The Germans did not escape the bloodletting either, losing 1,300 captured and another 2,000 casualties. For both sides the first round in the Huertgen was a gory stalemate.[18]

At First Army headquarters Courtney Hodges remained adamant that Schmidt fall into American hands. The First Army commander wanted VII Corps to concentrate entirely on preparations for its upcoming offensive, so on 25 October he adjusted unit responsibilities in the Huertgen so that the Schmidt area fell entirely within the zone of General Gerow's V Corps. For the new attack on Schmidt, Gerow selected his most rested unit, the 28th Infantry Division commanded by the newly promoted Maj. Gen. Norman D. Cota. The "Keystone Division" traced its lineage to the Pennsylvania National Guard and would add a bitter chapter to its history while conducting the second American effort to capture Schmidt.[19]

First Army and V Corps exerted excessive control in planning the new battle. Hodges dictated that the 28th Division had to capture Vossenack as well as the treeline facing the village of Huertgen. Gerow ordered Cota to commit an entire regiment in the attack toward Huertgen and a second regiment in an attack southeast from Raffelsbrand. The 28th Division's final attack plan complied with the demands of higher headquarters. On the left, the 109th Infantry would attack northward and occupy positions overlooking Huertgen. On the right, the 110th Infantry would clear out Raffelsbrand and continue attacking to the southeast. The 112th Infantry would conduct the main effort in the center. One battalion was to attack eastward from Germeter, sweep through Vossenack, and take up positions just beyond the village. The remaining battalions were to attack eastward from Richelskaul, then swerve left and move into the woods along the Kall Trail. The attackers would cross the Kall River gorge, capture the village of Kommerscheidt, and use it as a jump-off position for the final attack on Schmidt. From beginning to end, the 112th Infantry would have to cross three miles of wooded, difficult terrain to reach the objective. One battalion from the 1171st Engineers was to support each regiment. Except for one tank company that was to help capture Vossenack, all other tanks and TDs were to augment the division's artillery fire. Fighter-bombers were to isolate Schmidt with a sustained battlefield interdiction effort.[20]

In dictating the parameters of the attack, First Army and V Corps meant to prevent a repeat of the 9th Division's experience. But the real effect was to leave Cota and the 28th Division almost no initiative in planning or conducting the battle. The fundamental problem was that the 28th Division was not concentrating a maximum effort against the primary objective. Instead, its three regiments were to attack along separate, diverging axes over some of the most heavily wooded and broken terrain in Western Europe. General Cota was aware of the problems caused by the constraints from First Army and V Corps. His best endorsement of the plan was to say that it had a "gambler's chance" of success.[21]

The enemy situation also forebode ill for the impending attack. The Germans were now more willing than before to commit to a slugfest in the forest and came to believe that forest fighting was preferable to defending more open ground. German generals desired to chew up U.S. manpower while preventing the full employment of American air, artillery, and armor firepower and hoped to keep the Americans from detecting preparations for the attack in the Ardennes. Primary responsibility for defending the Vossenack-Schmidt area remained with the three regiments of Generalleutnant Schmidt's 275th Division. The 89th Infantry Division defended the West Wall around Monschau and another unit was scheduled to relieve it in late October. The fortunes of war were to thrust the 89th Division into the fight at Schmidt with dire consequences for Cota's 28th Division. To the north, the 116th Panzer Division was in army group reserve and within supporting distance of the Schmidt battlefield. The 116th Panzer Division was one of the Wehrmacht's stalwart units in the west, and its tanks, assault guns, and infantrymen would have a lot to do with the final outcome. In all, the Germans had roughly three divisions with which to throw back the American regimental-sized attack on Schmidt.[22]

As preparations for the attack progressed, the 28th Division received considerable added brawn for the fight. Gerow assigned the entire 1171st Engineer Combat Group with three battalions to assist in clearing obstacles and improving roads and trails. The 707th Tank Battalion and two tank destroyer battalions joined the Keystone Division. Both V and VII Corps artillery stood ready with added firepower from as many as eight battalions. First Army ordered IX TAC to put a maximum effort toward Schmidt. Quesada's flyers prepared to commit six fighter-bomber groups for battlefield interdiction and CAS missions around the village. To assist in supply and medical evacuation efforts over the rough terrain, V Corps gave forty-seven special cargo carriers to the 28th Division. The small, tracked vehicles were known to the troops as "weasels" and proved worth their weight in gold during the battle.[23]

General Cota's attack was originally scheduled to begin on 31 October, but rain, fog, and poor visibility forced postponement. First Army ordered the 28th Division's offensive to start not later than 2 November, so as to support Collins's main drive in the north ten days later. But when VII Corps' attack was postponed by several days, Hodges saw no reason to delay the Keystone Division's attack on Schmidt and it went forward as scheduled on 2 November. Bad weather grounded fighter-bombers, and at 0800 hours corps and division artillery began belching forth a preparatory bombardment that shook the entire forest. Within an hour the American artillery dumped more than 11,000 shells onto the Germans. At 0900 hours the indirect fire lifted, and the riflemen of the 28th Division climbed out of their foxholes and moved forward.[24]

Over the next few days fighting on the division's flanks accomplished little. The 109th Infantry tried to reach the woods overlooking Huertgen but only had success west of the Germeter-Huertgen highway. A large minefield south of Wittscheidt blunted the nose of the offensive and was to hold up all attacks in the sector for more than three weeks. Prepared German defenses in the Weisser Weh valley proved almost impregnable. By the evening of the second day the course of the 109th's attack was set. Neither side could go forward; both refused to fall back. The 110th Infantry's experience in the south was even more frustrating and costly. Heavy enemy fire, thick minefields, mud, a lack of roads, and the dense woods stalled the attack from the beginning. At the end of the first day, several units had not yet moved beyond their initial positions. Because of the surprise capture of Schmidt on 3 November, Cota decided to commit his only reserve—one rifle battalion—in the south to try to get the 110th moving. It was a key mistake, for over the next few days other, more urgent crises arose that cried out for the commitment of the division's reserve. For several days the 110th Infantry and the division's reserve butted their heads against German defenses until they reached the point of exhaustion. By 13 November all the officers in the regiment's rifle companies had been killed or wounded. One battalion had only fifty-seven men left.[25]

The real drama unfolded in the 112th Infantry's sector. At H-hour on 2 November, the 2d Battalion and one company of the 707th Tank Battalion attacked east from Germeter to capture Vossenack. Tank-infantry teams swept through the village, which was about a city block wide and almost 2,000 yards long. By early afternoon the attackers had overcome light resistance, cleared Vossenack, and had begun to dig in beyond the village. Around noon the remainder of the 112th Infantry attacked eastward from Richelskaul through the woods in a column of battalions. Almost immediately, heavy German fire pinned down the lead company. The attack remained stalled for the rest of the day, and it appeared as though the division's main effort would follow the pattern of stalemate now common in the Huertgen.[26]

However, the next day's events seemed almost too good to be true. The 112th Infantry's commander decided to bypass Richelskaul by rerouting his battalions through Vossenack and then toward the entrance to the Kall Trail. The advance jumped off at 0700 hours on 3 November with Lt. Col. Albert Flood's 3d Battalion in the vanguard. The leading infantrymen passed into Vossenack, turned right at the village center, and headed toward the Kall Trail. Behind Flood's troops came Maj. Robert T. Hazlett's 1st Battalion. By 0900 hours Flood's riflemen had started to cross the Kall River and had begun the sharp climb toward Kommerscheidt. They met only light resistance and by 1300 hours had captured the village. With Schmidt in sight, Colonel Flood urged his troops forward. The final American effort took the village around 1430 hours. Captured German soldiers seemed utterly surprised by the attack. Because of Schmidt's exposed location atop a high ridge, the Americans formed a perimeter defense. Tired from their exertions and flushed with success, Flood's men failed to dig in and carelessly strewed mines along the roads leading into town. Meanwhile, Major Hazlett's battalion took up defensive positions in and around Kommerscheidt. Jubilation broke out in division headquarters when word came in of Schmidt's capture.[27]

Almost immediately things began to turn for the worse. Bad weather prevented IX TAC from isolating Schmidt, and the fear that German tanks might appear to retake the village required American armor to cross the Kall River. Around sundown on 3 November, Company A, 707th Tank Battalion, made a first attempt at negotiating the Kall Trail. The company commander, Capt. Bruce M. Hostrup, reconnoitered the route, and what he saw revealed the trail's unsuitability for moving reinforcements and supplies. The narrow, treacherous roadbed could barely handle tanks, and in one place a stalled vehicle blocked the way. The 20th Engineer Combat Battalion soon went to work with orders to improve the trail and have it open for traffic by the next morning, but the engineers lacked power tools and heavy equipment and accomplished little. Sunrise on 4 November saw the two forward battalions of the 112th Infantry without additional supplies or reinforcements, although a full eighteen hours had elapsed since the capture of Kommerscheidt and Schmidt.[28]

With the dawn of 4 November came an even more serious and deadly situation. Unknown to the 28th Division, the enemy's 89th Infantry Division had been relieved of duties around Monschau on 3 November and was moving to a rest area north of Schmidt. When the 112th Infantry captured Schmidt, it had unknowingly cut off the 89th Division's line of withdrawal. Around midnight on 3 November German soldiers confirmed that Schmidt was in enemy hands, and the 89th Division soon organized a counterattack to begin early the next morning. Senior German commanders also released the reserve 116th Panzer Division so it could help with efforts to recapture Schmidt, Kommerscheidt, and Vossenack as well as adding robustness to the defenses of the village of Huertgen. A German artillery barrage around 0730 hours on 4 November signaled the beginning of the 89th Division's attempt to recapture Schmidt. Thirty minutes later the Germans charged into Schmidt with three infantry battalions and about ten armored vehicles. Alone and unsupported, Colonel Flood's 3d Battalion was overwhelmed. By 1100 hours the Germans had control of Schmidt. Many American troops managed to make it back to Kommerscheidt where Major Hazlett's men stood ready to repel the next assault. The artillery was on call and clearing skies permitted fighter-bombers to pummel Schmidt with several air strikes around 1230 hours. More important, a portion of Company A, 707th Tank Battalion, had arrived. During the early morning the tankers had tried once again to negotiate the Kall Trail, but only three Shermans under 1st Lt. Raymond E. Fleig managed to get through. The rest of the company lay disabled along the narrow, twisting trail, with thrown treads, mechanical failures, or the victims of mines. Unfortunately, the tanks completely blocked the Kall Trail. Help had arrived, but the 112th Infantry's only line of supply and reinforcement was now gone.[29]

The defense of Kommerscheidt saw the only fully combined arms operation in the 28th Division's sector and proved what the combat arms could do in the Huertgen when they had a chance to operate together. In early afternoon five German tanks and about 150 infantry attacked the village. The tanks stayed beyond American bazooka range and pumped shells into buildings while the infantry pressed the attack. Lieutenant Fleig's tanks were the ace up the 112th Infantry's sleeve; their luck and aggressiveness made a difference. The tanks fired from locations around the village, constantly shifting and shooting from new positions while masking their movements behind folds in the earth. Meanwhile, American infantrymen stubbornly held on to Kommerscheidt and engaged German tanks with bazookas and grenades. Artillery and P-47s also provided valuable defensive firepower. By 1600 hours the Germans were in full retreat, having lost all their armor. Fleig's tanks claimed three kills, a bazooka team took out another Panther, and a 500-pound bomb from a P-47 destroyed yet another. The next morning the Germans again attempted to capture Kommerscheidt, but the American combined arms team stood fast, destroyed another Panther, and sent the Germans back toward Schmidt. American CAS made a strong showing on 5 November, claiming ten German armored vehicles destroyed in and around Schmidt.[30]

On 4 and 5 November, General Cota ordered immediate attacks to recapture Schmidt, but everyone at Kommerscheidt realized that was next to impossible. The situation beyond the Kall only worsened. The Germans infiltrated the Kall Trail, interfering with the engineers' work to improve the pathway and disrupting resupply and medical evacuation efforts. Engineers had the mission of guarding the trail but seemed content to provide only local security to their own work details. As a result, the Germans had great freedom in interdicting and moving along the trail's entire length. Without resupply and reinforcement, the situation grew more desperate by the hour. General Cota threw together at least two different ad hoc task forces that had orders to clear the Kall Trail and reinforce Kommerscheidt, but for various reasons both failed.[31]

While the majority of the 112th Infantry held on at Kommerscheidt, a debacle at Vossenack threatened to destroy the rest of the regiment. Since 2 November Colonel Hatzfeld's 2d Battalion had been dug in at the eastern end of Vossenack. For several days the troops were exposed to foul weather and almost continuous shelling. The sound of battle beyond the Kall River gorge convinced everyone that the Germans would soon mount a counterattack. The battalion had an unusually large number of replacement troops, and the psychological and mental stresses of holding the position began to take their toll. Company commanders reported that their soldiers' nerves were shattered; some cried uncontrollably while others refused to eat. The officers were disturbed to see Colonel Hatzfeld sitting in his command post, head in hands, an apparent combat exhaustion casualty. Daybreak on 6 November brought disaster. When a few enemy artillery shells struck, one company began to break and run. The desire to head for the rear spread like wildfire. Panic and fear took control, as troops raced down Vossenack's main street and headed for the rear. Officers tried to stem the tide, and by 1030 hours they had established a tenuous defensive line about halfway back through the village. General Cota ordered the 146th Engineer Combat Battalion into Vossenack to restore order. The engineers moved swiftly and took up defensive positions as infantrymen. By noon the Germans had mounted an attack against Vossenack and managed to capture half of the village. The next day saw one of the more unusual combined arms attacks in the ETO: a tank-engineer counterattack by the 707th Tank Battalion and the 146th Engineers. Behind a heavy artillery barrage, the tankers and engineers attacked with enthusiasm to push the Germans out of Vossenack. By early evening the Americans had cleared Vossenack, inflicted 150 casualties, and taken up defensive positions in buildings on the eastern end of town.[32]

On 7 November the 112th Infantry's position beyond the Kall became untenable. Determined to wipe out the American defenses at Kommerscheidt, the 89th Division struck at dawn with full force. After an intense, hour-long artillery bombardment, two battalions of German infantry and fifteen tanks moved against the village. A savage fight went on for several hours, but by noon the Germans had gained the upper hand. The defenders began to give, and in early afternoon they abandoned Kommerscheidt and withdrew to a treeline west of the village. Now even General Cota realized that renewing the attack on Schmidt was impossible. He called General Gerow and received permission to withdraw behind the Kall River. That night the 112th Infantry began a torturous retreat marked by misery, fear, and confusion. Order and discipline broke down as frightened and fatigued soldiers made their way back across the Kall River gorge. More than 2,200 soldiers had crossed the Kall River; just over 300 made it out with the final withdrawal.[33]

In addition to a flawed battle plan that had troops attacking in three different directions over broken and difficult terrain, other factors combined to produce the Schmidt catastrophe. Most commanders in the 28th Division believed the unsuitability of the Kall Trail as a resupply line was "the greatest single factor bringing about the failure of the entire operation." Others believed that German observation from the higher Schmidt and Brandenberg-Bergstein ridge lines was "one of the greatest single causes" for the defeat. Rain, snow, and low-hanging clouds kept fighter-bombers grounded, turned trails into rutted, slippery quagmires, and filled foxholes with water. Without the proper gear to protect themselves from the cold and wetness, soldiers fell prey to the elements, and the division surgeon reported 750 cases of trench foot. The 28th Division had many new replacements with little or inadequate training as infantrymen. The root cause for the panic at Vossenack was probably the high number of inexperienced, untrained replacements. Air power failed to keep the enemy from moving toward Schmidt, and with no threats in any other sector, the Germans were free to concentrate remarkable strength against Schmidt and Kommerscheidt.[34]

The performance of American troops was mixed. Combined arms action always resulted in success. The initial defense of Kommerscheidt and the tank-engineer counterattack at Vossenack show the efficacy of the combined arms team in the Huertgen. But bad weather and the large fir trees tended to keep the combat arms separated and impotent. Units floundered when infantry, tanks, artillery, engineers, and air support operated independently. The engineers' inability to improve and protect the Kall Trail was a key shortcoming. The best performance by American units was the valiant, stubborn defense of Kommerscheidt, while the low point was the collapse of the 2d Battalion, 112th Infantry, at Vossenack. In the end the raw courage and perseverance of American soldiers could not overcome the broader flaws of a battle plan that many believed was doomed from the start.

The 28th Division's casualties reveal the magnitude of the disaster at Schmidt. Total losses for the division and its attachments reached 6,184 casualties. The division surgeon reported 738 cases of trench foot and another 620 casualties from combat exhaustion. Hardest hit was the 112th

Infantry, which suffered a whopping 2,093 casualties: 167 killed, 719 wounded, 431 missing, 232 captured, and another 544 casualties from trench foot and combat exhaustion. The losses among Kommerscheidt's defenders show just how bad the disaster was beyond the Kall River. Out of an authorized strength of 871 men, the 1st Battalion, 112th Infantry, came away from Kommerscheidt with 364 survivors. The rifle companies lost all their officers save one lone lieutenant, and only the supply officer survived on the battalion staff. The combined strength of all three rifle companies was only 225 soldiers. The battalion lost every one of its mortars and machine guns and retained only a few BARs. The Germans captured the battalion headquarters, complete with maps, orders, staff journals, and all classified materials. In terms of equipment, more than half of the 28th Division's armored vehicles were destroyed, and losses in trucks, equipment, and weapons were staggering.[35]

After the 28th Division left the Huertgen, it took a hard look at its performance in the woods. The 110th Infantry drew from its experience to develop new forest combat tactics. Tactical innovations sought to solve the problems of maintaining direction and positive command and control. Rifle companies were to attack using tight formations that permitted maximum control and mutual support. Two rifle platoons deployed abreast with two squads forward acted as the assault element. Individual squads moved in wedge formation. Every rifleman was to be alert and act as a scout, while the squad leader controlled his men from the center of the wedge and maintained direction with a compass. Squad leaders were to reduce the sense of isolation among the trees by calling their soldiers by name, and riflemen were required to answer. The company moved in a rectangular formation with the wide base toward the Germans. A rifle platoon with two squads forward covered a front of 125 to 175 yards, a company from 250 to 350 yards, and a battalion from 500 to 600 yards. Squads in column protected the flanks. To the rear, the company commander kept tight control over his third rifle platoon and the weapons platoon. A training memorandum from the 110th Infantry specified that each rifle squad and platoon would conduct rehearsals through dense woods using the new formations "until each man in the squad understands his role in the formation and the squad leaders have had sufficient practice to control their squads." Without doubt the 28th Division made a concerted effort to learn from its experience in the Huertgen.[36]

Even before the debacle beyond the Kall had run its course, Maj. Gen. Raymond O. Barton's 4th Infantry Division was sucked into the dark, green maelstrom. When V Corps heard of the disaster at Vossenack, General Gerow ordered a regiment from the 4th Division to head for Germeter. Col. James S. Luckett's 12th Infantry drew the assignment of relieving the 109th Infantry and moved into the 109th's positions north of Germeter during the dark, wet night of 6 November. Attacks over the next few days went nowhere. On the morning of 10 November, the Germans launched a large counterattack that cut off and surrounded many rifle companies, and not until the evening of 15 November was Luckett able to restore order. In nine days of furious, bitter fighting, the 12th Infantry lost 1,600 men to enemy fire, combat exhaustion, and trench foot.[37]

In anticipation of joining the fight in the Huertgen, the 4th Division spent time in a rest area in Belgium preparing for combat in the dense woods. On 28 October division headquarters issued Operations Memorandum Number 23, "Notes on Woods Fighting," that outlined the hazards of forest combat and recommended attack methods. As in other divisions, commanders were to divide their units into assault and support teams. The memorandum discussed tank-infantry coordination at some length. Each tank platoon received one infantry squad, one engineer mine removal squad, and a bazooka team to provide continuous security. Just as in the 9th Division, methods used in Normandy reappeared. Soldiers affixed field phones to tank back decks and developed prearranged hand, pyrotechnic, and smoke signals to control movement and to coordinate direct fire. Assault teams were to lay wire back to company command posts. The wire also would mark a safe lane for messengers, resupply teams, and litter bearers, and assault teams tied cloth tags to the wire every 100 yards to measure their movement through the woods. The memorandum also advised soldiers on details such as standing behind trees during shellings and getting overhead cover as protection against tree bursts.[38]

While the 12th Infantry bled in the woods north of Germeter, the balance of the 4th Division moved into the Huertgen and launched a large attack through the heart of the forest. As in previous operations in the Huertgen, the 4th Division lacked the resources required to achieve the overly ambitious objectives outlined by corps headquarters. Still, on 16 November the main attack went ahead. Battalions, companies, and platoons attacked in column to increase command and control and to concentrate their firepower. The pattern of previous battles predominated: small slugging matches that brought heavy losses with few gains. In a five-day attack the 4th Division made very little progress and suffered terribly. Some rifle companies were reduced to 30 percent strength. The two attacking regiments lost 1,500 battle casualties, while another 500 soldiers were evacuated for combat exhaustion, trench foot, and other maladies. Between 7 November and 3 December, the 4th Division poured out its lifeblood in the Huertgen, losing over 7,000 men—about 110 soldiers per regiment for each day engaged. Most rifle companies had turnover rates in excess of 100 percent. Replacements flowed in to compensate for the losses, but the Huertgen's voracious appetite for casualties was greater than the army's ability to provide new troops.[39]

A number of problems caused the 4th Division to bog down. The large trees denied the infantry artillery and air support and kept the combat arms from cooperating together. There were few roads and trails for movement and resupply efforts. The Germans blocked all of them with mines and obstacles, or they soon turned into muddy quagmires. The cold, wet weather became almost too miserable to endure. Commanders realized that their units were unprepared to fight in the dense woods, and replacements were thrust directly into the fight without refresher training or the opportunity to adapt to conditions on the front lines. Many died in artillery barrages before they even had a chance to fight. Fighting without any reserve, General Barton could not pull troops off the line for a rest. Excessive fatigue made troops sluggish and careless, and combat exhaustion became commonplace as the dark, deadly forest blanketed soldiers with a sense of gloom and desperation.[40] One company commander reflected on the combat exhaustion cases in his unit: "An officer should be quick to realize a combat fatigue case . . . [one] man had discarded his equipment, including his helmet. He sat on the edge of his hole shaking and staring into space. He made no attempt to get down in his hole when the company was shelled."[41] Division veterans who had fought among the Normandy hedgerows believed the Huertgen was the worst combat they had yet seen. The 4th Division enjoyed an exceptional fighting reputation in the ETO, but the Huertgen Forest managed to place a blemish on its outstanding combat career.[42]

While the 4th Division tried to slash its way through the center of the forest, Maj. Gen. Donald A. Stroh's 8th Infantry Division moved onto the front lines to relieve the shattered Keystone Division. On 19 November First Army had begun its long awaited offensive toward Cologne, and General Hodges was looking for other places along his front to exert pressure on the Germans. First Army ordered V Corps to commit the fresh 8th Division to yet another attempt to capture Huertgen and assigned Combat Command Reserve (CCR), 5th Armored Division, to add punch to the attack. Two regiments of the 8th Division took over defensive positions manned by Cota's soldiers around Simonskall, Raffelsbrand, and Vossenack. General Stroh's third regiment, the 121st Infantry, was to relieve the 12th Infantry in the sector facing north toward the village of Huertgen. The 8th Division experienced two significant developments in the Huertgen Forest campaign: the commitment of massed armor in an effort to break the deadlock and the capture of the village of Huertgen.[43]

The 121st Infantry was over 100 miles away when it received orders to move to the Huertgen. On 20 November the regiment made the grueling trip, riding in open trucks in freezing rain and snow. The convoys arrived at their drop-off points just as the sun fell, and the half-frozen riflemen still faced a brutal seven-mile hike to the front lines. The agony of the night march over muddy trails strewn with rocks and tree limbs convinced everyone that the relief of the 12th Infantry could not occur until daylight. Finally, the trudging columns came to a staggering halt, and soldiers fell into ditches to sleep on their weapons as a cold, driving rain soaked everything. Commanders received word in the darkness that the relief would commence at sunrise followed by a major attack at 0900 hours. The light of the gathering dawn slowly revealed the horrors of the Huertgen, and the surroundings unnerved the 121st Infantry. Large trees lay broken and torn from artillery airbursts. The trunks of other trees, stripped of bark and foliage by shell blasts, stood like stone pillars. The burned-out hulks of vehicles destroyed by mines dotted roadsides. A wide variety of battlefield trash littered the forest floor, including helmets, rifles, ammunition boxes, and discarded clothing, some of which bore large splotches of dried blood. But there was little time to take in all the surrounding horrors, as the infantrymen struggled to their feet and pressed ahead to gain their attack positions.[44]

At 0800 hours V and VII Corps artillery began throwing 4,500 rounds at the Germans. By a great dint of effort the 121st Infantry was in position when the shelling lifted, and at 0900 hours they attacked. The fighting quickly degenerated into the grueling patterns experienced by other regiments, and the close combat began to fray everyone's nerves. A mishap on 24 November prompted the regimental commander to relieve a battalion and a company commander. By the end of 24 November another battalion commander and two company commanders had lost their commands. In four days of bitter fighting the 121st Infantry failed to make much headway while suffering 650 battle casualties, and units evacuated just as many more soldiers for exposure or combat exhaustion. By sundown on 24 November the 121st Infantry was a spent regiment.[45]

That night General Stroh realized that the only way to get the main attack moving was to commit his armored forces, so he ordered CCR, 5th Armored Division, to move into positions behind the 121st Infantry and to bash its way through to Huertgen at daylight the next day. CCR's commander, Col. Glen H. Anderson, had grave misgivings about the attack. The 121st Infantry had not cleared the tree lines on either side of the Germeter-Huertgen highway, and Anderson feared that Germans with panzerfausts would wreak havoc on his tanks. A huge bomb crater blocked the road about halfway to Huertgen and surrounding trees made it an impassable obstacle. Engineers would have to clear a path around the crater, install a bridge span, or fill in the crater to make way for CCR's Shermans. Throughout the night of 24 November, riflemen of the 47th Armored Infantry moved into positions within the 121st Infantry's lines.

From there they were to clear the woods ahead to make the going easier for the 10th Tank Battalion. When CCR gained the treeline overlooking Huertgen, the 10th Tank was to lead the attack on the village followed by the armored infantry.[46]

But bad luck plagued CCR's attack from the beginning. Minutes before H-hour the Germans began pouring intense and accurate artillery and mortar fire onto the infantry. A column of Shermans from the 10th Tank Battalion soon appeared on the main highway moving north toward Huertgen, but they came to a halt when they reached the road crater. Despite assurances that it was now passable, no work had been done to fill or bridge the crater. The lead tank tried to cross the crater, but it slid into the hole, thrashed around, and wound up on its side on the far edge of the crater's rim. Shell fire punished the stalled tank column, as German and American infantry became intermingled in savage, close-quarters fighting on either side of the road. Finally, an engineer unit came forward and managed to span the crater with a section of treadway bridging. The next tank crossed the crater around 1030 hours, drove less than 50 feet, and hit a mine. Another Sherman pressed ahead, but minutes later the Germans disabled it with panzerfausts. Colonel Anderson saw that his tanks could make no further progress until his infantry cleared the woods. He directed the 10th Tank Battalion to withdraw and ordered the 47th Armored Infantry to make a fresh attack down both sides of the Germeter-Huertgen highway. The riflemen launched a second effort at 1630 hours, but minefields, machine guns, and artillery and mortar fire kept them from advancing. At sundown Colonel Anderson ordered the infantry to withdraw and regroup. In a single day's action, CCR had lost 3 tanks and incurred 150 casualties. CCR went on to perform well during the later stages of the Huertgen Forest campaign, but on 25 November weather, trees, and the German defense won the day.[47]

By the evening of 25 November the stage was set for the capture of the village of Huertgen. As CCR began its withdrawal, elements of the 4th Division had managed to capture the woods west of Huertgen. German commanders feared their troops might be cut off, so they began a partial withdrawal. The next day the 8th Division gained the woods overlooking Huertgen with little difficulty. When the 121st Infantry tried to push its way across the 1,000 yards of open ground between the treeline and the village, heavy German fire threw soldiers back into the woods. A new plan called for the 2d Battalion, 121st Infantry, to execute a frontal attack against Huertgen while another battalion tried to swing wide and enter the village from the rear. On 27 November the riflemen attempted to reach Huertgen from the west, but German fire pinned down the lead platoons one hundred yards from the outskirts of town. After dark an American patrol entered the village and verified the presence of large numbers of Germans.[48]

The next day the 8th Division managed to coordinate a tank-infantry attack that finally captured Huertgen. Around mid-morning on 28 November, Company A, 709th Tank Battalion, moved from the treeline south of Huertgen with close support from Companies E and F of the 121st Infantry. The tanks moved across open ground relying on shock effect and raw firepower to smash their way into the village, and the riflemen pinned down the previous day had a chance to join the advance. The moving spirit behind the attack was Lt. Col. P. D. Ginder, a fresh, aggressive officer newly assigned to the 8th Division, who organized the ad hoc task force for the final push into Huertgen. Ginder's drive made the difference. During the attack he admonished a rifle company commander who seemed hesitant; "Well, damn it, captain, if you get wounded, you'll get a nice rest in the hospital. If you get killed, you won't know anything more about it. If neither happens, you have nothing to worry about. Let's get going!"[49]

Soldiers knew they were about to capture a key objective for which so many Americans had bled and died. Flushed with the sense that victory was near, soldiers felt a rush of emotion and adrenaline that produced an orgy of carnage and violence. Infantrymen and tankers worked their way from house to house in a frenzy, shooting at anything that moved and knocking down walls and buildings with direct fire. One company commander remembered:

> It was a wild, terrible, awe-inspiring thing, this sweep through Huertgen. Never in my wildest imagination had I conceived that battle could be so incredibly impressive—awful, horrible, deadly, yet somehow thrilling, exhilarating. Now the fight for Huertgen was at its wildest. We dashed, struggled from one building to another shooting, bayoneting, clubbing. Hand grenades roared, rifles cracked— buildings to the left and right burned with acrid smoke. . . . The wounded and the dead—men in the uniforms of both sides—lay in grotesque positions at every turn. From many the blood still flowed.[50]

By the time it was all over the Americans had taken 200 prisoners. The end came at 1800 hours on 28 November when the 121st Infantry reported that the village that had come to symbolize the suffering and bloodletting of the Huertgen Forest campaign was finally in American hands.[51]

The 1st Infantry Division was one of the last major formations to get a taste of the Huertgen Forest. Huebner's Big Red One took the lead in a second effort by Collins to break out onto the Cologne Plain. The division was to attack through the northern fringes of the Huertgen along the axis Schevenhuette-Langewehe and then make for crossing sites on the Roer River some three miles distant. Despite its outstanding combat record in North Africa, Sicily, and Normandy, the division had considerable difficulties in the forest. Units pushed off from positions around Schevenhuette on 15 November. The 1st Division managed to reach Langewehe and Merode by 29 November but could go no further. In a 4-mile advance that took almost two weeks, the Big Red One suffered 3,400 casualties. German defenses, bad weather, and dense woods managed to drain the élan and vitality from yet another first-rate combat formation.[52]

In its drive through the northern edge of the Huertgen, the Big Red One managed to learn several lessons about forest combat. German outposts fired on American units not to cause casualties, but to force riflemen to hit the dirt in places where Germans had preplanned artillery concentrations. Soldiers learned to avoid German shell fire by pushing ahead as best they could against light resistance. Night patrols were useless in the thick woods. Many got lost in the pitch-black, and others returned to friendly lines unable to report accurately on where they had been or what they had seen. Company commanders learned to withdraw most of their troops after dark from forward positions gained during the day. By pulling back 400 to 500 yards, commanders removed the majority of their troops from areas most likely to receive the heaviest German indirect fire. A reinforced platoon manned strong outposts until companies moved forward again just before dawn.[53]

As November passed into December, American units began to reach the far-northern boundary of the Huertgen Forest and to take up positions overlooking the Roer River and the Cologne Plain. For all practical purposes, the hell of the Huertgen Forest was over. The campaign lasted almost ninety days with heavy involvement from six divisions: the 1st, 4th, 8th, 9th, and 28th Infantry and the 5th Armored. The butcher's bill was appalling. More than 24,000 Americans were killed, wounded, captured, or reported missing, while another 9,000 fell victim to trench foot, combat exhaustion, and disease. Units suffered an average of 25 percent casualties. The 28th Division endured the worst losses at Schmidt. The only other comparable division-sized debacle in World War II occurred in the Pacific in November 1943 when the 2d Marine Division suffered 3,318 casualties during the amphibious assault on Tarawa. The Keystone Division's attack on Schmidt was the Tarawa of the ETO.[54]

Compared to other types of operations in Europe, the American combined arms team failed to learn or to adapt as well in forest combat. Infantry units had only mixed success in meeting the Huertgen's challenges. Commanders quickly determined that maintaining command and control was their most serious problem. They kept formations closer together, designated map and compass specialists, and relied on wire communications to maintain control over their soldiers. Units had little success in adapting tactics to overcome the Germans' forest defense. Divisions had no chance to conduct special training on attacking through the dense trees, and units that adapted did so during combat. Many regiments organized their rifle companies into attack and support teams that tried to push through the woods. Regimental and battalion commanders realized that infiltration tactics could achieve only limited gains. For major efforts, it was better for battalions and regiments to attack in column so as to increase command and control and concentrate firepower. Most of the learning took place after units had left the Huertgen, too late to have any influence on the campaign's outcome.

The engineers had an especially difficult time because they lacked the heavy equipment required to improve roads and trails. The huge job of removing thousands of German mines taxed their capabilities and courage, and too many American troops and vehicles fell victim to mines. The inability of the 1171st Engineer Group to improve and protect the Kall Trail for the 28th Division was the single greatest engineer failure in the campaign. Engineer units trained to support the infantry had difficulty working with armor, and tank-engineer cooperation was much better in units where the two arms had fought together over a longer period. Heavy losses in riflemen and extended frontages meant that engineers often had to fight as infantry. The campaign's best engineer action occurred on 6 November, when the 146th Engineer Combat Battalion counterattacked as infantry to regain Vossenack.

Still, some lessons did emerge. Doctrine specified that armor had only two roles in forest combat: tank units were to sweep around a forest mass and attack it from the rear, or they were to stay in reserve until the infantry had cleared the forest and then assist in pushing beyond the forest's far boundary. Experience in the Huertgen suggested a third role. Tank battalions moved into the dense woods, dispersed into small teams, and supported the infantry in clearing the woods. Armor commanders believed that the shock effect their tanks had on German troops and the confidence they gave to American infantry far outweighed the disadvantages of limited mobility and firepower imposed by the woods. Cooperation between tank and infantry units varied in proportion to the length of time they had worked together. The best tank-infantry coordination occurred between infantry divisions and supporting tank battalions that had been together since Normandy. In infantry units with little armor experience, commanders usually misused their supporting tanks.[55]

The army's preference for problem solving at the lowest level did not serve it well in the Huertgen. Although a great number of units across the entire front had to come to grips with the best ways to attack fortifications, rivers, and urban areas, only a handful of divisions saw action in the

Huertgen. Because of the smaller number of units engaged, 12th Army Group and First Army expressed less interest in examining the difficulties of forest combat. On the battlefield, units had few opportunities to learn from each other. Divisions went into the forest in succession, not simultaneously, so they were unable to exchange ideas and experiences. Even worse, regiments tended to turn over their sectors to fresh units very quickly, usually at night and during bad weather. Units free to leave had little stomach for remaining and passing on to fresh battalions the benefit of their experience. Officers and NCOs usually gathered and disseminated the combat lessons small units learned, but in the Huertgen these men fell at an alarming rate. New units coming into the lines found few functioning leaders remaining in battle-torn battalions. Green replacements and the few surviving veterans were able to pass on little if any of what they had learned.

First Army's handling of the campaign indicates a lack of understanding of the difficulties divisions faced in the dark woods. Senior commanders were slow to realize that the summer pursuit was over. Army and corps headquarters routinely assigned missions far beyond the capacity of their subordinate units. Instead of chasing a beaten enemy on a broad front, American units now had to concentrate their power in deliberate attacks against prepared defenses. Yet, in the Huertgen Forest the exact opposite occurred. From the beginning, divisions routinely had to disperse their combat power against multiple objectives. Only rarely did a division attack with all its three regiments directed against a single objective. The struggle for Schmidt, in which First Army forced the 28th Division to attack in three different directions, is the best example of a dispersion of effort during the campaign.

The battles in the Huertgen Forest show that weather and terrain alone can force an army to search for new tactics and combat techniques. More than anything else, thick trees, difficult ground, and atrocious weather determined the torturous course of events. Tall, dense fir trees were formidable barriers that kept tanks and infantrymen separated and prevented the use of normal fire and maneuver tactics. Close-quarters combat and poor observation prevented American units from bringing artillery and CAS to bear. The dense forest made it difficult for units to maintain proper direction and orientation. Poor trails and a lack of roads made resupply and medical evacuation difficult. Rain transformed the entire forest into a slippery morass, and fog and early morning mists reduced visibility. Mud and snow concealed mines and booby traps while adding frostbite and trench foot to the other discomforts troops had to withstand. In addition to losses from enemy fire, the stress of combat, bad weather, horrid living conditions, and gloomy surroundings inflicted psychological and physical casualties at alarming rates.

The campaign taught the army much about the limits of firepower. Poor observation and bad weather kept artillerymen and aviators from influencing the battle. Shelling and bombing enemy LOCs probably hampered German freedom of action but had little influence on battles deep in the forest. The Germans' ability to mass troops and armor against Schmidt and Kommerscheidt suggests air power's inability to interdict and isolate small, discreet portions of a larger combat zone.

The Huertgen exacerbated the army's manpower problems. Combat exhaustion soared amidst the forest's perpetual gloom and slaughter, as soldiers experienced a repetition of the isolation and hopelessness first felt among the Normandy hedgerows. Troops reached the breaking point and became dysfunctional after several days on the line without any hope of rest or relief. Combat exhaustion made men careless and docile. They began to lose the instinct for self-preservation and failed to follow the fundamentals of combat training. The overall result was a higher casualty rate than infantry commanders normally expected. Trench foot and respiratory diseases further ravaged the ranks. Lacking proper coats and foot gear, soldiers had inadequate protection against the elements.[56]

The army also became acutely aware of inadequacies in the replacement system. In October, lulls on most fronts and good weather kept the ETO's total casualties down to around 60,000 men. November offensives in the Huertgen and Lorraine and around Aachen combined with worsening weather to almost double casualties to 118,698, and the replacement system sagged under the strain. New troops fed into the Huertgen inferno came from two sources: soldiers already in the theater who were transferred from other military specialties and retrained as infantrymen and new replacements from stateside. The flight of 2d Battalion, 112th Infantry, from Vossenack showed how fragile units filled with retrained soldiers could become during extended operations. Individual replacements fared even worse. After making a long journey of several weeks through replacement depots, new troops found themselves thrust onto the front lines almost overnight. Many became instant casualties, and numerous wounded replacements could not tell doctors with which unit they had fought.[57]

The problems that the Americans encountered in the Huertgen Forest raises questions about the campaign's validity. First Army originally plunged into the forest with two objectives: to bleed further German forces west of the Rhine and to secure the right flank of the army's main effort toward Cologne. The American army did clear the forest and bruise the Germans, but the price was too high. At a time when manpower was reaching dangerous lows, the American leadership was too willing to engage the enemy in a war of attrition. The Germans possessed an almost decisive advantage in fighting on terrain of their choosing in an environment that gave every advantage to the defender. Because of the high casualties and low gains, the Huertgen Forest was one campaign the army should not have fought.

What did the Germans think of their enemy's willingness to plow into the dense woods? To the Germans, the American willingness to conduct a sustained offensive through such an extensive, thick forest came as a surprise. Most German generals could not understand the American fixation with the Huertgen and were critical of their enemy's fighting ability. A training memorandum of the 183d Volks Grenadier Division summarized German attitudes on the performance of American units: "In combat in wooded areas the American showed himself completely unfit."[58]

The opposing sides had little time to reflect on their experience in the Huertgen. The first days of December saw American units attacking to clear out the eastern portion of the forest and to get control of the Roer River dams. On the morning of 16 December, the rumble of hundreds of artillery guns firing in the Ardennes reverberated through the Huertgen. Rumors began to spread that something—something big—was going on in the Ardennes. Units began preparing to move by foot and by truck, but instead of moving east toward the Rhine, they were to head south into the Ardennes and the largest battle in the history of the American army.

CHAPTER EIGHT

Defense in the Ardennes

Normal procedure[s] in countering enemy armored attacks on Rocherath and Krinkelt were to take enemy armor under fire with medium artillery before it reached our lines; then to hit individual tanks from the flanks with our tanks, TDs, and 57-mm antitank guns, and mop up infiltrations. . . . The close teamwork between infantry, artillery, tanks, and TDs accounted for 69 known enemy tanks, plus several armored trucks and scout cars.
—*After-action report of the 38th Infantry,*
2d Division

On Saturday, 16 September 1944, Hitler's personal staff gathered in the conference room at the Wolf's Lair, the Fuehrer's East Prussian headquarters, for the daily operations briefing. With the situation in the East relatively quiet, the briefing soon turned to the Western Front. A senior staff officer reviewed the strengths and weaknesses of German units rallying on the West Wall and the continuing buildup of Allied forces on the Continent. The briefer went on to report on the withdrawal of German forces from southern France when Hitler suddenly cut him short. After a long, tense pause Hitler spoke. "I have just made a momentous decision. I shall go over to the counterattack," he told the stunned listeners. Pointing at a large map on the table in front of him, the German warlord told his audience that he intended to attack "here, out of the Ardennes, with the objective—Antwerp." While the senior officers sat in stunned disbelief, Hitler went on to outline the basics of what would become Operation WACHT AM RHEIN, the great German counteroffensive in the Ardennes.[1]

Considering the situation on the Western Front, Hitler's scheme was not as incredible as it first sounded. The Fuehrer's intuition told him that Germany could not go on defending in the west indefinitely against growing Allied strength. An unexpected, mass offensive was probably the only way the Third Reich could regain the initiative or at least upset Allied plans. Hitler also saw that time was running out along his western border. Just five days before, a patrol from First Army's 5th Armored Division had crossed over into Germany, the first American soldiers to set foot on enemy soil. With a counterattack out of the Ardennes, Hitler hoped to repeat the miraculous survival of Prussia brought on by Frederick the

Great's spectacular battlefield victories and to recreate the German army's stunning defeat of the Allies in May 1940. Ironically, the failed Ardennes counterattack would go a long way toward hastening Germany's final defeat.

The Battle of the Bulge presented the American army with two new challenges. Many units had not yet fought defensive battles, and commanders lacked experience in coordinating the combined arms team on the defensive. The surprise German onslaught in the Ardennes tested the army's ability to throw together formations quickly and to fight them as a smooth-functioning defensive team. Second, winter warfare tested the army's capacity to operate under adverse conditions and challenged the endurance and adaptability of American GIs. How well U.S. forces could perform under conditions of snow and extreme cold was an unanswered question as winter began to settle on the Western Front.

To the American army, defensive operations had two purposes: to gain time until forces could resume the offensive or to economize on one front while massing for attacks elsewhere. FM 100-5 taught soldiers that defensive tactics consisted of concentrating maximum firepower to stop the attacker's advance or to repel the enemy with counterattacks. Units established defensive positions by carefully selecting terrain that offered the greatest advantages: adequate observation, good fields of fire, concealment, and natural obstacles. A line of adjoining battle positions constituted the MLR. Heavy shelling and small arms fire were expected to stop the enemy short of American lines. Doctrine held that tanks were "essentially offensive weapons," better held in reserve for counterattacks rather than used along the MLR. Towed antitank guns fought forward along the MLR, while TD battalions occupied supporting positions to the rear. On the defense, air power's main role was to interdict the battlefield, not to fly CAS missions.[2]

FM 100-5 spent some time discussing combined arms operations during "antimechanized defense." Infantry and artillery were the backbone of normal defensive operations, but other combat arms predominated against enemy tanks and mechanized infantry. Antitank guns were of "first importance," and commanders were to employ a minimum of antitank guns forward and to use all others in a mobile reserve. Tank units were kept off the MLR and only used in large numbers for counterattacks. Air power was to strike deep against enemy reinforcements and supply lines. Minefields, antitank ditches, and demolitions were needed to slow mechanized forces. Doctrine called for artillery to play a significant role against enemy armor but suggested that shell fire might not be able to stop tanks and halftracks.[3]

The battles in the Ardennes forced American commanders to improvise and adapt defensive techniques and methods much more sophisticated than those outlined in FM 100-5. Instead of fighting to regain the initiative, units battled to deny the Germans access to key roads, intersections, and bridges. There was no time to organize a solid defensive line along the most suitable terrain supported by preplanned artillery fire and reserves. In the carnage and confusion of the Bulge's first days, commanders established hasty defenses on the best terrain available and coordinated supporting fires any way they could. The German onslaught required commanders to use every available soldier and weapon in combined arms defensive battles that saw infantry, tanks, artillery, fighter-bombers, antitank gun crews, and engineers working together frantically to stem the enemy tide.

Bitter winter weather posed a threat to American troops just as real as German shells and bullets. Field manuals on operations in snow and extreme cold taught soldiers how to function during winter warfare. Four major challenges existed: keeping soldiers warm, moving across snow and ice, transporting and preserving supplies and equipment, and preventing the malfunctioning of weapons and equipment. The army identified two broad categories of solutions to these problems. First, adequate quantities of winter clothing, equipment, and cold weather supplies had to be available. Soldiers also needed training in how to care for themselves and their supplies and equipment. Marching and fighting in snow and ice required special skills, and troops needed training on how to keep weapons functioning in bitter cold.[4]

The army believed that operations in snow and extreme cold did not "vary in principle" from other types of operations, but that the harsh environment did require "certain differences" in many procedures. Doctrine called for a "large part" of the troops to operate on snowshoes and for the use of "specially trained" ski soldiers. Commanders had to allow more time for movement of convoys and cross-country marches. Snow was an obstacle to maneuver, while cold weather often permitted movement across soft ground, streams, and lakes frozen solid by frigid temperatures. Deep snow restricted maneuver and resupply activities to established roads and made camouflage difficult to obtain. Lengthy exposure to the cold made soldiers lethargic, apathetic, and sapped their physical and mental stamina. Whenever possible, U.S. troops were to deprive the enemy of every source of food, rest, and shelter. On the defensive, well-built positions were to provide cover, concealment, and shelter.[5]

Hitler believed that a successful counteroffensive in the West would restore Germany's deteriorating strategic situation. The attack had many objectives. First, Hitler thought a major blow against the Anglo-American armies would shatter the Allied coalition and create conditions for a negotiated peace. A diplomatic settlement in the West would solve Germany's dilemma with a two-front war and free the Third Reich to concentrate all of its efforts against the Red armies. A victory would also keep the line of the Rhine River secure and protect the vital Ruhr industrial area. Militarily, Hitler hoped to punch through the Ardennes and paralyze the Allies by capturing the main supply base at Antwerp. His choice of the Ardennes as the site of the impending attack had several merits. The forest lay not far from the major boundary between the British and American armies. An attack along the seam would split Montgomery's 21st Army Group from Bradley's 12th Army Group and might permit the quick destruction of the British before the Americans could react. The heavy forest and broken ground would mask preparations for the offensive and conceal German forces in the campaign's early stages, and Hitler planned on bad weather to negate Allied air superiority.[6]

The Ardennes is not a distinctly defined region but a continuum of rolling hills and patches of heavy fir trees lying within a swath that starts between Liege and Dinant on the Meuse River and sweeps westward toward the German border. In general, the highest hills stand just inside the German border, and the ground becomes more even as it approaches the Meuse. Roughly a third of the Ardennes is covered by thick forests that stand in scattered patches. A number of rivers and streams flow generally from south to north, often through narrow, steep gorges that are considerable obstacles. Paved roads usually followed high ridges, twisted and turned into river gorges, crossed waterways over stone bridges, and eventually led to a number of key road junctions like those at St. Vith and Bastogne. The typical village had a number of stone houses and narrow streets, all centered about a large road intersection, with the largest villages numbering between 2,500 and 4,000 dwellers. The weather in the Ardennes is raw and cold with heavy rainfall, deep snows, and biting winds. In winter, the days are short with early morning fog and mists that linger well into the morning.

The nature of the terrain in the Ardennes had a significant influence on the conduct of the campaign. Ridge lines tended to block and compartmentalize major troop movements from east to west. Scattered forests and streams fragmented the lay of the ground, making command and control and sweeping maneuvers very difficult. The road network was adequate, but numerous villages and bridges were all potential roadblocks. Hitler hoped poor weather would conceal the advance of German units and keep Allied air power grounded. In 1940 the German army proved that a large mechanized force could quickly negotiate the Ardennes when the weather was good and enemy resistance sparse. However, whether or not the Germans could successfully attack through the Ardennes during bad weather, over muddy and snow-covered ground, and against a stubborn enemy defense was another question.

The ultimate outcome of the titanic struggle in the Ardennes lay in the skill and determination of the opposing forces. The Germans managed to mass the equivalent of twenty-nine infantry divisions and twelve panzer divisions organized into four separate armies. Overall responsibility for the conduct of the offensive fell to Hitler's old war horse, western Commander in Chief Gerd von Rundstedt. Army Group B, commanded by Field Marshal Walter Model, exercised operational control over the armies. The newly formed Sixth Panzer Army, under Generaloberst der Waffen-SS Josef "Sepp" Dietrich, had the mission of penetrating the northern portion of the Ardennes, crossing the Meuse, and then attacking to capture Antwerp. To the south, General der Panzertruppen Hasso von Manteuffel's Fifth Panzer Army would support Dietrich's main attack with an offensive through the heart of the Ardennes. Two other German armies—the Seventh in the south and the Fifteenth in the north—were to hold open the shoulders of the main effort.

Compared to the huge German forces massing for the offensive, American units in the Ardennes were spread thin. The army used the Ardennes as a rest area for divisions that had taken heavy losses and as a place where new divisions arriving in the ETO could adjust to the rigors of living on the front lines. In the northern portion of the Ardennes, Maj. Gen. Walter Lauer's 99th Infantry Division held a wide, twenty-mile front from Monschau in the north to Losheimergraben in the south. Lauer's division had arrived in Europe in November and was assigned to Gerow's V Corps to occupy the southern portion of the corps sector. Below V Corps, Middleton's VIII Corps manned the remainder of the Ardennes sector. The 106th Infantry Division around St. Vith held the northern portion of the corps zone along a twenty-two-mile front. Cota's 28th Division occupied the center of the corps sector. The Keystone Division was still recovering from the Huertgen Forest debacle and manned a thin, north-south line through the center of the Ardennes. Below Cota's troops the 4th Infantry Division occupied the southern portion of the VIII Corps' zone all the way to the Belgium-Luxembourg border, where the First and Third army sectors joined. Middleton had only one unit in reserve, CCA of the 9th Armored Division, positioned to support the corps' left and center. Normally, divisions defended along a ten-mile front, but in the Ardennes, division sectors were twice as wide. Commanders had to put all of their troops forward and were unable to form a solid front of uniform strength. Instead, units occupied a series of widely dispersed company- and platoon-sized strongholds positioned to control high ground and the road network.

While American divisions settled into the routine of defending the quiet sector, German commanders completed their plans for the Ardennes offensive. Sepp Dietrich's Sixth Army would attack on a narrow front in order to concentrate power for the drive to the Meuse. The I SS

Panzer Corps, operating in the army's southern zone, would spearhead the offensive. The attack plan called for three infantry divisions to breach the American lines, then the I Corps' armored divisions—1st and 12th SS Panzer—were to pour through the opening followed by Dietrich's army reserve, the II SS Panzer Corps. While the panzer divisions swept toward Liege, the infantry divisions were to shift northward and establish a series of defensive positions to protect the panzer divisions' westward routes and repel American counterattacks from the north. According to Dietrich's timetable, the panzer divisions had until the evening of the fourth day to establish firm bridgeheads over the Meuse. The Sixth Panzer Army was relatively well equipped and trained, its main offensive punch consisting of about 500 tanks and self-propelled assault guns.

The control of dominating terrain was a key factor in the outcome of Dietrich's attack. Two roads in the southern portion of the I SS Panzer Corps' sector that would carry German armor westward were especially critical. To the north, the Elsenborn Ridge was the most prominent terrain feature. (See Map 8.1.) Its highest point, just over 2,000 feet, lies midway between Elsenborn and Wirtzfeld. The Germans realized the defensive value of the ridge and designated it a prime objective of initial infantry attacks. The 277th Volks Grenadier Division was to make its way west along forest roads, capture the twin villages of Krinkelt-Rocherath, and then occupy the hill mass beyond. By seizing the Elsenborn Ridge, the Germans hoped to block American ripostes from the north, capture or drive off U.S. artillery units spotted near Elsenborn, and prevent American observation of the Sixth Army's rear area.

While attacking the Elsenborn Ridge, the Germans would face portions of three U.S. infantry divisions. General Lauer's 99th Division occupied forward defenses around Losheimergraben and Lanzeroth and bore the brunt of the offensive's opening fury. Two other divisions, the 1st and 2d Infantry, would enter the battle from the north. General Robertson's 2d Division would break off an eastward attack toward the Roer dams and march to the defense of Krinkelt-Rocherath. The 1st Division moved hastily from rest areas in the north to take up defensive positions around Butgenbach. The fight for the Elsenborn Ridge, as carried out in the battles at Krinkelt-Rocherath and Butgenbach, saw some of the most bitter defensive battles in the ETO. The engagements are also outstanding examples of how the American combined arms team performed on the defensive.

The main effort of Hitler's offensive started at 0530 hours on 16 December, when massed artillery struck the 99th Division around Losheimergraben. Ninety minutes later columns of German infantry and tanks appeared out of the trees and early morning fog to attack General Lauer's 394th Infantry. American commanders were not concerned over

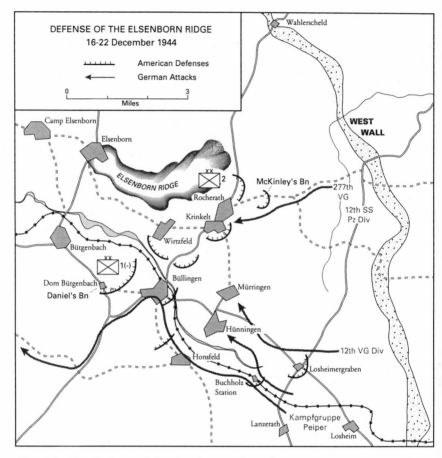

Map 8.1. The Defense of the Elsenborn Ridge, 16–22 December 1944 (Sherry L. Dowdy)

the shelling, but the size and intensity of the ground attack convinced them that something else was afoot. The character of the fighting throughout most of the Battle of the Bulge surfaced in the first day. Surprise and confusion reigned as American units became intermingled, and isolated pockets of defenders fought desperately. Though shaken and bloodied, the 99th Division prevented a total rupture of its defenses and maintained a fighting front while slowly withdrawing.[7]

By the late afternoon of 16 December, General Gerow realized that the situation in the southern part of his corps' sector was rapidly deteriorating. His concerns went beyond the 99th Division's survival. Since 13 December the 2d Infantry Division had been attacking northeastward from the center of the V Corps sector toward the Roer dams. By the evening of 16 December, the bulk of General Robertson's "Indianhead Division" was concentrated for an attack around Wahlersheid. Robertson's supply lines ran south from Wahlerscheid to Krinkelt-Rocherath, due west past the division command post at Wirtzfeld, then northwest along a single-lane forest trail that climbed over the Elsenborn Ridge and then descended toward the division's main base at Elsenborn. Gerow feared that the capture of the Elsenborn Ridge would not only result in the destruction of the 99th Division, but the isolation and encirclement of the 2d Division as well. At 0730 hours the next morning, Gerow ordered Robertson to break off operations around Wahlerscheid and to march south to join in defending the Elsenborn Ridge.[8]

General Robertson had a firm grasp on what his division had to do and how to go about it. His main concern was to keep his supply line, and now his only escape route, out of German hands, so he decided to establish a series of defensive positions centered on Wirtzfeld and Krinkelt-Rocherath. A stubborn defense there would slow down the German attack, give the 99th Division a position on which to rally, and furnish more time to organize a comprehensive defense of the Elsenborn sector. From the twin villages, as Krinkelt-Rocherath became known, Robertson could either fall back onto the Elsenborn Ridge or conduct a withdrawal all the way back to Elsenborn. Robertson lost little time in extricating his battalions from around Wahlerscheid, and by 1000 hours on 17 December many units were moving south. In addition to the 9th and 38th Infantry, Robertson had available three companies of the 741st Tank Battalion and two companies of the 644th TD Battalion. His third regiment, the 23d Infantry, was already engaged on opposite ends of the Krinkelt-Rocherath-Wirtzfeld position, throwing up the first firm breakwater against the German offensive and receiving groups of 99th Division survivors.[9]

The first crisis in the battle of the twin villages came at 1600 hours. Robertson received a report that elements of the 277th Volks Grenadier and 12th SS Panzer divisions had broken through forward U.S. positions east of Rocherath and were moving on the village. The occupation of Rocherath would block the 2d Division's line of withdrawal and disrupt all plans for the defense of the Elsenborn Ridge. Robertson drove out onto the Wahlerscheid road and commandeered the first unit he came upon, Company K, 9th Infantry. He briefed the company commander on the situation and ordered the unit to block the German advance by taking up defensive positions about a mile east of Rocherath. With a promise that reinforcements were on the way, Robertson headed north along the road as Company K moved out on its new, hazardous mission. Moments later the division commander came upon the head of the column of the 1st Battalion, 9th Infantry. Robertson ordered the battalion commander,

Tactical and technical adaptations during the Battle of the Bulge helped Americans defeat the enemy and operate under extreme weather conditions. A column of infantrymen clad in snowsuits moves down a Belgian road. (U.S. Army Military History Institute)

Lt. Col. William D. McKinley, to join Company K, to defend east of Rocherath, and not to abandon the position "until ordered otherwise."[10]

Over the next twenty-four hours, McKinley's troops fought one of the most desperate defensive battles of the Ardennes campaign. In the gathering twilight on 17 December, the rifle companies occupied their new defensive positions and began to dig in. The weather was extremely cold, about a foot of snow covered the ground, and a fog began to settle with sundown. All together, McKinley had about 600 soldiers. A platoon from the 644th TD Battalion joined the infantrymen. Soldiers laid clusters of mines forward of their positions, as the officers sited machine guns and stationed bazooka teams at critical points. The battalion fire support officer developed a defensive fire plan and established radio contact with the 2d Division artillery. Unknown to McKinley or his fire support officer, General Robertson had ordered the division artillery to give top priority to all of McKinley's fire support requests. In the meantime, three battalions of 155-mm howitzers from V Corps artillery joined the 2d Division artillery near Elsenborn, so that eighty-four guns were available to support McKinley's battalion.[11]

The first German attackers appeared around 1930 hours. Company B heard some tanks approaching through the fog and darkness and, thinking they might be American tanks falling back on Rocherath, soldiers held their fire. Not until the tanks were right on top of the infantrymen did they recognize them as enemy. Three panzers, with about a platoon of infantry following close behind, slipped through the battalion's positions and headed into Rocherath. These tanks were the advance guard of a much larger force, and soon the Americans heard a large number of tanks moving about in the woods to the east. Minutes later a large column of German tanks and infantry from the 12th SS Panzer Division hit McKinley's battalion head on. The first tanks hit mines, but soon other panzers were moving cross country in a broad attack. The German effort seemed confused and uncoordinated, probably because the advance guard had passed through to Rocherath without reporting the American positions. Darkness and a thick fog created more confusion that played into American hands. A wild melee ensued for several hours as the opposing forces became intermingled. American bazooka teams roamed the battlefield and knocked out several panzers, the flames lighting the battlefield with an eerie glow. While the battle raged within McKinley's positions, American artillery savaged German forces trying to reach the battlefield. Around midnight the Germans broke off the attack and withdrew eastward. McKinley reported that his battalion had been "strenuously engaged," but that everything was "under control at the present."

A strange silence settled on the battlefield as McKinley's troops recovered from their ordeal. Soon all of the companies began preparing for further action. Soldiers improved their positions, cared for the wounded, and brought ammunition forward. Units established contact with those on the flanks and replaced fallen leaders. Commanders sent patrols forward of their positions to detect German infiltration. In the middle of the night the commander of the 38th Infantry contacted McKinley to say that his troops were beginning to move in behind the 1st Battalion. McKinley's troops were to withdraw from their exposed positions just as soon as the 38th Infantry could establish a firm defensive line.

The real test for McKinley's battalion came the next morning. Around 0600 hours the full force of a German tank-infantry attack struck along the entire battalion front. Heavy fog and darkness again aided the defense, and American troops and artillery succeeded in separating German panzers from their accompanying infantry. Hand-to-hand combat between the opposing infantry was widespread, while American bazooka teams stalked wandering panzers. Sunlight and lifting fog around 0830 hours tipped the battle in the Germans' favor. A platoon of enemy tanks attacked across the 1st Battalion's front, smashing almost every machine-gun position. By this time, the Germans had all but overrun both Companies A and K, taking many prisoners. Just before 1100 hours the Company A commander reported that his unit was all but wiped out and that he was destroying his radios and wanted artillery put on his own position. McKinley agreed to the request and moments later a tremendous barrage plastered the area. Company A no longer existed. Other units continued to hold their own against ever-increasing pressure.

At 1100 hours the commander of the 38th Infantry contacted McKinley with orders to fall back on Rocherath. However, McKinley responded that without help from tanks or TD withdrawal was impossible. Almost miraculously, a platoon of Shermans from the 741st Tank Battalion appeared on the scene. McKinley quickly devised a withdrawal plan that hinged on combined arms coordination. A thirty-minute bombardment would stun the enemy, then the Shermans would counterattack to destroy a number of German tanks that had pinned down much of the battalion. Once the tank-artillery riposte broke the enemy's grip on the battalion, McKinley would pull back through the 38th Infantry. Soon massed artillery fire began delivering a terrific bombardment. At 1145 hours the bombardment stopped, and the Shermans attacked three German tanks still in the battalion's perimeter, destroying two and driving off the third. Under the cover of the counterattack, the majority of the battalion began to withdraw. With all guns blazing, the tanks and the final elements of McKinley's battalion fell back through the 38th Infantry's lines and began to regroup in Krinkelt.

With their defense east of Rocherath, McKinley's troops achieved two important goals. First, they bought valuable time for the remainder of the 2d Division to rally on Krinkelt-Rocherath. And by delaying the German advance, the 1st Battalion gave the beleaguered troops of the 99th Division more time to fall back and rally at Elsenborn. McKinley's battalion paid dearly for its stand at Krinkelt-Rocherath, entering the fight with about 600 soldiers and departing eighteen hours later with 197 survivors.

On 19 December McKinley reorganized the remnant of his battalion into a composite rifle company, the only reserve available within the 2d Division. In fading twilight that day, McKinley's tired troops trudged northward over the Elsenborn Ridge to begin organizing the 2d Division's final defensive positions around Elsenborn.

Several factors made McKinley's heroic stand possible. American artillery fire was decisive. It separated German tanks from infantry and inflicted heavy casualties while maintaining a defensive shield in front of the 1st Battalion's positions. During the fight on the night of 17 December, artillery units fired 8,000 rounds. Without armor support from the 741st Tank Battalion, McKinley's unit might have been destroyed during the daylight withdrawal. American tanks, artillery, and infantry knocked out seventeen panzers and an undetermined number of the enemy, but German infantry casualties were certainly heavy. Fog and darkness confused the enemy attack and frustrated German commanders. There was sufficient ammunition available, and antitank mines and bazooka teams were essential to defeating German armor.

On 18 December the struggle for Krinkelt-Rocherath broadened and intensified. The Germans concentrated the bulk of two divisions, the 277th Volks Grenadier and the 12th SS Panzer, to grab control of the villages. Several armor battalions were ready to do battle, armed with formidable Panther and Tiger tanks. On the American side, the 2d Division occupied solid defensive positions centered on the twin villages. The infantry regiments would not fight alone. The 741st Tank Battalion, one of the army's most seasoned armor units that had landed on Omaha Beach on D-Day and had seen extensive fighting ever since, was ready for the enemy's armor assault. The M10s of the 644th TD Battalion were on hand as well as the towed antitank guns of the 612th and 801st TD battalions. The heavy concentration of artillery that had supported McKinley's battalion widened its sector of fire and prepared to fire missions all across the narrow division front.[12]

The main struggle for Krinkelt-Rocherath began in earnest on the morning of 18 December. Waves of German tanks and infantry charged at the twin villages. American artillery tore at the enemy and had great success in separating foot soldiers and tanks. American 155-mm howitzers played havoc on several panzers. Tank and TD crews knew they could not take on the big German tanks toe-to-toe. Instead, they let the panzers close on their positions where an intricate game of cat and mouse took place among the twin villages' streets and alleys. Shermans and M10s remained hidden and quiet behind walls, buildings, and hedgerows, waiting for a Panther or a Tiger to cross their sites. Sometimes they sallied forth from hiding positions to stalk a panzer slowly, shooting only when they had good flank or rear shots. Most engagements took place at ranges of less than 25 yards. The 741st Tank Battalion knocked out twenty-seven panzers and lost eleven Shermans. The 644th TD Battalion destroyed seventeen tanks at a cost of two M10s.

Infantrymen defended the twin villages with every weapon and tactic possible. Soldiers fought doggedly with their reliable M1 rifles and .30-caliber machine guns. Much of the fighting took place at close quarters with liberal use of rifle butts and hand grenades. One of the most important roles of the infantry was to kill or capture German tank crews trying to escape after their vehicles had been put out of action, and soldiers used antitank mines to stop a number of vehicles. Hasty minefields emplaced to protect the rear and flank of several units were effective. The 57-mm towed antitank gun, however, performed poorly. Too immobile in the snow and mud, they could not respond quickly enough to unexpected threats and did not have enough punch to pose a serious threat to enemy armor. The best infantry antitank weapon was the bazooka. During darkness, bazooka teams could work their way close to panzers to get in a killing shot and they did their best work when finishing off tanks already disabled in some way by artillery, tanks, or TDs.

By the night of 18 December, General Robertson believed his mission at Krinkelt-Rocherath had been fulfilled. The supply line and escape route to Elsenborn was secure and the last organized remnants of the 99th Division had fallen back through the 2d Division's positions. General Gerow gave Robertson permission to withdraw to Elsenborn the next day. The withdrawal order went out at 1345 hours on 19 December, and the first units began falling back under modest pressure around 1730 hours. The 741st Tank and the 644th TD battalions formed a rear guard, with the last tank platoon passing through Wirtzfeld and heading for the safety of Elsenborn around 0200 hours on 20 December.

After the fight, General Robertson credited his success to bold execution and combined arms coordination. The stubborn defense was to a large degree attributable to the "wide and effective employment" of the artillery, for it was the key factor in turning back most German infantry assaults on 18–19 December. Tanks and TDs performed their missions superbly. Infantrymen fought stubbornly, fueled by stories that the Germans were killing PWs. The 2d Division had successfully reversed its direction of attack, fought a stubborn defense, and then conducted a gradual withdrawal under pressure. Robertson told an interviewer, "Leavenworth would say it couldn't be done," then added, "[but] I don't want to have to do it again."[13]

While the battle for the twin villages raged on 18–19 December, the stage was being set for another desperate fight in defense of the Elsenborn Ridge. By midnight on 16 December, VII Corps headquarters realized the gravity of the situation in the V Corps' sector. VII Corps released an uncommitted unit, the 1st Division's 26th Infantry, and loaded it on trucks for a quick overnight trip to Elsenborn, arriving around 0900 hours the next morning. The Germans were advancing in force northward along the Honsfeld-Bullingen road and seemed ready to make a swing around the 2d Division's right flank to capture the Elsenborn Ridge and the road network around Elsenborn. The 26th Infantry's mission was to move south and occupy defensive positions around Butgenbach to block the German thrust and to protect General Robertson's right flank. Soon the 26th Infantry was heading south to occupy defensive positions on two hills midway between Butgenbach and Bullingen.[14]

In the vanguard of the column marched the 2d Battalion, 26th Infantry, still commanded by Lt. Col. Daniel, who had led the battalion in the attack through downtown Aachen and in several actions in the Huertgen Forest. Daniel seemed to have a knack for showing up at the scene of a crisis and would now lead his troops in one of the most desperate engagements of the Battle of the Bulge. The battalion was at 80 percent strength, but because of heavy losses in the Huertgen Forest, more than half of the troops were new replacements. Since 7 December the battalion had conducted refresher training for new soldiers while imbuing them with the spirit and traditions of the 1st Division. By sundown the 2d Battalion was digging in on high ground near the tiny hamlet of Dom Butgenbach. Reinforcements soon joined the battalion: a platoon of antitank guns from the 26th Infantry's Antitank Company, a platoon of M10s from the 634th TD Battalion, and a platoon of Shermans from the 745th Tank Battalion.[15]

While the companies took up initial positions, Colonel Daniel conducted a reconnaissance and formulated his plan. There was little cover in the area and the prospect of heavy fog in the evening and early morning prompted him to defend forward with little depth to the position. The battalion front extended almost 2,100 yards, another reason for putting everything forward. Expecting a German tank attack along his lines, Daniel positioned his antitank guns and TDs across his front, orienting them on likely armor approach routes. He kept the tank platoon in reserve and held it under his control near the battalion command post. The battalion headquarters established itself in the main building in Dom Butgenbach, a stone structure with thick walls. Daniel decided to keep one rifle platoon in reserve. He did not develop a counterattack plan because he did not have enough troops available to eject German penetrations; any counterattack force would have to come from another unit in the 1st Division. He requested division engineers to emplace obstacles and minefields, but they were still far to the north. The artillery fire support officer planned targets on likely German assembly areas, attack positions, and approach routes. That night Daniel called his company commanders to the battalion command post, told them what he knew of the strength of the German attack, and issued his orders for the defense of Dom Butgenbach. He also told the officers of the new battalion motto for the upcoming fight— "We fight and die here."

The next day the 2d Battalion continued to prepare its fighting positions. Soldiers camouflaged and dug deep foxholes and gun emplacements and put overhead cover on as many as possible. Communications personnel laid wire between all positions. No one had winter clothing, so commanders instituted a round-the-clock rotation plan to move soldiers back to a warming house in Butgenbach. The 3d Battalion, 26th Infantry began digging in off to the far left of Colonel Daniel's position, while his right flank remained exposed. Colonel Daniel and his officers moved among the troops, supervising defensive preparations, telling the riflemen all they knew about the Germans' big offensive, and doing what they could to dispel fear and anxiety. The fire support officer established radio contact with artillery units, whose numbers increased as the day passed. Unknown to the 2d Battalion, artillery commanders were expending extraordinary effort to prepare for the defense of the Elsenborn Ridge. The artillery battalions of four divisions—the 1st, 2d, 9th, and 99th Infantry— were rallying north of Elsenborn, as V and VII Corps artillery battalions began displacing to the scene of the crisis.

During the night of 18 December, elements of the 12th SS Panzer Division and the 12th Volks Grenadier Division began arriving in Bullingen to begin a series of attacks northward toward Elsenborn. The first probing attack against the 2d Battalion came at 0225 hours on the morning of 19 December. A German tank company and an infantry battalion conducted a frontal assault. Artillery, antitank fire, and bazooka teams kept the panzers at bay, while shell fire tore gaps in the German ranks. The German attack accomplished its purpose: commanders discovered that the road toward Elsenborn was blocked and that to push the defenders aside would require a coordinated, deliberate attack. Over the next forty-eight hours the Germans made at least three major efforts to overrun Daniel's battalion, usually attacking with tank-infantry teams supported by varying amounts of shell fire. The pattern of the American defense emerged during the ensuing battles. Artillery and mortars put what Daniel described as a "ring of steel" around his positions. Shells tore at German units trying to form for attacks and continued to punish them during assaults. Indirect fire consistently managed to strip the German infantry away from their tanks. Panzers managed to penetrate the MLR but fell prey to antitank guns, bazooka teams, and TDs. Antitank gunners especially distinguished themselves. By firing into the flank and rear of German panzers at close range, the gun crews made several kills. One gunner, Cpl. Henry F. Warner, moved from gun to gun, destroyed three tanks and drove off another after he killed the tank commander with his .45-caliber pistol. (He died the next day trying to stop another tank and was awarded the Congressional Medal of Honor posthumously.) Tanks that did manage to break into Daniel's rear area were hit by artillery fire or destroyed by the reserve tank platoon.

The fight at Dom Butgenbach reached its crescendo on 21 December. The Germans tore a page out of American tactics manuals and delivered an intense bombardment with artillery and direct fire weapons beginning well before dawn and lasting three hours. The heavy shelling inflicted many casualties, shattered gun positions, and tore large holes in the lines. At dawn an infantry regiment and a tank battalion from the 12th Volks Grenadier Division assaulted Daniel's position. Ten battalions of American artillery roared back at the Germans. A number of tanks made it into the right side of the battalion's perimeter, smashed several antitank guns, and then systematically moved down the infantry line wiping out machine-gun positions and foxholes. Several more German tanks poured through the gap and advanced on Dom Butgenbach, slamming shells into Colonel Daniel's command post. The battalion commander and his staff dropped their radios and maps, picked up rifles and bazookas, and joined the fight. At Elsenborn, artillery battalions lost radio contact with Daniel's command post and believed the Germans had overrun the position. The muzzle of every available gun swung toward Dom Butgenbach, as the artillery began a three-hour saturation shelling of the battalion sector.

Meanwhile, Colonel Daniel directed the fight against the panzers about to overrun his position. The reserve Shermans and remaining TDs joined the battle, knocking out several panzers before they were put out of action. When things seemed all but lost, the Americans heard the crack of 90-mm cannons from the north, and a platoon of M10s from the 613th TD Battalion appeared down the Butgenbach road and assisted in clearing the German tanks away from the battalion command post. By early afternoon the front had stabilized, and the German attack seemed to have lost its impetus. The battalion left had held, but the right was still open. Daniel was considering a partial withdrawal to strengthen his lines when reinforcements arrived. Company C, 26th Infantry, moved in to occupy the smashed positions on the battalion right. Another unit, Company E, 18th Infantry, showed up in late afternoon. A large part of the 1st Engineer Combat Battalion soon followed, and in the gathering twilight began laying a huge, hasty minefield forward of Daniel's positions. Strengthened by fresh troops and a new confidence based on the repulse of the German attack, Daniel decided to stay in position. The next day the Germans attacked two more times, but the bolstered American defense stood firm. By the end of 22 December, the commander of the 12th Volks Grenadier Division had had enough and believed no further attacks toward Elsenborn were possible unless he received heavy reinforcements.

The fight at Dom Butgenbach exacted a heavy toll on both sides. Colonel Daniel reported the loss of three tanks, one TD, and five antitank guns, as well as over 250 killed, wounded, and missing. The Germans had impaled themselves on American defensive firepower. The burned-out hulks of forty-seven panzers littered the battlefield. An American patrol counted 300 dead sprawled in the snow forward of one company sector, and by Christmas Eve American burial teams had counted 782 German bodies throughout the 2d Battalion's sector.

In the aftermath of the battle, Colonel Daniel and Maj. Thomas J. Gendron, the battalion operations officer, credited the successful stand at Dom Butgenbach to the full integration of the combined arms team. They believed the "adequate and timely delivery" of artillery fire was "the greatest single factor" in the battalion's success. Shelling struck areas where the Germans were forming for attacks, broke up the coherency of their tank-infantry assaults, and helped eject them from the battalion's perimeter. The greatest amount of artillery support arrived during the crisis on 21 December; as many as twelve battalions fired over 10,000 rounds. Colonel Daniel later remarked that the artillery "did a great job" and that "we wouldn't be here now if it wasn't for them." When German tanks made it into the perimeter, antitank guns, TDs, and tanks drove them back. Crews of the towed 57-mm antitank guns relied on raw courage to take on panzers at close quarters. The battalion's leaders also believed the grim determination of the average soldier was a key factor in the success. Everyone knew they were in a desperate situation and that only the 2d Battalion stood between the enemy and the American rear area at Elsenborn.[16]

The defense of the Elsenborn Ridge knocked Sepp Dietrich's forces far enough behind schedule to cause a major shuffling of responsibilities among the German armies. On 20 December the mission of crossing the Meuse and capturing Antwerp passed from the Sixth Panzer Army to von Manteuffel's Fifth Panzer Army in the south. There another roadblock was forming that would slow von Manteuffel's advance—the 101st Airborne Division's defense of Bastogne. Although the tenacity and courage of American paratroopers had much to do with the outcome at Bastogne, the final success was a combination of many factors. Within the perimeter, American commanders hammered together a cohesive defensive force from parts of three separate divisions. The result was a combined arms team of paratroopers, tanks, artillery, and TDs that proved stronger than the Germans' most powerful blows. Air power played a significant role as fighter-bombers struck at the surrounding enemy and air transports delivered desperately needed supplies.

The gathering of U.S. forces at Bastogne reflects the prevailing confusion of the first days of the Battle of the Bulge. (See Map 8.2.) By the after-

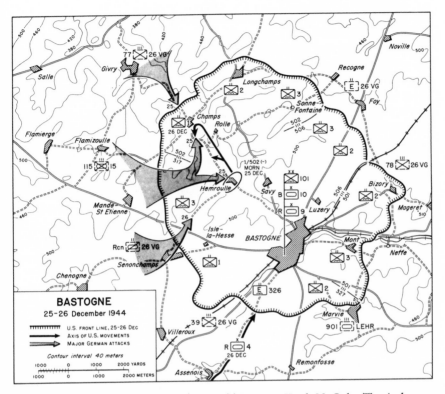

Map 8.2. Bastogne, 25–26 December 1944 (*Source*: Hugh M. Cole, *The Ardennes* (Washington, D.C.: U.S. Army, Office of the Chief of Military History, 1965; reprint ed., Washington, D.C.: U.S. Army Center of Military History, 1988), 473.)

noon of 17 December, General Middleton began to form a picture of enemy operations in the VIII Corps' sector. Believing that the Germans were attacking to gain control of the road intersection emanating from Bastogne, the corps commander sent his armored reserve, CCR of the 9th Armored Division, to establish a series of roadblocks several miles east of Bastogne. At the same time, CCB of the 10th Armored Division began arriving, and Middleton deployed them in support of the 9th Armored's defensive shield. Still, enemy armor from the XLVII Panzer Corps came on strong, inflicting heavy casualties on the 9th and 10th Armored divisions. By the morning of 19 December the German tide was threatening to sweep over and around the defenders and flow on into Bastogne.[17]

Fortunately, the 101st Airborne Division began arriving at Bastogne just as the situation east of town seemed all but lost. On the afternoon of 17 December, Bradley asked Eisenhower to release the only units in SHAEF reserve—the 82d and 101st Airborne divisions—to deal with the crisis in the Ardennes. Eisenhower acquiesced reluctantly, and on the afternoon of 18 December truck convoys began moving the 101st Airborne from rest areas around Rheims toward Bastogne. The "Screaming Eagles" made the 107-mile trip riding in mostly open trucks, in darkness and bitter cold. The first soldiers arrived in the division's assembly area, some four miles west of Bastogne, around midnight on 18 December, and by 0900 hours the next morning all of the division's four regiments had arrived. The 101st Airborne's mission was to stop the German advance and prevent American roadblocks from being surrounded or overrun. Actually, the three German divisions approaching Bastogne were more interested in bypassing the city and pushing on toward the Meuse. As events unfolded, German efforts on 19–21 December to go around the city converted the 101st Airborne's linear defense east of Bastogne into a perimeter defense centered on the town.[18]

As the 101st Airborne began establishing a defensive line east of Bastogne, the command relationships and forces available for the coming fight coalesced. Because Maj. Gen. Maxwell D. Taylor, the commander of the 101st Airborne, was on leave in the United States, the division's artillery commander, Brig. Gen. Anthony C. McAuliffe, took command. The next major unit in Bastogne was CCB, 10th Armored Division, commanded by Col. William Roberts. On 19 December Roberts and McAuliffe clashed over command arrangements, so Middleton settled the dispute on 20 December by formally assigning CCB to the 101st Airborne. The 101st Airborne's four regiments—the 501st, 502d, and 506th Parachute Infantry and the 327th Glider Infantry—would bear the brunt of the fighting. Under Colonel Roberts's leadership the remnants of CCB, 10th Armored, and CCR, 9th Armored, reorganized into a fighting force of about forty tanks. A welcome addition to the force was the 705th TD Battalion, which rushed to Bastogne on the evening of 18 December from positions 60 miles to the north. The 705th's TDs were armed with new, long-barreled 76-mm cannons that enabled them to take on panzers head-on. Besides the four battalions in the 101st Airborne's division artillery, two other artillery battalions armed with big 155-mm howitzers and a battalion of self-propelled howitzers from the 10th Armored Division would add their weight to the fight. A handful of antiaircraft artillery assets made it into the perimeter, and their quadruple-mounted .50-caliber machine guns turned back several enemy assaults with authority. Other battalions falling back on Bastogne or caught in the perimeter by chance fell under McAuliffe's control. A large number of stragglers also flowed into Bastogne, and Colonel Roberts organized them into an ad hoc reserve force called Team SNAFU, which in 1944 stood for "Situation Normal, All Fouled Up."[19]

The early defensive battles were uncoordinated and chaotic. Paratroopers, tankers, and TD crews did not work well together. Facing heavy German attacks, units had to concentrate on turning the enemy back before they could work on improving combined arms coordination. By the nature of their mission and training, paratroopers were more used to fighting from encircled positions, while armored troops found their situation disconcerting. The 101st Airborne took fierce pride in its role as an elite parachute unit and looked with some contempt on tank and TD crews, who the paratroopers believed benefited from the protection of steel plate between themselves and the enemy. But the key role Shermans and M10s played in repulsing panzer attacks on 19–21 December began to give the paratroopers a new respect for armored crewmen.[20]

Colonel Roberts took some of the first steps to convert the collection of units into a coordinated, combined arms force. Early in the war he had been an instructor in armored warfare at the Command and General Staff College at Fort Leavenworth and possessed a keen grasp of the problems and capabilities of tank-infantry forces. The 101st Airborne was in particular need of this knowledge, because the paratroopers had never worked with tanks and knew little about their proper employment, capabilities, or limits. Roberts moved among Screaming Eagle units, talking to commanders about tank-infantry cooperation, and was especially helpful as an armored adviser in the 101st Airborne's command post. Noticing that infantry commanders tended to use tanks as immobile pillboxes to block roads, Roberts told them to keep the tanks moving and to disengage them as quickly as possible after each fight so the armor could act as a mobile reserve. He worked on a training memorandum on the proper employment of armor that went out on 28 December to all units in the division.[21]

Despite their best efforts, the Americans were unable to keep the Germans from closing the ring around Bastogne. By the evening of 21 December, the Bastogne garrison was completely encircled. Increasing pressure on 22–23 December resulted in a major reorganization on Christmas Eve. Lt. Col. Harry W. O. Kinnard, the 101st Airborne's operations officer, devised a comprehensive plan to shorten and strengthen the defenses. Readjustments put soldiers in mutually supporting battle positions on prominent terrain along a 16-mile perimeter encompassing Bastogne. More significantly, Kinnard organized each of the four infantry regiments into a combined arms team, and each received a permanent attachment of tanks, TDs, and antitank guns. Colonel Roberts retained control over a central combined arms reserve that could take advantage of interior lines to move quickly between threatened points on the perimeter. Plummeting temperatures on 21 December froze the ground solid, enabling armored vehicles to maneuver cross-country against German encroachments.[22]

By 25 December the 101st Airborne Division and all other units in the perimeter felt a new sense of confidence in their ability to drive back the Germans with defensive combined arms tactics. The greatest challenge to the paratrooper-armored force came on Christmas Day. Von Manteuffel was becoming more and more concerned over the situation at Bastogne and finally ordered a major effort to capture it on 25 December. The task fell to the 15th Panzer and 26th Volks Grenadier divisions, and the main blow would fall in the northwest around Champs, where the Germans believed the perimeter was thinly manned. The offensive would begin with a supporting attack by the 26th Division against Champs, with the main effort attacking along the axis Flamizoulle-Hemroulle and then continuing on in to capture Bastogne.[23]

The 1st Battalion, 502d Parachute Infantry, and the 1st Battalion, 327th Glider Infantry, held the perimeter targeted for the German attack. At 0245 hours on Christmas Day, enemy artillery began falling on the two forward battalions. In the 1st Battalion, 502d Parachute Infantry's sector, Company A was defending forward around Champs, while companies B and C were further back in reserve. An hour later German troops in white snowsuits attacked Company A, and before long an entire battalion from the 26th Division was pushing into Champs. The paratroopers began falling back into the village as the reserve companies began to move forward to join the fight. A desperate, close-quarters, house-to-house slugfest developed as the outnumbered paratroopers tried to hold their ground. The Americans had an ace up their sleeve in the form of two M10s from the 705th TD Battalion. While one vehicle took up a firing position that allowed it to keep more Germans from reaching the village, the other moved in to give the infantry close support. Like TDs in Brest, Aachen, and hundreds of other urban fights, the vehicle buoyed the infantry's spirits and added considerable firepower to the action. Sgt. Lawrence Valletta of the 705th TD Battalion used canister and high explosives to punish the Germans, and his M10 blew apart at least six houses the enemy were using as strongholds. By dawn, Company A and the TDs had stabilized the front in Champs.

The main crisis of the day was yet to come. At 0710 hours a large German tank-infantry attack rolled through companies A and B of the 327th Glider Infantry. Eighteen panzers hit the paratroopers with all guns blazing, and grenadiers riding on the tanks added small arms fire to the melee. Paratroopers huddled in their foxholes, unable to stop the big panzers. Within minutes the enemy overran the 1st Battalion command post and headed into the American rear area. Suddenly, two M10s from the 705th TD Battalion opened up, destroying two enemy tanks. The Germans fired back, stopping both M10s. German tankers now advanced boldly, confident that they had eliminated the only serious antitank threat in the area.

Fortunately, companies B and C of the 502d Parachute Infantry were marching northward along the road from Hemroulle with the intention of reinforcing Champs. When the commanders realized that something was wrong off to the left in the 327th's sector, they ordered their men to take up hasty defensive positions to face the German threat from the west. As paratroopers scooped out fighting positions in the snow, they could hear approaching enemy tanks. Company C, commanded by Capt. George R. Cody, took up positions in a stand of woods next to the Champs-Hemroulle highway. To his surprise, Cody discovered two TDs hidden in the woods waiting for a chance to get a shot at the Germans. Paratroopers and armored crewmen manned their vehicles, machine guns, bazookas, and rifles, waiting for the storm to break. Moments later the enemy panzers came rolling through the gathering early morning fog. Cody's men opened up with everything they had, and the heavy volume of fire inflicted severe casualties on the German infantry. The enemy attack began to stall, and suddenly the German force split in two directions. Apparently the tankers wanted to break off the engagement and seek cover, so half of them headed north for the protection of Champs while the others spun right for Hemroulle. As the tanks pivoted, they presented perfect flank shots to the M10s. The TDs quickly destroyed three panzers, and bazooka teams from Cody's outfit knocked out two more. The German column heading for Champs then ran straight into the teeth of Company B's defenses. Before long the entire German force that had turned north was eliminated. Seven tanks lay smoking, and Cody's paratroopers counted sixty-seven German dead and took another thirty-five prisoners.

The enemy force that veered toward Hemroulle met an even more sudden and violent death. The 1st Battalion, 327th Glider Infantry, had quickly recovered from its ordeal earlier in the morning and organized a counterattack force. Four M10s, two Shermans, and a large group of paratroopers headed east in pursuit of the enemy. Meanwhile, artillery fire had managed to stall the enemy advance just short of Hemroulle, and the pursuing force hit them in the flank and rear. Tanks, TDs, machine guns, bazookas, and artillery tore into the German column. A battery from the 101st Airborne artillery positioned in fields just east of Hemroulle knocked out two German tanks with direct fire. The enemy armor took so much fire from so many directions that American gunners could not claim individual kills. A portion of the 101st Airborne's armored reserve moved from Bastogne toward the battlefield, but by the time it reached Hemroulle the fight was over. Eleven more German tanks had been destroyed, with heavy casualties among the escorting infantry. Around 0900 hours the 101st Airborne command post received word that the German attack around Champs had been defeated and that paratroopers would reoccupy the original perimeter sometime during the afternoon.

Air-ground operations also played a significant role in the defense of

Bastogne. A huge aerial resupply effort during the second week of the battle helped guarantee success. One of the most unfortunate events of the encirclement took place on 19 December, when German raiding parties captured almost all of the 101st Airborne's medical supplies and killed or captured most of the division's medical company. The shortage of medical supplies and personnel became acute. After the Germans closed off all the roads on 21 December, other shortages developed, and food, artillery ammunition, gasoline, and petroleum products became scarce. General McAuliffe informed VIII Corps of the developing supply crisis, and COMZ logisticians and the Ninth Air Force's IX Troop Carrier Command worked furiously to organize an air bridge into the perimeter.[24]

With cold, clear skies over Bastogne on 23 December, soldiers began to hear approaching aircraft about mid-morning. Around 0900 hours a small pathfinder team, the vanguard of any airborne operation, descended into the perimeter and reported to Colonel Kinnard that a huge armada of C-47 air transports was headed for Bastogne. The pathfinders deployed fluorescent panels to mark a mile-square drop zone west of Bastogne, turned on their radios and directional beacons, and waited for the aircraft. Around 1150 hours, the first C-47s in a long stream of transports appeared. Over the next six hours 241 aircraft dropped 1,446 bundles weighing 144 tons, and a tight drop pattern resulted in the swift recovery of approximately 95 percent of all supplies. German flak knocked down a number of aircraft, but transport pilots pressed the attack without taking evasive action. Another 160 C-47s made drops on Christmas Eve, and on Christmas Day 11 gliders braved bad weather to bring in a team of four surgeons and petroleum products. The biggest effort came on 26 December when 289 transports delivered their cargo, and the next day another 130 C-47s dropped their loads into the perimeter. By 28 December relieving forces had opened ground routes into Bastogne and supplies began to arrive by truck.[25]

Air power gave many types of assistance to the besieged. The first fighter-bombers appeared as escorts for the supply armada on 23 December. As the C-47s cleared Bastogne, P-47s turned their attention to the enemy. During the afternoon, eighty-two fighter-bombers struck at the Germans with fragmentation bombs, napalm, and machine guns. The next day P-47s from XIX TAC hammered German positions on all points of the compass. An air support party that had been rushed to Bastogne on 18 December integrated CAS into the fight throughout the siege. The chief air controller was Capt. James E. Parker, a veteran fighter-bomber pilot with considerable experience in both the Pacific and European theaters. Parker talked to flight leaders en route to Bastogne, gave them approach instructions, and helped them identify intended targets. P-47s came in low and fast, catching the Germans by surprise. On more than one occasion, ground troops received CAS within fifteen minutes of requesting an air strike. Aircraft also flew eastward to attack German routes toward Bastogne and to collect intelligence for McAuliffe's command post. Enemy flak was heavy and elusive, with German batteries apparently moving from position to position around the perimeter. On 28–29 December, Captain Parker coordinated a series of combined arms air-artillery attacks that finally silenced the threat.[26]

At 1645 hours on 26 December, the lead element of the 4th Armored Division made contact with 101st Airborne paratroopers on the perimeter. Much more fighting around Bastogne was to come, but the German grip on the city had been broken. The courage and doggedness of American paratroopers was an important element in the defense of Bastogne, but the ability of the encircled units to hammer together a defensive combined arms team of paratroopers, tankers, TD crews, and artillerymen supported by aerial resupply and fighter-bombers was the real reason for success. The 101st Airborne and its attached tank and TD units quickly organized themselves for combat and learned how best to work together. They quickly gained a healthy respect for one another's capabilities. Armored crewmen admired the paratroopers' aggressive attitudes, and the infantrymen gained a healthy respect for those who had to stand face to face against the big German tanks. Colonel Kinnard later called CCB, 10th Armored Division, a "splendid unit and full of fight" and the 705th TD Battalion a "super fine" outfit. He also credited the presence of additional artillery units for part of the success. Kinnard believed the availability of shelter within the perimeter gave the defenders a great advantage. Americans had places to get warm, change out of wet clothes, and have a cup of hot coffee. The Germans had no shelter, and Kinnard added that the 101st Airborne was simply not about to let the enemy "run us out of the houses."[27]

Air operations around Bastogne were only a small part of the total air effort during the Battle of the Bulge. When the weather cleared on 23 December, fighter-bombers flew 696 sorties to establish air superiority, to interdict German LOCs, and to assist ground units. In addition to operations around Bastogne, fighter-bombers from IX TAC flew CAS and armed reconnaissance missions along the Bulge's northern shoulder. On Christmas Eve, Ninth Air Force P-47s flew 1,100 sorties. By 26 December American air power was taking a toll on the enemy, as aircraft cratered and cut highways and railroads, destroyed bridges, rubbled villages that choked German supply lines, and demolished vast quantities of enemy vehicles and rolling stock. Sustained air support buoyed American morale, supported ground operations, and provided commanders with valuable intelligence. The enemy suffered heavy losses, began to lose confidence in the offensive's outcome, and found it increasingly difficult to move during daylight. During 23–31 December Ninth Air Force fighter-bombers and medium bombers flew 10,305 sorties and dropped 6,969 tons of bombs while losing 158 aircraft. The Ninth claimed the destruction of 2,323 enemy trucks, 207 armored vehicles, 173 gun positions, 620 railroad cars, 45 locomotives, 333 buildings, and 7 bridges.[28]

Throughout the Ardennes fighting, units adapted and improvised various means of coping with the rigors of living and fighting in snow, ice, and cold. The army learned that after forty-eight hours of combat in extreme cold, the efficiency of the average soldier dropped below 50 percent. Providing basic creature comforts to troops was a formidable challenge. Most units developed small rest areas where soldiers could change out of wet clothes, warm themselves, and get hot food and drinks. Infantry regiments tried to provide each soldier with one pair of dry socks daily. Warming tents went up just behind the front lines, while many units used buildings as rest areas. Digging foxholes for shelter in the frozen ground was a backbreaking chore that took hours, and many units learned to use explosives to hasten the process. Troops desired two- and three-man foxholes for maximum warmth and safety. The best defensive positions were wide enough and deep enough for three infantrymen and covered with logs and earth.[29]

Infantrymen discovered several ways to ensure their combat effectiveness. Olive drab uniforms stood out in the snow, so riflemen rummaged through Belgian homes and tore up white sheets to use as improvised snowsuits. Soldiers learned to keep outer garments dry because clothing became stiff and bulky once it froze. The lack of overshoes prompted troops to wrap their feet in burlap bags to prevent trench foot and frostbite. Leaders learned not to talk directly into radio handsets because their breath could condense and freeze on the diaphragms of radio microphones. Infantrymen kept a thin coat of oil on weapons or operated moving parts regularly to prevent jamming. GIs improvised several ways of using tin cans to construct small stoves for heating rations and coffee. Outposts learned to listen for enemy movements; they could easily hear the sounds of German soldiers laboring through the deep snow at long distances, especially on cold, still nights.[30]

Armor units learned ways to keep their units moving over the ice and snow. Columns had to creep along at speeds of less than ten miles per hour, and commanders had to keep slow travel rates in mind when planning movements. Roads and trails well defined on maps were hard to find in deep snow, and daily reports on road conditions and snow depth in the battle area were essential. Despite their heavy weight, armored vehicles slid and spun on icy roads, so tankers and mechanics improvised two methods to give their steel monsters better traction. Maintenance sections welded a short piece of angle iron to every fifth or sixth track block that acted like a cleat, gripping snow and chopping through ice. Other crew-men removed several rubber pads from their tracks, so the track's steel frame clawed into the ground. Tanks parked in mud overnight could be-come frozen to the ground, so crewmen learned to park on hard surfaces or to pull up onto logs. Tankers mixed their own homemade whitewash to camouflage their vehicles. A lack of antifreeze was a problem throughout the winter, so mechanics learned to add alcohol or kerosene to cooling systems to keep engines from freezing.[31]

The other combat arms learned cold weather lessons as well. Deep snow decreased the lethality of artillery surface bursts and increased the bursting height of proximity fuse ammunition. Cold temperatures made powder less stable, and rounds fired with cold powder had excessive dis-persion. Artillery units found ways to keep powder stocks warm and dry, and mortarmen learned to keep powder rings warm by stuffing them in-side their shirts. Medics could not treat casualties with frozen water, and they discovered that putting drops of liquor in their canteens prevented freezing. Snow was a great aid in helping pilots spot and follow enemy movement. Tank tracks running into thick woods usually pointed the way toward German armor, so pilots bombed and strafed woods suspected of containing enemy vehicles. Large fir trees caught fire easily, and fighter-bomber pilots learned to use napalm in an effort to burn the Germans out of hiding.[32]

The army might not have performed as well in the Ardennes if com-manders and soldiers had not adapted a series of tactical and technical in-novations that helped defeat the German counteroffensive. Commanders at division level and below relied on their knowledge of defensive doc-trine to improvise more sophisticated combined arms tactics that took full advantage of mobility and firepower and integrated CAS into defensive battles. Technical lessons emerged as well. Soldiers learned that some weapons and equipment items did not perform up to expectations in con-ditions of extreme cold and limited visibility, so they improved tech-niques to keep these items operating properly. Soldiers quickly discov-ered which weapons worked best during close-quarters combat in darkness, fog, and low light conditions. At the individual level, soldiers improvised a wide variety of techniques that allowed them to function in extreme weather conditions and provided protection against the dangers of prolonged exposure to the snow and bitter cold.

The Battle of the Bulge illustrates one of the greatest advantages of a de-centralized approach to organizational adaptation: the rapid development of solutions to immediate, unexpected problems. Soldiers learned and adapted in combat during a period of great uncertainty and confusion, and their capacity for independent thinking and action served the army well during the December battles. Units initiated change and improvements on their own rather than waiting for orders and guidance from senior commanders and their staffs. There was no time for the army to analyze the difficulties of winter combined arms warfare or cold weather survival techniques for individual soldiers. An army operating under more centralized planning and staffing procedures might not have been able to respond as quickly to the sudden difficulties encountered in the Ardennes.

The nature of the battles in the Ardennes prompted American commanders to ignore or revise many of the defensive warfare tactics prescribed in FM 100-5. The size and swiftness of the German attack forced units into defensive combined arms battles on terrain chosen quickly with little time for planning or preparations. Locked in desperate battles, commanders violated doctrine by bringing to bear every gun they had without holding anything in reserve. Tanks and TDs were rarely held back but went forward to support the infantry and to take on German panzers. Not until the latter stages of the Bulge could corps and division commanders concentrate enough armor for big counterpunches. Antitank guns performed unevenly. Under conditions of low light and visibility they took on enemy armor with an even chance of survival but in daylight were no match for German tanks. Bazooka teams had good luck against unescorted or immobilized German tanks. Infantry actions throughout the Bulge illustrate what disciplined riflemen with an effective, hand-held antitank weapon can achieve against enemy armor.

The defensive battles also illustrate that doctrine must keep pace with the capabilities of combat units; when it fails to reflect the enhanced abilities of modernized forces, commanders must make adjustments that exploit the advantages of new weapons and equipment. Prewar doctrine maintained that infantry and artillery fought defensive battles while antitank guns countered enemy mechanized forces. In reality, commanders in the Ardennes had a much broader array of modern weapons available. Tanks and TDs played a vital role by moving quickly to threatened points or to establish roadblocks across the path of advancing panzers. Armored vehicles again proved their worth in the first line of defense instead of remaining in reserve. CAS was crucial in punishing German units, as exemplified by the air strikes against the outer perimeter at Bastogne. When antitank guns did not work well, infantrymen picked up the bazooka, a relatively new weapon in the fall of 1944. Modern communications were a key element in promoting the American defense. Commanders were able to maintain control over fluid battlefields, to move forces quickly from one danger point to the next, and to keep close, constant touch with supporting artillery battalions. Without improved radio communications, the army might not have been able to maintain order over the chaos produced by the sudden, violent, German counterattack.

In some cases doctrine failed to describe accurately the roles of weapons in the defense. FM 100-5 warned that artillery had only limited effect against enemy armor, but in the Bulge American artillery performed brilliantly on the defensive. Guns attacked German LOCs and assembly areas, punished enemy units during assaults, and put solid walls of hot steel in front of U.S. defensive positions. The artillery's greatest contribution was to separate German tanks and infantry. Panzers that made it into American positions without infantry support fell victim to antitank guns and bazooka teams. Artillery fire was also effective in crippling enemy tanks and armored vehicles. The artillery's ability to concentrate and shift vast quantities of firepower was extraordinary: by 21 December artillery commanders had assembled twenty-three battalions behind the Elsenborn Ridge. The four infantry divisions defending the northern shoulder of the Bulge received continuous support from the 348 guns massed around Elsenborn. This unanticipated gathering of howitzers and cannons was probably the greatest concentration of artillery firepower in the ETO, if not in all of U.S. military history.[33]

Air units proved that they could play a much larger role in defensive warfare than the battlefield interdiction mission outlined in FM 100-5. Once skies cleared, air-ground operations played a great part in the victory. Using improved air control systems, fighter-bombers flew valuable CAS missions and provided ground commanders with timely intelligence. Air power supported ground units and attacked German LOCs with devastating effects. The aerial resupply of Bastogne was one of the most dramatic and important air-ground operations of the campaign.

Doctrine maintained that combat in ice, snow, and extreme cold required special equipment and the use of specially trained ski troops, but the army just did not have special troops or equipment for cold weather operations. Instead, commanders fought with the standard equipment and regular soldiers that filled the ranks. American troops were not trained in cold weather operations or how to live in such conditions. Cold weather clothing was unavailable, most of it lying in warehouses in the COMZ because of the autumn supply crisis. In the absence of ski troops, aircraft kept ground formations updated on the enemy situation, and commanders learned that they had to account for the snow and cold when planning and fighting engagements. Instead of adversely affecting morale, the cold weather seemed to bring out the American soldier's best fighting qualities. The ferocity of the German onslaught, fear of atrocities, newfound hatred for the enemy, and uncertainty and danger in a confused situation infused most Americans with a grim determination to hold their ground at all costs.

The Battle of the Bulge is usually portrayed as the best example of the tenacity of the American fighting man. However, the army's performance in the Ardennes also reflects the American soldier's ability to adjust rapidly to the sudden surprise demands of the battlefield. A broader analysis of the army's performance in the ETO reveals the entire spectrum of improvisations and new ideas generated by soldiers of all ranks to overcome the enemy and to survive in battle.

.

CHAPTER NINE

The American Soldier

In the first few days we threw the book away. It didn't work the way we'd
been taught. In combat we learned from what was going on at the time.
— *Sgt. Al Oyler, Company K, 333d Infantry*

The most vital component of the American combined arms team was the
officers and men that closed with and destroyed the enemy. As an organization, the American army excelled in innovating and adapting technical
and tactical solutions to a wide variety of problems. However, a third category of change took place throughout the army that was just as important. From corps commanders to individual riflemen, soldiers of all ranks
created new techniques and changed a great number of established practices that enabled them to prevail in battle. The ability of the American
soldier to change his behavior under fire as the living, thinking component of the combined arms team was often critical to success. These adaptations helped soldiers to bridge the gap between the doctrine and the actual practice of warfare and to adapt to the many differences that existed
between peacetime training and combat action.

A wide range of problems at all levels of organization challenged and
adversely affected the fighting power of GIs. As an institution, the army
attempted to repair several broad manpower problems. The inefficiencies
of the replacement system and huge losses from cold weather injuries and
combat exhaustion reduced the quality and quantity of soldiers available
on the front lines. Senior commanders tried to devise better methods for
employing firepower and maneuvering their major combat formations,
and junior officers worked to institute more effective leadership styles.
The enlisted ranks focused on adapting to the everyday hazards of living
and fighting on the front lines while seeking techniques that would make
them more effective in battle.

A key American philosophy motivated much of the changes in behavior
that occurred in the ETO. Although a variety of attitudes and values kept
men fighting day after day, one pervasive belief focused all of the military's efforts. From George C. Marshall sitting in his office in the Pentagon
to the lowest foot soldier huddled in a foxhole in Western Europe, Ameri-

cans believed the best way to win the war was to end it as quickly as possible with a minimum of casualties while inflicting maximum damage on the enemy. All ranks believed that huge offensives aimed at the annihilation of the German army would carry American troops closer to the Third Reich and naturally hasten the war's end. Such a view was not an impersonal concept imposed by higher authority, but a living idea that guided the daily activities of many commanders and soldiers.

The main tenets of this war-fighting philosophy—short time, maximum damage, minimum casualties—go a long way in explaining many of the changes made throughout the army. Perhaps the military's greatest conceptual challenge was to reconcile the conflicting demands between conserving manpower and the need to end the war as soon as possible through relentless, offensive action. American generals showed a willingness to stay on the attack whenever possible in the hope of quickly destroying the German army. When battles of maneuver were impossible, they developed powerful methods of bringing all their combat power together against the enemy's prepared defenses. The willingness to attack did not mean Americans had a reckless disregard for their own safety. Commanders employed firepower and maneuver so as to minimize risks to their troops and unleashed heavy caliber weapons and demolitions with wild abandon rather than needlessly exposing their troops to danger. Soldiers instinctively realized that the only way for them to end the war and go home was to keep pushing forward. Col. James E. Rudder, who led the elite 2d Ranger Battalion in the assault on Pointe du Hoc on D-Day, summarized the attitudes of many soldiers in an open letter to his troops: "There is only one reason for our being here and that is to eliminate the enemy that has brought the war about. There is only one way to eliminate the enemy and that is to close with him. Let's all get on with the job we were sent here to do in order that we may return home at the earliest possible moment."[1] Americans devised a number of techniques to ward off danger and fear and to husband their mental and physical strength. In prolonged campaigns in which the dead and wounded fell at alarming rates, the need to conserve and sustain soldiers' stamina was paramount.

Senior commanders deploying to Europe carried with them the American army's conventional views on waging war. Prewar doctrine envisioned a fluid battlefield on which divisions tailored for mobility maneuvered against the enemy, always seeking the flanks or trying to bypass stiff resistance. Doctrine declared that maneuver was always preferable to battles of attrition and assumed that mobile armies could easily maneuver under all types of conditions. Commanders believed the purpose of offensive operations was to destroy the enemy's army rather than seizing terrain. However, the battles in the ETO forced generals to refine some of their views on theater operations. Opportunities for maneuver warfare were more rare than anyone had imagined. The Germans sought to cancel American advantages in mobility and firepower by defending the most inhospitable terrain available. Bold flanking actions in the bocage, around fortifications, and through urban centers and dark forests sounded good in theory but were impossible in practice. Bad weather hampered maneuver across the countryside and turned roads into rutted tracks. All too often American generals lacked the forces to fix and bypass the enemy simultaneously. Senior commanders soon learned that destroying a competent enemy battling from prepared defenses required more hard fighting than maneuver. Mobility did play a key role on several occasions—the COBRA breakout, the pursuit across France, and the counterattack in the Ardennes—but dismantling Germany's army called for a surprising amount of close-quarters fighting.

In battles between large armies deployed on extended frontages, senior commanders found it difficult to destroy enemy forces without first capturing key terrain features. In Europe, the opposing armies relied heavily on road networks for troop movements and logistical support. Often, the control of highway systems dictated the conduct of campaigns. Bradley wanted desperately to destroy German forces in Normandy, but he could not do so before gaining control of the web of roads emanating from St. Lo. Cities were often obstacles too large to ignore. Both Hodges and Patton believed they could not afford to bypass Aachen and Metz before pushing on toward Germany, and for moral and political reasons the Allies had to divert troops to liberate Paris rather than pushing all units toward the German border. American generals also learned that gaining ground and destroying the enemy were not mutually exclusive goals but went hand in hand. Capturing important terrain features put American forces in more advantageous positions from which to destroy their enemies.

Rather than keeping their forces always dispersed for mobile operations, American corps commanders learned to concentrate overwhelming combat power for big assaults against prepared defenses. As a group, they were quick to devise the best ways of employing massed formations. One favorite technique was to attack with divisions in column. Corps used infantry divisions to rupture German defenses and armored divisions to exploit the breach. After the infantry had blown a hole in the defenses, American armored divisions attacked through friendly troops with combat commands in column and kept pushing forward. Attacks by divisions in column were common in the ETO. The 2d Armored Division followed the 30th Division through the Siegfried Line, and the 10th Armored Division exploited the 90th Division's gains in the Koenigsmacher bridgehead. The best example is the 4th Armored Division's breakout from the 80th Division's perimeter in the Dieulouard bridgehead.

During prolonged operations, corps commanders kept the pressure on the Germans with continuous attacks for several days or weeks across the fighting front. Generals learned that the only way to keep moving forward was to combine massed fire support with fresh troop units. In extended operations, corps attacked a single objective using their divisions in a series of alternating thrusts along converging axes. The flexibility of CAS and artillery permitted corps commanders to shift priority of fire support between different divisions on a daily basis. Only rarely did one division remain in the vanguard of a corps attack for an extended period. Middleton's attack on Brest is the best example of an American corps using alternating thrusts to shoulder its way toward a single objective.

When the situation required maximum combat power, corps commanders learned to mass forces along a common division boundary near the center of the corps' sector. Each division concentrated an attacking regiment on a narrow front along their adjoining boundaries. The corps staff then coordinated all divisional and corps firepower to support the main attack. Across a corps front of 10–20 miles, two regiments pushed ahead on a front as narrow as 1–2 miles supported by every fighter-bomber and artillery tube available. A good example of a massed attack astride a division boundary occurred on 11 July when the 29th and 2d divisions joined forces to capture high ground east of St. Lo. The 116th Infantry of The Blue and the Gray Division went for the Martinville Ridge, while the 38th Infantry of the Indianhead Division captured Hill 182. The attack was astride a division boundary as well as a corps boundary, so the entire fire support of the V and XIX Corps was available to the two leading battalions. On 11 July the artillery battalions of the 29th and 2d Divisions, assisted by V and XIX Corps and First Army artillery units, fired 33,000 rounds in support of the infantry.[2]

Division commanders had to revise the army's doctrine for offensive operations to capture stubbornly defended positions on close terrain. Prewar doctrine called for two attacks against enemy positions. (See Figure 9.1.) The purpose of the main attack was to capture the objective, while supporting attacks diverted the enemy's attention and resources to other sectors. Regimental frontages were fairly uniform across the division sector. Reserves stood ready to exploit opportunities or repel counterattacks. In the ETO, attack plans based squarely on doctrine saw little use. Much of the fighting took place on close terrain that prevented the use of maneuver and the long-range fires needed to implement the offensive concepts doctrine recommended.

When division commanders needed more fighting punch than maneuver, they took extraordinary measures to concentrate combat power and maintain positive command and control. Divisional main attacks with small frontages allowed for maximum concentration of fire support. A fa-

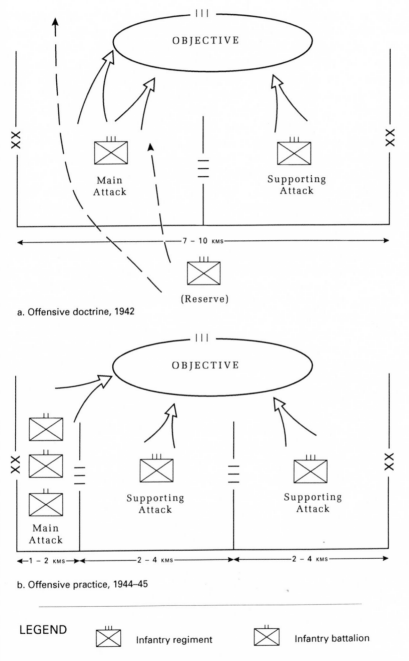

a. Offensive doctrine, 1942

b. Offensive practice, 1944–45

LEGEND   Infantry regiment   Infantry battalion

Figure 9.1. Battlefield Maneuver: Doctrine and Practice (Sherry L. Dowdy)

vorite practice was to weight the division's attack in one narrow sector rather than spreading combat power uniformly across the front. Other regiments manned wide sectors of the division front or constituted a small reserve. The attacking regiment concentrated all its battalions against the flank of a German position. Regiments conducting main attacks sometimes advanced with two battalions abreast, but the most popular formation was to attack with battalions in column. On close terrain battalion columns permitted utmost command and control and maximum concentration of organic weapons. When the lead battalion hit stiff resistance, the next battalion in column pushed straight ahead to get the attack moving again or maneuvered around against the enemy's flanks. For the actual assault on the objective, the two trailing battalions moved forward and came abreast on either side of the lead battalion. All three commands then swept across the objective. Corps often passed the control of all organic artillery units and CAS sorties to one headquarters to concentrate maximum firepower. An infantry battalion in the vanguard of a division's main attack could expect fire support from as many as five to twelve battalions of artillery and dozens of CAS sorties.

Divisions attacking with regiments in columns of battalions supported by massed firepower were common in Europe and usually got the job done. The 29th Division's 116th Infantry plowed through the hedgerow country in columns of battalions and helped push the Germans out of St. Lo. The 30th Division attacked with two regiments abreast, battalions in column, during its successful breaching of the Siegfried Line. The 80th Division at Dieulouard forced the Moselle with columns of battalions, and in the Huertgen Forest, regiments routinely attacked in column. One of the few times a regimental attack with battalions in column did not succeed was the 112th Infantry's spectacular failure at Schmidt.

One of the great tasks facing air and ground generals was the coordination of tremendous amounts of firepower. For moral and expedient reasons, American generals preferred to expend munitions rather than lives. The use of massed firepower was also viewed as one of the best ways to inflict maximum damage on the enemy while exposing U.S. troops to a minimum of danger. However, merely throwing huge stocks of bombs and shells at the Germans did not guarantee success. The military had to learn the best ways to blend mortar, artillery, and aerial firepower into a coordinated whole for maximum efficiency. Prewar doctrine did not tell commanders how to coordinate firepower from a wide variety of sources, and staffs devised increasingly sophisticated fire support plans as the war progressed.

An army or corps in a deliberate attack could expect fire support from different types of air and ground units. On selected occasions, the AAF committed heavy and medium bombers to augment fighter-bombers.

Armies massed artillery tubes from army, corps, and division field artillery units. Developing a comprehensive fire support plan meant more than just bringing planes and guns to bear. Staffs organized fire support plans by type of weapons system, and it became standard practice to echelon firepower in depth and to apply it in successive waves.

Attacks supported by lavish firepower saw the employment of fire support systems from heavy bombers to rifle company mortars, and staffs organized the attack zone into target areas arrayed in depth. (See Figure 9.2.) The attack zone began just beyond friendly lines and extended deep into enemy territory. Attacks usually began with heavy bombers striking deep against enemy reserves, command posts, and LOCs. Ordnance from the closest heavy bomber strikes was to fall beyond a bomb safety line 2,000 yards from friendly troops, and the attack could stretch for several miles. As the heavies cleared the target area, medium bombers came in at lower altitudes to focus on more critical or hard-to-hit targets. While the mediums did their work, fighter-bombers attacked initial objectives designated for the ground attack. When medium bombers droned away, the fighter-bombers shifted beyond their initial targets to fly armed reconnaissance. Artillery went to work once aircraft cleared critical sectors of airspace. Massed battalions from corps and army struck deep against a variety of targets in a broad sector that began within 1,000 yards of friendly troops and stretched into the enemy's rear areas. Meanwhile, division artillery and any number of reinforcing artillery battalions began hammering at the first ground objectives. Bombardments varied in length, but the usual preparatory fire lasted about an hour. Artillerymen ended their attack at H-hour by pausing for several minutes in the hope that the Germans would come out of their dugouts and man weapons in the open. Moments later the division artillery dumped one last volley on the objective and then shifted its guns to targets further to the rear. Shelling behind the objective sought to destroy counterattack forces and to isolate forward defenses from the rest of the battlefield. When division artillery began shelling beyond the objective, organic mortars shifted their fires forward to the first enemy positions. The splash of mortar rounds on the objective signaled the beginning of the ground attack. Only a few operations incorporated all types of aircraft and indirect fire support, the best examples being the COBRA and QUEEN air-ground attacks. Staffs planned many others, but they ran afoul because of bad weather or aircraft availability. By the spring of 1945 staffs were fully prepared to orchestrate firepower into fire support plans much more elaborate than anything envisioned before the war.

The army learned that there were limits on what firepower could achieve. Ground units watched tremendous outpourings of bombs and shells with awe but knew that firepower alone could not get the job

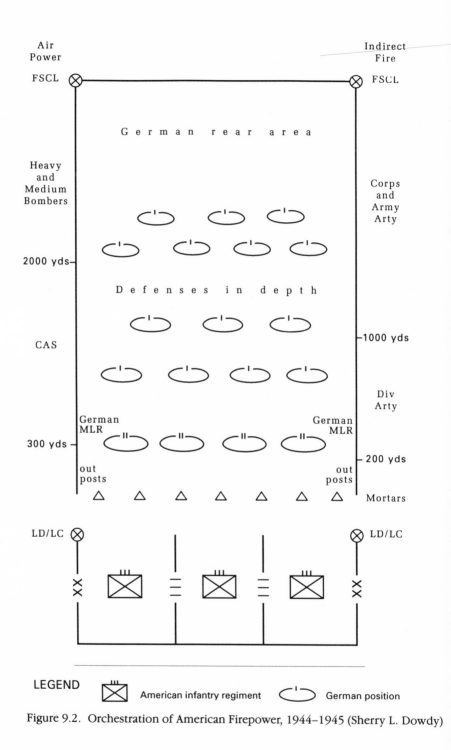

Figure 9.2. Orchestration of American Firepower, 1944–1945 (Sherry L. Dowdy)

done. No matter how much ordnance the army expended, some Germans survived to defend their positions. Air and artillery bombardments were area weapons that were not precise enough to destroy German strongholds. Carpet bombing could make an area almost impassable and decrease an attacker's mobility. The most valuable aspects of ferocious bombardments were to disrupt German command and control, stun enemy defenders, and buoy the morale of attacking units.

Another departure from prewar doctrine was the need to fight without adequate reserves. Doctrine advised commanders to commit two-thirds of their strength into the fight and to hold the remainder in reserve. But constant attrition whittled away at combat units, and the demands of attacking prepared German defenses prompted generals to throw every man they had into the fight. Fighting with every unit committed became standard practice, and generals learned to live with the calculated risks of fighting without a reserve. When XX Corps attacked with three divisions across the Moselle north of Metz in November, General Walker had only one infantry battalion in corps reserve, not a division, and soon had to commit it at Thionville to force another crossing. When the 30th Division breached the Siegfried Line north of Aachen, it attacked with no reserves. The 1st Division cleared Aachen with all troops forward. Divisions in the Huertgen Forest had to fight on extended fronts without relief because reserves were not available. When the Germans counterattacked in December, 12th Army Group and First Army had no reserves to influence the action. Even as late as the spring of 1945, a lack of reserves hindered operations. One of the reasons for the slow buildup in the Remagen bridgehead was that there were no reserves readily available to exploit the success.

Lack of reserves also meant that units had to stay on the fighting line for long periods without relief or rest. By May of 1945 American forces in the ETO included forty-six infantry and fifteen armored divisions. Between D-Day and V-E Day stretched 337 days, during which many divisions endured near continuous commitment in battle. (See Table 9.1.) Half of the infantry divisions spent over 150 days in combat, and 40 percent spent 200 days or more. Two divisions saw more than 300 days of action. The 2d Division marched across Omaha Beach on 8 June and went on to spend an incredible 303 days in battle. The 90th Division saw its first fight in Normandy and in a stormy combat career managed to accumulate 308 days of combat, the highest of any division in the ETO. The armored divisions also had to endure long periods under fire. Of the fifteen armored divisions in the ETO, four saw more than 200 days of battle.

While generals learned new ways to use combat power, officers discovered several important lessons about combat leadership. Peacetime training overemphasized the need for leaders to motivate their troops through

TABLE 9.1. Comparative Statistics of Army Divisions in the ETO

			Infantry Divisions			
				Casualties		
	Entered Combat	Days in Combat	Battle	Non-Battle	Total	% of Turnover
1	6 JUN 44	292	15,003	14,002	29,005	205.9
2	8 JUN 44	303	15,066	10,818	25,884	183.7
3	15 AUG 44	233	13,101	15,299	28,400	201.6
4	6 JUN 44	299	22,454	13,091	35,545	252.3
5	16 JUL 44	270	12,475	11,012	23,487	166.7
8	8 JUL 44	266	13,458	7,598	21,056	149.4
9	14 JUN 44	264	18,631	15,233	33,864	240.4
13	NO COMBAT	0	—	—	—	—
17	25 DEC 44	45	3,166	834	3,020	
26	12 OCT 44	199	9,956	6,895	16,851	119.6
28	27 JUL 44	196	15,904	8,936	24,840	176.3
29	6 JUN 44	242	20,111	8,665	28,776	204.2
30	15 JUN 44	282	17,691	8,347	26,038	184.8
35	11 JUL 44	264	15,406	10,082	25,488	180.9
36	15 AUG 44	227	11,238	14,919	26,157	185.7
42	17 FEB 45	106	3,598	2,351	5,949	42.2
44	24 OCT 44	230	6,111	7,637	13,748	97.6
45	15 AUG 44	230	10,458	15,991	26,449	187.7
63	6 FEB 45	119	4,547	3,472	8,019	56.9
65	9 MAR 45	55	1,052	1,250	2,302	16.3
66	1 JAN 45	91	1,098	849	1,947	13.8
69	11 FEB 45	65	1,556	1,791	3,347	23.8
70	3 FEB 45	83	3,996	4,235	8,201	58.2
71	6 FEB 45	49	788	1,081	1,869	13.3
75	25 DEC 44	94	3,954	4,062	8,016	56.9
76	19 JAN 45	95	3,126	2,430	5,556	39.4
78	13 DEC 44	125	7,890	4,367	12,257	87.0
79	19 JUN 44	248	14,875	8,582	23,457	166.5
80	8 AUG 44	239	14,460	11,012	25,472	180.8
83	27 JUN 44	244	15,248	8,732	23,980	170.2
84	18 NOV 44	152	6,561	3,250	9,811	69.6
86	29 MAR 45	34	760	473	1,233	8.8
87	13 DEC 44	134	5,555	6,032	11,587	82.2
89	12 MAR 45	57	1,006	1,074	2,080	14.6
90	10 JUN 44	308	18,460	9,157	27,617	196.0
94	17 SEP 44	183	5,607	5,203	10,810	76.7
95	20 OCT 44	151	6,307	3,834	10,204	72.4
97	1 APR 45	31	934	384	1,318	9.4
99	9 NOV 44	151	6,103	5,884	11,987	85.1
100	9 NOV 44	163	4,790	7,425	12,215	86.7
102	26 OCT 44	173	4,867	3,958	8,825	62.6
103	11 NOV 44	147	4,543	4,826	9,369	66.5
104	24 OCT 44	178	7,011	6,396	13,407	95.1
106	10 DEC 44	63	8,163	2,508	10,671	75.7

TABLE 9.1. *Continued*

		Armored Divisions				
2	2 JUL 44	223	6,751	7,116	13,867	95.9
3	9 JUL 44	231	10,105	6,017	16,122	111.5
4	28 JUL 44	230	5,988	4,508	10,496	98.4
5	2 AUG 44	161	3,554	3,592	7,146	67.0
6	28 JUL 44	226	5,526	7,290	12,816	120.1
7	14 AUG 44	172	6,150	4,352	10,502	98.4
8	23 FEB 45	63	1,313	1,141	2,454	23.0
9	16 DEC 44	91	3,952	1,459	5,411	50.7
10	2 NOV 44	124	4,697	3,684	8,381	78.5
11	23 DEC 44	96	3,216	1,921	5,137	48.1
12	7 DEC 44	102	3,436	2,540	5,976	56.0
13	10 APR 45	16	493	246	739	6.9
14	20 NOV 44	133	2,896	1,400	4,296	40.3
16	5 MAY 45	3	12	231	243	2.3
20	24 APR 45	8	76	319	395	3.7

Source: Order of Battle, United States Army in World War II—European Theater of Operations, Office of the Theater Historian, ETO, December 1945.

personal example. Older career officers especially clung to the belief that a commander's bold but calm presence on the front lines instilled the troops with confidence. During the construction of the first treadway bridge across the Rhine at Remagen, the engineer group commander, Col. Harry Anderson, arrived to watch engineers build the bridge under heavy fire. Anderson was one of the army's most senior engineers and had seen action during Pershing's raid into Mexico in 1916 and in the trenches of World War I. The crusty, straight-backed veteran had a reputation for never wavering or flinching under fire. When artillery shells landed near the bridge, Anderson stood erect on the riverbank, even after several NCOs asked him to take cover. Then a number of Luftwaffe airplanes streaked by strafing and bombing, but when the smoke cleared the old colonel still stood in the same spot. Word that Anderson had defied the air strike spread through the engineer battalion "like wildfire." Such methods fell into disfavor during the war, but many officers still persisted in the dangerous practice.[3]

The army began to realize that the gutsy "follow me" style of leadership in which officers led from the front was too costly. Company grade officers at the very forefront of attacks suffered high casualty rates, and their loss seriously affected unit efficiency and morale. The commander of CCB, 7th Armored Division, summarized the problem: "Too much emphasis has been placed on leadership. . . . Leaders got the idea that they must always be in front. We lost many platoon leaders, company commanders, and even our best infantry battalion commander for that reason.

I do not mean by this that leaders should not show themselves well forward. They should. But to make a habit of continuously staying in front is foolish."[4] Still, many senior commanders persisted in wanting their officers forward in battle. One regimental commander in Normandy told a group of newly arrived lieutenants, "As officers, I expect you to lead your men. Men will follow a leader, and I expect my platoon leaders to be right up front. Losses could be very high. Use every skill you possess. If you survive your first battle, I'll promote you. Good luck."[5]

But as the fighting progressed, beliefs on leading from the front softened. Company officers learned to direct the battle from less exposed positions, and captains and lieutenants took calculated risks to show troops that mission accomplishment took priority over personal safety. When circumstances required, officers knew the worth of physical bravery and conspicuously took bold steps to get attacks moving or to calm soldiers who were about to break. The 7th Armored Division issued a training memorandum in February 1945 that warned leaders not to expose themselves foolishly: "You don't have to prove how brave you are—it's too hard on your friends, and besides, your courage isn't questioned—we take it for granted."[6]

Officers soon learned that their own troops did not expect them to lead from the front. Men in the ranks thought it was foolhardy when officers needlessly exposed themselves to danger. Soldiers instinctively knew the importance of keeping key leaders alive and often asked them not to lead the way in hazardous situations. When Capt. Charles B. MacDonald tried to move to the head of his rifle company during a night march through a dangerous area in the closing stages of the Battle of the Bulge, one of his sergeants intervened. "Goddamit, Captain," he said, "you've got to stay further back. At least get some scouts out front." Similar incidents of soldiers' concern for the safety of their officers were common throughout the ETO.[7]

If troops did not expect officers to lead from the front, they did look for several qualities in their officers. Soldiers believed that officers should fight alongside them and share all of their hazards. The best officers did not order or ask men to expose themselves needlessly or to attack in the face of overwhelming odds. Troops desired self-control and emotional stability in their captains and lieutenants. An excitable officer was ineffective. Officers learned that speaking in a calm, firm voice during tense situations was the best way to reassure soldiers. Cheerfulness and laxity in periods of low danger lulled troops into carelessness, while commanders who appeared nervous or gloomy during a crisis unnerved their troops. Whether in dire or favorable circumstances, officers on the front lines learned to speak and give orders in sober, straightforward tones.[8]

One of the greatest emotional challenges for inexperienced officers came in the aftermath of battle. They tended to brood over feelings of direct, personal responsibility for each casualty. Training publications took a hard line in dispelling their anxieties. Junior officers were to "steel" themselves against losing men and to realize that "casualties are an expected product of war and must be accepted as such." Officers and troops began to accept the reality of casualties. The commander of an engineer company with the mission of building a bridge under fire told his soldiers that the infantry had already taken heavy casualties while establishing the bridgehead, and now it was the engineers' turn to suffer. Everyone understood the risks and forged ahead to build the bridge. By May 1945 officers accepted the fact that casualties were inevitable, and the adage "it costs casualties to take objectives" became widespread in the army.[9]

A survey of casualties in the ETO shows why officers may have been so worried over their losses. Overall, U.S. army air and ground forces suffered 936,259 battle casualties in all theaters during World War II. The European theater alone accounted for the loss of 586,628 soldiers and airmen. Over 78 percent of the losses, or a total of 456,779 casualties, came from fighting divisions. The resulting picture is sobering: of the total American air and ground casualties in World War II, 49 percent occurred in the ETO's ground units between 6 June 1944 and 8 May 1945. The final body count of the ETO's casualties included 80,211 killed, 325,969 wounded, 40,271 prisoners of war, and 10,328 missing in action. Leaders in the ETO's ground units could take little consolation in the fact that they were participating in the greatest American bloodletting since Grant's 1864 drive on Richmond.[10]

A review of divisional casualties conveys the intensity of the fighting. Of the sixty-one divisions in the theater, twenty had a personnel turnover rate of 100 percent or higher due to battle and nonbattle casualties. The infantry divisions suffered horribly; eighteen out of forty-six lost the equivalent of an entire division's worth of troops. Five divisions—the 1st, 3d, 4th, 9th, and 29th—had the dubious distinction of suffering more than 200 percent casualties during their careers in the ETO. The 4th Division had the unenviable distinction of being the most blooded division in Europe, suffering a ghastly casualty rate of 252.3 percent. In early 1945, forty-seven infantry regiments serving throughout nineteen divisions had sustained casualty rates between 100 and 200 percent. The armored divisions lost fewer in total numbers, but the proportion of the suffering was also grim. The 3d and 6th Armored Divisions had a turnover rate exceeding 100 percent. Three others followed close behind with casualty rates above 95 percent, so that one-third of the armored divisions had a turnover rate of 95 percent or higher.

To study the wounded and the dead is, to a great extent, to study the infantryman's burden; they represented 14 percent of the army's overseas strength but suffered 70 percent of the total battle casualties. Before D-Day army planners estimated the casualty rate for riflemen at around 70 percent. In reality the rate was much higher, about 83 percent, and the typical rate of loss in infantry platoons exceeded 90 percent. Riflemen accounted for 68 percent of an infantry division's authorized strength, but suffered almost 95 percent of its casualties. An AGF study on casualties concluded that in a typical battle, 90 percent of a division's casualties took place in the forward sectors assigned to the rifle battalions.[11]

The other combat arms suffered much less than the infantry. Artillerymen were 16 percent of an infantry division' authorized strength but only absorbed 3 percent of its casualties. The lion's share of artillery casualties took place among FO teams operating on the front lines rather than among gun crews. Engineers composed 4 percent of the division and lost only 2 percent of the casualties. Definite patterns emerged during tank-infantry operations. Armored infantry equaled 29 percent of an armored division's authorized strength but suffered an average of 62 percent of all casualties. Likewise, tankers filled 20 percent of authorized spaces but accounted for only 23 percent of the casualties. Losses between tankers and infantrymen varied in direct proportion to the tactical situation, as whoever led the attack absorbed the brunt of the losses. In one attack in Europe, tank battalions pushed ahead and suffered 50 percent of an armored division's losses, while the infantry absorbed 40 percent of the casualties. When armored infantry led attacks they suffered as much as 66 percent of the division's losses, the tankers just over 16 percent. The pattern of tanker to infantry losses holds true for the entire ETO. For all of the infantry and armored divisions that fought in Europe, the average rates of battle casualties per thousand men per day of combat were 3.2 and 2.7, respectively.[12]

Two types of casualties caught the army off guard and caused serious problems throughout the European campaigns. The first was an epidemic of cold weather casualties that occurred in the form of trench foot and frostbite. Cold weather injuries usually took place in combat units forced to live in cold and wetness during static periods in which soldiers could not warm themselves, change socks and footgear, or receive warm food and hot drinks. Long periods of inactivity manning defenses and the constriction of blood flow to the extremities caused by poor clothing and footgear made troops vulnerable to cold weather injuries.[13]

Cold weather injuries ravaged the American ranks like a medieval plague. In all of World War II, air and ground forces suffered a total of 91,000 cold weather casualties, and the lion's share of these occurred in the fighting units in the ETO. Between November 1944 and April 1945, hospitals in Europe admitted 45,283 cold weather casualties, just under

50 percent of all air and ground cold weather injuries for the war and about 9 percent of the total ground battle casualties suffered during the same period. In general, for every 1,000 soldiers in the ETO, 76 suffered a cold weather casualty. During November and December 1944, the American armies lost 23,000 soldiers to cold weather causes. In raw numbers the losses equaled the strength of one-and-a-half infantry divisions. However, most of the injuries took place among the 4,000 riflemen in a division, so cold weather injuries in reality incapacitated the equivalent fighting power of five-and-a-half divisions. Between November 1944 and March 1945, First and Third armies suffered 115,516 battle casualties and another 32,163 losses to cold injuries, a ratio of roughly 4 to 1.[14] General Patton captured the flavor of the trench foot crisis in a memorandum of 21 November 1944 sent to all Third Army corps and division commanders: "The most serious menace confronting us today is not the German Army, which we have practically destroyed, but the weather which, if we do not exert ourselves, may well destroy us through the incidence of trench foot. . . . To win the war we must conquer trench foot."[15] The explosion of cold weather injuries eroded the army's combat power and put unbearable demands on the replacement and medical evacuation systems.

A number of factors precipitated the cold weather injury epidemic. The winter of 1944 was the coldest, wettest period Europe had experienced in thirty years. Heavy rains in October and November and winter months with long periods of record-breaking cold caused frostbite and trench foot cases to mount. The American army was slow to gather and disseminate lessons learned on cold weather injuries in other theaters. Stateside and overseas training programs paid little attention to cold weather injury prevention, and soldiers did not know enough about the care and treatment of their own feet. General Bradley took a calculated risk in the early fall of 1944 and deliberately gave priority of shipment to ammunition and gasoline to sustain the drive into Germany rather than moving forward stocks of winter clothing and supplies. When the German army stopped the Allied advance and bad weather set in, American troops were ill equipped for it.[16]

Information, training, and command emphasis became the cornerstones of an aggressive trench foot control program. In January 1945 all major commands published materials on the nature and control of trench foot that gave soldiers the basics of how to avoid cold weather injuries. In retraining and replacement training centers, soldiers received instruction on how to prevent and treat frostbite and trench foot. Units on the front lines implemented training programs with varied success. Many divisions created trench foot control teams to assist in the training and supervision of preventive measures. Units learned to reduce trench foot by rotating small groups of soldiers off the front lines back to tents or dugouts where they could dry or exchange their wet clothes and receive warm food and hot drinks. The army believed the effectiveness of control measures reflected the level of a unit's discipline, and that responsibility for cold weather injury prevention and treatment fell squarely on unit commanders. In the winter of 1944 commanders of several units that continued to have high losses to cold weather injuries lost their positions. The army's success in controlling cold weather injuries is hard to gauge, but whatever the result, solutions to the epidemic of cold weather casualties came too late to prevent an unnecessary drain on manpower.[17]

The army also suffered heavy losses to a much more serious and complicated disease—combat exhaustion. American forces in World War I learned to cope with the effects of "shell shock," but 1941 found the army unprepared to deal with large numbers of soldiers suffering from combat-related mental disorders. At the time of Pearl Harbor the army lacked a treatment system, a definition, or even a name for a vexing problem that by 1945 would drain combat power from fighting units at an alarming rate. Large numbers of cases developed during the Tunisian campaign when the army first coined the term "combat exhaustion." The army's chief neuropsychiatrist graphically described the distinctive symptoms of a combat exhaustion casualty: "Typically he appeared as a dejected, dirty, weary man. His facial expression was one of depression, sometimes of tearfulness. Frequently his hands were trembling or jerky. Occasionally he would display varying degrees of confusion, perhaps to the extent of being mute or staring into space. Very occasionally he might present classically hysterical symptoms."[18] Medical channels believed the "social and psychological background of the individual" helped determine the incidence and severity of combat exhaustion cases. Other determining factors were a soldier's military training and experience as well as the cumulative effects of fatigue, hunger, and fear. Perhaps the most telling indication that the army was not prepared to deal with the problem is that throughout the war it never considered combat exhaustion as a category of disease for reporting purposes.[19]

Psychiatric casualties winnowed the ranks at an alarming rate. The armies in Europe evacuated 151,920 cases of neuropsychiatric disorders to hospitals in 1944 and 1945, and combat units discovered that on average, for every three men killed or wounded, one other soldier became a psychiatric casualty. High incidences of combat exhaustion paralleled peak fighting periods and was most prevalent in units in action for the first time. First Army suffered a combat exhaustion epidemic in July and August during the fighting to break out of the Normandy bridgehead and to repulse the German counterattack at Mortain. Cases among Hodges's troops peaked in early August when almost 17 percent of all hospital admissions were for combat exhaustion. All armies experienced declines during the summer pursuit followed by a resurgence during the autumn battles. Third Army experienced its peak of combat exhaustion cases—11 percent of all hospital admissions—during the September battles to cross the Moselle. The Huertgen Forest campaign caused First Army's combat exhaustion rate to reach double digit figures again. The Battle of the Bulge, despite its intense combat and bitter weather, saw a marked decline in combat exhaustion. In the spring of 1945 a feeling that the war would soon be over and better methods of preventing and treating psychiatric disorders resulted in a marked decrease in rates. The armies lost about 5 percent of all casualties to combat exhaustion during the late winter of 1945, and after the breakout from the Remagen bridgehead incidents trailed off steadily until the end of hostilities.[20]

Combat exhaustion casualties usually fell into two broad categories. The first type occurred among new soldiers just before entry into combat or during their first five days on the front lines. Infantry replacements without adequate training or proper integration into their new units experienced unusually high combat exhaustion rates. Acute, traumatic incidents of fear or carnage induced combat exhaustion in many new soldiers. In the Huertgen Forest a new replacement in the elite 2d Ranger Battalion saw the head of a fellow ranger less than three feet away blown completely off. The new soldier became speechless, did not know his name, and could not recognize anyone around him. The unit evacuated the replacement, who finally ended up in a stateside psychiatric ward.[21]

A second type of combat exhaustion occurred among experienced veterans who had endured continuous, severe fighting for four months or more. In the spring of 1945, First Army determined that the longest any man could remain in combat and retain his wits was about 200 days. The first indications of developing combat exhaustion among veterans were increased irritability, apathy, inefficiency, and carelessness about their own safety. Soldiers easily identified the phenomenon among veterans and began to call it the "old sergeant syndrome." Although this second kind of combat exhaustion developed over time, a specific occurrence usually brought on the final breakdown. A platoon leader in a rifle company of the 1st Division observed a classic, graphic example of the syndrome. In late March 1945 his company was fighting within the Remagen bridgehead. One of the squad leaders had landed on Omaha Beach on 6 June, was never wounded, and had not missed a day of action in all of the 1st Division's battles across Europe. But on 22 March the sergeant finally succumbed to combat exhaustion. The platoon leader wrote, "Now more than 270 combat days after first engagement, he suddenly reached the limit . . . the woods were silent except for his sobbing. Clutching his rifle he sat at the foot of a tree completely hysterical. He refused to release the rifle, apparently heard no commands, was unaffected by solicitude, and was incapable of further action."[22] Fearing that the sergeant's collapse would demoralize the other men, the platoon leader evacuated him to the rear. After a few days of rest the squad leader rejoined the company but was never again "an effective fighting man."[23]

Attitudes toward men suffering from combat exhaustion varied widely. Even the army's senior leaders held mixed opinions. Bradley believed that every soldier had his breaking point. The infamous Patton slapping incident during the Sicilian campaign personified the attitudes of many others who contended that combat exhaustion casualties really suffered from cowardice, poor motivation, or weakness of character. Soldiers in fighting units were much more understanding. Most officers in leadership positions believed that combat exhaustion and extreme reactions to fear were medical, not disciplinary, problems and required treatment rather than punishment. In 1944 as many as 77 percent of the officers assigned to two infantry divisions in the ETO indicated that combat exhaustion casualties should be treated as sick men, and a clear majority of the enlisted men held the same view. But there was little tolerance toward those trying to use combat exhaustion or extreme fear reactions to avoid combat. Troops expected everyone to make an effort to overcome fear and exhaustion. Soldiers visibly shaken by danger, who trembled and cried openly, were not considered cowards if they made an effort to regain their composure and to go back to their duties. If a man showed exhaustion symptoms and simply declared that he could not go any further and required evacuation, other soldiers branded him a coward and expressed their contempt and scorn.[24]

Treatment methods and systems emerged slowly early in the war because many senior leaders tended to ignore or minimize the depth of the problem. But by 1944 the need for an organized medical response was clear to everyone. Commanders and medical channels had to improvise and experiment to develop effective treatment programs. Three principles guided treatment regimes: immediacy, proximity, and expectancy. Commanders learned to evacuate combat exhaustion casualties as quickly as possible for immediate treatment. Early in the war the army evacuated these soldiers far to the rear, where patients lost touch with their comrades, began to question their own worth and esteem, and tended to exaggerate the seriousness of their problem. In the ETO the army learned that by treating soldiers at the lowest adequate level of care and keeping them close to the front, most patients maintained a desire to return to their old units. Medical channels also conveyed to soldiers that their condition was temporary and treatable, and that after proper care they would return to the fighting. Many of the psychiatric care channels required to treat combat exhaustion were not included in the army's prewar force structure, and surgeons and commanders had to reorganize personnel and equipment to form treatment channels from scratch.[25]

Battalion aid stations within 400 yards of the front lines were the army's most forward treatment centers. Battalion surgeons knew most of the troops in the unit and took a personal approach to their care. Common treatments included a few hours' rest, hot coffee, warm food, and a chance to wash. For more serious cases, surgeons administered sedatives from whiskey to morphine. Drug-induced sleep and food seemed the best remedies for mild cases and brought most soldiers back to full duty status. Battalion surgeons also separated malingerers and soldiers suffering temporary effects of extreme fear reactions from those with combat exhaustion symptoms. It was not unusual for troops to undergo immediate treatment and to return quickly to their unit. When soldiers did not respond to treatment, battalion surgeons evacuated them further to the rear. Regimental aid stations served as triage points for a more careful investigation of cases suspected of malingering and as rest areas for soldiers with persistent symptoms. The next level of evacuation was division clearing stations, where doctors tended to focus on battle casualties and the sick and hesitated to divert their time and resources to neuropsychiatric cases. Most divisions began to segregate physical casualties from mental cases and created separate combat exhaustion triage and treatment centers operated by the division's neuropsychiatrist. Most soldiers responded to treatment and moved on to division retraining centers that prepared them for return to the front lines. The most severe mental patients went on to newly formed hospitals controlled by the field armies or the COMZ. Patients responding to rehabilitation went back to their divisions for reassignment. Those who did not improve went to the ETO's central neuropsychiatric hospital at Ciney, Belgium, for more extensive treatment or rehabilitation.[26]

The improved methods for treating combat exhaustion cases seemed to bear fruit. Between June and December 1944, First Army reported 28,475 cases of combat exhaustion, and medical channels managed to return 52 percent of these—14,788—to normal duty. From its activation on 1 August 1944 until the end of the war, Third Army had 19,536 combat exhaustion cases and returned 70 percent of them to full duty. Seventh Army lost just over 5,000 soldiers to combat exhaustion with about half returning to their units. Seventy-five percent of the patients evacuated to the COMZ returned to normal duty. Of course, not all soldiers returned to combat performed well. A First Army report showed that four months after 708 combat exhaustion cases had returned to their units in July and August, 217 remained with their units, more than 200 were killed or wounded, 108 had been evacuated for sickness, and 278 had experienced a relapse of combat exhaustion.[27]

One of the army's greatest challenges was to keep battle-torn divisions up to strength with a constant flow of individual replacements. Fresh troops usually came from two sources: stateside replacements who entered the ETO through the Replacement System, which was a separate command within the COMZ, or soldiers from a variety of overstrength specialties retrained within the ETO to fight in critically short combat positions. The theater attempted to support a replacement pool of 70,000 troops. The key challenge was to maintain a manpower pool containing the right number of soldiers in the correct military specialties. Before D-Day the ETO determined that 64 percent of the replacement pool should consist of infantrymen, but after the heavy fighting in Normandy, the number went up to almost 80 percent. Casualty rates and the tempo of operations were variables that caused fluctuations in manpower demands. Matching the military specialties of incoming troops against the numbers and types of soldiers out of action was a balancing act commanders and personnel officers had a hard time mastering. Not until April 1945, when the stockage of replacements reached 86,000 men, was the Replacement System entirely capable of meeting the theater's demands.[28]

Responsibility for administering the ETO's replacement infrastructure fell to the Replacement System, which was composed of a series of depots. By January 1945 twelve depots assisted in the movement of troops. The key nodes were four forward depots that supported the major field armies. Behind the army depots a varying number of intermediate depots assisted in the flow of replacements. Two depots acted as receiving stations for hospital returnees, commonly known as "casuals." The typical replacement set foot in the ETO through one of the entry depots at Le Havre or Marseilles. There he had a stop of several hours or an overnight rest while awaiting transportation to another depot further inland. At intermediate depots troops received individual weapons and equipment, clerks updated personnel records, and instructors gave lectures and classes. Replacements finally reached army depots where they underwent administrative processing before loading on trucks for the final leg of their trip to the front. Replacements ended their odyssey through the human pipeline under a variety of conditions. The lucky ones joined divisions in rest areas where they had a chance to become part of their unit before going into combat, while others went directly onto the firing line with little knowledge of their location, unit, or mission.[29]

Replacements voiced acute dissatisfaction with the depot system. The army seemed incapable of providing quality amenities, and soldiers began to refer derisively to depots as "repple depots." The spartan facilities provided little more than the most basic shelter, sanitation, and dining comforts. Replacements moved from depot to depot in open trucks or in unheated and crowded train cars normally used to haul cargo or livestock.

With little to do, soldiers became bored or frustrated and worried about what lay ahead. Lengthy delays in transit gnawed at replacements' physical conditioning, mental keenness, and discipline. Morale suffered tremendously, and casuals returning to units were quick to fuel replacements' anxieties with horror stories of what it was like at the front.[30] A new officer replacement remembered talking to veterans in one repple depot:

> I met several individuals who had come back from the line. Invariably they recounted their hair-raising experiences—their outfits had been "wiped out," or "pinned down for days"; "officers didn't have a dogs' chance of survival," etc. One platoon sergeant . . . said his platoon had lost sixteen officers in one two-week period. I expected confidently that I would be blown to bits within fifteen minutes after my arrival at the front.[31]

For the average soldier, life in the Replacement System was a hardship that seemed meaningless and unnecessary.

By the late fall of 1944 there were enough complaints about the poor physical and mental quality of replacements to cause concern. The COMZ made a concerted effort to provide better billets, recreational facilities, mess halls, and transportation. Improvised training programs attempted to reduce boredom, and the army began to segregate replacements from the dour casuals. A consensus developed that the term replacement had an adverse impact on morale because it suggested a soldier's expendability. In late December fresh troops became known as reinforcements, an effort to emphasize the replacement's function as a combat reserve rather than as a human repair part. The most fundamental reform did not come until March 1945. Recognizing the replacement system's adverse effects on the morale, discipline, and training of individual soldiers, the ETO began to move troops through depots in organized groups. Reinforcements became members of ad hoc squads, platoons, or companies organized for movement to the front. When possible, soldiers remained in these units until they reached their final destination. Keeping soldiers grouped together successfully warded off the impersonal nature of the depot system, but the reform came too late to indicate any other real benefits.[32]

The army transferred soldiers from a variety of military specialties to the combat arms to provide additional replacements. The ETO drew from three sources in an effort to fill critical shortages: noninfantry replacements, men taken from overstrength units, and troops reassigned from COMZ and AAF units. As combat casualties grew, the theater vigorously retrained these soldiers as infantrymen and sent them to the front lines. Commanders everywhere seemed displeased with the retraining pro-

gram. Most division commanders preferred to receive infantry replacements from stateside than from the ETO's retraining centers, complaining
that soldiers released by the COMZ and AAF were of poorer quality than
those coming from the United States. Undoubtedly, both the COMZ and
AAF used the retraining program to clean house. Many troops transferred
to the infantry were undesirables. In April 1945 First Army complained
that of 514 retrained soldiers received from AAF, 231 had court-martial
convictions. Later that month an investigation revealed that 22 percent of
all AAF airmen transferred to the infantry had records of court-martial
conviction.[33]

The differences between peacetime training and actual combat was a
topic of interest to all soldiers. One of the common tendencies among officers approaching the fighting front, or reflecting back on their initial
fight, was to think of gaps in their training or what types of training would
have better prepared them for combat. Lt. Col. Dave Pergrin, whose 291st
Engineers built America's longest tactical treadway bridge at Remagen,
had a typical reaction upon seeing his first battlefield. He had trained his
battalion for eleven months, and on 23 June it entered the ETO across
Omaha Beach. Pergrin remembers that "only when I first set foot on
Omaha did it dawn on me that I might not have known enough, might
not have done enough."[34] George Wilson, a platoon leader in the 4th Division, vividly recalled his first hours in combat: "The shooting of my
first man, face-to-face, was not covered by the infantry school at Fort Benning, and I was deeply shaken. I'm glad I didn't kill him . . . I was still
trembling a few hours later. . . . My first hour in combat had been enough
for my lifetime, and I was wondering if I'd last the day."[35] Wilson later had
a chance to reflect on his first battle and believed the army's training was
"thorough and practical" but had "some serious gaps." The new lieutenant did not know enough about how to fight a unit reduced to half
strength by casualties, to recognize and treat combat exhaustion cases,
and to replace disabled leaders.[36]

Although the army had trained many of its divisions for as long as two
years with the full realization that they were headed for a combat zone,
the best efforts could not completely close the gap between training and
battle. Officers felt they had received adequate tactical training but
needed more instruction on leadership methods and how to train their
own soldiers. A majority of rifle company officers in three divisions preparing to deploy overseas felt they did not know enough about developing pride and motivation in soldiers or how to cope with troops' personal
problems. They also wanted more instruction on how to train troops on
specific soldier skills. They believed physical training and conditioning,
close order drill, and military courtesy and discipline were the strengths
of American training programs. The enlisted ranks were more thorough

and critical in evaluating training. A slim majority of combat veterans believed their overall training had been "about right," while 30 percent thought it had not been demanding enough. Most soldiers felt that field exercises with tough, realistic battle conditions, regular and rigorous physical fitness training, running obstacle courses, and long field marches of 25 miles with full field equipment best prepared them for battle. These activities reflected the broad consensus that the single best way to prepare a soldier for combat was to improve his stamina and physical strength.[37]

Veterans were quick to point out training shortcomings. Inadequate knowledge of the enemy was one of the army's greatest training deficiencies. Approximately 80 percent of soldiers said that they did not know enough about German weapons or how to defend against them. Knowledge of German tactics was deficient, and soldiers lacked training on how to attack various types of enemy defenses. Almost two-thirds of American soldiers felt they were weak on aircraft identification. Many veterans criticized their precombat training for not giving them enough exposure to live fire ammunition. Almost 90 percent of American soldiers indicated that they were unprepared for mine warfare. The detection and removal of mines and booby traps challenged units in the ETO and resulted in heavy losses in men and equipment. Veterans felt they did not know enough about how to deal with trench foot. Considering the army's heavy trench foot losses, it is no surprise that training on the prevention and treatment of the malady was one of the military's greatest training oversights.[38]

A broad consensus existed among enlisted men on the best and worst aspects of training. Soldiers felt that weapons training, instruction in seeking cover and concealment, how to stay dispersed and not bunch up, and skills in digging foxholes and defensive positions helped them the most. Soldiers held the view that close order drill, military courtesy, inspections, bayonet and hand-to-hand combat drills, and chemical warfare training had little relevance to their work on the battlefield. A paradox in soldiers' evaluations of training programs is that those areas in which officers felt training programs excelled—close order drill and military courtesy and discipline—were perceived by the troops as not very important in preparing them for combat. The opposing views probably reflected the officer corps' attitude that instilling discipline was a vital function of training programs, while the enlisted ranks tended to believe that the exclusive purpose of training was to teach them the specific skills required for combat.[39]

Actual combat revealed a number of defects in American battlefield performance. New units experiencing their baptism of fire in the ETO failed to follow close behind supporting artillery fire, tended to slow down upon initial enemy contact, and allowed German indirect fire to pin them down in the open. Tank-infantry cooperation was poor across the board but improved over time. Commanders put excessive emphasis on protecting their flanks and maintaining contact with adjacent outfits. Units put too much faith in artillery firepower and often failed to generate enough fire with their own organic weapons. The performance of individual soldiers indicated other training weaknesses. The tendency of soldiers to bunch together under fire was a universal complaint. American troops displayed carelessness in close proximity to the enemy and tended to expose their locations because of poor noise and light discipline.[40]

Commanders believed that their soldiers did not fire enough and that units needed better fire discipline and training in distributing fire throughout objective areas. Soldiers trained on known-distance rifle ranges found many reasons for not shooting in combat. Instead of placing fire in the general area of the objective, many wanted to identify specific targets before firing, while others preferred to remain under cover rather than exposing themselves while trying to get off a few shots. Some soldiers believed that firing at anything other than a good target was a waste of ammunition. Lt. Col. John A. Hentges, commander of the 3d Division's 7th Infantry, summed up the views of many as to why soldiers did not shoot enough:

> Our greatest need in training is to get riflemen to fire their weapons. New men will not fire. This is caused primarily by not wanting to disclose their position and inability to see the enemy or something to aim at. I believe our policy of putting so much of our basic weapon training on known distance ranges where men are cautioned so often on holding, squeezing and marking the target causes this.[41]

A training memorandum of the 78th Division told commanders that "new men must be told and re-indoctrinated" that aggressive fire kept the Germans pinned down and allowed their own units to advance. It reminded soldiers that "the M-1 and the BAR throw a lot of lead" and that "the unit that keeps firing intelligently" could always move on the battlefield.[42] Col. S. L. A. Marshall, one of the leading combat historians in the ETO, interviewed many units after engagements and came up with a surprising and controversial finding on infantry firepower. Marshall believed that in an "average experienced infantry company" only 15 percent of soldiers fired their weapons, while the best units under extreme, heavy combat managed to produce fire from 25 percent of all soldiers.[43]

The army adopted a technique known as "marching fire" to increase infantry firepower and aggressiveness. In attacks across open ground, infantry platoons deployed into skirmish lines with their BARs and light machine guns scattered along the line. The idea was for soldiers to keep pressing forward while throwing a wall of lead before them. Marching fire seemed most popular in Third Army. Patton told his soldiers:

> The proper way to advance . . . is to utilize marching fire and keep moving. . . . One round should be fired every two or three steps. The whistle of the bullets, the scream of the ricochet . . . have such an effect that his small arms fire becomes negligible.
> . . . the most foolish thing possible is to stop under such fire. Keep working forward . . . shooting adds to your self-confidence, because you are doing something.[44]

One battalion commander said he had never heard of marching fire until he "landed in Third Army." Advancing on the enemy with all guns blazing kept the Germans' heads down and prevented accurate counterfire. Soldiers' morale and confidence increased with the feeling that they were part of an attacking force pumping out "invincible fire" that smothered the enemy. One unit reported that marching fire "paid off 100 percent in diminishing casualties, improving self-confidence of our men, and enabling us to take many difficult objectives" and went on to add that "many men are really sold on this system of battle."[45]

The need to train soldiers in the theater of operations was not fully appreciated before the war but took on great importance as the fighting progressed. Training programs in the combat zone strove to repair weaknesses and to teach new skills needed on the battlefield. Four types of training programs emerged. Units preparing to attack certain types of German defenses conducted drills and rehearsals on the best way to assault the positions. Many divisions established rigorous, remedial training programs during rest periods or lulls in the fighting to fix problems identified in battle. Divisions also conducted refresher training for replacements. Last, soldiers reassigned from various military specialties to fill shortages in the combat arms required extensive retraining.

Stateside training programs that emphasized cross-country maneuvers did not prepare soldiers for the many types of close combat they faced in Europe. Although the army quickly improvised solutions to the problems encountered in close combat, units needed rehearsals and training on new tactics and techniques. Divisions in Normandy rehearsed novel hedgerow tactics while at the same time improving tank-infantry coordination. The 29th Division might not have captured St. Lo without the extensive rehearsals and training in hedgerow fighting the Blues and Grays conducted in early July. The 30th Division's training program on how to reduce German pillboxes made for much easier going against the

Siegfried Line in October. The 90th Division's success in the early stages of the river crossings at the Koenigsmacher bridgehead resulted from infantry-engineer refresher training in river crossing tactics. Almost every division in Europe conducted specialized training to further their success against a specific type of German defense.

The army learned several lessons as it tried to implement unit training programs. Division commanders realized that continuous combat induced a numbing fatigue and stress that dulled soldiers' physical and mental edges. Senior commanders realized that short breaks and refresher training could revitalize units, but they made several early mistakes. Division commanders initially rotated regiments off the front lines for remedial training but also designated them as a reserve or gave them a contingency mission, so commanders felt compelled to spend time preparing for their new missions rather than training. Battalions and regiments leaving the fight for short periods could not get far enough away from combat to concentrate solely on training. At first, units tended to go directly from combat into intensive training sessions, but tired, hungry, dirty soldiers had little enthusiasm for training. By the end of 1944 the army had corrected these problems, and whenever possible, entire divisions came off the line to train. Commanders also realized that clean, rested soldiers responded much better to training, so units tried to spend the first day or two off the front lines resting, feeding, and cleaning up.[46]

Several themes ran through division training programs, and tactical exercises at battalion level and below were common. Units put emphasis on receiving and issuing oral combat orders and rehearsing fire and maneuver tactics. If the division anticipated combat in a particular environment, such as pillbox positions, rivers, or dense forests, units prepared for these missions. Weapons firing was widespread with emphasis on training flamethrower, bazooka, and demolition teams. Divisions also conducted schools for officers and NCOs on reconnaissance and patrolling techniques, calling for artillery fire, and lessons recently learned in combat. A key goal of refresher training was to integrate replacements who had joined the division in combat. The army discovered that battle-torn divisions needed a minimum of ten days to recoup their fighting edge enough to perform basic missions.[47]

Commanders noticed that replacements needed remedial training on a variety of subjects, and many divisions began to give proficiency tests to new soldiers. Replacements knew how to fire their weapons but were short on weapons maintenance skills and correcting malfunctions. Knowledge in map reading and compass work was especially weak, and new soldiers did not know enough about handling prisoners or challenging with passwords. Strengths included the care of their personal equipment, first aid, and individual movement techniques. Divisions felt an obligation to give replacements remedial training before shoving them into battle. If a division was off the line or had a less demanding mission, it usually established a fixed training facility under the auspices of the division's operations staff.[48]

The quality and scope of division training centers varied greatly. The 83d Division administered two-and-a-half days of refresher training to all replacements. New troops were put into groups of twelve and given intensive training in digging foxholes, field sanitation, grenade practice, and weapons firing. The 104th Division ran one of the best division training centers under the close eye of its flamboyant commander, Maj. Gen. Terry Allen. Relieved of command of the 1st Division in Sicily, the mercurial Allen returned to Europe with the 104th "Timberwolf" Division. Whatever his other faults, he was a pragmatic combat soldier who realized the value of hard training, and the 104th's training site had a name commensurate with their commander's theatrical style—the Timberwolf Reinforcement Training Center. Allen's replacements went through ninety hours of intensive training over a twelve-day period. Weapons firing consumed a great portion of time, and other topics included squad tactics, scouting and patrolling, detection and removal of mines and booby traps, march discipline, and night maneuvers. Instructors spent considerable time answering replacements' questions about what combat was like and the common traits of German soldiers and equipment. Overall, division replacement training centers were one of the best training innovations devised in the ETO.[49]

While the army as an institution changed its ways of employing combat power, individual soldiers tried to adjust to life in the combat zone. Soldiers instinctively knew that increasing their own survivability and effectiveness would make the combined arms team more powerful and help hasten the war's end. A number of tremendous stresses faced soldiers on the battlefield: getting used to the notion of killing or being killed; the incessant presence of danger, noise, and confusion; living in a world of frustration and uncertainty; and having to always depend on others for personal safety and welfare. Veterans came to realize that the combat zone was a forbidding, tiring place, and constant threats to life and limb drained their mental stamina and will to fight. Lack of shelter, wetness, extreme hot or cold, filth, and sleep deprivation caused misery and mind-numbing fatigue. The loss of friends and the sights and sounds of the dead and wounded unnerved even the strongest. Isolation from loved ones, normal social activities, and female companionship bothered many soldiers. Conflicts between fundamental values—the paradox between morality and the horrors of war and loyalty between duty and friends—confused and distressed many soldiers. Soldiers had to learn to deal with all of these problems while pushing ahead against the enemy.

Without a doubt coping with fear was the greatest human challenge soldiers faced on the battlefield. During stateside training the army tried to
reduce adverse reactions from fear in three ways. Trainees underwent systematic psychological screening to weed out those mentally unfit for
combat, and about 10 percent of all draftees were rejected on psychiatric
grounds. The army also encouraged soldiers to take a permissive attitude
toward their own symptoms of fear. Soldiers were taught that feeling
afraid in dangerous situations was not shameful and that fear was normal
and felt by everyone. Training stressed that even though a man felt fear he
could overcome it and that eventually the symptoms of fear would
abate.[50] A handbook issued to all trainees conveyed these notions in easy-
to-understand language:

> YOU'LL BE SCARED. Sure you'll be scared. Before you go into battle,
> you'll be frightened at the uncertainty, at the thought of being
> killed. . . . If you say you're not scared, you'll be a cocky fool.
> Don't let anyone tell you you're a coward if you admit being scared.
> Fear before you're actually in the battle is a normal emotional reac-
> tion. . . . After you've become used to the picture and the sensations
> of the battlefield, you will change. All the things you were taught in
> training will come back to you. . . . That first fight—that fight with
> yourself—will have gone. Then you will be ready to fight the en-
> emy.[51]

Last, the army tried to reduce the disruptive effects of fear by ingraining
soldiers with automatic responses to certain kinds of dangers and exposing them to simulated battle conditions. Instructors drilled trainees time
and time again on how to clear weapons malfunctions, don gas masks,
"hit the dirt" when taken under fire, move with "your head down," and
dozens of other reflex responses to danger. Trainees had to crawl over
rough ground for about 80 yards with live machine-gun bullets clipping
over their heads. Sometimes the army exposed infantry trainees to close
artillery shelling to give them a feel for the noise and concussion of exploding rounds. The efficacy of such steps is hard to measure, but veterans believed that more exposure to fear in training would have better
prepared them for combat.[52]

On the front lines, commanders saw that fear and anxiety before battle
were just as great as when bullets began to fly, and officers and NCOs
learned specific leadership techniques to reduce fear before it overwhelmed their troops. Before combat, soldiers tended to multiply and exaggerate the unknown dangers that lay ahead. Almost 70 percent of veterans admitted to worrying about becoming a casualty in the next fight.
Commanders counteracted prebattle fear by giving soldiers as much in-

Soldiers had to adjust to the fear and confusion of small unit actions and other battlefield realities. Infantrymen of the 89th Division crouch low in their assault boat to avoid enemy fire during a river crossing. (U.S. Army)

formation as they could about the tactical situation while explaining their battle plans in detail. Leaders appealed to teamwork and cooperation, the sense of responsibility for the welfare of others, unit pride, the hope of winning and going home, and hatred for the enemy. However, commanders discovered that troops did not respond well to patriotic appeals, and though humor worked to dispel fear, those in charge learned to never joke about death or wounds. Leaders making promises they could not keep—telling soldiers the fight would be over in a few days or promising a rest period after the battle—created morale problems. Officers learned that they could not threaten or browbeat soldiers into overcoming fear and that it was impossible to talk rationally to men panicked or hysterical with fear. Soldiers preparing for battle did not have time to dwell on their anxieties, so leaders kept them busy with weapons and equipment maintenance and inspections. Commanders talked informally with troops and found that humor, encouragement, prayer, and talking about any variety of subjects diverted attention from the dangers ahead.[53]

Training could not introduce soldiers to stark fear, so they felt the physical symptoms of fear for the first time in battle. The most common physiological sign of fear experienced by roughly 80 percent of troops was violent pounding of the heart. A majority of soldiers also felt a "sinking feeling" in the stomach, shaking or trembling of the hands and body, cold sweat, and nausea. Fewer than 20 percent of soldiers admitted to losing control of their bowels, another 10 percent said that they urinated in their pants, and runaway bodily functions may have been even more common.[54] A new replacement was next to a veteran when a German 88 fired on them. The older sergeant swore, and the new troop asked him if he was hit:

> He sort of smiled and said no, he had just pissed his pants. He always pissed them, he said, when things started and then he was okay . . . and then I realized something wasn't quite right with me. . . . There was something warm down there and it seemed to be running down my leg . . . I told the sarge. I said, "Sarge, I've pissed too," or something like that and he grinned and said, "Welcome to the war."[55]

A survey of 277 wounded in the ETO revealed that some symptom of fear at one time or another kept 65 percent of them from performing adequately, and almost half admitted recurring incidents of disruptive fear reactions.[56]

Training did not prepare soldiers for coping with the fear of enemy weapons. Enemy machine guns and mines inflicted heavy casualties, but Americans' familiarity with the weapons made them less fearful. GIs identified the 88-mm gun, German aircraft, and mortars as the most fearful weapons they faced. Soldiers seemed to respect most the weapons they could not hear coming or take protection against, and they linked fear with a weapon's noise. Enemy machine guns had a high cyclic rate of fire that Americans said sounded like a sheet being torn in two, while their own machine guns had a slower, thumping rhythm. A weapon that struck widespread fear was the German Nebelwerfer, a mobile, multibarreled rocket launcher that induced fear not from its accuracy or ordnance, but because its shells made a terrifying, moaning noise in flight. Soldiers learned to detect the accuracy of incoming artillery from the noise of the shells in flight. Veterans came to fear German mortars more because their shells exploded without warning. Over time, fear of weapons often changed to healthy respect as soldiers got used to enemy weapons, listened for approaching dangers, and learned to take cover.[57]

Despite the army's best efforts to provide realistic training, soldiers still had to learn fundamental survival lessons and were quick to discover ways to stay alive in combat. Veterans stated emphatically that staying put under fire was one of the best ways to get killed. Soldiers had to overcome the tendency to freeze upon initial enemy contact, and units learned to minimize casualties by moving quickly through preplanned mortar and artillery fire and by maneuvering aggressively against enemy defenses. The Germans tended to return fire when fired upon, so troops learned to use reconnaissance by fire to detect enemy positions at long range. Soldiers stressed the importance of proper cover and concealment and taught replacements to avoid open fields, roads, and paths. The easiest route forward was often the quickest way to get killed or wounded. Soldiers learned to dig deep foxholes—two feet or more to provide adequate protection—and to get some type of overhead cover against shell fragments. Despite warnings that they had to stay dispersed under fire, soldiers sought mutual protection by crowding together during engagements.[58] A wounded rifleman warned, "The minute you bunch up they let you have it. Men bunch up for company. When you get into battle you just naturally want to get close—but we learned the hard way—don't bunch."[59] Soldiers learned better light and noise discipline to avoid giving away their positions. Riflemen tried to remain calm when wounded because panicked shouting and thrashing about endangered themselves and the lives of others nearby. New troops learned that the Germans often booby-trapped abandoned weapons and tempting souvenirs. Moving forward to take custody of surrendering Germans could be hazardous, and Americans learned always to make prisoners come to them. Soldiers also developed a wariness for overly friendly civilians.[60]

The maintenance of troop morale in fighting units was one of the army's greatest concerns. Soldiers with high morale had a zeal to accomplish tasks, a discipline that allowed them to subordinate individual interests to those of the group, a confidence in themselves and their equipment, and an absence of discontent and worry regarding their duty position and role in combat. Soldiers with low morale were lethargic and ineffective, had discipline problems, and contributed little on the combined arms battlefield. Mental anxiety was perhaps the greatest cause of low morale. The army learned that war fostered worries that could drain a soldier's working and fighting efficiency. Troops thousands of miles from home, living and fighting under heartbreaking and nerve-wracking conditions, worried about immediate problems and the welfare of loved ones at home. Common concerns among officers and enlisted men included being gone from the United States for long periods, family matters at home, and the overall progress of the war. Footsoldiers seemed to worry about very practical matters: their overall mental and physical health, fear of wounds or death, the uncertainties that came with each day on the front lines, and a concern that America might not achieve its war aims. Officers tended to worry more about the future than the present and about how they would resume normal lives and careers after the war.[61]

Commanders on the front lines learned that they could do much to maintain esprit. Soldiers responded readily to measures that promoted teamwork, unit pride, and improved officer-enlisted relations. Soldiers respected and followed leaders who looked after their needs, and boasts from troops that they had "a damn good company commander and a fine first sergeant" were one of the best indicators of high morale. Teamwork existed in units where officers led by example, enlisted men cooperated with one another, and everyone pulled together to get through tough times. Leaders who remained calm under fire and maintained a sense of humor fostered high morale. Efforts to give soldiers adequate meals, shelter, rest, and recreation whenever possible also paid great dividends, while the absence of any or all of these conditions made morale suffer. A thoroughly trained, physically fit soldier with high morale responded to training, maintained discipline during periods of quiet and boredom, and performed well in battle.[62]

The army's greatest cause of low morale was far beyond the power of frontline commanders to repair: extended periods overseas and the lack of a rotation policy for ground soldiers. As units moved across France combat troops came to realize that only peace, wounds, or death would bring release from the war's burdens. Veteran infantrymen believed they had done their part and that others should come forward to assume their share of the burden. Soldiers began to talk about the "million dollar wound," one serious enough to require evacuation to rear areas or even stateside but inflicting no permanent disfigurement or injury.[63]

Officers detected a distinct lack of animosity for the enemy among their troops, and postwar surveys revealed that Americans had fairly moderate attitudes toward enemy troops and the German people. A substantial minority of soldiers admitted that some hatred for the Germans motivated them in combat, but most soldiers were not vindictive. More than half the riflemen in one division in Europe admitted that viewing enemy prisoners close up made them realize that Germans were "men just like us" and that it was "too bad we have to be fighting them."[64] The War Department seemed appalled by American soldiers' tepid feelings of hatred and cautioned commanders, "Many soldiers who lack vindictiveness are probably standing on the shaky ground of too much identification with the enemy as a human being. . . . These men need to be convinced that America's very survival depends upon killing the enemy with cold, impersonal determination, that the enemy must be destroyed if America is to live."[65] Despite the army's desire to perpetuate hatred for the enemy, about two-thirds of American soldiers believed that after the war the Allies should punish Nazi leaders but not the German people.[66]

Outside the parameters of combat, behavior between Americans and Germans ranged from savagery to compassion. Only 13 percent of a sample of riflemen from Europe observed atrocities, but sometimes Americans found it difficult not to kill their enemies in the heat of passion. At Brest a German sniper shot a medic square in the center of the red cross on his helmet, so infantrymen avenged his death by refusing to take prisoners for the next several hours. North of Aachen a surrendering German officer killed a soldier of the 30th Division with a concealed pistol. The other members of the platoon threw the officer against a pillbox, killed him with a volley from almost every one of their weapons, and then continued the attack. Not all captured Germans made it into PW handling channels, and some rifle companies developed reputations for taking few prisoners. At the other end of the spectrum, opposing forces often held short truces to evacuate the dead and the wounded. In the midst of the gruesome fighting in the Huertgen Forest, German troops blocking the 28th Division's supply line along the Kall Trail let medical vehicles and stretcher teams pass unharmed.[67]

The high number of incidents in which small numbers of isolated Germans and Americans encountered one another without firing a shot was one of the more peculiar aspects of soldiers' behavior. When small groups unexpectedly ran into one another at close quarters, both sides tended to back off quickly without firing a shot and to go about their business somewhere else.[68] During the Battle of the Bulge, two American riflemen moving through the woods came upon a line of skirmishers moving in the opposite direction. One of the soldiers remembers:

> I say to Carl, "Hey, look at the long overcoats." Carl turns, takes one quick look, and says, "Oh, my God, those are Germans!" . . . I whisper "What do we do now?" And Carl, he was an old-timer, says to me, "Don, we don't do nothing, we just keep going." They passed us, we passed them. I think both [Carl] Bauer and I were scared stiff. I know I was. We kept this to ourselves, we never told anyone.[69]

Soldiers on both sides seemed to believe that killing one another as a result of a meaningless, unexpected encounter was folly. They tended to save their hostilities for days when they could fight as a unit and when their killing might have some bearing on the war's outcome.

If American soldiers were unemotional about the enemy, they also held sober attitudes toward their own work. Soldiers viewed the war in pragmatic terms and rarely discussed the broader values and principles for which they were fighting. All across Europe, Americans manned guns, drove vehicles, and marched against the enemy with a matter-of-fact attitude toward the fighting. They faced combat with grim determination. During the bloody fighting in the Huertgen Forest, a group of squad leaders in the 4th Division received another attack order from their platoon leader. When the lieutenant finished, an awkward silence fell over the men. One sergeant stood up with his rifle, said "Well, we can't do a damn thing sitting here," and walked away to get his men ready for the attack.

Soldiers agonized over losses but rarely celebrated their victories. Those decorated for valor seldom dwelled on their heroics and believed that any other man would have done the same under similar circumstances. After the crossing of the Rhine a correspondent approached Sgt. Alex Drabik, the first man over the Remagen bridge, to get the sensational details of the crossing. When the reporter asked several questions about the bridge's capture, Drabik summed up his part by saying, "All I know is that we took it."[70]

An attack by one rifle company of the 84th Division experienced much of what hundreds of other units faced throughout the ETO. In mid-November the 84th Division held the extreme left flank of the Ninth Army's sector with the mission of reducing the northern portion of the West Wall. Company K, 333d Infantry, operated on the division's far left in a narrow sector that included the west bank of the Wurm River. On 19 November the 333d Infantry captured the large town of Geilenkirchen. Company K followed close behind to help clear the town and then moved beyond it into forward attack positions. The sweep through the town was the company's first minor combat action.[71]

The real baptism of fire came at noon on 21 November when Company K attacked beyond Geilenkirchen. Under the leadership of Capt. George Gieszl, the soldiers pushed forward against light opposition. Three tanks from the British Sherwood Forest Yeomanry Regiment provided armor support and gave the Americans their initial experience in tank-infantry coordination. The company captured its first objective of the war in the form of Chateau Leerodt, a large, three-story brick building with an inner courtyard. After spending thirty minutes clearing the chateau and reorganizing, they pushed forward again. The line of infantrymen advanced fifty yards beyond the chateau when the Germans opened up with an artillery and mortar bombardment that overwhelmed the green troops with its "violence, surprise, and intensity." Machine-gun fire from distant pillboxes and shells from 88s added to the fury. One soldier remembered that nothing had prepared them for the noise and shock of the battlefield or for the loss of control, bewilderment, and the sense of total helplessness it induced. Riflemen clawed frantically into the wet ground to create shallow trenches. During the bombardment, soldiers noticed the differences in sounds between types of ordnance: the whistle of artillery shells gave a few seconds advance notice before impact, mortar rounds were almost silent, and shells from 88s could not be heard until they had already passed. Before long Company K had suffered a dozen casualties, and Captain Gieszl ordered his platoons to fall back slowly toward the chateau.

After some time to regroup, the company attacked again at 1600 hours. The bombardment had taught everyone the value of pushing forward and not stopping. Gieszl told his troops to keep moving, to reorganize on the run, and not to bunch up. When they attacked the second time, the Germans answered with a mortar volley. But now the company rushed through the Germans' preplanned fires with ease, as most of the shells fell just behind the advancing troops. The company pushed forward several hundred yards, and around nightfall took up defensive positions in a marsh thick with underbrush. Soon German flares illuminated the marsh with an eerie, green glow, while mortars delivered a methodical pounding and thousands of machine-gun bullets whipped through the underbrush. Soldiers tried to dig in on the marshy ground but struck water. The night became colder, the wind more intense, and a stinging rain began to fall. Gieszl realized that any forward movement was impossible and received permission to withdraw to the protection of Chateau Leerodt.

The company's overnight stay at the chateau brought many incidents typical of the fighting throughout Europe. Medics tended the wounded as the infantrymen dug in. Company K suffered its first combat exhaustion case when one soldier broke down hysterical with fear. A friend tried to console him but with no success. Another remembered he was torn between sympathy for the soldier's hysteria and disdain for his inability to control fear. A second soldier soon succumbed to combat exhaustion and begged a rifleman to shoot him in the leg to get him off the front lines. Around midnight another soldier put himself out of action with a self-inflicted wound. Because many men had lain in water-filled holes in the marsh, the company lost twelve men to trench foot. The supply sergeant managed to come forward in the dark with ammunition and three replacements, one of whom was hit the next day. Captain Gieszl received word that Company K was to attack again the next day because division headquarters had ordered the final objective to be taken "at all costs." The division also passed down a new directive: "Henceforth all commanders are prohibited from using the term 'pinned down' in situation reports." Reflecting on his first day in combat, Gieszl laughed at the new policy, called it "crap," and then went about preparing for the next day's fight.

After sunrise a thundering artillery barrage shook the German positions. When the shelling lifted, Company K attacked for the third time. The bombardment did the trick, as Gieszl's men advanced over the open ground and through the swamp where they had suffered the previous day. Resistance stiffened as the advance neared the small village of Kogenbroich, and the riflemen began to encounter mines and German log emplacements among a series of hedgerows. In the heat of battle one American whose best friend had just been killed shot four German prisoners, claiming they had tried to escape. By late afternoon Company K had captured and cleared Kogenbroich. The soldiers were soon on the attack again, but before long they encountered stout defenses. Captain Gieszl was anxious to keep the attack moving and to reach his final objective. The company commander managed to get some machine guns forward, but they had little effect. Gieszl sensed that his unit was bogging down, and that the time had come for decisive action. Before anyone realized it, the company commander raised to a half-crouch and charged the German position. He made it about 20 feet before he went down wounded. Lt. Harold Linebaugh took command and assembled the company's leaders, while others crawled out and pulled Captain Gieszl to safety. Linebaugh outlined several courses of actions to the other officers and senior NCOs, then they took a vote. The new commander realized that it "was not the approved way to make a military decision" but he wanted full support for the decision. Everyone believed a limited withdrawal was best, so under the cover of darkness Company K pulled back to Kogenbroich and settled in for the night.

Over the next few days the company supported other attacking units, and on the night of 24 November received orders to pull back to Geilenkirchen for rest and reorganization. After coming off the front lines, the men began to feel pride in their first action and to realize what a beating they had taken. In six days of battle Company K suffered eleven men killed and forty-two wounded. Eighteen others had been evacuated for sickness, trench foot, combat exhaustion, and self-inflicted wounds, and two were reported missing. Losses occurred in all ranks. The commander and one lieutenant fell wounded, and two of the four original platoon sergeants were gone as well as their replacements. Some of the company's staff sergeants were killed or wounded, along with six squad leaders, and many privates now led remnants of their original squads. Nearly half of the riflemen in the rank of private who had jumped off in the first attack on Chateau Leerodt did not make it back to the rest area in Geilenkirchen. In its first major combat action, Company K, 333d Infantry, suffered almost 40 percent casualties, a rate not especially high for the severe fighting in Europe.

Company K's experience was typical of the first combat action of many infantry units. Soldiers were quick to adapt to the realities of combat, and they realized that training had not fully prepared them for all of the sights and sounds of battle. They learned to listen for incoming shells and discovered that the best way to avoid enemy barrages was to keep advancing. Captain Gieszl tried the "follow me" leadership style, for which he paid a heavy personal price, and the company attack stalled soon after his loss. Casualties were heavy and came from a variety of sources: bullets, shell fragments, trench foot, and combat exhaustion. Troops had to endure the miseries of rain and mud. The savagery of war surfaced when a soldier killed four German prisoners out of revenge. Replacements showed up in the middle of the night, probably unsure of their location, new unit, or tactical situation, and one fell wounded the next day. Most of the 1,242 rifle companies that served in the ETO shared many of the same experiences Company K went through north of Geilenkirchen.

In retrospect, the army's philosophy of getting the war over with as quickly as possible while inflicting maximum damage on the Germans and minimizing its own casualties motivated much of what went on in the ETO. Soldiers knew the only way to get the war over and go home was through hard fighting. When Creighton Abrams stood on the west bank of the Moselle River at Dieulouard and told his superiors that the shortest way to end the war and go home was to attack and capture the hills on the far bank, his words personified the attitudes of most soldiers. Americans stayed on the offensive as much as logistical constraints and the enemy situation would allow. GIs closed with the enemy with a sense of grim determination but without developing a consuming hatred for their opponents.

The army excelled in inflicting maximum damage on the Germans. Merely throwing troops and ordnance at the enemy could be costly and wasteful, and the army discovered the best ways to coordinate and synchronize firepower and maneuver for maximum affect. Corps and division commanders learned new ways to combine and concentrate fire support with ground maneuver, and the better integration of CAS into ground engagements greatly enhanced the combined arms team's combat power. Firepower sought to eliminate the enemy and reduce friendly casualties, and when it failed to achieve its purpose, ground units finished the job. Often fighting at close quarters, soldiers used point-blank heavy-caliber fire, explosives, and other weapons to demolish enemy defenses and inflict the greatest number of casualties.

The army adapted several measures meant to minimize losses and to husband soldiers' physical and mental stamina. The flow of replacements and retrainees, as well as divisional and theater training programs, attempted to sustain the drive toward Germany. Leadership based on trust rather than discipline kept soldiers motivated, and commanders discovered techniques that dispelled fear and maintained morale. The army implemented better ways of preventing and treating cold weather injuries and combat exhaustion but with mixed results. Soldiers learned to keep moving under fire, to dig deep, and to watch and listen for enemy weapons as the best techniques for reducing casualties. Aggressive use of organic weapons revealed enemy positions and kept the Germans' heads down.

The army used both centralized and collective problem-solving processes while attempting to repair defects in the utilization and employment of manpower. Senior leaders engaged the problems of the Replacement System, hoping to allocate resources and implement changes that would better preserve the fighting spirit of soldiers and make the network less impersonal. The ETO realized the magnitude of losses in infantry units and developed large retraining programs designed to produce more riflemen. Divisions identified problems with the proficiency level of replacements and instituted their own training centers free from the direction and control of higher headquarters. The prevention and treatment of combat exhaustion saw both improvised and directed efforts, as commanders and physicians in fighting units learned to watch for the early signs and discovered that sleep, food, and morphine usually relieved symptoms. At the same time, the ETO organized new, separate treatment and evacuation channels for soldiers with more severe cases. Commanders experimented with new tactics and techniques for concentrating combat power by channeling ground attacks and massing firepower against narrow sectors of the enemy's front. Soldiers on the front lines took the initiative in developing techniques to avoid casualties, to cope with fear and the many dangers of battle, and to make themselves more effective fighters.

As soldiers improvised better weapons and tactics for combined arms operations, they discovered more effective ways of using their own minds and bodies, changes that resulted in significant improvements to the combined arms team that were just as important as technical or tactical innovations. Any broader conclusions on the successes of American soldiers must be made within the framework of the entire war effort and the lessons learned during the battles of 1944–1945.

CHAPTER TEN

The Schoolhouse of War

Here lie the bones of Lieutenant Jones,
A graduate of this institution,
He died on the night of his very first fight,
While using the school solution.
                    —*Epitaph on a tombstone in a mock cemetery at*
                    the U.S. Army Infantry School, Fort Benning,
                    Georgia, 1944

In early 1942 a construction project of almost unparalleled size unfolded on the west bank of the Potomac River, not far from Arlington National Cemetery. As many as 13,000 workers labored around-the-clock to complete a behemoth of a building capable of accommodating America's rapidly expanding military nerve center. The massive structure did not have a name yet, but the world would come to know it as the Pentagon. Not far from the construction site, 300 architects in an abandoned airplane hangar toiled over the building's floor plans. Architects and construction workers raced to stay ahead of one another, and construction foremen were seen snatching blueprints from drafting tables before architects could finish their work. One day a puzzled designer asked a fellow architect, "How big should I make that beam across the third floor?" The other man looked at the blueprint, said he was not sure, and suggested that the best way to find out was to walk over to the Pentagon and look at the beam because workmen had installed it the day before. Despite such confusion, workers completed the Pentagon in early 1943, the largest office building in the world, capable of holding 40,000 people but conceived, funded, designed, and constructed in little more than a year.[1]

The Pentagon construction project is an apt metaphor for America's military effort in World War II. The raising and deployment of major field forces was a project almost without precedent that sometimes defied central planning or succeeded in spite of it. If architects drawing plans for the Pentagon sometimes fell behind construction workers, so too did the military staffs that eventually occupied the monster headquarters building fail to keep pace with what was going on in the overseas theaters. One of the major reasons American soldiers did well in World War II is that when they faced unexpected challenges on the battlefield, they needed little guidance from higher headquarters on what to do. Soldiers were quick to learn, adapt, and improvise and to get on with the fighting. Construction workers did not need completed blueprints from architects to finish the Pentagon, and neither did American soldiers require much guidance from their superiors on the best ways to go about defeating the enemy.

Any analysis of army operations in World War II must be made within the context of the tremendous growth and expansion of the ground forces. On 1 January 1941, the authorized strength of what eventually became the AGF stood at 356,000 troops; by 31 January 1945, the AGF had grown 760 percent and achieved a troop strength of 2.7 million men. The effort to get troops overseas was staggering. AGF training centers handled 2.1 million new soldiers, while the service schools conducted specialized training for 108,000 officers and 229,000 enlisted men. During the mobilization for war the army activated 3,800 ground units with an authorized enlisted strength of 1.7 million men. Between 9 March 1942 and 28 February 1945, the AGF sent 5,900 units with an aggregate strength of 2.1 million men to ports of embarkation and during the same period shipped out 36,900 officer and 726,000 enlisted replacements. In addition to managing vast pools of manpower, the AGF developed, modified, accepted, or rejected over 10,000 items of equipment. The army shipped 89 divisions overseas, and all but one saw combat. Between 6 June 1944 and 8 May 1945, an average of 5,000 Americans per day entered the Continent. When the Germans capitulated, American ground forces in Europe included 61 divisions and all their supporting units, giving the ETO a standing strength of 1,703,613 soldiers.[2]

One of the army's greatest advantages in World War II was the validity of its conceptual approach to waging war. Commanders discovered that the army's offensive and defensive doctrines were correct, and that success hinged on how well senior commanders applied doctrine to specific circumstances. After the war a special board of general officers reported:

> The tactical doctrines and principles set forth in *Field Service Regulations* and in various service manuals were proved successful in combat. Operations in the European Theater emphasized the fact that basic doctrines of troop leading and staff functioning as outlined in our service manuals and as taught in our service schools are correct . . . the degree of success attained continues to be dependent upon the ability of the individual commanders to apply these doctrines properly.[3]

Commanders in the ETO fought with the confidence that their approach toward operations was correct. When unique problems arose, successful commanders applied doctrine with flexibility, combined it with their own training and judgment, and produced effective solutions.

Sound doctrine gave the Americans another significant advantage. Because the army did not have to devise and learn a whole new approach to battle, it was able to expend time and resources fixing internal shortcomings and problems. Combat formations concentrated on improving their battlefield performance rather than significantly revising their broad approach to operations. Because the need for changes was usually at the tactical level of war, local commanders were in a good position to identify problems and find solutions. They focused on fixing problems with tank-infantry coordination, air-ground operations, employment of TD units, the prevention and treatment of excessive cold weather and combat exhaustion casualties, and the broad spectrum of problems posed by German defenses. If the army had been unable to orient all its efforts on institutional and tactical problem-solving, the war might have turned out differently or continued on for much longer.

No military establishment can assume that its doctrine is correct. During the twentieth century, several armies have suffered because of flawed doctrine. In the opening stages of World War I the French and the Germans relied on offensive doctrines that machine guns, trenches, and barbed wire rendered invalid. Both sides had difficulty devising tactical alternatives to trench warfare. The Germans initially made good gains with infiltration tactics, while the Allies restored mobility to the battlefield with the combined arms team. In 1940 the French remained bound to the slower battlefield tempo of the First World War, as the German blitzkrieg outpaced the French army and destroyed the Third Republic. After 1945 several armies had problems devising effective doctrine to counter insurgencies and "wars of national liberation." The American army began World War II with sound doctrines and did not have to endure the trauma of revising its approach to war while at the same time mobilizing, deploying, and fighting large field forces.

Although an army's tactics must be consistent with its broad approach to waging war, doctrine does not impart to soldiers the specific techniques that they should use on the battlefield, especially when confronting unique problems. Americans applied doctrinal tenets with flexibility or violated them entirely while improvising new combat formations and tactics. Corps and division commanders devised better ways of massing troops and firepower together in strong attacks against prepared defenses. Regimental and battalion commanders adapted flexible, columnar formations that permitted maximum command and control and the massing of combat power. Forced together among the confines of the Normandy hedgerows, units went beyond doctrine to develop better tactics for tank-infantry coordination. While attacking village strongholds, Americans developed sophisticated combined arms techniques that became the basis for the army's modern fire and maneuver tactics. During urban and forest combat and the attack of fortifications, units rejected normal formations and reorganized into assault and support teams. Techniques that had American soldiers moving from building to building instead of down city streets, attacking the rear rather than the front of fortifications, and bypassing forest strongholds all violated doctrine but worked well in practice. The attack of rivers convinced commanders to amend doctrine, and they emplaced heavy bridging early and put antitank capabilities into bridgeheads as quickly as possible. On the defense, Americans surpassed doctrine to integrate the combat arms into a more effective team. Without a coordinated combined arms defense, the army might not have stopped the Germans in the Ardennes. Doctrine failed to describe air-ground operations in any detail, yet soldiers and airmen worked together to integrate tactical air power into ground combat in ways unheard of before the war.

Technical improvisation also abounded in the ETO. Soldiers discovered new devices as well as better ways of employing standard weapons. In the bocage, hedgerow cutters and back deck telephones solved mobility and communication problems. A host of innovations resulted in better air support. Air and ground units found new ways to mark enemy targets and identify friendly troops. Enhanced radio communications between air and ground FACs and bomber and fighter-bomber formations improved coordination and command and control. In river crossings, commanders discovered the benefits of screening crossing and bridging sites with smoke generators. Aerial artillery observers performed brilliantly in bringing fire on German units and in counterbattery work. Improvements in photo reconnaissance provided ground commanders with better tactical intelligence. Tanks and tank destroyers performed well in providing both close-quarters and long-range fire support. TD battalions also fought effectively in an artillery role, and on occasion point-blank self-propelled artillery fire eliminated stubborn defenses. Firepower from antiaircraft artillery battalions shooting in a ground mode supported river crossings and played an important defensive role in the Battle of the Bulge. Soldiers learned how well reconnaissance by fire revealed enemy positions, and bazookas and explosives at close quarters became an important part of battlefield techniques.

Not only did the army expand rapidly to meet global missions, but forces modernized at the same time. The flow of modern weapons into units added to the need for tactical and technical adaptations. The U.S. infantry-based army of World War I had to learn very quickly how to integrate tanks, armored cavalry, TDs, and CAS into battle plans. In retrospect, it is hard to believe that infantry formations of 1944 had very little training or experience with armored forces, and in many cases, battlefield commanders were the first to develop the specific tactics and techniques for armored and mechanized warfare. The first time infantry and armored forces had to fight closely together was in the bocage, and the new combined arms tactics developed in Normandy set the standard for tank-infantry cooperation for the remainder of the war. Even in armored divisions, there was considerable experimentation to determine the best methods for employing tanks and armored infantry. The development of new TD forces and technological improvements in communications and aircraft demanded changes in the use of antitank assets and air-ground operations. A myriad of other modern weapons and equipment required additional changes in combined arms tactics and techniques.

The army's problem-solving processes had a number of common characteristics. First, the army put no restrictions on the source of new ideas, and contributions came from enlisted ranks, officers, and generals alike. The best example of a single soldier's influence on battlefield adaptation was Sergeant Culin's hedgecutter invention, while General Quesada's commitment to finding better ways to bring air power to bear personifies the contributions of general officers. The army promoted initiative and problem solving at the lowest level. Rarely dictating the use of new tactics or ways to employ weapons, corps, army, and army group headquarters instead provided subordinate units with ideas and information and then held subordinate commanders responsible for getting things done. Commanders incapable of overcoming the enemy or resolving internal problems usually did not last long. All innovations and ideas shared the same purpose—to inflict maximum damage on the Germans while minimizing U.S. casualties and getting the war over with as quickly as possible.

If the army excelled in tactical and technical improvisation, it performed equally well in disseminating new ideas and lessons learned. Formal and informal channels carried information between units. Within battalions and regiments, new ideas probably traveled best by word of mouth. Divisions constantly produced training bulletins to get information to soldiers on methods and techniques that worked well in battle. They also published elaborate training memoranda, complete with diagrams and explanatory notes, telling subordinate commanders how to train and implement new tactics. It was common for divisions to publish small booklets that contained the unit history, leadership philosophy, and combat tips. The booklets went to every soldier in the division and were small enough to fit in their shirt pockets. Corps and divisions put on demonstrations and rehearsals for officers so that they could actually see the workings of new tactics. During lulls or rest periods, some divisions took officers on staff rides over ground they had just fought on to hammer home the lessons of recent combat.

At army level and higher, the sharing of lessons learned became more structured. Almost from the beginning, higher headquarters gave subordinate units as much information as they could on successful tactical methods. First Army published a series of "Battle Experiences" in Normandy. Each report was a few pages in length and contained succinct advice on German defensive tactics and the lessons Americans were learning on the battlefield. A masthead on each document told First Army units: " 'Battle Experiences' will be published regularly by this headquarters to enable units in training to profit from the latest combat experience of our troops now fighting the Germans in France . . . the items published will be those based on practical experience and are recommended for careful consideration by units which may encounter similar problems."[4] First Army published the first "Battle Experiences" on 12 July 1944 and issued twelve more reports by 1 August. The 12th Army Group took the lead in disseminating combat lessons upon its activation in early August and by November 1944 had issued seventy-seven more of its own "Battle Experiences." ETO Headquarters also produced a series of "Battle Experiences" between July 1944 and April 1945. Perhaps the best example of the ETO's ability to disseminate lessons learned occurred after the guns fell silent. On 17 June 1945, the ETO established a special General Board of general officers and experienced commanders whose purpose was "to prepare a factual analysis of the strategy, tactics, and administration employed by the United States forces in the European Theater." By the time it had fulfilled the provisions of its charter, the General Board had produced 131 authoritative reports on almost every aspect of the army's efforts. Copies of the reports were distributed throughout Europe, AGF Headquarters, and the entire army schools system.[5]

The highest echelons of command took a great interest in gathering and distributing battlefield lessons. AGF Headquarters used a wide network of combat observers to gather information for the War Department on the performance of troops and equipment. The information helped to link together divisions fighting overseas with the War Department, the army's schools system, and units training for overseas deployment. By the end of the war AGF observers in Europe had sent back over 1,500 reports filled with the details of combat in the Mediterranean and European theaters. The War Department's Operations Division published thirty-two issues of an "Information Bulletin" to inform senior commanders of the lessons learned in other theaters. The War Department told commanders the material did not constitute authority to depart from established doctrine but did encourage them to use the information to adjust doctrinal tenets to fit local circumstances. A second set of Operations Division publications, small booklets entitled *Combat Lessons*, provided individual soldiers with tactical information. The first issue appeared in early 1944, and eight more followed about once a month until the summer of 1945. *Combat*

Lessons communicated ideas, tips, and soldiers' experiences in authentic, easy to understand prose and hammered home concepts with caricatures and photos. Other War Department publications covered a wide variety of topics on the organization of the German army and the enemy's weapons and equipment.[6]

Tactical adaptation, technical innovation, the dissemination of lessons learned, and experience allowed the army to achieve unparalleled levels of professional competence. As the separate combat arms learned to use their own weapons and tactics more effectively, improvements in combined arms operations significantly enhanced the army's combat power. As units moved across Europe, tank-infantry coordination improved, TDs took on new combat roles, and CAS became a deadly combined arms partner. Artillery-infantry cooperation became even more responsive and powerful. Engineers were competent at mine warfare and in emplacing obstacles and bridging and gained a reputation as tough fighters when committed as infantry. Individual soldiers learned the best ways to survive and to keep fighting day after day.

The aggregate effect of all these changes was to bring victory quicker and with fewer casualties. By late 1944 improved combined arms operations enabled the army to carry the war to the enemy with maximum affect. To compare the performance of units in North Africa with the battles in the Ardennes is to analyze the actions of two very different armies. The experience and knowledge levels of the leaders of 1942 probably would not have been up to the tasks that confronted the defenders of Bastogne. Coordinating a perimeter defense of infantrymen with tanks, TDs, and artillery from as many as three different divisions while at the same time orchestrating CAS and aerial resupply into the battle would have probably confounded the prewar officer corps. The complexity of combined arms operations at the Remagen bridgehead, with the simultaneous employment of tank, TD, infantry, artillery, engineer and antiaircraft units, is another case in point.

By the spring of 1945 coordinated combined arms battles were the norm. One company commander in the 2d Division recalled his battalion's attack on a defended village in Germany. He watched with professional pride as artillery, mortars, and three P-47s rocked the village with a coordinated preparatory bombardment that was "something for the book." Then the ground assault began. On one flank the tanks and infantry of an adjacent company moved with such precision that it reminded him of "diagrams in the army's manuals." Then his company attacked:

My own men met the tanks at the rendezvous point with split-second precision. The tanks infiltrated their steel monsters into the for-

mation and adjusted their speed to the slower pace of the foot soldier. . . .
The timing, the formations were perfect. I looked at the men
around me, and they looked at me and each other. The last time we
had seen an attack like this was in the training films back in the
States.[7]

Improved combined arms operations permitted units to achieve their missions quicker while keeping friendly casualties to a minimum and inflicting maximum damage on the enemy.

The many tactical and technical adaptations that occurred in the ETO
invalidates the popular notion that the army won battles because of overwhelming matériel superiority. If the army had been able to crush the
Germans with an abundance of resources alone, there would have been
no need for changes in battle techniques. Clearly, the matériel advantages
the army possessed did not mean much during close combat in the Normandy hedgerows, in the Huertgen Forest, or during urban battles. The
army was adequately equipped, but in many cases a variety of shortages
hampered operations. In early 1945 General Patton complained that he
was being forced to fight with "inadequate means" and told the War Department that shortages in replacements, ammunition, and the number of
combat divisions were hindering the war effort. Huge expenditures of
firepower and munitions during certain large, key operations are usually
held up as examples of American logistical superiority and the heavy reliance on firepower. But to create stockpiles for firepower extravaganzas in
support of critical battles, air and artillery units had to husband their ammunition. Most of the time, artillery units fired under very strict ammunition rationing plans, and manpower and gasoline shortages hampered several operations.[8]

Innovations in tactics and the use of weapons were the main reasons
American forces were able to turn their limited advantages in matériel into
good effect against the Germans. Joining the efforts of the separate combat arms into a coordinated, combined arms team produced an aggregate
force more powerful than the sum of all the capabilities found in each
combat arm. At the same time, Americans discovered improved methods
for using their weapons and equipment. The creative employment of explosives, smoke, small arms, tank dozers, TDs, and an array of other weapons innovations permitted U.S. troops to keep pushing forward. All of
these improvisations and adaptations permitted Americans to gain a com-
petitive edge over the Germans without the benefit of overwhelming
matériel superiority.

Despite its proven capacity for overcoming challenges, the army failed
to solve all its problems. Changes in combined arms operations in Nor-

mandy are the best examples of the army's success in battlefield adaptation. Soldiers developed a wide variety of tactical and technological innovations to overcome German defenses in the hedgerows. Solutions to problems came from a number of sources and spread throughout First Army's divisions. Units conducted extensive rehearsals and training periods to make sure that everyone understood the increased tank-infantry coordination required by the hedgerow battles. At the opposite end of the spectrum, units had little luck in devising new ways of overcoming German defenses in the Huertgen Forest. The large firs proved more of a barrier than the hedgerows, preventing units from maneuvering and keeping the combined arms team separated. Divisions went into the Huertgen, bled themselves white, and left without learning much about forest combat. Some of the lessons and techniques learned in Normandy reappeared in the forest, but they were not significant enough to alter the course of events.

The army also had mixed success in improving various institutional problems. In the North African and Mediterranean campaigns the lack of a viable air-ground control system was perhaps the military's greatest problem. By 1945 ground and air units had converted a significant liability into one of their greatest strengths. The air-ground battle team that evolved in Europe permitted the most effective CAS yet seen in warfare. Air support parties with ground units, airborne FACs, liaison officers between major air and ground staffs, and better methods of communication and target identification allowed the fighter-bomber to become an integral partner in the combined arms team. The mutual cooperation and increased knowledge of one another's capabilities and limitations that soldiers and aviators acquired in battle was the bedrock upon which they built effective air control systems.

On the other hand, the army's inefficient and impersonal replacement system eluded improvement until near the end of the war. The system appeared sensible enough on paper but drained replacement troops of their fighting edge and provided poor personnel sustainment to the fighting divisions. The manpower shortages of late 1944 prompted some reforms that eventually had troops moving to the front in small groups under proper supervision, but the changes came too late to make much of a difference. A system that better maintained replacements' morale, discipline, and proficiency, even at the cost of bureaucratic efficiency, would have served the army's purposes much better.

An examination of how the German and Soviet armies have implemented change during wartime provides a basis for comparison with the American experience of adaptation in the ETO. During the latter part of World War I, the German army adapted a new form of offensive warfare known as infiltration tactics. By the end of 1917, the German high command knew it had to defeat the British and French armies before American forces began arriving on the Continent. Bolstered by reinforcements from other fronts, German armies hoped to end the war with a series of large offensives in the West during the spring of 1918. The German leadership believed the new infiltration tactics could produce results dramatic enough to alter favorably Germany's deteriorating strategic situation.

The German methodology for finding solutions to the stalemate of the trenches had distinct characteristics and phases. First, there was a widespread perception that change was needed to break the deadlock. The Germans observed Allied attempts at overwhelming the trenches with tanks and massed artillery and rejected both methods. The German high command defined the types of changes required as well as the desired results. Talented, articulate officers collected new ideas from fighting units and staffs, and with the high command's goals in mind, generated new regulations and training literature describing the specifics of infiltration tactics. The new doctrine became the basis for combat zone training programs, and units were expected to train in compliance with the new techniques and tactics. At the same time, commanders identified and recommended changes in equipment and small unit organization to make infiltration tactics more effective. The offensives of 1918 were the real test of how well the tactics worked. After the battles, the Germans refined their infiltration methods with various improvements.[9]

Ideas for infiltration tactics came from a number of sources, but the actual development of doctrine was a centralized process within the German high command. Experts in storm trooper operations and infantry-artillery cooperation provided valuable ideas and suggestions to a small group of officers who put pen to paper and developed a final product that defined and described the new tactics. On 1 January 1918, the high command published *The Attack in Position Warfare*, which became the basic source document on infiltration tactics. The regulation went to all units, who were to comply with its contents and use it as a basis for developing new training programs.

The winter of 1917 was a period of intense activity as German divisions implemented rigorous training regimes in infiltration tactics. In accordance with directives from the high command, units conducted exercises in assault tactics and the coordination of the combat arms. Special storm battalions acted as a training cadre for other units. Training emphasized individual initiative, and the use of live-fire ammunition increased realism. When possible, units came off the front lines to train in rear areas, and in some cases, entire divisions left the trenches to practice infiltration tactics. Each field army on the Western Front established special facilities where units arriving from the East trained in accordance with the new doctrine. The German high command ensured that officer schools and training for new recruits included instruction in infiltration tactics.

The first test of the new attack methods came with the great German Peace Offensive that began on 21 March 1918 against British positions near Amiens. After an intense five-hour bombardment, storm battalions went over the top hoping to accomplish a major breakthrough of the Allied lines. After infantry probes identified British positions, elite storm trooper units attempted to push through weak areas and envelop enemy positions from the flank or rear. A second wave of storm troopers armed with heavier weapons followed close behind to support assault units by fire. Behind the storm battalions came regular infantry who reduced pockets of resistance bypassed by the storm troopers and added momentum to the overall attack. By World War I standards, the results of the infiltration tactics were impressive. The Germans ruptured the Allied lines but failed to achieve a strategic breakthrough. After the Peace Offensive stalled, the Germans initiated other offensives along the Western Front for several weeks. Again, storm troopers accomplished substantial advances, but they could not produce results of strategic significance. By August 1918, the German army was exhausted and forced to resume the defensive against increasing Allied supremacy.

A number of traits characterized the German process of adapting and implementing infiltration tactics. Development of doctrine was a collective, corporate effort that drew ideas from many talented officers. A selected few actually wrote the doctrine, but no single officer or group championed or took credit for inventing infiltration tactics. There was great precision in defining the terms and aims of doctrine, and at all times the Germans tried to relate doctrine to actual battlefield conditions. After final approval by the high command, the doctrine provided thorough, consistent principles for the organizing, equipping, and training of storm trooper units. The German army was cautious and prudent about change and did not seek to make change for its own sake. The training effort that converted theory into battlefield practice was thorough and controlled. The high command went to some lengths to develop and supervise training programs, often stipulating the specific tasks that units were to include in their training plans, but the actual conduct of training remained in the hands of unit commanders. Once in combat, commanders of storm trooper units were left alone to fight the battle as they saw fit with little interference from higher headquarters.

A more dramatic example of how a military institution can change during wartime was the transformation of the Soviet army during World War II. The Soviets' great accomplishment was to implement sweeping doctrinal changes while fielding large, modernized forces capable of translating new doctrine into action. The Soviets focused on the operational rather than the strategic or tactical level of war and implemented the doctrine of deep battle at the operational level against Hitler's legions. Soviet theorists first identified the operational art during the 1920s. The growing sophistication of modern warfare and the scope and scale of operations in World War I and the Russian Civil War, where armies of millions operated across thousands of square miles, compelled the Soviets to view large-scale operations as a distinct level of warfare. Military thinkers began to believe that in modern warfare single, decisive battles of annihilation were becoming an anachronism and that only a series of successive offensives could destroy enemy armies.[10]

The primary advocate of the operational art and deep battle concepts was Marshal Mikhail N. Tukhachevsky. To Tukhachevsky and other theorists, the object of deep battle was to seize the initiative throughout the enemy's defensive zone by an onslaught of combined arms forces. Deep battle called for simultaneous assaults against enemy defenses, complete penetration of the defensive zone, and expansion of tactical gains into operational success that would ultimately result in the enemy's encirclement and annihilation. By 1936 the Soviet General Staff had published regulations making the doctrines of operational art and deep battle the fundamental tenets of Soviet military thinking. But Stalin's military purges of 1937–1938 liquidated Tukhachevsky and the generation of officers who had formulated the new concepts. Deep battle doctrine fell under a shadow, and those officers who survived the purges were conservative, inexperienced, and reluctant to embrace the doctrine of those who had felt Stalin's wrath.

Defeat is a powerful agent of change, and in the face of the German onslaught of 1941–1942, the Soviets undertook the daunting tasks of rebuilding and reforming the army while fighting a desperate battle for survival. While commanders grappled with the crisis at the front, the Soviet General Staff analyzed the army's strategy, doctrine, and tactics. They concluded that deep operations would become the focal point of Soviet military thinking and provide the means for converting tactical success into operational and strategic victory. The Soviets began to form fronts and shock groups as the instrument of deep battle. At the same time, the General Staff gathered, studied, and analyzed strategic, operational, and tactical lessons learned. The result was a series of directives, regulations, and instructions to units on better ways to conduct operations. A new generation of commanders emerged, whose knowledge, drive, and ambition overshadowed the prewar officer corps. The USSR also started a massive modernization effort. During 1942 the Soviets began to form tank armies and mechanized corps for large-scale exploitations. These huge formations became the offensive punch of the Soviet army and carried out the Stalingrad counteroffensive that caused the strategic initiative in the East to pass from German to Russian hands.

Armed and organized with new units and equipment, commanded by competent officers, and guided by deep battle doctrine and the experience of lessons learned, the Soviets used 1943 as a year of experimentation and transformation. By the summer of that year, the Soviets had created five new tank armies, each armed with 700 tanks. The tank armies were to function as front mobile groups to exploit success and saw their first action during the Soviet counterattack at Kursk. The tank armies were the means for implementing the deep operations and deep battle doctrines first articulated during the interwar years. With the huge battles of 1943, commanders learned to coordinate large-scale operations on a broad front that resulted in multiple penetrations of German defenses. Senior commanders tested and perfected operational techniques, while subordinate units improved tank-infantry coordination, artillery support, engineer operations, communications, and small unit tactics.

The huge Soviet counteroffensives of 1943 set the stage for even larger operations in 1944–1945. The Soviet General Staff incorporated lessons learned into the deep battle doctrine of 1942 and issued new directives in 1944 that formed a comprehensive view of deep operations and brought to full fruition the theories of Tukhachevsky. A central theme of operations in 1944 was the execution of tactical penetrations and the exploitation of gains by mobile groups into the operational and even strategic depth of German defenses. Combined arms armies became more refined in their organization and weapons mix, and the Soviets added logistical and combat support units to better sustain operations. Command and control increased in span and effectiveness to maintain touch with far-flung forces. A multifront offensive in June 1944 used a series of successive encirclements to crush the German Army Group Center and propelled Soviet forces to the borders of East Prussia. In the last two years of the war, operations by groups of fronts involved as many as 200 divisions, 2.5 million soldiers, 6,000 tanks, 40,000 guns, and 7,500 aircraft. Deep operations spanned frontages of 300–850 miles, thrust to a depth of 300–360 miles, and could destroy as many as one hundred German divisions. The final campaigns of 1945 were the culmination of Soviet doctrinal reform and unit modernization, as Soviet forces projected their power into Berlin, where they crushed the political and military head of the Third Reich.

A number of common threads run through the story of the Soviet renaissance during World War II. Soviet doctrine precisely defined the concepts of the operational art and deep battle, and there was little debate or disagreement about doctrine's purpose or intent. Soviet understanding of doctrine drew heavily from the writings of Tukhachevsky and others, reflecting the Soviet tendency for individuals rather than institutions to act as agents of change. The Soviet General Staff acted as both proponents and guardians of deep battle. They transmitted and imposed doctrine with numerous directives and regulations and issued materials on the use of combined arms forces. The Soviets had a keen interest in collecting and disseminating lessons learned, and the General Staff ultimately collected more than sixty massive volumes of lessons learned that became the basis for the reforms of 1942–1944. The high command also ordered the field forces to perform systematic analyses of their experiences. Another major characteristic of the reforms was major changes in combat units. The organization of forces changed drastically, new weapons and equipment flowed into units, and a new breed of commanders emerged.

A comparison of the ways the American, German, and Soviet armies have implemented wartime change reveals certain characteristics about each military institution and its parent society. The German method of developing and implementing infiltration tactics was centralized and formal, while American adaptation in the ETO was decentralized and informal. Both armies sought as much information as possible from a variety of sources before making changes in doctrine and tactics. The Germans used established channels of communication and formal regulations and directives to disseminate new doctrine. On the other hand, American headquarters treated information in an advisory manner and allowed subordinate units to use the knowledge in any manner that would help ensure success. The Germans were very prudent and cautious in making changes, while U.S. forces were more bold and confident in their search for new methods. Combat zone training programs taught both German and American soldiers new skills and converted theoretical concepts into specific tactics and techniques. The Germans more closely monitored training, but in both armies small unit leaders had the freedom to train their own soldiers. For the German army, infiltration tactics failed to produce results of strategic significance, while American adaptations went a long way toward winning the war faster and reducing casualties. In all, the German experience shows an army comfortable with direction from above and reflects what many believe is a German social preference for compliance with higher authority and the search for orderliness.

The Soviet implementation of deep battle doctrine reveals a number of significant military and societal differences between East and West. The Soviets believed doctrine should be precisely defined, well understood by all, and not subject to change. In the American army, soldiers believed doctrine was a flexible guide and subject to interpretation and redefinition as circumstances warranted. Soviet reforms took place at the operational level of war, were sweeping in both concept and scope, and were intended to produce strategic results. U.S. adaptations were more tailored to specific situations, incremental in nature, and sought to make the best use of resources as a means of hastening the war's end. The Soviet General Staff was the sole executive agent for formulating, articulating, and disseminating deep battle doctrine. At no comparable level of authority did the U.S. army attempt to change doctrine or control the actions of units in the field. The Soviet experience of managing wartime change with authoritarian methods reflects the long tradition of czarist Russia. And in World War II, the central authority wielded by Stalin and the Communist party further ensured that change would come from the top down instead of from the lower ranks.

A comparison of American, German, and Soviet organizational adaptation reveals unique aspects of the U.S. military's approach to war. The American process of learning and adapting was decentralized and nondirective. Major headquarters did not dictate solutions to problems down to their subordinate units. Instead, senior staffs collected lessons learned and disseminated the information to all units. Commanders at division level and below were expected to use their judgment, training, experience, and creativity to find solutions to the problems confronting the combined arms team. Unlike the Germans and the Soviets, there was no expectation in the American army that soldiers were to comply strictly with doctrine and training. Flexibility was encouraged, and the army recognized and rewarded soldiers of all ranks for innovation and results. Americans were primarily interested in the efficacy of solutions and paid less attention to where ideas originated. Ideas and information spread from unit to unit through both formal and informal channels. Often, informal networking replaced formal channels of communication, whether among soldiers in a division or in a particular combat arm. Adaptations occurred most often during intense fighting with no lulls between major campaigns. There simply was no time available to produce army-wide solutions to the many new problems encountered on the battlefield. A key component of adaptation was combat zone training that instructed soldiers in new combined arms tactics, taught them new ways to use their weapons, and provided lifesaving refresher training to replacements.

In contrast to the Germans and Soviets, Americans did not have to make major changes to their fundamental doctrines. Still, U.S. operations in Europe saw the maturation and revision of many practices and techniques normally specified in doctrine. Compared to the European armies, Americans had a permissive view toward the authority of doctrine and considered blind obedience to doctrine a vice, not a virtue. Commanders believed the flexible application of sound doctrine helped them solve problems. Unlike European forces, the U.S. army's major field headquarters tolerated and encouraged departures from established doctrine during the search for solutions to problems. Senior commanders built upon basic doctrine to develop more sophisticated, effective tactics and techniques for maneuvering large formations and integrating massive firepower from multiple weapons systems into large ground offensives.

The speed with which units adjusted to challenges was one of the great advantages of the American adaptive process. Centralized control of change requires time for the study, dissemination, and implementation of new ideas. The tempo of operations in the ETO did not permit time for thorough staffing of unexpected problems. Units encountering difficult terrain and enemy defenses acted quickly to develop their own new tactics and techniques. Small unit leaders had no expectation that higher headquarters would become involved to any great degree in the problem-solving process. Solutions to the problems of hedgerow combat and urban battles, as well as new techniques for defensive battles in the Ardennes, emerged quickly because fighting units forged ahead in their search for new, effective combined arms techniques. Soldiers rapidly devised a large number of methods that increased their personal protection, endurance, and effectiveness.

Armies on campaign must respond and adapt to a wide variety of dynamic forces. In the ETO, terrain, weather, and novel German defensive tactics were the major catalysts for change. The environment of the Normandy hedgerows, thick forests, urban settings, and heavy fortifications presented significant challenges that required changes in tactics, reorganization of units, and the novel employment of weapons and equipment. German expertise in planning and executing different types of defensive schemes required Americans to institute major adaptations. The weather alone caused American soldiers to devise a number of new techniques that permitted them to function in extreme cold, snow, rain, mud, and conditions of low light and visibility.

A military institution must have the means of evaluating the results of adaptation. In World Wars I and II, the German and Soviet General Staffs served as the mechanism for observing and measuring the effectiveness of change. The U.S. army had a less formal and structured means for measuring results. American units developed and implemented their own ideas, then observed how well the new techniques worked in battle. Instead of senior staffs, unit commanders were responsible for determining the success of adaptations. Higher headquarters helped facilitate the flow of ideas among units but did little to determine the actual effectiveness of adaptations. In general, the army believed the evaluation of results was a command function. Senior commanders held their subordinates responsible for identifying problems, developing solutions, and implementing adaptations that worked. Officers incapable of solving problems were often subject to relief from command.

A decentralized approach to adaptation works best when incremental change is necessary. The army realized that its basic land warfare doctrine was correct and that radical, new approaches to operations were not required. Implementing fundamental changes to its doctrine and tactics would have required a centralized, concerted effort and considerable expenditure of time and resources. Because commanders were confident that the army's doctrine was correct, they were free to concentrate their efforts on repairing defects in combined arms operations or responding to the specific challenges posed by terrain, weather, and enemy defenses. Soldiers had faith in their training and weapons, so they concentrated their creative efforts on developing practices that better sustained and protected them during extended operations.

Decentralized adaptation may be inadequate, however, when combat units face obstacles that are far beyond their capacity to surmount. Despite their best efforts, fighting units could not compensate for the Replacement System's serious problems, and tentative solutions did not emerge until near the end of the war. The army did not have the right types of equipment and weapons to overcome heavy fortifications. No matter how much units improvised new equipment and tactics, reinforced steel and concrete often confounded their efforts. Close combat in the Huertgen Forest presented formidable challenges that defied solution. Instead of allowing units to keep on failing, the army should have mustered its collective staffing, technical, and logistical energies to devise army-wide solutions for the reduction of fortifications and forest combat. On the other hand, air and ground units implemented sweeping changes in air doctrine and procedures for CAS without centralized direction. Suitable aircraft and communications systems for effective air-ground operations were already available. Soldiers and airmen analyzed the problems of CAS, invented new procedures, refined others, and made functional air support a vital part of the combined arms team.

A spontaneous approach to problem solving can cause high casualties, as fighting units identify problems and work toward solutions. Divisions in Normandy suffered severely before they discovered techniques for overcoming the hedgerows and the German defense. Early crossings of the Moselle by unsupported infantry were stunning defeats. Only after heavy losses did commanders find ways to integrate the combined arms team into river crossings that succeeded with much lower casualties. The forbidding environment and the German defense in the Huertgen Forest confounded the Americans, and heavy losses persisted throughout the campaign because units discovered few solutions to the difficulties of forest combat. Deliberate problem-solving procedures make for slower results but often at a smaller cost to frontline units.

The U.S. army's process of managing change reflects several predominant characteristics of American society. The fact that ideas for change came from a wide number of sources reflects the American values of individual freedom, free speech, and the entrepreneurial spirit. Coming from a society that tends to resist centralized control, it was natural for American soldiers to use a collective, decentralized approach to problem solving. The army's permissive attitude toward changes in established doctrine reflects the values of a society that often questions higher authority. The adaptations that took place also suggest that Americans are a people who respect innovation and are comfortable with change. The great number of technical improvements in the use of weapons and equipment reflects the particularly American aptitude for operating and repairing machines. While Yankee ingenuity is a hallmark of U.S. commercial production and manufacturing, it is an American trademark that also accompanies soldiers to the battlefield.

The interpretations of the army's performance in the ETO found in Russell Weigley's *Eisenhower's Lieutenants* have stirred considerable debate. Weigley argues that America's military heritage as an army organized for mobile constabulary operations with a strategic tradition of direct assault against the enemy's armed forces greatly influenced the war in Europe. The army's preference for a strategy of powerful offensives aimed at confronting the enemy's main body using forces designed for mobility rather than direct, sustained combat resulted in costly tactical deadlocks in Normandy and along the West Wall. Weigley is also critical of American generalship, arguing that it was unimaginative, addicted to playing it safe, and undecided on the use of maneuver or overwhelming force as the best way to win the war. *Eisenhower's Lieutenants* concludes that the American army "rumbled to victory" because of a preponderance of matériel resources, and that the war dragged on longer than it should have "because American military skills were not as formidable as they could have been."[11]

There can be little disagreement that the U.S. army wanted to attack Nazi Germany at the earliest possible moment along a direct route across the European continent. The tradition of Gen. Ulysses S. Grant's direct, head-on assaults against the Confederacy in 1864–1865 and Gen. John J. Pershing's offensives aimed at the German army during World War I convinced American military leaders that the quick, decisive defeat of the enemy's field forces was the best way to secure victory. Thinking along these lines produced plans in 1942 that envisioned a rapid buildup of forces in England and an immediate cross-channel attack while air forces bombed the German homeland and gained air superiority over the Continent. But Americans did not stubbornly cling to their strategic heritage. A number of constraints and realities soon modified their plans. The British were reluctant to return to the Continent as quickly as the Americans, and the creation and deployment of trained and equipped ground and air forces took longer than expected. The political decision to send U.S. forces to North Africa and the Mediterranean postponed plans for a landing in France. Americans remained fixed in their aim of attacking Germany directly, but they realized that certain requirements dictated that the march to victory would circle through the Mediterranean rather than along a direct path through northwest Europe. In the end, the delay of OVERLORD best served Allied interests by permitting the further weakening of German air and ground forces while allowing U.S. formations to gain considerable combat experience.

Eisenhower's Lieutenants argues that the army was confused in its approach to warfare and could not decide if a doctrine of direct application of superior power or a doctrine of mobility and maneuver was the best way to win the war. The mix of battles of maneuver and attrition that occurred in the ETO resulted from considerations of the specific conditions of enemy defenses, terrain, weather, logistics, and the availability of friendly forces, and not out of some mental confusion over the best way to defeat the Germans. The army clearly preferred battles of maneuver over attritional slugging matches, but often a clear choice between the two was not available.

One of the frustrations American generals endured was the lack of opportunities for mobile warfare. In 1944–1945 the army attempted to maneuver against the Germans whenever possible, but often circumstances would not allow it, and hard fighting resulted. Tank units in particular were unable to conduct the exploitations, breakthroughs, and pursuits that were the lifeblood of mechanized warfare. The Germans consciously tried to negate American advantages in mobility and firepower by fighting on difficult terrain. German defenses in the bocage, fortified areas, urban centers, dark forests, and city streets drew American units into bloody encounters on types of terrain they normally tried to avoid. The desire to destroy German forces compelled American commanders to attack the enemy's defenses, rather than bypassing resistance and attacking terrain features further to the rear. The mobile operations of the Normandy breakout, the pursuit across France, and the counterattack in the Ardennes were notable exceptions in a war that required more hard fighting than maneuver.

The fighting in the ETO suggests that U.S. commanders might not always be able to conduct mobile warfare instead of battles of attrition. Maneuver warfare is more than a mental mindset and seems to have certain physical preconditions. Before carrying out mobile operations an attacker must fix, weaken, or immobilize the enemy, a process that may be more costly in terms of time and resources than most commanders realize. Terrain is a major inhibiting factor. Mechanized units require suitable space on which to deploy and maneuver. The ground cannot be broken and compartmentalized because inhospitable terrain impedes mobility and makes long-range fires and observation impossible. Road networks are needed to support the logistical infrastructure required by mechanized forces. Commanders may have to conduct preliminary offensives to reach better terrain or gain control of road networks before they can begin mobile operations. Bad weather restricts cross-country maneuver, keeps vehicles roadbound, and adds to soldiers' miseries. First Army units fighting in Normandy and the Huertgen Forest or Patton's divisions trying to break out of bridgeheads along the Moselle could easily explain to contemporary soldiers the many impediments to maneuver warfare.

Eisenhower's Lieutenants maintains that the army did not have the right force structure and types of divisions appropriate for the large offensives in Europe. The argument is that the triangular infantry division lacked staying power, promoted mobility at the expense of offensive punch, and was incapable of overcoming strong defensive positions. The prewar military tailored the smaller, triangular division for mobile battlefields by keeping organic, heavy weaponry to a minimum and gathered heavier combat forces like tanks, tank destroyers, combat engineers, and antiaircraft battalions into unit pools controlled by army headquarters. The pooling concept sought to give senior commanders maximum flexibility in tailoring their forces for specific missions while retaining the mobility inherent in the triangular division.

In actual practice the army relied neither on the mobility of the triangular division nor on the flexibility of the pooling concept. Commanders quickly realized that heavy weapons were needed on the front lines to bolster the infantry, not held in reserve in unit pools. The constant moving of heavy units around the theater and their assignment to different divisions that the pooling concept called for precluded the development of the coordination and teamwork required for effective combined arms operations. Commanders in the field realized that they needed better battlefield teamwork and increased firepower. Their solution was to improvise heavier, more capable organizations by forfeiting the mobility of the infantry division and the flexibility of the pooling concept in favor of an ad hoc arrangement that saw the semipermanent assignment of heavy forces to infantry divisions. A close study of the battles in the ETO shows that infantry divisions seldom fought without heavy reinforcement and demolishes the notion that the triangular infantry division as employed in the theater was not up to the task. By late 1944 division commanders consistently had a mix of infantry, tank, TD, antiaircraft, and engineer units to influence the battle. For the crossing of the Moselle River at Koenigsmacher, the 90th Division had with it six additional artillery battalions, two TD battalions, one armor battalion, and an entire engineer group. When the 99th Division crossed the Rhine and went into the Remagen bridgehead, it took with it a tank battalion, a TD battalion, and an antiaircraft battalion. Historians often hold up Patton's assault of the Metz fortifications as the best example of the inability of American divisions to generate enough combat power. However, one of Third Army's most flawed engagements, the 5th Division's assault on Fort Driant, failed because of a lack of proper equipment, poor intelligence, and the small size of the assault force, not because of some defects in the army's force structure.

An analysis of the processes of change and adaptation that took place in U.S. units adds a new perspective to the argument that the prewar army was not fashioned for high-intensity combat in Europe. The army of 1942, with its triangular divisions and pooling concepts, may not have been an effective instrument for generating the sheer power many believe was at the heart of American strategic concepts. But the series of adaptations that took place during 1944–1945 shows that American commanders became masters of reorganizing and shaping their units into powerful, cohesive, combined arms formations capable of generating awesome firepower and effective ground maneuver. It is clear that a learning process took place for each type of operation and environment on which the army fought the Germans. The adaptation process adds an important qualification and a new dimension to the argument that the army was not properly organized for combat. The army of 1942 may not have been suited for European warfare, but as the campaigns of 1944–1945 unfolded, the army successfully transformed itself into an effective fighting organization with a whole host of innovative adaptations.

After the war, the army sought to institutionalize the ad hoc changes in the triangular division's structure that had occurred in the ETO. In late 1945 a board of general officers and experienced infantry commanders convened in Germany to review the "organization, equipment, and tactical employment" of the triangular division and to recommend changes based on combat experience. Proposals were a compromise between retaining the maneuverability and flexibility of a smaller organization and the need to facilitate better combined arms operations by adding other combat units to the division. The board rejected outright the notion that a fourth regiment was needed. Adding an additional infantry regiment would make the division too unwieldy without corresponding increases in combat power.[12]

Instead, the board recommended that more combat arms be included in a new division structure. The "unanimous opinion of the combat leaders of the European Theater" contended that organic armor units were essential. The board called for the elimination of TD units and light tank companies and recommended that a tank regiment with three tank battalions become part of the division. An antiaircraft artillery battalion was also needed. The board believed division engineers lacked the resources to support fighting units, enhance mobility, emplace obstacles, and maintain supply lines, and they advised the addition of a second engineer battalion. The problem of the Replacement System also drew the board's attention. They advocated that postwar divisions contain a cadre replacement battalion of thirty-six officers and enlisted men. In wartime the cadre battalion would expand to full strength and receive new troops coming into the division. The replacement battalion would give new soldiers additional training while indoctrinating them with the "division spirit" and a sense of "higher morale and more efficient teamwork."[13]

The board also called for numerous changes to enhance the division's firepower. Commanders saw the terrific punch of the division artillery and wanted to make it even more potent. Additional firepower would result from increasing the number of guns in a battery from four to six. Self-propelled guns that would better allow the artillery to keep pace with advancing units and allow artillery commanders to move and mass firepower even faster were needed. Board members roundly criticized the inadequacy of towed antitank guns, which were not powerful enough, lacked mobility, and were not worth keeping. The addition of tank battalions to divisions would more than compensate for the loss in antitank capability. Infantry battalions also required additional weapons. Battalion commanders needed their own platoon of heavy mortars to provide continuous fire support to the rifle companies. Because of the army's many experiences with close combat, the board recommended that each rifle company contain a nineteen-man assault section armed with six bazookas. Their mission would be to knock out pillboxes, obstacles, and prepared defenses and to give rifle companies a more credible antitank capability. To the board, fighting in Europe validated the basic composition and weaponry of the rifle squad. Looking toward future technology, the board called for the army to explore the use of more recoilless weapons and rocket launchers for "infantry supporting fires and antitank defense."[14]

Historians and military analysts have put too much emphasis on the army's mobility, believing that the use of tracked and wheeled vehicles gave the army a degree of mobility that was inappropriate for the heavy fighting in Europe. Trucks did give the army operational mobility, but motorized movement had no influence on the battlefield. The most common uses of trucks in 1944 were to keep a strained logistical system functioning, to move new units and replacements from Normandy to the front, and to transfer forces laterally across corps and army sectors. Higher headquarters tended to strip their divisions of truck units to haul cargo or troops, leaving the divisions with little organic transport. The army used trucks to shift divisions about or to get troops to crisis points like the 101st Airborne's hasty convoy to Bastogne. In general, staff planners kept truck units out of harm's way, and infantrymen deposited along roadsides often found they had to march several miles before reaching the front lines. In combat, tankers were slaved to the slow tempo of the infantry because riflemen walked into battle. Infantry units did enhance their battlefield mobility by improvising ways to ride on the backs of tanks. In reality, the army's means of logistical and operational mobility had no direct influence on combat.

Eisenhower's Lieutenants concludes that American generalship was unimaginative and preferred conservative, safe campaign plans, while more aggressive action might have ended the war sooner. In theory, American generals should have conducted encirclements, breakthroughs, and exploitations, but in reality a number of factors reduced such opportunities. A large dilemma faced U.S. generals: they had to stay on the offensive but also had to keep casualties to a minimum. The desire to get the war over with as quickly as possible while at the same time reducing losses and husbanding manpower prompted senior commanders to follow more conservative courses of action. Great flanking actions and mobile exploitations were filled with risk, exposed U.S. forces to greater casualties, and had no certainty of returns commensurate with the risks involved. Boldness is an important trait in a general, but prudence also has a place in campaign planning. By 1944 the Allies were closing the circle around Germany in the air and on the ground. Given the overall strategic situation, Eisenhower's decision to advance on a broad front was the best way to defeat Germany while reducing unnecessary risks to Allied troops.

Logistics and terrain also constrained American generals. Overall, the army was adequately supplied and sustained, but a number of shortages in petroleum products, ammunition, and personnel replacements plagued the campaign almost from the beginning. Bad weather and difficult terrain also made the going difficult. In many cases, rain, mud, swollen rivers, thick forests, broken and compartmentalized ground, and urbanized terrain prevented commanders from conducting maneuver warfare. During the fighting in Alsace-Lorraine, bad weather and supply shortages alone compelled General Walker to craft new plans for the reduction of the Metz fortified zone.

In *Fighting Power*, Martin van Creveld presents his findings on the relative combat performance of the German and American armies in World War II. He argues that the American army regarded war not as a struggle between opposing forces, but as a contest in which machines and firepower would largely determine the outcome. To Creveld, the army viewed soldiers as little more than adjuncts of machines, overlooked their most elementary psychological needs, and placed bureaucratic efficiency ahead of troop morale or unit cohesion. *Fighting Power* maintains that the U.S. personnel replacement system, with its tendency to treat soldiers like spare parts, and insufficient numbers of combat divisions were serious deficiencies that greatly inhibited the army's fighting ability.

Many of Creveld's evaluations of the U.S. army's performance have substantial merit but fail to measure the improvements the army made on the battlefield. Certainly, the military's key decision to field only ninety divisions resulted in an inadequate number of fighting units. The army had planned for a force of 213 divisions, but American policymakers whittled down that number to ninety based on optimistic estimates that Allied air power and the Russian army would gravely weaken the Germans. Fewer major formations meant that divisions had to stay on the front lines longer with no prospect of relief. Generals were forced to fight without reserves, and vast numbers of casualties reduced the fighting power of American divisions at an alarming rate. The decision to field only ninety divisions was influenced by other huge, competing demands on U.S. manpower. The Soviets and Germans fielded hundreds of army divisions, but only the United States had to form a global army, a two-ocean navy, and multiple strategic and tactical air forces. The shortage of American manpower required women to enter the workplace on the production lines. Criticisms of the lack of U.S. ground forces often neglect the fact that America successfully distributed its human resources to create a global, joint military organization backed by enormous manufacturing facilities.

Creveld's critical views on the army's soldier replacement system are more than justified. The policy of providing standing divisions with replacements rather than raising new divisions was a concept carried to extremes. Although the replacement system made good bureaucratic sense and promoted efficient management, it is hard to imagine a system more detrimental to the individual soldier's discipline, morale, and training. Replacements were the army's lost orphans, and they personified a tremendous waste of combat power. The army's handling of personnel matters was perhaps its greatest institutional blunder in World War II. However, it is inaccurate to conclude that the army was content with the replacement system; the army was aware of the deficiencies in the replacement system and tried to make improvements. Depots and transportation systems became more hospitable and comfortable, and replacements received refresher training. The greatest change was that by war's end replacements moved to the front in ad hoc squads and platoons where they joined divisions as a group. While it may be difficult to measure the results of these reforms, they do indicate that American commanders were aware of existing problems in the replacement system and made efforts to improve conditions.

Fighting Power argues that the American army ignored the needs of its soldiers and placed too much emphasis on the use of weapons and machinery. However, a study of combined arms operations in the ETO shows that the army was aware of its manpower deficiencies and decided to maximize the use of weapons, firepower, and machinery. The full use and integration of firepower compensated for shortcomings in the personnel system. The technical and tactical adaptations that took place throughout the ETO best illustrate American superiority in employing weapons and equipment. Americans had a special flair for bringing their resources to bear in devastating land and air attacks. Reliance on special equipment, weapons, and firepower was not a major American deficiency but a great strength.

Adaptations in air-ground operations best illustrate the American military's superior aptitude for using its machines and weapons. Tactical and technical innovations permitted the air-ground battle team to generate a tremendous amount of coordinated combat power. Americans found ways to solve target acquisition problems and to prevent the attack of friendly troops by supporting aircraft. The development of tank-mounted air controllers and improvements in the HORSEFLY system resulted in some of the best air-ground cooperation ever conducted. Army and air leaders eventually discovered effective techniques for integrating the tremendous weight of heavy bombers into the ground battle. Aviators and soldiers learned to coordinate their efforts against enemy positions under varying conditions. Great progress occurred in the use of tactical air reconnaissance. The full synchronization of bombers, fighter-bombers, massed artillery, and the organic weapons of forward units during overwhelming preparatory bombardments best displays American superiority in the employment and coordination of weaponry. The adaptations airmen and soldiers invented and implemented to make air power part of the combined arms team shows the extraordinary ability of Americans to make the best use of their weapons and equipment.

A survey of combined arms battles in Europe reveals that too much has been made over the notion that Americans did not shoot enough. S. L. A. Marshall's findings in *Men against Fire* were accepted as gospel at one time, but veterans and historians have called Marshall to task in recent years. Marshall's findings resulted from intuitive and subjective means rather than quantitative or scientific methods. Because of a lack of hard data, his conclusions can be neither proven nor disproven, and his personal style often included bluster and hyperbole as he tried to drive home the force of his convictions to listeners and readers. A close survey of after-action reports and training memoranda from the ETO does reveal that volume of fire was a problem in many units. But Marshall's belief and grave concern that only 15–25 percent of soldiers fired their weapons does not appear among the voluminous reports and writings of the participants. An exhaustive review of anecdotal evidence, unit after-action reports, and training literature suggests that Marshall's figures on the numbers of active firers are too conservative and that many more soldiers were pulling the trigger. Furthermore, it is hard to believe that an army attacking prepared defenses for the better part of an entire year could have accomplished much of anything with only one quarter of its soldiers firing their weapons. While many soldiers probably never did fire their weapons, the problem was perhaps not as great as Marshall believed.

If Americans did not fire their weapons, it was because of training inadequacies rather than some innate inability or lack of courage. Many infantrymen believed that marksmanship training under controlled conditions on known-distance rifle ranges taught soldiers little about firing in combat, where fear and confusion reigned and the enemy was hard to spot. It should come as no surprise that new soldiers forced through an impersonal replacement system or other troops hastily retrained as infantrymen may have had problems firing their weapons. After the war, infantrymen took a long, hard look at their marksmanship training. One article in the *Infantry Journal* told readers that "a soldier experienced in combat knows that such marksmanship training has nothing to do with combat training." The army's success with marching fire and Marshall's own advocacy of better training methods convinced the army to implement more realistic marksmanship programs that required firers to acquire obscure and fleeting targets and to estimate ranges.[15]

A strange parallel exists between soldiers' understanding of S. L. A. Marshall's main themes and the other training deficiencies identified in the ETO. Too many professional soldiers and historians have forgotten most of Marshall's other main points. In addition to his views on small arms firepower, Marshall observed that unit cohesion keeps soldiers present and functioning on the battlefield, that fatigue breeds fear, and that excessive loads of equipment and ammunition drain soldiers' physical stamina and courage. In the same way, commanders in the ETO saw many training deficiencies they considered just as damaging as the lack of infantry firepower. Troops bunching together under fire, freezing upon initial enemy contact, failing to follow artillery barrages close enough or not moving out from underneath enemy shell fire, and not digging deep enough all had grave consequences. A comprehensive picture of the problems of soldier performance on the battlefield must include all of these points rather than concentrating solely on why soldiers may not have fired their weapons enough.

Writers and historians have recently assaulted S. L. A. Marshall's honesty regarding his own career and historical findings, and a tendency has developed to discredit his arguments along with his integrity. Professional historians and soldiers must remember that the broader questions Marshall raised are probably more significant than any facts about his personal career. Disciplined thinkers must separate the man from his arguments and perform critical analyses of Marshall's ideas based solely on their own merits and available evidence. On balance, it appears as though Marshall's writings about the broad experience of men under fire are much more often right than wrong. To forget or disregard Marshall's main theses solely because of concerns over his personal integrity is to throw the baby out with the bath water. And in Marshall's case, the issues contained in the bath water may be far more significant than questions about the infant's personal integrity.[16]

While historians are quick to point out the army's reliance on vast firepower, soldiers in Europe were more struck with the limits of firepower than with its omnipotence. The army learned that vast amounts of ordnance could hurt, demoralize, and disrupt the Germans, but that firepower alone was not decisive. No matter how many bombs and shells were unleashed, riflemen and tankers still had to root the Germans out of their prepared positions. Firepower served as a catalyst to help keep units moving forward but was not powerful enough to let American troops merely step over the enemy's broken remnants. The COBRA bombardment and the subsequent ground attack is probably the most dramatic example of the effectiveness of massed firepower and ground units working in concert. Firepower had a terrible effect when Americans mistakenly opened fire on other Americans. Artillery battalions had good reputations for fire discipline despite the occasional shelling of friendly units, and improvements in target identification kept bombers and fighter-bombers off the backs of friendly ground units. Ironically, the COBRA bombardment caused the enemy the most harm but also produced perhaps the largest single incident of American casualties to friendly fire in all of World War II.

Two aspects of the use of firepower are little known. Units in Europe quickly discovered the effectiveness of heavy-caliber fire delivered at point-blank range, and commanders had no reservations in using tank and TD main guns as well as self-propelled artillery to batter German strongholds into submission. Heavy-caliber weapons used at close quarters physically dismantled German defenses and greatly bolstered soldiers' morale. Tanks and TDs wrecked pillboxes as well as hedgerow, forest, and urban strongholds, while direct fire artillery blasted away at heavy fortifications. Soldiers also discovered a number of creative ways to use explosives. Demolitions gapped hedgerows, blew passageways through buildings, and fractured steel and concrete defenses. Americans used close-quarters firepower without restraint or any regard for humanitarian considerations rather than risking their own lives. To average soldiers, blasting the enemy into oblivion at point-blank range was one of the best ways to minimize casualties and to get the fighting over with as quickly as possible.

Combat zone training programs that increased soldier's capabilities and proficiency are one of the army's unsung success stories of World War II. A variety of training activities helped improve and sustain combat power. The ETO as a whole mustered resources to run an extensive retraining program for soldiers newly reassigned to combat duties. Divisions trained during lulls in the fighting to prepare for specific battlefield challenges, to hone skills dulled due to heavy losses, and to provide replacements with refresher training. One of the most significant functions of training was to introduce soldiers to new organizations and equipment. Companies and platoons reorganized into assault and support teams and rehearsed new tactics and techniques devised for attacking through hedgerows and forests, down city streets, and against fortifications. Combat zone training programs repaired many of the problems of tank-infantry coordination and air-ground cooperation. Soldiers learned how to use bangalore torpedoes, bazookas, and flame throwers. Units rehearsed for specific operations in the days just before the actual attack, while units new to the theater used training sessions to familiarize themselves with lessons other units had already learned. The best way to assimilate new troops was through tough training before battle. The army did not recognize the need for these training functions before the war, but everyone came to realize the importance of training conducted in the combat zone.

Training programs near the front lines taught commanders two important lessons. Prewar doctrine often spoke of the need for "special units" or "special troops armed with unique equipment" for certain types of operations. Officers facing the formidable tasks of attacking stubborn defenses realized that special troops and equipment were a mirage. They had to attack with only the troops and equipment readily available. Training permitted regular units to learn and sharpen the special skills required for urban combat, the attack of fortifications, and a number of other unique operations. Second, leaders learned that combat zone training is a legitimate requirement that must be anticipated in peacetime. Armies cannot believe that they train to peak proficiency before war and then expend their expertise in battle, or that training ceases with the beginning of hostilities. The need to maintain readiness extends into wartime, so commanders and trainers must think about how to hone soldiers' skills, teach troops new techniques, and assimilate replacement troops with combat zone training programs.

It did not take long for commanders to realize that the best peacetime training programs have distinct limits in preparing soldiers for battle. No matter how thorough or rigorous, training could not simulate battlefield conditions realistically. Soldiers under fire for the first time were struck with the sense of fear, confusion, and helplessness that shelling and direct, heavy fire induced. Commanders and leaders had to learn how to maintain command, control, and communications, while keeping their soldiers moving despite the paralyses of fear and confusion and a hail of enemy shot and shell. The noises of battle are all new to unseasoned troops. The sights and sounds of the dead and wounded and the notion that soldiers had to kill or be killed could not be a part of training programs, yet these factors had a profound, emotional impact on most soldiers. No peacetime army can come to believe its training methods fully approximate battle. In a world where lasers and electronics make battle simulations more realistic, commanders and trainers must resist the tendency to think their mock battles are just about the same as real war. No matter how hard an army prepares for war, the physical and emotional shocks of the sights and sounds of battle are challenges soldiers cannot confront and overcome until their first fight.

Combat was far different from what many soldiers had expected. In peacetime exercises groups of soldiers moved together rapidly in mock attacks, but the opposite was true in battle. The tempo of combat was much slower, with single attacks often taking hours rather than minutes. A myriad of tasks slowed units in battle: gathering intelligence, coordinating direct and indirect fires, evacuating casualties, and handling PWs. Even in small unit actions, detailed planning achieved success more effectively than élan or adrenaline. The battlefield was a lonely place that tended to isolate rather than unify soldiers. Fear and confusion were more prevalent than anyone had expected and tended to hold units back. Much more combat took place at close quarters than on open terrain, and the combat arms had to work much closer together than in peacetime. Commanders discovered that combined arms attacks not only increased their combat power but improved soldiers' morale and confidence. Infantrymen felt better with tanks and TDs nearby, while artillery barrages and air strikes gave footsoldiers confidence. The numbers and types of casualties took commanders by surprise. Hypothetically, a twelve-man infantry squad eliminated in combat would suffer two soldiers killed, five wounded, one missing, two evacuated for trench foot, and two others incapacitated by combat exhaustion.

Junior officers faced two significant leadership challenges in Europe. The U.S. army was a mass conscript force drawn from a liberal, democratic society, and the first problem facing officers was the fundamental conflict between the need for military discipline and draftees' desire to retain some form of individual freedom. Officers felt compelled to instill discipline through tough training, inspections, punishment, and military courtesy while remaining somewhat aloof from the troops. On the other hand, soldiers felt that discipline was almost a vice and desired more familiarity with their officers. The incongruence in values between a professional officer corps and a mass conscript army has always existed, and the American army in Europe was no exception. When it came to the problems of leading conscripts into battle, young officers had much in common with their professional forebears in the Civil War and World War I.

Company grade officers learned not to accept at face value the simplistic battlefield leadership style implied in the cry "Follow me!" They had to lead by example but also had to exercise common sense and judgment in how to influence tactical situations. Officers who led from the front with a reckless disregard for their own safety quickly became casualties, and battalions and companies that lost their leaders in the early stages of battle became bogged down and confused. Yet junior officers knew that at crucial times mission accomplishment came before their own personal safety. Many captains and lieutenants grabbed their carbines and led the way against German defenses; some survived, most did not. Officers came to understand that their troops did not expect them always to lead from the front. In fact, most soldiers felt better knowing that their officers were alive and doing all they could to control the fight and to bring the other combat arms to bear.

Of all the types of operations in Europe, the army was least prepared to reduce fortifications, and doctrine on the attack of fortified positions had the least relevance to actual combat. Vague training materials on how to reduce strongholds and pillboxes and the failure to develop and deploy special equipment are other indicators of unpreparedness. The army had no heavy artillery, armored bulldozers, or combat engineer vehicles, and no experience in the Mediterranean campaigns made the army more aware of the special challenges of attacking fortifications. As the army built the forces and major weapons systems it would use in World War II, there was much anticipation of an eventual assault of the Siegfried Line, but aside from some training at the Infantry and Engineer schools and at a few special sites, little else was done to prepare for attacking the West Wall.

The most fundamental reason for the army's unpreparedness to attack fortifications lay in its historical roots. The army had only limited experience in manning, attacking, or defending heavy fortifications; its greatest involvement with fixed, reinforced defenses armed with heavy guns was the forts defending the principal harbors along the Eastern seaboard. Hasty field fortifications were a big part of the army's combat legacy, and the Civil War and World War I were filled with engagements against entrenchments. The sieges of Vicksburg and Petersburg saw savage assaults against reinforced works of earth and wood but did not involve the systematic reduction of stone masonry fortresses. During the interwar period, the American military followed the trend of the European armies in eschewing positional trench warfare in favor of a mobile, mechanized battlefield. In the campaigns envisioned by B. H. Liddell Hart, Maj. Gen. J. F. C. Fuller, and their disciples, there was no place for deliberate assaults against heavy defenses. America's wars did include some isolated incidents where troops assaulted fortresses, but the operations were not significant enough to ingrain the army with a sense that the reduction of fortifications should be part of its battlefield skills.

The varied roles of TD battalions were one of the army's great surprises. TD units rarely saw employment in their intended role of killing enemy tanks. Instead, they ignored prewar doctrine and went on to perform well as indirect fire artillery and gave their most valuable service as infantry support weapons. In the Bulge, tank destroyers played a key role in blunting German attacks at Krinkelt-Rocherath, Dom Butgenbach, and Bastogne. A sampling of TD battalions revealed that the average unit in Europe destroyed thirty-four German tanks and self-propelled guns, seventeen artillery and antitank guns, and sixteen pillboxes.[17]

After the war the validity of TDs came under fire for two reasons. First, improvements in U.S. tanks negated the advantages M10s and M36s enjoyed in firepower and mobility. The fielding of the M26 Pershing tank in February 1945 brought to Europe a vehicle with heavier armament and better protection than the Shermans or TDs. The armor community began to believe that an improved tank fleet was equally capable of offensive and defensive operations. The army also began to view the failure of TD doctrine as an indictment of the TD force. The army's senior leaders saw that TDs had not performed in the ways envisioned before the war and concluded that the TD force was no longer needed. Tank destroyers became a casualty of postwar demobilization. The Tank Destroyer Center at Camp Hood closed its doors in November 1945, and the army inactivated the last TD battalion a year later.[18]

The success of air-ground operations in the light of an almost total lack of doctrine on CAS is one of the great paradoxes of World War II. And when considered against the backdrop of air power theory between the World Wars, the dichotomy looms even larger. The air power advocates of the interwar period saw their new weapon as an alternative to the ghastly trench stalemate of World War I. According to the Italian theorist Giulio Douhet and his followers, strategic bombing forces in the next war were to produce quick victories and avoid long, attritional conflicts. In reality, the great strategic air campaigns over Germany degenerated into an aerial war of attrition, and the only use of air power in Europe that avoided huge losses and produced immediate destructive effects was tactical aviation. In the ETO heavy and medium bombers as well as fighter-bombers bloodied German units and materially helped ground units advance. Ironically, American air theorists not only failed to foresee the importance of tactical aviation, but their writings openly ridiculed the only form of air power that best achieved direct, short-term results. But wartime experience changed the theorists' minds, and a conclusive postwar report on air power determined that a requirement existed for new field manuals and training literature "covering the methods and techniques of operations of a tactical air force . . . based on principles proved sound in the European Theater." The study also recommended that the organization of the Ninth Air Force and its subordinate TACs become the standard model for building future tactical air forces. To air theorists and AAF leaders, the successful employment of air power in a ground support role was one of the great surprises of World War II.[19]

Controversies over the use of heavy bombers in support of ground operations raged in army and air circles during and after the war. Aviation advocates viewed the heavy bombers' tactical role as a waste of air assets better directed against the enemy's homeland, while ground commanders wanted the big aircraft to augment their firepower. The actual results of preparatory bombardments were mixed and seemed less decisive than both airmen and aviators had desired. Heavy bomber attacks represented tremendous expenditures of resources and were used in the hope of influencing the outcome of campaigns rather than assisting in the attack of limited objectives. Ground formations learned that they had to advance on the heels of bomber strikes in order to take full advantage of a bombardment's effects.

The World War II experience in using heavy bombers to support ground troops reveals a key characteristic of America's approach to fighting wars. Differing opinions about the tactical use of strategic air assets in the ETO failed to prevent heavy bombers from supporting ground troops in Korea and Vietnam. Formations of B-29 Superfortresses in Korea and B-52 Stratofortresses in Vietnam and the Persian Gulf War conducted extensive sustained air campaigns to help prosecute ground operations. The collective, twentieth-century experience in using heavy bombers against enemy ground troops shows the American willingness to pull no punches in unleashing conventional firepower. It also suggests that a heavy bomber is a value-laden weapons system that personifies American might and determination in winning battles in both total and limited wars. The willingness of air leaders to use heavy bombers in a ground support role shows their eagerness to play a full role in conventional wars. Such employment also helps to justify the need for maintaining expensive, strategic weapons systems that have never fired a nuclear shot in anger. The United States' future enemies should anticipate America's use of strategic air assets not only against their homeland but against installations and troop formations in the combat zone as well.

Despite significant changes in warfare since 1945, the U.S. military's recent war in the Persian Gulf has many close parallels with World War II
and suggests the timeliness of a number of the attitudes and characteristics of the American way of war. The 1941 edition of FM 100-5 had served
as a broad guide for the conduct of operations in the ETO, and fifty years
later the new FM 100-5 outlined the principles of AirLand Battle, which
proved effective in the open desert of Southwest Asia. U.S. troops in
Saudi Arabia wanted to get the fighting over with and go home as quickly
as possible while defeating the enemy and suffering as few casualties as
possible, and American soldiers attacking Omaha Beach, crossing the Moselle River, or breaching the Siegfried Line had said the exact same things.
In both wars, soldiers at all levels displayed a flair for devising innovative
ways to use their weapons. The adaptations devised by U.S. troops to help
breach Iraqi defenses beg comparison with similar developments that occurred in the bocage a half a century earlier. The army again displayed a
capacity to collect and disseminate lessons learned, to coordinate the use
of overwhelming firepower, and to conduct combined arms operations.
Once deployed to Saudi Arabia, combat zone training programs gave soldiers confidence in living and fighting in the desert and imparted them
with a number of new skills in much the same way divisional training centers had done in Europe. In both campaigns, air power helped hasten the
enemy's defeat by attacking both rear areas and forward combat units.
The pilots and FACs of DESERT STORM could trace the historical roots of air-
ground cooperation back to the Normandy campaign and the HORSEFLY
air control system. Once the ground war began the attack scenario was
not unfamiliar: the U.S. VII Corps conducted the main attack, assisted by
tremendous fire support and aircraft from the U.S. Ninth Air Force, just as
General Collins's VII Corps had tackled German formations in the ETO.
Perhaps the most ironic of all these similarities was that American troops,
for the first time since World War II, were fighting the forces of an authoritarian dictator whom many compared to Adolf Hitler.

    The legacy of the fighting in Europe, reinforced by the recent DESERT
STORM experience, points to several characteristics of the American way
of war that may become prevalent in future conflicts. Within the bounds
of political objectives and constraints, the American war machine is relentless in achieving its goals. Commanders stay on the offensive to destroy their opponents even if it means fighting the enemy under disadvan-
tageous conditions. The army prefers to maneuver but does not shirk
from plodding battles of attrition. Americans concentrate overwhelming
combat power to win quickly and to keep casualties to a minimum, and
firepower will remain a key ingredient to success. Massed artillery and air
power will bleed the enemy and help keep ground units moving forward.
Modern battlefield technologies, such as enhanced sensors and communi-

cations, precision-guided munitions, night vision equipment, and a host of other improvements, will help commanders destroy the enemy even faster with fewer friendly losses. However, the tremendous effects of fire-power and technology still will not relieve ground troops of the burden of closing with the enemy. On the offensive and the defensive, American units will employ the most effective combined arms tactics possible. Training in the combat zone will improve morale and make soldiers more confident and proficient.

The greatest single trait of Americans in any future conflict may once again be their ability to adapt and innovate on the battlefield. The pattern of problem solving and adaptation that occurred in the ETO is likely to re-peat itself during extended operations. Americans will revise doctrine, in-vent new combined arms tactics, and innovate changes in weapons and equipment in order to respond to varying conditions of terrain, technol-ogy, enemy defenses, and weather. Ideas will come from a wide number of sources and spread among units through both formal and informal channels. Soldiers will have success in finding techniques to improve their performance and survivability and will improvise quick remedies to manageable problems. More significant challenges may defy easy solu-tion, and commanders and small unit leaders must have the competence and expertise to identify and find solutions to unexpected challenges without major involvement from higher staffs. Senior commanders will hold subordinates responsible for the results of battlefield adaptation.

The notion that a successful army must be capable of making adjust-ments in its tactics and methods after the shooting starts was not lost on the combatants in the ETO. The veterans of one unit reflected back on their experience and remembered, "K Company's war was far different from the one we'd been trained to fight . . . some things had definitely changed. Gone was the blind faith in the manuals, in the infinite wisdom of senior officers. What counted instead was experience, sheer bloody ex-perience."[20] Soldiers of all ranks relied on their experience, training, and judgment to find better ways of bridging the gaps between theory and practice and training and fighting. Innovations in tactics and the use of weapons and equipment helped soldiers take objectives easier with fewer casualties.

In the immediate aftermath of World War II, the army clearly recog-nized the importance of critical analysis and the need to adapt in battle. In reflecting on the successes in Europe, the theater's General Board chal-lenged America's future military leaders:

> While operations in the Western European Campaign have indi-cated no necessity for changes in our present tactical doctrines, it can be expected that these doctrines will require modification with the

future development of improved weapons and equipment. . . . The tactics and techniques of the various arms, and of the combined arms, must be reviewed constantly in the light of new developments. . . . Only by this means can we hope to be fully prepared for the next war.[21]

Perhaps the greatest lesson the army learned in World War II was that the learning process itself is an integral part of any conflict and can spell the difference between victory and defeat. It is a lesson contemporary American soldiers should never forget.

U.S. Army Organization and Weaponry

In 1940, the army adopted a new divisional organization on the premise that the infantry division should be simple, mobile, and trimmed of all nonessential troops and equipment. Called the triangular division because of the use of three infantry regiments as its basis, the new division became the army's workhorse during World War II. Lean, agile, and optimally suited for the attack, it became the blueprint for Regular Army infantry divisions, and National Guard divisions adopted the new structure after the U.S. entered the war.

The basic composition of the triangular division was three infantry regiments and a variety of combat and combat support troops at the division level. Taken together, the weaponry gave commanders at all levels vast amounts of firepower. Foremost in combat power at division level, the artillery had four battalions: three 105-mm howitzer battalions with twelve guns each and a 155-mm howitzer battalion with twelve guns. The standard infantry regiment, the next major command below division level, consisted of three infantry battalions, an antitank company, a cannon company, a headquarters company, a service company, and a medical detachment. The next organizational level was the infantry battalion: three rifle companies, a heavy weapons company, and a headquarters company composed an 871-man battalion. The rifle company consisted of three rifle platoons, a weapons platoon, and a small headquarters section and had a total manpower strength of 6 officers and 187 enlisted men. The weapons platoon was armed with one .50-caliber and two .30-caliber machine guns, three 60-mm mortars, and three 2.36-inch bazookas. Three infantry squads composed a rifle platoon. Each rifle squad consisted of twelve men armed with ten M1 Garand rifles, one Browning automatic rifle, and one M1903 bolt-action Springfield rifle. Despite the awesome aggregate firepower of the weapons within a triangular division, the lifeblood of the infantry division was the 5,211 officers and combat infantrymen who manned its 27 rifle companies.

Ironically, in emphasizing the leanness and toughness of the triangular division, army planners denied it the organic support of the weapon that would prove so important in ground combat in World War II—the tank. Despite the impressive array of weaponry within the triangular division, the firepower and mobility of tanks were necessary to augment the division's combat power. The need for effective combined arms operations was one of the principal tactical lessons of World War I and had been reaffirmed by the Wehrmacht's victories early in World War II. For this reason, army planners had not neglected tanks, neither in their role nor in their organizational composition.

At the outbreak of World War II, American armor had two combat roles, infantry support and exploitation. With the founding of the Armored Forces in July 1940, the army laid the groundwork for the creation of the American armored division, whose intended, primary role was offensive operations against hostile rear areas. By 1943, the combat power of the armored division was based on an equal number of tank, infantry, and artillery battalions within the division. Thus, the armored division, unlike its counterpart the triangular infantry division, was a true combined arms unit.

The army realized, however, that the triangular division needed armored support. Adamant in preserving the agility of the infantry division, army planners refused to incorporate a tank battalion into its standard organization. Instead, independent tank battalions were formed and became known as General Headquarters (GHQ) tank units. The theory ran that GHQ tank battalions could be attached to infantry divisions singly or in groups for specific operations, or that army and corps commanders could mass GHQ tank units for exploitations in much the same way as they might employ an armored division.

Regardless of whether a tank battalion served in an armored division or as a GHQ tank unit, the organization was the same. A standard tank battalion consisted of a headquarters company, a service company, three medium tank companies, and a light tank company. Every tank company had three platoons and a headquarters section of two tanks. Each tank platoon had 5 tanks—two tanks in a "light" section and three tanks in a "heavy" section. The medium tank company had a total strength of 5 officers and 116 enlisted men and was equipped with seventeen M4 Sherman tanks. The light tank company had 5 officers and 91 enlisted men and was equipped with the M5 Stuart light tank.

Single GHQ tank battalions were normally assigned to divisions to provide infantry support. In turn, the tank companies were attached to the infantry regiments and operated closely with the battalions in each regiment. In an infantry division, the separate elements of the combined arms team came together at the regimental level. A GHQ tank unit, detachments from the division's engineer battalion, fire support elements from the division artillery and supporting combat aviation, and the rifle battalions of the infantry regiment were the active participants in the combined arms team of World War II. Supporting elements often were not held at the regimental level but were passed on to the rifle battalions, which might be augmented by tanks, combat engineers, artillery support, and fighter-bombers.

U.S. Army Doctrine and Tactics

FM 100-5, *Field Service Regulations, Operations*, was the conceptual foundation for the army's battle doctrines that were conceived and implemented before and during World War II. The manual described the fundamental doctrines of combat operations, the basic concepts of battlefield leadership, and the principles of employment for the combat arms. Additionally, FM 100-5 was the common link between all training and instruction carried out at the various service schools.

The military subject matter covered by the 1941 edition of FM 100-5 was broad and diverse. However, two root concepts occur again and again throughout discussions about the roles of the combat arms and the conduct of military operations. The first was the critical importance of dynamic, competent leadership. Commanding troops in combat was a complex task that required leaders to possess "will power, self confidence, initiative, and disregard for self," as well as superior knowledge about technical and tactical matters. In the introduction to FM 100-5, Army Chief of Staff Gen. George C. Marshall stressed that it was a function of competent leadership to combine doctrinal concepts with battlefield experience to produce plans that would ensure success in battle.

Ironically, the coordination of the combat arms, which was deficient in the beginning phases of the war, was the second theme that ran throughout FM 100-5. Officers of the expanding, modernizing U.S. Army of the early 1940s were aware of the importance of coordinated, concerted action by the combat arms. FM 100-5 stated that "no one arm wins battles." The "combined action of all arms and services" was the key to success, and unit commanders were held responsible for coordinating the "tactics and techniques of the various arms" and for developing in their units the combined arms teamwork "essential to success."

According to FM 100-5, the sole purpose of offensive operations was the destruction of hostile armed forces. To achieve this purpose, a commander established a clearly defined physical objective toward which he could direct all efforts. Attacks were grouped into two categories: envelopments and penetrations. Of these two attack forms, envelopment was the more preferable. The design for an attack consisted of a plan of maneuver and a plan of fire. FM 100-5 stated that the best guarantee for success in an attack was the effective cooperation between the troops in the attacking echelon and fire support from artillery and combat aviation. The "superior commander" was the battle leader who could coordinate his fire support with his plan of maneuver.

From the doctrinal framework provided by FM 100-5, the army's various combat arms, working under the supervision of the War Department, generated detailed offensive doctrines for their respective arms. The techniques and procedures developed specifically described how each arm would perform in battle and interact with other combat arms during operations. In turn, these doctrines served as the basis for combat training conducted in the army's service schools and maneuver units.

The primary ground-gaining arm was the infantry. Because of its ability to seize or retain major objectives, the infantry battalion was the army's most basic combat unit. Infantry doctrine prescribed that battalions usually attacked in daylight to seize terrain objectives. Although envelopments were preferred over penetrations, infantry doctrine admitted that battalion-size attacks were usually nothing more than frontal assaults against enemy defenses. Battalions attacked along a frontage of 500–1,000 yards in width, depending on terrain and enemy dispositions. Normally, battalions were to attack with two companies abreast, the third company acting as the battalion reserve. One company conducted the main attack, while the other supported it with secondary attacks. The rifle companies performed the actual tasks of seizing objectives and closing with the enemy; a single rifle company's zone of attack was usually 200–500 yards wide.

Army doctrine recognized that the infantry was capable of only "limited independent action" through the employment of its organic weapons. The other combat arms had to augment the infantry's offensive power, so each developed doctrine in support of the infantry's attacks.

FM 17-36 outlined the techniques used by armored forces when operating in conjunction with the infantry. Like FM 100-5, this manual stressed the need for closer cooperation and coordination between the ground forces. FM 17-36 insisted that since the role of tanks and infantry "[is] linked so closely," it is essential that the "doctrine, powers and limitations of both" be understood by those involved.

Tanks operating with infantry during offensive operations assisted the infantry by destroying the enemy with firepower and by keeping the attack moving using their inherent armored protection and mobility. The combat capabilities of tanks and infantry were complementary. Prewar doctrine specified that infantry-armor attack formations consisted of two separate echelons. Armor led when the terrain was suitable and when antitank weapons and obstacles were absent or neutralized, infantry led over difficult terrain and when strong enemy minefields and antitank defenses were present. When armor led, the first attacking echelon was composed solely of tanks, while the second comprised infantry and tanks. Similarly, if infantry led the attack, the first wave was composed solely of infantry formations, while the second comprised tank-infantry teams. Despite the firepower produced by small arms, machine guns, and tank main guns in tank-infantry forces, tactical doctrine acknowledged that this firepower in no way minimized the need for close support from the other combat arms.

Foremost among the support provided by the other combat arms was the firepower of the field artillery. Commanders fully integrated supporting fires into the attack so that they would coincide with the time of attack and the scheme of maneuver. Artillery's role in the combined arms attack was to neutralize enemy crew-served weapons, to destroy field fortifications, and to prevent enemy infantry from manning their defenses as the assault approached its objective. When tank-infantry forces were prepared to conduct the final assault, they lifted artillery fires and shifted them onto other enemy targets beyond the objective.

Combat engineers formed another important adjunct to the tank-infantry team by increasing combat effectiveness through acts of construction or demolition designed to facilitate friendly movement or to hinder the enemy's mobility. When operating with tank-infantry forces in offensive operations, engineers usually had a mobility enhancement mission, which meant they were to remove or breach obstacles such as antitank ditches, wire entanglements, and minefields.

A NOTE ON SOURCES

The literature of World War II presents both the serious scholar and the casual reader with a skewed perspective of the campaigns in the ETO. The D-Day landings and the Battle of the Bulge have tended to overshadow the historiography of the fighting in Europe because of their strategic significance and their vastness. But to the soldiers of 1944–1945, a number of other battles were just as important and arduous. Commanders and soldiers trying to push through the bocage, to move down the streets of Brest and Aachen, to reduce the Siegfried Line fortifications, to jump major rivers, or to slug their way through the Huertgen Forest believed their efforts were equally critical to the final victory. An appreciation of battles other than Normandy and the Ardennes is required to paint a complete picture of unfolding events in the ETO. The present work tries to rectify the imbalances in the American historiography of World War II by providing a more even analysis of all of the types of battles that the army fought, rather than focusing primarily on OVERLORD and the Ardennes.

Any study of soldiers at war must draw heavily from primary source materials, the writings and reports of the men who actually pulled the triggers and endured the shellings. But, with few exceptions, many of the most renowned studies of American participation in World War II have failed to draw adequately from the many superior primary sources that are available. The U.S. Army did a thorough job of recording the events of combat and the lessons learned in battle. The present study draws heavily from several previously untapped primary sources in an attempt to provide a more thorough, analytical picture of Americans at war.

Participants of all ranks in the ETO produced the best materials. Frontline units and their higher headquarters made a concerted effort to record lessons learned and to circulate them throughout the rest of the army. The *Reports of the Army Ground Forces Observers Board* is an indispensable source of information on how the army actually fought the war. Teams of observers from the AGF produced six huge volumes containing reports on both tactical and technical innovations during combat from Tunisia to Bavaria. This series of more than 1,500 reports discusses a vast range of topics from the best ways to heat rations to how junior officers were to cope with battle-fatigue cases. In the ETO all of the major headquarters cataloged and distributed lessons learned in battle. The best of these are

Battle Experiences, first published by 12th Army Group and then later by Headquarters, ETO, U.S. Army. At war's end the Supreme Commander convened a Special General Board "to prepare a factual analysis of the strategy, tactics, and administration employed by the United States forces in the European Theater." The board produced 131 detailed studies that address all aspects of the army's functions, from administration and logistics to equipment and force structure issues. The *Reports of the General Board* espoused several reforms that influenced the army in the postwar period, giving proof that an army can focus on future challenges rather than thinking of ways to refight the last war. Any analysis of American combat performance in World War II is incomplete without reference to the above series of authoritative reports.

The words and writings of the actual combatants provide a second, vast pool of primary source materials. Foremost is the huge collection of combat interviews and after-action reports housed at the Military Reference Branch of the National Archives in Records of the Adjutant General's Office, World War II Operations Reports, 1940–1948. Teams of historians from the Historical Office of the ETO worked under the auspices of the War Department's Historical Section and did a superb job of interviewing combatants not long after engagements. Their combat interviews reek of the sweat, blood, and gunpowder of battle. Combat historians in the ETO also did an excellent job of capturing the key details of several small but significant engagements in a series of "Small Unit Studies." All headquarters in the ETO, from SHAEF to battalion level, produced after-action reports and training memoranda of great value.

After the war the army moved to a peacetime footing by requiring officers to return to appropriate levels of schooling within the professional military education system. Instructors in the army's branch schools and at Fort Leavenworth attempted to teach their lieutenants, captains, majors, and lieutenant colonels the specifics of military science. But they discovered that most of the officers had already commanded companies and battalions in some of the army's largest battles of the twentieth century. Aware of the great experience that sat in their classrooms, the service schools and the Command and General Staff College decided to have students record their wartime experiences as part of the curriculum. The result was a mother lode of committee reports and individual accounts of battle at the regimental, battalion, and company level. The archives at Forts Benning, Knox, and Leavenworth are gold mines of information on what it is like to fight and lead men in a major war.

Official publications from the U.S. War Department tell much of how America fought the war. The field manuals referred to throughout this study contain the authoritative theoretical knowledge about how the military intended to fight World War II. Of these, FM 100-5, *Field Service*

Regulations: Operations, is by far the most important. War Department Pamphlet No. 20-17, *Lessons Learned and Expedients Used in Combat*, is a revealing review of what the army learned on the front lines. A series of official publications provided units in the field with updates on enemy forces as well as tactical and technical lessons learned by combat troops in all theaters. These periodicals include *Combat Lessons, Tactical and Technical Trends*, and *Intelligence Bulletins*.

Memoirs, paper collections, diaries, and oral histories round out the primary source materials available. Omar Bradley's *A Soldier's Story* and the semi-autobiographical *A General's Life* provide good overviews of the campaign strategies and major battles. Patton's *War as I Knew It* provides a gritty chronology of Third Army operations. Gavin's *On to Berlin* relates much of the airborne's contributions in Europe and provides frank analyses of American successes and failures. At the foxhole level, Charles B. MacDonald's *Company Commander* remains a stalwart in relating the experiences of one small unit commander. A more recent unit memoir, *The Men of Company K*, graphically tells the story of how one rifle company fought and endured. It deserves to take its place alongside *Company Commander* as one of the two best American memoirs of small unit actions in World War II. The archives of the U.S. Army Military History Institute at Carlisle Barracks, Pennsylvania, are an invaluable source for World War II paper collections, diaries, and oral histories. The William C. Sylvan and Chester B. Hansen Diaries, the Arthur S. Nevins Papers, and Elwood R. Quesada's oral memoirs of air-ground operations give good views of the fighting from the perspectives of SHAEF, 12th Army Group, and First Army Headquarters.

The start and end point of the secondary sources on the war in Europe is the magisterial series United States Army in World War II. Perhaps the largest historical venture ever undertaken in the United States, the army's efforts produced a thorough, balanced history of the war. The six volumes on the ETO—Harrison's *Cross-Channel Attack*, Blumenson's *Breakout and Pursuit*, Cole's *The Lorraine Campaign* and *The Ardennes: The Battle of the Bulge*, and MacDonald's *The Siegfried Line Campaign* and *The Last Offensive*—are indispensable accounts of the war in Europe. At least two volumes—*Cross-Channel Attack* and *The Ardennes*—remain the best works available on their respective topics. Other volumes in the series provide insights on varying aspects of the war. *The Organization of Ground Combat Troops* and *The Army Ground Forces: The Procurement and Training of Ground Combat Troops* explain how the United States manned, organized, and trained its combat formations. Two volumes by Ruppenthal, *Logistical Support of the Armies*, tell how the nation equipped and sustained its far-flung forces. *The Corps of Engineers: Troops and Equipment* is particularly good on the hardware and functions of engineer units, while *The Corps of Engineers: The War against Germany* relates the contributions of engineers in the ETO. *Europe: Argument to V-E Day*, a key volume in the official air force history of World War II, relates the significant events of air-ground operations against the Germans.

A number of books lead the pack in recounting and analyzing the war in Europe. MacDonald's *The Mighty Endeavor* remains the best single-volume overview of America's second war with Germany. Russell Weigley's *Eisenhower's Lieutenants* is clearly the best study of the ETO, although his conclusions are far from definitive. Shelby Stanton's *Order of Battle, United States Army, World War II* is a definitive source of information on army organization and unit histories. A number of other books tell about the battles: Hastings's *Overlord*, Kemp's *The Unknown Battle: Metz, 1944*, Whiting's *The Battle of the Huertgen Forest*, MacDonald's *A Time for Trumpets: The Untold Story of the Battle of the Bulge*, and Hechler's *The Bridge at Remagen*.

The literature on the experiences and fighting abilities of the America GI continues to expand. The start point for studying how Americans viewed and endured combat is the definitive *The American Soldier: Combat and Its Aftermath* by Samuel Stouffer. *What the Soldier Thinks* came from the War Department's Morale Services Division in the Pentagon and gives a revealing wartime look at the motives and attitudes of Americans in battle. A number of recent books—Ellis's *The Sharp End: The Fighting Man in World War II*, Kennett's *G.I.: The American Soldier in World War II*, and Fussell's *Wartime*—enrich our knowledge of what men experience in war. Van Creveld's *Fighting Power*, Weigley's *Eisenhower's Lieutenants*, and Hastings's *Overlord* fuel the debate over American versus German fighting prowess and the effectiveness of the U.S. war machine. S. L. A. Marshall's *Men against Fire* is a long-standing but controversial work on the performance of the American infantry. As of late, Marshall's scholarship has been closely scrutinized, and a flurry of articles in military and popular journals have criticized his professional and personal honesty.

Several War Department and Department of the Army publications are noteworthy. After the war the War Department's Historical Division published the outstanding American Forces in Action Series that details over a dozen of World War II's more significant operations. Two works in the series—*St. Lo* and *Omaha Beachhead*—remain the best studies available on those battles. In the late 1940s and early 1950s, the Armor Force School at Fort Knox produced a series of committee reports that are required reading for anyone interested in how American tankers performed in the war. The Armor School's best products are "The Battle of St. Vith, Belgium, 17–23 December 1944" and "The Remagen Bridgehead." The army's Command and General Staff College at Fort Leavenworth has sponsored two series of manuscripts that contain much analysis of World War II operations: the Combat Studies Institute's "Battlebooks" and the master's theses resulting from the college's Master of Military Art and Science program.

The professional military journals of the period contain a large number of articles on a variety of subjects. *Infantry Journal, Armored Cavalry Journal, Field Artillery Journal, Military Review*, and the *Military Engineer* between 1944 and 1950 are especially helpful. Fort Benning also published two training periodicals that provide rich details on infantry combat: *The Mailing List* and the *Infantry School Quarterly*.

Unit histories provide valuable, detailed accounts of battles and engagements; unfortunately, good division histories are few in number. The best include *29 Let's Go! A History of the 29th Infantry Division in World War II, Work Horse of the Western Front: The Story of the 30th Infantry Division*, and *The Fifth Infantry Division in the ETO*. Two corps histories on specific campaigns are exceptional: XX Corps' "The Reduction of Fortress Metz, 1 September–6 December 1944, An Operational Report," and XIX Corps' "Breaching the Siegfried Line." The best division level study of a single operation is the 4th Armored Division's "Nancy Bridgehead."

NOTES

INTRODUCTION

1. *Small Unit Actions*, American Forces in Action Series (Washington, D.C.: War Department, Historical Division, 1946; reprint ed., Washington D.C.: U.S. Army Center of Military History, 1986), 177. The U.S. Army Center of Military History is hereafter cited as USACMH.

2. Michael Howard, "Military Science in an Age of Peace," *Journal of the Royal United Services Institute for Defense Studies* 119 (March 1974): 3–9.

3. B. H. Liddell Hart, *History of the First World War* (London: Pan Books, 1972), 337–39.

4. Russell Weigley, *Eisenhower's Lieutenants* (Bloomington: Indiana University Press, 1981), 727–30.

5. For an interesting comparison of how the articulation and presentation of American military doctrine has changed since World War II, compare the 1941 and 1986 editions of the U.S. Army's Field Manual 100-5, *Operations*.

6. U.S. Army Infantry School, *Infantry in Battle* (Washington, D.C.: Infantry Journal, 1934), vii. The U.S. Army Infantry School is hereafter cited as USAIS.

CHAPTER 1: LESSONS LEARNED IN THE NORTH AFRICAN AND MEDITERRANEAN CAMPAIGNS

1. Alfred D. Chandler, Jr., ed., *The Papers of Dwight D. Eisenhower: The War Years*, 5 vols. (Baltimore: Johns Hopkins Press, 1970), 1:66.

2. George F. Howe, *Northwest Africa: Seizing the Initiative in the West*, United States Army in World War II (Washington, D.C.: United States Army, Office of the Chief of Military History, 1957; reprinted, Washington, D.C.: USACMH, 1985), 671–74; U.S. War Department, *Lessons from the Tunisian Campaign* (Washington, D.C.: Government Printing Office, 1943), 1–2; Allied Force Headquarters, Training Memorandum no. 50, "Lessons from the Sicilian Campaign," 20 November 1943, 1; Headquarters, Mediterranean Theater of Operations, United States Army, Training Memorandum no. 2, "Lessons from the Italian Campaign," n.d., 1–2, 19, 55–56; and Courtney H. Hodges, U.S. Third Army, *"Report of Visit to North African Theater of Operations,"* n.d., 5–6.

3. Omar N. Bradley, *A Soldier's Story* (New York: Rand McNally, 1951; reprint ed., New York: Rand McNally, 1978), 83–88; Ernest F. Fisher, Jr., *Cassino to the Alps*, United States Army in World War II (Washington, D.C.: United States Army, Office of the Chief of Military History, 1977; reprint ed., Washington, D.C.: USACMH, 1984), 77–78; U.S. War Department, *Lessons from the Tunisian Campaign*, 2–5; and Headquarters, 9th Infantry Division, U.S. Army, "Reports

on Combat Experience and Battle Lessons for Training Purposes," 21 June 1943, 1.

4. Ernest N. Harmon, "Notes on Combat Experience during the Tunisian and African Campaigns," n.d., 3–4; and "Lessons from the Italian Campaign," 18, 22.

5. Weigley, *Eisenhower's Lieutenants*, 26–27; Harmon, "Notes," 15–17; U.S. War Department, *Lessons from the Tunisian Campaign*, 3; 9th Infantry Division, "Battle Lessons for Training Purposes," 4–5; and "Lessons from the Italian Campaign," 81.

6. "Lessons from the Italian Campaign," 81; 9th Infantry Division, "Battle Lessons for Training Purposes," 3–4; and "Lessons from the Sicilian Campaign," 14–15.

7. "Lessons from the Sicilian Campaign," 15.

8. Harmon, "Notes," 15–17; "Lessons from the Sicilian Campaign," 13–14; "Lessons from the Italian Campaign," 77–79; and United States Army Ground Forces Observers Board, North African Theater of Operations, *Reports of the Army Ground Forces Observers Board*, North African Theater of Operations, Rept. no. 3, 22 August 1943, Appendix A, "Notes on Infantry," 5–7, hereafter cited as AGF Obs. Bd. followed by the applicable theater of operation, the report number, and the report title. There were AGF Observer Boards for each World War II theater of operations; at one point observers were operating for both the War Department and the Army Ground Forces and filed their reports under the aegis of the War Department while intending them for the AGF. The six-volume collection of AGF Observer Board reports at the United States Army Military History Institute at Carlisle Barracks, Pa., contains reports bearing both headings but is considered representative of AGF reports. The United States Army Military History Institute is hereafter cited as USAMHI.

9. Headquarters, 9th Infantry Division, United States Army, "Reports on Combat Experiences and Battle Lessons for Training Purposes Learned during the Sicilian Campaign," 4 September 1943, 2–3; Harmon, "Notes," 3; "Lessons from the Sicilian Campaign," 13–14; and "Lessons from the Italian Campaign," 77–79.

10. U.S. War Department, *Lessons from the Tunisian Campaign*, 35–39; Albert N. Garland and Howard McGaw Smyth, *Sicily and the Surrender of Italy*, United States Army in World War II (Washington, D.C.: U.S. Army, Office of the Chief of Military History, 1965; reprint ed., Washington, D.C.: USACMH, 1986), 418; and Peter C. Hains III, "Tanks in Tunisia," *The Cavalry Journal* 52 (July-August 1943): 13.

11. Harmon, "Notes," 11–13; and "Lessons from the Italian Campaign," 22–27.

12. "Lessons from the Sicilian Campaign," 11–12.

13. Charles E. Heller and William A. Stofft, eds., *America's First Battles, 1776–1965* (Lawrence: University Press of Kansas, 1986), 261–65; and "Lessons from the Italian Campaign," 22–27.

14. Harmon, "Notes," 6–9; "Lessons from the Sicilian Campaign," 11–12; and "Lessons from the Italian Campaign," 22–27.

15. Charles M. Baily, *Faint Praise: American Tanks and Tank Destroyers during World War II* (Hamden, Conn.: Archon Books, 1983), 54–60; Christopher R. Gabel, *Seek, Strike, and Destroy: United States Army Tank Destroyer Doctrine in World War II*, Leavenworth Papers, no. 12 (Fort Leavenworth, Kans.: Combat Studies Institute, U.S. Army Command and General Staff College, 1985), 24–41; Heller and Stofft, *First Battles*, 263; U.S. War Department, *Lessons from the Tunisian Campaign*, 56–58; and "Lessons from the Italian Campaign," 34–

41. The U.S. Army Command and General Staff College is hereafter cited as USACGSC.

16. Gabel, *Seek, Strike, and Destroy*, 24–41; and "Lessons from the Italian Campaign," 34–41.

17. U.S. War Department, *Lessons from the Tunisian Campaign*, 16–21.

18. Ibid.; Garland and Smyth, *Sicily*, 418; "Lessons from the Sicilian Campaign," 25; and "Lessons from the Italian Campaign," 84–85.

19. Martin Blumenson, *Salerno to Cassino*, United States Army in World War II (Washington, D.C.: United States Army, Office of the Chief of Military History, 1969), 411, 441; Garland and Smyth, *Sicily*, 418; Harmon, "Notes," 3; "Lessons from the Sicilian Campaign," 25; and "Lessons from the Italian Campaign," 22.

20. "Lessons from the Italian Campaign," 22.

21. U.S. War Department, *Lessons from the Tunisian Campaign*, 7–8; "Lessons from the Sicilian Campaign," 22; "Lessons from the Italian Campaign," 95; and 9th Infantry Division, "Battle Lessons for Training Purposes," 3.

22. Kent R. Greenfield, *Army Ground Forces and the Air-Ground Battle Team Including Organic Light Aviation*, Study no. 35 (Fort Monroe, Va.: Historical Section, AGF, 1948), 45–46; Daniel R. Mortensen, *A Pattern for Joint Operations: World War II Close Air Support, North Africa* (Washington, D.C.: Office of Air Force History and U.S. Army Center of Military History, 1987), 66–71, 78–83; Walton H. Walker, Headquarters, AGF, "Report of Visit to the North African Theater of Operations," 29 June 1943, 1–2; Howe, *Northwest Africa*, 673; Garland and Smyth, *Sicily*, 421; and Harmon, "Notes," 10–11.

23. AGF Obs. Bd., North African Theater of Operations, Rept. no. 309-A-1/29, "Air-Ground Support in North Africa," 20 June 1943, 1–2; Greenfield, *Air-Ground Battle Team*, 45–46; Harmon, "Notes," 10–11; "Lessons from the Sicilian Campaign," 61–64; "Lessons from the Italian Campaign," 51–52; and 9th Infantry Division, "Battle Lessons for Training Purposes," 7.

24. "Lessons from the Sicilian Campaign," 64–66; AGF Obs. Bd. Rept. no. 309-A-1/29, 1–2; and "Lessons from the Italian Campaign," 51–52.

25. AGF Obs. Bd., Mediterranean Theater of Operations, unnumbered report, "Lessons Learned in the Battle from the Garigliano to North of Rome," 21 September 1944, 13–16; Greenfield, *Air-Ground Battle Team*, 78–85; "Lessons from the Italian Campaign," 53–55.

26. Blumenson, *Salerno to Cassino*, 409–17, 441; and "Lessons from the Italian Campaign," 47–50.

27. "Lessons from the Sicilian Campaign," 6–7; and "Lessons from the Italian Campaign," 19.

28. U.S. War Department, *Combat Lessons*, no. 2 (Washington, D.C.: Operations Division, Combat Analysis Section, n.d.), 1–2.

29. Ibid., 2.

30. Ibid., 5; "Lessons from the Sicilian Campaign," 6; and Harmon, "Notes," 2.

31. Harmon, "Notes," 5.

32. Ibid.

33. "Lessons from the Italian Campaign," 19.

34. Harmon, "Notes," 5.

35. "Lessons from the Italian Campaign," 19.

36. "Lessons from the Sicilian Campaign," 66–67.

37. U.S. War Department, *Lessons from the Tunisian Campaign*, 3–4; "Lessons from the Sicilian Campaign," 21–23; Harmon, "Notes," 6; AGF Obs. Bd., Mediterranean Theater of Operations, Rept. no. A-M-89, "34th Infantry Division,

Lessons Learned in Combat, 8 November 1942–1 September 1944," n.d., 91; AGF Obs. Bd., Mediterranean Theater of Operations, unnumbered report, "Replacements," 27 February 1944, 1; and 9th Infantry Division, "Battle Lessons Learned for Training Purposes during the Sicilian Campaign," 2.

38. U.S. War Department, *Lessons from the Tunisian Campaign,* 9, 60–61; "Lessons from the Sicilian Campaign," 10–11; 9th Infantry Division, "Battle Lessons for Training Purposes," 4; AGF Obs. Bd., North African Theater of Operations, Rept. no. 309-A-1/27, "Report of Visit to the North African Theater of Operations," 27 May 1943, 2–3; and AGF Obs. Bd., Rept. no. A-M-89, 93.

39. Hodges, "Report of Visit to North African Theater of Operations," 2–4, 12; AGF Obs. Bd., Rept. no. 309-A-1/37, 9; Walker, "Visit to North African Theater of Operations," 5–6; AGF Obs. Bd., Rept. no. A-M-89, 94–96.

40. Harmon, "Notes," 14; Walker, "Visit to North African Theater of Operations," 7–8; AGF Obs. Bd., Rept. no. A-M-89, 94–96; AGF Obs. Bd., Rept. no. 309-A-1/27, 6; and AGF Obs. Bd., unnumbered report, "Replacements," 3.

41. Robert R. Palmer, Bell I. Wiley, and William R. Keast, *The Army Ground Forces: The Procurement and Training of Ground Combat Troops,* United States Army in World War II (Washington, D.C.: U.S. Army, Office of the Chief of Military History, 1948), 1–13; Allan R. Millett and Williamson Murray, eds., *Military Effectiveness,* 3 vols. (Boston: Allen and Unwin, 1988) 3: 59–61; and Harmon, "Notes," 14–15.

42. Harmon, ibid.; and Walker, "Visit to North African Theater of Operations," 7–8.

43. Howe, *Northwest Africa,* 674.

CHAPTER 2: BUSTING THE BOCAGE

1. Forrest C. Pogue, *The Supreme Command,* United States Army in World War II (Washington, D.C.: U.S. Army, Office of the Chief of Military History, 1954), 52–53.

2. Martin Blumenson, *Breakout and Pursuit,* United States Army in World War II (Washington, D.C.: U.S. Army, Office of the Chief of Military History, 1961), chaps. 1–3 passim. All factual background material on the Normandy campaign is from the cited reference unless otherwise noted.

3. Ibid., 178.

4. Omar N. Bradley and Clay Blair, *A General's Life* (New York: Simon and Schuster, 1983), 247–59.

5. Ibid., 262–64.

6. Ibid., 266–71.

7. "Appreciation on Possible Development of Operations to Secure a Lodgement Area: Operation OVERLORD," a terrain analysis study of the Cotentin Peninsula, 3 May 1942, 7, Arthur S. Nevins Papers, USAMHI; and Blumenson, *Breakout and Pursuit,* 177.

8. "Operations to Secure a Lodgement Area," Nevins Papers, 5; Chester B. Hansen Diaries, 8–9 June 1944, USAMHI; James M. Gavin, *On to Berlin: Battles of an Airborne Commander, 1943–1946* (New York: Viking Press, 1978), 121; Charles D. Folsom, "Hedgerow Fighting near Carentan," U.S. Army Armor School Library Report 41–53 (Fort Knox, Ky.: Advanced Officers' Class no. 1, U.S. Army Armor School, 1948), 1; and AGF Obs. Bd., ETO, Rept. no. 171, "Normandy

Hedgerows," 1–2. The U.S. Army Armor School is hereafter cited as USAARMS.

9. Blumenson, *Breakout and Pursuit*, 48–50.

10. AGF Obs. Bd., ETO, Rept. no. 138, "Notes on Hedgerow Warfare in the Normandy Beachhead," 1–2; AGF Obs. Bd., ETO, Rept. no. 141, "German Defense in Hedgerow Terrain," Exhibit A; AGF Obs. Bd., ETO, Rept. no. 195, "Lessons from Present Campaign," 1–4; U.S. Army, XIX Corps, "The Tank-Infantry Team," 24 June 1944, 2–3, available at USAMHI; and U.S. Army, 1st U.S. Army Group, "Battle Experiences," no. 1, 1, available at USAMHI, hereafter cited as FUSAG, "Battle Experiences." During the Normandy fighting, 1st Army Group published and distributed a series of "Battle Experiences," reports that contained technical information and a synopsis of key lessons learned in combat by subordinate units.

11. Ibid.; FUSAG, "Battle Experiences," no. 1,3; and FUSAG, "Battle Experiences," no. 12, 2.

12. FUSAG, "Battle Experiences," no. 1, 2; AGF Obs. Bd., ETO, Rept. no. 195, 1–4; and United States Army, First Army, *First United States Army: Report of Operations, 20 October 1943–1 August 1944*, 7 vols. (Washington, D.C.: U.S. War Department, 1945?), 1:122–23, hereafter cited as *First Army Report*.

13. Ibid.

14. Ibid.

15. *First Army Report*, 1:117; AGF Obs. Bd., ETO, Rept. no. 157, "Notes on Interview with Various Infantry Commanders in Normandy," 1; and FUSAG, "Battle Experiences," no. 14, 1–2.

16. *First Army Report*, 1:117; FUSAG, "Battle Experiences," no. 1, 3; and FUSAG, "Battle Experiences," no. 14, 1–2.

17. FUSAG, "Battle Experiences," no. 10, 1.

18. Ibid., no. 19, 1.

19. AGF Obs. Bd., ETO, Rept. no. 157, 1, 4, 10.

20. William R. Campbell, "Tanks with Infantry," USAARMS Library Report 42-9 (Fort Knox, Ky.: Advanced Officers' Class no. 1, USAARMS, Fort Knox, Kentucky, 1947), 1; *First Army Report*, 1:121–22; and AGF Obs. Bd., ETO, Rept. no. 157, 5.

21. *First Army Report*, 1:121; and AGF Obs. Bd., ETO, Rept. no. 187, Exhibit B, 1.

22. *First Army Report*, 1:122; and AGF Obs. Bd., ETO, Rept. no. 195, 1–3.

23. Hansen, Diaries, 9 June 1944.

24. *First Army Report*, 1:122; and AGF Obs. Bd., ETO, Rept. no. 195, 1–3.

25. AGF Obs. Bd., ETO, Rept. no. 201, "Use of Dozer Tanks and Landing of Tanks in Amphibious Operations," 1; and U.S. Forces, European Theater, *Reports of the General Board*, Study no. 52, "Armored Special Equipment," 14–17. The Reports of the General Board are hereafter cited as USFET, *Reports*, and the study number.

26. AGF Obs. Bd., ETO, Rept. no. 191, "Notes on Interviews with Various Commanders in Normandy," 2–3, and Exhibits A, B, and C.

27. Ibid.

28. Ibid.

29. Ibid.

30. Ibid.

31. Folsom, "Hedgerow Fighting near Carentan," 5; AGF Obs. Bd., ETO, Rept. no. 191, 5; and Blumenson, *Breakout and Pursuit*, 206.

32. Max Hastings, *Overlord* (London: Michael Joseph, 1984), 252; and Blumenson, *Breakout and Pursuit*, 206–7.

33. Omar N. Bradley, *A Soldier's Story* (New York: Rand McNally, 1951; reprint ed., New York: Rand McNally, 1978), 342; William C. Sylvan Diaries, 14 July 1944, USAMHI; and *First Army Report*, V, 200–201.

34. James J. Butler, "Individual Tank-Infantry Communications," *Armored Cavalry Journal* (July-August 1947), 43–45; U.S. War Department Field Manual 17-36, *Employment of Tanks with Infantry* (Washington, D.C.: Government Printing Office, 7 July 1944), 93–100; and Blumenson, *Breakout and Pursuit*, 43.

35. Butler, "Communications," 43–45; and *First Army Report*, 1:122.

36. Folsom, "Hedgerow Fighting near Carentan," 7; and AGF Obs. Bd., ETO, Rept. no. 120, "Employment of Tanks with Infantry," 4–5.

37. Butler, "Communications," 44–45; AGF Obs. Bd., ETO, Rept. no. 120, 4–5; and FUSAG, "Battle Experiences," no. 13, 1–2.

38. USFET, *Reports*, Study no. 50, "Organization, Equipment, and Tactical Employment of Separate Tank Battalions," 6–7.

39. AGF Obs. Bd., ETO, Rept. no. Misc.-19, "Information Regarding Air-Ground Joint Operations," 8; and United States Army, G-3 Staff, Historical Branch, Programs Division, "Historical Survey of Army Fire Support," I-B-2; *First Army Report*, 1:123; and AGF Obs. Bd., ETO, Rept. no. 192, "Corps Artillery," 5.

40. Gordon A. Harrison, *Cross-Channel Attack*, United States Army in World War II (Washington, D.C.: U.S Army, Office of the Chief of Military History, 1950; reprint ed., Washington, D.C.: U.S. Army, Office of the Chief of Military History, 1977), 381–84.

41. Ibid.

42. Forrest W. Creamer, "Operations of the XIX United States Army Corps in Normandy," USAARMS Library Report 42-8 (Fort Knos, Ky.: Advanced Officers' Class no. 1, USAARMS, 1947), 31; and AGF Obs. Bd., ETO, Rept. no. 191, Exhibit A.

43. AGF Obs. Bd., ETO, Rept. no. 138, Exhibit A.

44. Ibid.

45. Ibid.

46. Blumenson, *Breakout and Pursuit*, 153–57; and *St. Lo*, American Forces in Action Series (Washington, D.C.: War Department, Historical Division, 1946; reprint ed., Washington, D.C.: USACMH, 1984), 54–58.

47. Ibid.

48. Ibid.; and AGF Obs. Bd., ETO, Rept. no. 191, 1.

49. Blumenson, *Breakout and Pursuit*, 149–53; and *St. Lo*, 58–69.

50. FUSAG, "Battle Experiences," no. 8, 1–2.

51. Blumenson, *Breakout and Pursuit*, 149–53; and *St. Lo*, 58–69.

52. Ibid.

53. Ibid.; and FUSAG, "Battle Experiences," no. 8, 2.

54. Creamer, "Operations," 18–22.

55. Ibid.

56. AGF Obs. Bd., ETO, Rept. no. 141, Exhibit A.

57. Ibid.

58. Creamer, "Operations," 20–28.

59. Ibid.

60. *First Army Report*, 1:117.

61. Hastings, *Overlord*, 210; AGF Obs. Bd., ETO, Rept. no. 191, 2; and Blumenson, *Breakout and Pursuit*, 175–82.

62. Blumenson, *Breakout and Pursuit*, 175–76.

63. S.L.A. Marshall, *Men against Fire: The Problem of Battle Command in Future War* (Gloucester, Mass.: Peter Smith, 1947; reprint ed., Gloucester, Mass.: Peter Smith, 1978), 108.

CHAPTER 3: THE AIR-GROUND BATTLE TEAM

1. U.S. War Department, Field Manual 100-20, *Field Service Regulations: Command and Employment of Air Power* (Washington, D.C.: Government Printing Office, 21 July 1943), 1–2.
2. Ibid., 10–12.
3. James A. Huston, "Tactical Use of Air Power in World War II: The Army Experience," *Military Affairs* 14 (Winter 1950): 171–75.
4. Wesley F. Craven and James L. Cate, eds., *The Army Air Forces in World War II*, vol. 3; *Europe: Argument to V-E Day, January 1944 to May 1945* (Chicago: University of Chicago Press, 1951; reprint ed., Washington, D.C.: Government Printing Office, 1983), 141; and Bradley, *A Soldier's Story*, 249.
5. Craven and Cate, *AAF in WW II*, 107–13.
6. Ibid., 196–97; and Blumenson, *Breakout and Pursuit*, 208.
7. Elwood R. Quesada, transcript, oral memoirs, Section III, 15–16, 34–35; and Bradley, *A Soldier's Story*, 250.
8. AGF Obs. Bd., ETO, Rept. no. Misc.-19, 2, 5–6.
9. Ibid., 4; Blumenson, *Breakout and Pursuit*, 208; and Quesada oral memoirs, Section IV, 9–11.
10. AGF Obs. Bd., ETO, Rept. no. Misc.-19, 2; and *First Army Report*, 1:119–20.
11. Air Effects Committee, 12th Army Group, "Effects of Air Power on Military Operations, Western Europe," (Wiesbaden, West Germany: 12th Army Group, 15 July 1945), 43–44; FUSAG, "Battle Experiences," no. 6, 1–2; *First Army Report*, 1:120; and AGF Obs. Bd., ETO, Rept. no. 195, 3.
12. Creamer, "Operations," 20; *St. Lo*, 62; and Blumenson, *Breakout and Pursuit*, 178.
13. *St. Lo*, 40–41; and Quesada oral memoirs, Section V, 3–5.
14. AGF Obs. Bd., ETO, Rept. no. Misc.-19, 4; and FUSAG, Operations Memorandum no. 3, "Observation of Artillery Fire by Fighter Type Aircraft," 1–2.
15. *First Army Report*, 5:200; and Quesada oral memoirs, Section III, 35–37.
16. Quesada oral memoirs, Section III, 35–37; Bradley, *A Soldier's Story*, 337–38; and "Employment of 2d Armored Division in Operation COBRA," USAARMS Library Report 45.2-3 (Fort Knox, Ky.: Advanced Officers' Class no. 1, Committee 3, USAARMS, 1950), 15.
17. Craven and Cate, *AAF in WW II*, 239–40.
18. Ibid.
19. *First Army Report*, 1:121; *First Army Report*, 5:220; 12th Army Group, "Effects of Air Power," 41–42; and *Condensed Analysis of the Ninth Air Force in the European Theater of Operations* (Washington, D.C.: Headquarters, Army Air Forces, March 1946), 26–27.
20. Craven and Cate, *AAF in WW II*, 238–43.
21. Ibid.; and Kent R. Greenfield, *American Strategy in World War II: A Reconsideration* (Baltimore: Johns Hopkins University Press, 1963; reprint ed., Malabar, Fla.: Robert E. Krieger Publishing Company, 1982), 109–11.
22. "Air-Ground Teamwork on the Western Front: The Role of the XIX Tactical

Air Command During August 1944," *Wings at War*, no. 5 (Washington, D.C.: Headquarters, Army Air Forces, n.d.), 4–14.

23. Ibid,; and George S. Patton, Jr., *War as I Knew It* (Boston: Houghton Mifflin, 1947; reprint ed., New York: Bantam Books, 1981), 96.

24. Craven and Cate, *AAF in WW II*, 552.

25. Hugh M. Cole, *The Lorraine Campaign*, United States Army in World War II (Washington, D.C.: U.S. Army, Office of the Chief of Military History, 1950; reprint ed., Washington, D.C.: USACMH, 1984), 598–600.

26. Ibid.; and Headquarters, XIX Tactical Air Command, "Tactical Air Operations in Europe," 19 May 1945, 3–4, 53–54.

27. 12th Army Group, "Effects of Air Power," 43.

28. Cole, *The Lorraine Campaign*, 600; and XIX Tactical Air Command, "Tactical Air Operations," 3.

29. USFET, *Reports*, Study no. 20, "Liaison Aircraft with Ground Force Units," 14–22.

30. Ibid.

31. Ibid.

32. IX Tactical Air Command, Air Statistical Control Section, "IX TAC in Review: European Theater of Operations, November 1943–May 1945," n.d., 10; 12th Army Group, "Effects of Air Power," 25; and Headquarters, XIX TAC, U.S. Army Air Forces, "Tactical Air Operations in Europe," 10–13.

33. USFET, *Reports*, Study no. 19, "The Utilization of Tactical Air Force Reconnaissance Units of the Army Air Forces to Secure Information for Ground Forces in the European Theater," 1–11; Army Air Forces Evaluation Board, ETO, "Tactics and Techniques Developed by the United States Tactical Air Commands in the European Theater of Operations," Section II, "Reconnaissance Operations of the Ninth Air Force," 1 March 1945, 25–37; and Greenfield, *Air-Ground Battle Team*, 92–93.

34. Ibid.

35. Bradley, *A Soldier's Story*, 338–39; and Huston, "Tactical Use of Air Power," 175–76.

36. Craven and Cate, *AAF in WW II*, 167, 190.

37. Ibid., 190–93; and 12th Army Group, "Effects of Air Power," 90.

38. Blumenson, *Breakout and Pursuit*, 213–15.

39. Bradley, *A Soldier's Story*, 330.

40. Bradley and Blair, *A General's Life*, 276–77.

41. Blumenson, *Breakout and Pursuit*, 229–33.

42. Bradley, *A Soldier's Story*, 347; and Bradley and Blair, *A General's Life*, 279–80.

43. Blumenson, *Breakout and Pursuit*, 234–41.

44. Ibid., 234–35; and Craven and Cate, *AAF in WW II*, 228–38.

45. Blumenson, *Breakout and Pursuit*, 234–41; and Bradley, *A Soldier's Story*, 348–49.

46. Ibid.; and 12th Army Group, "Effects of Air Power," 104.

47. *First Army Report*, 1:120–21.

48. Charles B. MacDonald, *The Siegfried Line Campaign*, United States Army in World War II (Washington, D.C.: U.S. Army, Office of the Chief of Military History, 1950; reprint ed., Washington, D.C.: USACMH, 1984), 390–92, 403–7; and 12th Army Group, "Effects of Air Power," 128–40.

49. Ibid.

50. Headquarters, Ninth Army, U.S. Army, "Operation Q," 23 January 1945, 2–7; U.S. Army, First Army, *First United States Army: Report of Opera-*

tions, 1 August 1944–22 February 1945, 4 vols. (Washington, D.C.: U.S. War Department, 1945[?]) 1:73–74, hereafter cited as *First Army Report*, Aug '44–Feb '45; and 12th Army Group, "Effects of Air Power," 105–8.

51. Ibid.

52. Craven and Cate, *AAF in WW II*, 631–33; and MacDonald, *Siegfried Line Campaign*, 411–16.

53. Headquarters, Ninth Army, U.S. Army, "Operation Q," 2–7; *First Army Report*, Aug '44–Feb '45, 73–74; and 12th Army Group, "Effects of Air Power," 105–8.

54. Ibid.; Craven and Cate, *AAF in WW II*, 631–33; and MacDonald, *Siegfried Line Campaign*, 411–16.

55. USFET, *Reports*, Study no. 54, "The Tactical Air Force in the European Theater of Operations," Foreword.

56. USFET, *Reports*, Study no. 26, "Air Power in the European Theater of Operations," 14; and 12th Army Group, "Effects of Air Power," 26–27.

CHAPTER 4: BATTLES OF BUILDINGS AND COBBLESTONES

1. U.S. War Department, Field Manual 100-5, *Field Service Regulations: Operations* (Washington, D.C.: Government Printing Office, 22 May 1941), 209–10; U.S. War Department, Field Manual 31-50, *Attack on a Fortified Position and Combat in Towns* (Washington, D.C.: Government Printing Office, 31 January 1944), 60–94; and USAIS, "Principles of Town and Village Fighting," *The Mailing List* 28 (July 1944): 171.

2. FM 100-5, 209–10; and FM 31-50, 60–94.

3. Blumenson, *Breakout and Pursuit*, 632–37.

4. Ibid., 638–39.

5. U.S. War Department, Military Intelligence Division, "German Combat Tactics in Towns and Cities," *Intelligence Bulletin* 2 (January 1944): 41–46; Headquarters, Ninth Army, U.S. Army, "Fighting in Cities," 26 October 1944, 1–3; and Headquarters, 2d Infantry Division, U.S. Army, "Street Fighting in Brest, France," 4 October 1944, 1.

6. Ibid.

7. Blumenson, *Breakout and Pursuit*, 640–46.

8. U.S. War Department, Operations Division, Combat Analysis Section, "Street Fighting," *Combat Lessons*, no. 6 (n.d.): 11–21; U.S. War Department, War Department Pamphlet no. 20-17, *Lessons Learned and Expedients Used in Combat* (Washington, D.C.: Government Printing Office, July 1945), 55–59; Ninth Army, "Fighting in Cities," 3–7; and 2d Infantry Division, "Street Fighting in Brest, France," 1–4.

9. Ibid.; and Blumenson, *Breakout and Pursuit*, 646–47.

10. U.S. War Department, *Combat Lessons*, no. 6, 11-21; War Department Pamphlet 20-17, 55–59; Ninth Army, "Fighting in Cities," 3–7; and 2d Infantry Division, "Street Fighting in Brest, France," 1–4.

11. Ibid.

12. Ibid.; and USAIS, "Principles of Town and Village Fighting," 178–81.

13. George H. Duckworth, "Operations of Company F, 23d Infantry Regiment at Brest, France, 8–14 September 1944," (Fort Benning, Ga.: Advanced Officers' Class no. 1, USAIS, 1948), 20–31; USAIS, "Operations of a Rifle Company at Brest, France," *Infantry School Quarterly* 32 (April 1948): 114–18; and *Combat History*

of the Second Infantry Division in World War II (Nashville, Tenn.: Battery Press, 1979), 64–65.

14. Ibid.

15. Duckworth, "Operations of Company F," 20–31; and USAIS, "Operations of a Rifle Company at Brest, France," 128–36.

16. Ibid.

17. Ibid.

18. Ibid.

19. Ibid.

20. MacDonald, *Siegfried Line Campaign*, 36–38, 251–52, 284–85.

21. Ibid., 281, 285, 307–9, 314.

22. Ibid., 307–9.

23. Derrill M. Daniel, "Capture of Aachen, Germany, 10–21 October 1944," Combined Arms Research Library Report N-2253.17 (Fort Leavenworth, Kans.: USACGSC, 1947), 5–7; and Monte M. Parrish, "The Battle of Aachen," *Field Artillery Journal* 44 (September-October 1976): 26–27.

24. Ibid.

25. MacDonald, *Siegfried Line Campaign*, 309–10.

26. Ibid., 310–14; Daniel, "Capture of Aachen," 9–15; and Parrish, "Battle of Aachen," 27–29.

27. Ibid.

28. Ibid.

29. Charles Whiting, *Bloody Aachen* (New York: Stein and Day, 1976), 185; Daniel, "Capture of Aachen," 15–16; and MacDonald, *Siegfried Line Campaign*, 317–20.

30. Daniel, "Capture of Aachen," 16–17; Parrish, "Battle of Aachen," 29–30; and U.S. War Department, *Combat Lessons*, no. 6, 18–19.

31. U.S. War Department, Field Manual 17-36, Supplement no. 1, *Employment of Tanks with Infantry, Illustrated Problems* (Washington, D.C.: Government Printing Office, 7 July 1944), 17–27.

32. United States Army Training and Doctrine Command, Liaison Office, German General Army Office, "Defense of Villages, A German Army 'How to Fight' Guide from 1944," Monograph M-22-83 (Cologne, Federal Republic of Germany: U.S. Army Training and Doctrine Command German Army Liaison Office, 7 December 1983), 1–7.

33. Headquarters, XIX Corps, U.S. Army, "XIX Corps Demonstration: 2d Armored Division in the Tank-Infantry Assault of a Tactical Locality and 30th Infantry Division in the Infantry Assault of a Fortified Village," 10 December 1944, 1–7.

34. Ibid.

35. Ibid.

36. Ibid.

37. Ibid.

38. Ibid., 9–18.

39. Ibid.

40. Ibid.

41. Hugh F. Young, "Reinforced Armored Infantry Team in the Attack of a Town," USAARMS Library Report 41-146 (Fort Knox, Ky.: Advanced Officers' Class no. 1, USAARMS, 1948), 2–9.

42. Wallace H. Woods, "Initial Actions in an Attack Against a Town," USAIS Library, Student Monograph no. 191 (Fort Benning, Ga.: Advanced Officers' Class no. 1, USAIS, 1956), 3–4, 21–22; Headquarters, 12th Army Group, U.S. Army,

"Battle Experiences," Report no. 319.1/165, 28 December 1944, 3-5; and War Department Pamphlet 20-17, 56-59.

CHAPTER 5: STRUGGLES AGAINST STEEL AND CONCRETE

1. Fred L. Walker, Jr., "Siege Methods: 1945," *Infantry Journal*, January 1945, 10.

2. FM 100-5, 182-92.

3. FM 31-50, 1-10, 42-50.

4. Blanche D. Coll, Jean E. Keith, and Herbert H. Rosenthal, *The Corps of Engineers: Troops and Equipment*, United States Army in World War II (Washington, D.C.: U.S. Army, Office of the Chief of Military History, 1958; reprint ed., Washington D.C.: USACMH, 1969), 12-26, 465-83; and Francis Marion Cain III, "Mobility Support of Offensive Maneuver: First U.S. Army Attack on the Siegfried Line—1944" (Master's thesis, USACGSC, Fort Leavenworth, Kans., 1985), 19-52.

5. Headquarters, VIII Corps, U.S. Army, "Attack of a Fortified Area," 9 October 1944, 2-4; and Joseph H. Ewing, *29 Let's Go! A History of the 29th Infantry Division in World War II* (Washington, D.C.: Infantry Journal Press, 1948), 137.

6. Ewing, *29 Let's Go!* 138.

7. Ibid.; and Blumenson, *Breakout and Pursuit*, 649-51.

8. Ibid.; Office of the Historical Section, ETO, U.S. Army, "Battalion and Small Unit Study No. 2: Action at Fort Montbarey," USACMH Historical Manuscript File 8-3.1 BA2 (Washington, D.C.: USACMH, n.d.), 2-4; and USFET, *Reports*, Study no. 52, "Armored Special Equipment," 29-30, Appendix 2.

9. Ewing, *29 Let's Go!* 138-40; and Blumenson, *Breakout and Pursuit*, 649-51.

10. Ibid.; and Office of the Historical Section, ETO, "Action at Fort Montbarey," 14-18.

11. U.S. War Department, Military Intelligence Division, "Breaching the Siegfried Line," *Tactical and Technical Trends*, no. 57 (April 1945): 60-64; MacDonald, *Siegfried Line Campaign*, 28-35.

12. Ibid.

13. Headquarters, XIX Corps, U.S. Army, "Breaching the Siegfried Line," 12 January 1945, 9; and MacDonald, *Siegfried Line Campaign*, 251-53.

14. XIX Corps, "Siegfried Line," 6-8; and U.S. War Department, *Tactical and Technical Trends*, no. 57, 62-68.

15. XIX Corps, "Siegfried Line," 9, 38; and Robert L. Hewitt, *Work Horse of the Western Front: The Story of the 30th Infantry Division* (Washington, D.C.: Infantry Journal Press, 1946), 110-11.

16. XIX Corps, "Siegfried Line," 37.

17. Ibid., 9, 37-38; MacDonald, *Siegfried Line Campaign*, 255-56; and Hewitt, *Work Horse of the Western Front*, 111-12.

18. Ibid.

19. MacDonald, *Siegfried Line Campaign*, 253-61; Hewitt, *Work Horse of the Western Front*, 108-113; XIX Corps, "Siegfried Line," 12-14, 23-25, 31, 62-65; and Craven and Cate, *AAF in WW II*, 615.

20. Ibid.

21. U.S. War Department, *Tactical and Technical Trends*, no. 57, 69-71; XIX

Corps, "Siegfried Line," 15–18; and Hewitt, *Work Horse of the Western Front*, 113–25.

22. XIX Corps, "Siegfried Line," 22–23, 45–46.

23. Ibid.; U.S. War Department, Military Intelligence Division, "Pillbox Warfare in the Siegfried Line," *Intelligence Bulletin* 3 (January 1945): 39–48; AGF Obs. Bd., ETO, Rept. no. 319.1/159, 2; U.S. War Department, *Tactical and Technical Trends*, no. 57, 71–74; 12th Army Group, "Immediate Report No. 61," 3; and War Department Pamphlet 20–17, 59–61.

24. Ibid.

25. MacDonald, *Siegfried Line Campaign*, 262–63; and XIX Corps, "Siegfried Line," 40.

26. Hewitt, *Work Horse of the Western Front*, 119–25; U.S. War Department, *Tactical and Technical Trends*, no. 57, 70–71; and MacDonald, *Siegfried Line Campaign*, 279.

27. XIX Corps, "Siegfried Line," 9, 31.

28. Ibid., 31, 68.

29. Cole, *The Lorraine Campaign*, chap. 1 passim. All factual background material on the Metz campaign is from the cited reference unless otherwise noted.

30. Anthony Kemp, *The Unknown Battle: Metz, 1944* (London: Frederick Warne, Ltd., 1981), 30–33.

31. Cole, *The Lorraine Campaign*, 122–27.

32. Ibid.; and Headquarters, XX Corps, U.S. Army, "The Reduction of Fortress Metz, 1 September–6 December 1944, An Operational Report," 1945, 7–9.

33. Cole, *The Lorraine Campaign*, 122–27.

34. XX Corps, "Reduction of Metz," 4–6; and Cole, *The Lorraine Campaign*, 258–60.

35. Kemp, *The Unknown Battle*, 107–9; XX Corps, "Reduction of Metz," 10; and Cole, *The Lorraine Campaign*, 264–65.

36. Headquarters, 5th Infantry Division, U.S. Army, 5th Division Historical Section, *The Fifth Infantry Division in the ETO* (n.p., 1945), n.p.; Kemp, *The Unknown Battle*, 107–9, 112–13; and Cole, *The Lorraine Campaign*, 264–65.

37. Cole, *The Lorraine Campaign*, 269–70; and *Fifth Infantry Division*, n.p.

38. Ibid.; and Office of the Historical Section, ETO, U.S. Army, "The Capture of Metz," USACMH Historical Manuscript File 8-3.1 AS (Washington, D.C.: USACMH, n.d.), 56.

39. *Fifth Infantry Division*, n.p.; and Kemp, *The Unknown Battle*, 116.

40. *Fifth Infantry Division*, n.p.; Kemp, *The Unknown Battle*, 115–19; Cole, *The Lorraine Campaign*, 271–73; and XX Corps, "Reduction of Metz," 10–11.

41. Ibid.; and Office of the Historical Section, ETO, "The Capture of Metz," 64.

42. Cole, *The Lorraine Campaign*, 272–73.

43. Ibid. 272–75; Kemp, *The Unknown Battle*, 120–26; XX Corps, "Reduction of Metz," 11–12; and *Fifth Infantry Division*, n.p.

44. Ibid.; Office of the Historical Section, ETO, "The Capture of Metz," 71; and Joe I. Abrams, *A History of the 90th Division in World War II, 6 June 1944 to 9 May 1945* (Baton Rouge, La.: Army and Navy Publishing Co., 1946), 30; R. Stephenson et al., U.S. Army, "The Battle of Metz," Combat Studies Institute Battlebook 13-A (Fort Leavenworth, Kans.: Combat Studies Institute, USACGSC, 1984), 29; XX Corps, "Reduction of Metz," 14; and *Fifth Infantry Division*, n.p.

45. XX Corps, "Reduction of Metz," Appendix 13; and Cole, *The Lorraine Campaign*, 373–74.

46. XX Corps, "Reduction of Metz," 26–29; Cole, *The Lorraine Campaign*, 405, 440–41; and Office of the Historical Section, ETO, "The Capture of Metz," 274–77.

47. Headquarters, XX Corps, U.S. Army, *The XX Corps: Its History and Service in World War II* (Halstead, Kans.: Webs, n.d.), 168–69; Robert L. Schmidt, "XX Corps Operations, 1 August–22 November 1944: A Study in Combat Power" (Master's thesis, USACGSC, Fort Leavenworth, Kans., 1985), 213–15; XX Corps, "Reduction of Metz," 29–30; and Cole, *The Lorraine Campaign*, 440–43.

48. Kemp, *The Unknown Battle*, 195–96, 208–12; Cole, *The Lorraine Campaign*, 441–43; and Office of the Historical Section, ETO, "The Capture of Metz," 278–81.

49. Ibid.

50. Ibid.

51. XX Corps, "Reduction of Metz," 38; and Cole, *The Lorraine Campaign*, 446–49.

52. Walker, "Siege Methods: 1945," 8.

53. MacDonald, *Siegfried Line Campaign*, 616–17.

CHAPTER 6: IN SPITE OF HELL AND HIGH WATER

1. FM 100-5, 192–95.

2. Ibid.

3. U.S. War Department, Field Manual 5-6, *Operations of Engineer Field Units* (Washington, D.C.: Government Printing Office, 23 April 1944), 97–110; Blanche D. Coll, Jean E. Keith, and Herbert H. Rosenthal, *The Corps of Engineers: Troops and Equipment*, United States Army in World War II (Washington, D.C.: U.S. Army, Office of the Chief of Military History, 1958; reprint ed., Washington, D.C.: USACMH, 1969), 42–53, 492–94; and David E. Pergrin and Eric Hammel, *First across the Rhine: The 291st Engineer Combat Battalion in France, Belgium, and Germany* (New York: Ballantine Books, 1989), 242–43.

4. FM 5-6, 260–65.

5. FM 100-5, 197–200; and FM 5-6, 85–97.

6. Cole, *The Lorraine Campaign*, 16, 57–60.

7. James J. Mullen, "The Operations of Company E, 317th Infantry 80th Infantry Division) in the Establishment of a Bridgehead across the Moselle River, vicinity of Dieulouard, France, 5 September–14 September 1944," USAIS Library, Student Monograph no. D505 (Fort Benning, Ga.: Advanced Officers' Course, Class no. 1, USAIS, 1950), 6; Headquarters, 80th Infantry Division, U.S. Army, "Moselle River Crossing: Engineer Terrain Analysis," n.d., 1; James D. Long, Jr., et al., "Dieulouard Bridgehead Operation," Combat Studies Institute Battlebook 22-C, (Fort Leavenworth, Kans.: Combat Studies Institute, USACGSC, 1984), 9–11; and Cole, *The Lorraine Campaign*, 62–65.

8. Cole, *The Lorraine Campaign*, 62–65.

9. Karlton Warmbrod, "The Operations of the 2d Battalion, 317th Infantry (80th Infantry Division) in the Crossing of the Moselle and the Establishment of a Bridgehead at St. Genevieve, France, 5–12 September 1944," USAIS Library, Student Monograph no. D513 (Fort Benning, Ga.: Advanced Officers' Course,

Class no. 2, USAIS, 1950), 12–15; and Mullen, "Company E, 317th Infantry," 7–10.

10. Warmbrod, "2d Battalion, 317th Infantry," 15–21; and Mullen, "Company E, 317th Infantry," 10–12.

11. Cole, *The Lorraine Campaign*, 63–65; and Long et al., "Dieulouard Bridgehead," 52.

12. Ibid.

13. Cole, *The Lorraine Campaign*, 75–78.

14. Ibid.; Mullen, "Company E, 317th Infantry," 12–14; and Warmbrod, "2d Battalion, 317th Infantry," 21–25.

15. Cole, *The Lorraine Campaign*, 78–81.

16. Ibid.

17. Headquarters, Combat Command A, 4th Armored Division, U.S. Army, "The Nancy Bridgehead," n.d., 3–8, 24–25; and Cole, *The Lorraine Campaign*, 84–89.

18. Ibid.

19. Cole, *The Lorraine Campaign*, 96–105; and 4th Armored Division, "Nancy Bridgehead," 13.

20. Cole, *The Lorraine Campaign*, 380–81.

21. Alfred M. Beck et al., *The Corps of Engineers: The War against Germany*, United States Army in World War II (Washington, D.C.: USACMH, 1985), 423–34; and Charles E. Wright, "Moselle River Crossing at Cattenom," *Armored Cavalry Journal* 57 (May–June 1948): 50–52.

22. Cole, *The Lorraine Campaign*, 381.

23. Ibid., 382–83; and Abrams, *90th Division History*, 34.

24. Wright, "Moselle River Crossing," 52; Cole, *The Lorraine Campaign*, 383–87; and Abrams, *90th Division History*, 34–36.

25. Ibid.; and Beck et al., *Engineers: War against Germany*, 424–25.

26. Cole, *The Lorraine Campaign*, 390–92.

27. Ibid., 384; Beck et al., *Engineers: War against Germany*, 425–26; and Abrams, *90th Division History*, 38.

28. Wright, "Moselle River Crossing," 52–53; Abrams, *90th Division History*, 38; and Cole, *The Lorraine Campaign*, 402.

29. Ibid.; and Patton, *War as I Knew It*, 164.

30. U.S. War Department, Operations Division, Combat Analysis Section, "River Crossing Suggestions," *Combat Lessons*, no. 7 (n.d.): 13–23; AGF Obs. Bd., ETO, Report no. 667, "River Crossings," 1–2; AGF Obs. Bd., ETO, Report no. 704, "Roer River Crossing," 1–4; War Department Pamphlet 20-17, 52–54; and USFET, *Reports*, Study no. 50, "Organization, Equipment, and Tactical Employment of Separate Tank Battalions," 7.

31. Levin B. Cottingham, "Smoke over the Moselle," *Infantry Journal*, August 1948, 15–19; and Charles B. MacDonald and Sidney T. Mathews, *Three Battles: Arnaville, Altuzzo, and Schmidt*, United States Army in World War II (Washington, D.C.: U.S. Army, Office of the Chief of Military History, 1952; reprint ed., Washington, D.C.: USACMH, 1985), 63–70.

32. Ibid.; and AGF Obs. Bd., ETO, Report no. 784, "River Crossing Tactics," 1–2.

33. Charles B. MacDonald, *The Last Offensive*, United States Army in World War II (Washington, D.C.: U.S. Army, Office of the Chief of Military History, 1973), 208–9.

34. Research and Evaluation Division, USAARMS, United States Army, "The Re-

magen Bridgehead," n.d., 7; and Ken Hechler, *The Bridge at Remagen* (New York: Ballantine Books, 1957), 63.

35. Committee no. 22, Armor Officers' Advanced Course, 1949–1950, "Armor in River Crossings," USAARMS Library Report 45.2-22 (Fort Knox, Ky.: Advanced Officers' Class, 1949–1950, USAARMS, 1950), 9; and Hechler, *Bridge at Remagen*, 62–63.

36. USAARMS, "Remagen Bridgehead," 3.

37. MacDonald, *The Last Offensive*, 212–17; USAARMS, "Remagen Bridgehead," 1–2; and USAARMS, "Armor in River Crossings," 11–12.

38. Ibid.; and Hechler, *Bridge at Remagen*, 128, 139

39. MacDonald, *The Last Offensive*, 217; and Hechler, *Bridge at Remagen*, 142.

40. MacDonald, *The Last Offensive*, 220; and USAARMS, "Remagen Bridgehead," 5, 10.

41. MacDonald, *The Last Offensive*, 227–28.

42. Pergrin, *First across the Rhine*, 266.

43. MacDonald, *The Last Offensive*, 227–28; and USAARMS, "Remagen Bridgehead," 22.

44. MacDonald, *The Last Offensive*, 228–29; USAARMS, "Remagen Bridgehead," 22; and Beck et al., *Engineers: War against Germany*, 509–10.

45. Beck et al., *Engineers: War against Germany*, 507; and Pergrin, *First across the Rhine*, 237–47.

46. Beck et al., *Engineers: War against Germany*, 507–9.

47. MacDonald, *The Last Offensive*, 229–30; Hechler, *Bridge at Remagen*, 189–92; and Pergrin, *First across the Rhine*, 288–91.

48. MacDonald, *The Last Offensive*, 220, 229, 233–35.

49. Cottingham, "Smoke over the Moselle," 15; Wright, "Moselle River Crossing," 52–54; and U.S. War Department, *Combat Lessons*, no. 7, 16–19.

CHAPTER 7: CONFUSION AND SLAUGHTER AMONG THE FIRS

1. FM 100-5, 211–13.

2. U.S. War Department, Military Intelligence Division, "German Forest Fighting," *Tactical and Technical Trends*, no. 54 (January 1945): 70–77; U.S. War Department, Military Intelligence Division, "How the Germans Fight in Wooded and Broken Terrain," *Intelligence Bulletin* 3 (January 1945): 65–71; and Milton L. Rosen, "Forest Fighting," *Infantry Journal*, April 1945, 8–10.

3. Ibid.

4. Charles B. MacDonald, *The Battle of the Huertgen Forest* (New York: Jove Books, 1963), 4.

5. Ibid., 3–6.

6. MacDonald, *Siegfried Line Campaign*, 323–24.

7. Ibid., 92–95.

8. Ibid., 323–28.

9. Ibid., 328, 331–32.

10. Frank J. Randall, "The Operations of the 1st Battalion, 39th Infantry (9th Infantry Division) in the Huertgen Forest, Vicinity of Germeter and Vossenack, 10–14 October 1944," USAIS Library, Student Monograph (Fort Benning, Ga.: Advanced Officers' Course, Class no. 2, USAIS, 1949–1950), 21; and 12th Army Group, "Battle Experiences," no. 62, 2.

11. MacDonald, *Siegfried Line Campaign*, 330–31.

12. Ibid., 332.

13. Ibid., 332–36.

14. Ibid.

15. Committee no. 7, Armor Officers' Advanced Course, 1948–1949, "Armor in the Huertgen Forest," USAARMS Library Report 45.1-7 (Fort Knox, Ky.: Advanced Officers' Class, 1948–1949, USAARMS, 1949), 12–33.

16. Ibid.

17. Charles Whiting, *The Battle of the Huertgen Forest* (New York: Pocket Books, 1990), 53, 58; and MacDonald, *Huertgen Forest*, 80.

18. MacDonald, *Siegfried Line Campaign*, 337–40; and Whiting, *Huertgen Forest*, 59.

19. MacDonald and Mathews, *Three Battles*, 251–52.

20. MacDonald, *Siegfried Line Campaign*, 343–48.

21. Ibid.; and Robert A. Miller, *Division Commander: A Biography of Major General Norman D. Cota* (Spartanburg, S.C.: Reprint Company, 1989), 117.

22. MacDonald and Mathews, *Three Battles*, 256–57; and MacDonald, *Siegfried Line Campaign*, 346.

23. Ibid.

24. MacDonald, *Siegfried Line Campaign*, 347–48; and Miller, *Division Commander*, 114.

25. MacDonald, *Siegfried Line Campaign*, 348–50, 366, 372.

26. MacDonald and Mathews, *Three Battles*, 259–71; and USAARMS, "Armor in the Huertgen Forest," 37–39.

27. MacDonald, *Siegfried Line Campaign*, 350–52; and Miller, *Division Commander*, 119–21.

28. Ibid.

29. MacDonald, *Siegfried Line Campaign*, 352–59; and MacDonald and Mathews, *Three Battles*, 305–9.

30. Ibid.

31. MacDonald, *Siegfried Line Campaign*, 359–64.

32. Ibid., 364–66; MacDonald and Mathews, *Three Battles*, 355; and USAARMS, "Armor in the Heurtgen Forest," 44–46.

33. MacDonald, *Siegfried Line Campaign*, 371.

34. Combat Interview no. 74, "Huertgen Forest Campaign of 28th Division," 10–13.

35. Combat Interview no. 75, "Vossenack-Kommerscheidt-Schmidt (2–8 November 1944), Action of the 28th Division," 1–2; Headquarters, 28th Infantry Division, Office of the Surgeon, United States Army, "Battle Casualties," 7 December 1944, 1; and MacDonald, *Siegfried Line Campaign*, 373–74.

36. Headquarters, SHAEF, "Immediate Report no. 16, Combat Observations," n.d., 1–3.

37. MacDonald and Mathews, *Three Battles*, 373; and MacDonald, *Huertgen Forest*, 137–42.

38. Headquarters, 4th Infantry Division, U.S. Army, Operations Memorandum no. 23, "Notes on Woods Fighting," 28 October 1944, 1–3; and 12th Army Group, "Battle Experiences," no. 83, 1–2.

39. MacDonald, *Huertgen Forest*, 142–48; and Combat Interview no. 34, "Huertgen Forest Battle, 4th Infantry Division, First U.S. Army, November 7 to December 3, 1944," n.d., 1.

40. James W. Haley, "The Operations of the 2d Battalion, 8th Infantry (4th Infantry Division) in the Huertgen Forest, Germany, 16–22 November 1944," USAIS

Library Student Monograph (Fort Benning, Ga.: Advanced Officers' Course, Class no. 1, USAIS, 1947–1948), 48–50; Frederic H. Oettinger, Jr., "The Operations of Company B, 12th Infantry Regiment (4th Infantry Division) in the Huertgen Forest, West of Gey, Germany, 28 November–5 December 1944," USAIS Library Student Monograph (Fort Benning, Ga.: Advanced Officers' Course, Class no. 1, USAIS, 1948–1949), 31–34; and George Wilson, *If You Survive* (New York: Ivy Books, 1987), 147–58.

41. Oettinger, "Operations of Company B, 12th Infantry," 31.

42. Wilson, *If You Survive*, 158.

43. MacDonald, *Siegfried Line Campaign*, 440–41.

44. Paul Boesch, *Road to Huertgen—Forest in Hell* (Houston: Gulf Publishing Company, 1962), 145–55, 157–58; and MacDonald, *Huertgen Forest*, 150–51.

45. MacDonald, *Siegfried Line Campaign*, 442–45.

46. MacDonald, *Huertgen Forest*, 155–56; and USAARMS, "Armor in the Huertgen Forest," 132–37.

47. Ibid.

48. MacDonald, *Siegfried Line Campaign*, 447–48; and Boesch, *Road to Huertgen*, 202–10.

49. MacDonald, *Siegfried Line Campaign*, 448; and Boesch, *Road to Huertgen*, 221–28.

50. Boesch, *Road to Huertgen*, 226–27.

51. MacDonald, *Siegfried Line Campaign*, 448.

52. MacDonald, *Huertgen Forest*, 171–72.

53. Headquarters, 1st Infantry Division, United States Army, "Report of Operations, 1–30 November 1944," 5 December 1944, 61–63.

54. MacDonald, *Huertgen Forest*, 195–96.

55. USAARMS, "Armor in the Huertgen Forest," 196–97.

56. *First Army Report*, Aug '44–Feb '45, 167–68.

57. Roland G. Ruppenthal, *Logistical Support of the Armies*, 2 vols., United States Army in World War II (Washington, D.C.: U.S. Army, Office of the Chief of Military History, 1959; reprint ed., Washington, D.C.: USACMH, 1987), 2: 317.

58. Cecil B. Currey, *Follow Me and Die* (New York: Military Heritage Press, 1984), 264; MacDonald, *Siegfried Line Campaign*, 333; and *First Army Report*, Aug '44–Feb '45, 166.

CHAPTER 8: DEFENSE IN THE ARDENNES

1. Hugh M. Cole, *The Ardennes: The Battle of the Bulge*, United States Army in World War II (Washington, D.C.: U.S. Army, Office of the Chief of Military History, 1965; reprint ed., Washington, D.C.: USACMH, 1988), 1–2.

2. FM 100-5, 137–59.

3. Ibid., 160–65.

4. U.S. War Department, Field Manual 31-15, *Operations in Snow and Extreme Cold* (Washington, D.C.: Government Printing Office, 18 September 1941), ii; and War Department, Field Manual 70-15, *Operations in Snow and Extreme Cold* (Washington, D.C.: Government Printing Office, 4 November 1944), 1–4.

5. FM 70-15, 84–86, 95, 125.

6. Cole, *The Ardennes*, chaps. 1–3 and 5 passim; and Charles B. MacDonald, *A Time for Trumpets: The Untold Story of the Battle of the Bulge* (New York: Ban-

tam Books, 1985), chaps. 1 and 4 passim. All factual background material on the Battle of the Bulge is from the cited references unless otherwise noted.

7. Cole, *The Ardennes*, 80–83.

8. Ibid., 103–5.

9. Combat Interview no. 20, "Interviews, 2d Division, Commanding General," 2–6; and MacDonald, *Time for Trumpets*, 371–74.

10. MacDonald, *Time for Trumpets*, 380.

11. William F. Hancock, "The Operations of the 1st Battalion, 9th Infantry, in the Hasty Defense against an Armored Attack North of Rocherath, Germany, 17–18 December 1944," USAIS Library Student Monograph (Fort Benning, Ga.: Advanced Officers' Class no. 1, USAIS, 1949–1959), 8–22; Combat Interview no. 20, "Interviews, 2d Division, 1st Battalion, 9th Infantry," 1–9; Cole, *The Ardennes*, 108–10, 115–17; and MacDonald, *Time for Trumpets*, 380–83, 395–98. All factual material on the 1st Battalion, 9th Infantry's fight at Rocherath is from the cited material unless otherwise noted.

12. Cole, *The Ardennes*, 115–28; and MacDonald, *Time for Trumpets*, 398–402. All factual material on the 2d Infantry Division's fight at Krinkelt-Rocherath is from the cited material unless otherwise cited.

13. Combat Interview no. 20, "Interviews, 2d Division, Commanding General," 8–10; and Combat Interview no. 20, "Ardennes, 2d Infantry Division, Narrative," 8–9.

14. Cole, *The Ardennes*, 86, 112–13.

15. Derrill M. Daniel, "The Operations of the 2d Battalion, 26th Infantry at Dom Butgenbach, Belgium, December 16–21, 1944," 9 June 1958, Charles B. MacDonald Papers, "1st Infantry Division," USAMHI, Carlisle Barracks, Pa., 1–19; Thomas A. Gendron, "Operations of the 2d Battalion, 26th Infantry at Dom Butgenbach, Belgium, 18–21 December 1944," USAIS Library Student Monograph (Fort Benning, Ga.: Advanced Officers' Class no. 2, USAIS, 1949–1950), 9–33; Cole, *The Ardennes*, 112–13, 128–35; and MacDonald, *Time for Trumpets*, 403–11. All factual material on the 2d Battalion, 26th Infantry's fight at Dom Butgenbach is from the cited material, unless otherwise noted.

16. Daniel, "Operations at Dom Butgenbach," 19–21; and Gendron, "Operations at Dom Butgenbach," 34–41.

17. Cole, *The Ardennes*, 294–305, 445–49.

18. Ibid., 305–9.

19. S. L. A. Marshall, *Bastogne: The Story of the First Eight Days* (Washington, D.C.: Infantry Journal Press, 1946), 107–8; and Cole, *The Ardennes*, 308–9, 460.

20. Cole, *The Ardennes*, 560–61; and Marshall, *Bastogne*, 107–9.

21. Cole, *The Ardennes*, 460–61; and "CCB, 10th Armored Division, Roberts Interview," 12 January 1945, Charles B. MacDonald Papers, "10th Armored Division," USAMHI, Carlisle Barracks, Pa., 6–7.

22. Cole, *The Ardennes*, 472–74.

23. Ibid., 475–81; Marshall, *Bastogne*, 157–69; and Clarence A. Thompson, Jr., "The Operations of the 1st Battalion, 502d Parachute Infantry at Champs, Belgium, 25 December 1944, 0330 to 0900," USAIS Library Student Monograph (Fort Benning, Ga.: Advanced Officers' Class no. 1, USAIS, 1946–1947), 13–19. All factual material on the 101st Airborne's fight at Champs is from the cited material unless otherwise noted.

24. Combat Interview no. 230, "Ardennes, 101st Airborne Division, G-4," 3–4; Cole, *The Ardennes*, 461, 467; and Marshall, *Bastogne*, 133–36.

25. Combat Interview no. 230, "Ardennes, 101st Airborne Division, G-4," 5–7; Cole, *The Ardennes*, 468–70; Marshall, *Bastogne*, 138–39; and Combat Inter-

view no. 229, "Ardennes, 101st Airborne Division, Report on Aerial Resupply to 101st Airborne Division at Bastogne," 1–3.

26. Cole, *The Ardennes*, 470, 474–75; and Combat Interview no. 230, "Ardennes, 101st Airborne Division, Air Support Party at Bastogne," 1–5.

27. Harry W. O. Kinnard, transcript, oral memoirs, 51–52.

28. Craven and Cate, *AAF in WW II*, 692–701.

29. Headquarters, ETO, "Battle Experiences," no. 33, 12 January 1945, 2; Headquarters, ETO, "Battle Experiences," no. 46, 26 January 1945, 1–2; and Headquarters, ETO, "Immediate Reports," no. 49, 7 February 1945, 1–2.

30. Headquarters, 394th Infantry, 99th Infantry Division, U.S. Army, "After Action Report," 1 February 1945, 1–3; and Cole, *The Ardennes*, 470.

31. Committee no. 26, Armor Officers' Advanced Class 1949–1950, "The Maintenance of Armor in World War II" (Fort Knox, Ky.: Advanced Officers' Class, 1949–1950, USAARMS, 1950), 51–56; and Headquarters, ETO, "Immediate Reports," no. 49, 7 February 1945, 1–2.

32. Headquarters, ETO, "Battle Experiences," no. 46, 1; Headquarters, ETO, "Immediate Reports," no. 49, 1–2; and Combat Interview no. 230, "Ardennes, 101st Airborne Division, Air Support Party at Bastogne," 1–5.

33. MacDonald, *Time for Trumpets*, 409.

CHAPTER 9: THE AMERICAN SOLDIER

1. Whiting, *Huertgen Forest*, 237.

2. *St. Lo*, 58, 67.

3. Pergrin, *First across the Rhine*, 266–67.

4. AGF Obs. Bd., ETO, Rept. no. 1120, "Tactics, Organization and Equipment, 7th Armored Division," 2.

5. Wilson, *If You Survive*, 10.

6. Headquarters, CCA, 7th Armored Division, U.S. Army, "Foolhardiness, Caution, and Recklessness," 28 February 1945, 1.

7. MacDonald, *Company Commander*, 171.

8. 12th Army Group, "Battle Experiences," no. 48, 2.

9. War Department Pamphlet 20-17, 2; and Hall, "Bridging at Thionville," 171.

10. U.S. Department of the Army, Office of the Adjutant General, Statistical and Accounting Branch, *Army Battle Casualties and Nonbattle Deaths in World War II, Final Report, 7 December 1941–31 December 1946* 5 (1 June 1953): 84–85.

11. Bradley, *A Soldier's Story*, 444; and Headquarters, AGF, Plans Section, "Study of AGF Battle Casualties," 25 September 1946, Appendix A, 6, 10.

12. "Battle Casualties," *Infantry Journal*, September 1949, 18–21.

13. John Boyd Coates, Jr., ed., *Cold Injury, Ground Type* (Washington, D.C.: Department of the Army, Office of the Surgeon General, 1958), 10–12; and USFET, *Reports*, Study no. 94, "Trench Foot," 1.

14. Coates, *Cold Injury*, 497–506.

15. Ibid., 529.

16. Ibid., 5, 136–38, 208–10.

17. Ibid., 167–78; USFET, *Reports*, Study no. 94, 6–8; and Lee Kennett, *G.I.: The American Soldier in World War II* (New York: Charles Scribner's Sons, 1987), 147.

18. Kennett, *G.I.*, 145.

19. USFET, *Reports*, Study no. 91, "Combat Exhaustion," 1.

20. William S. Mullins, ed., *Neuropsychiatry in World War II* (Washington, D.C.: Department of the Army, Office of the Surgeon General, 1973), 2:286, 311, 995, 1015.

21. USFET, *Reports*, Study no. 91, 1; and Whiting, *Huertgen Forest*, 151–52.

22. USAIS, "Rifle Platoon in Combat," *Infantry School Quarterly* 35 (July 1949): 10–11.

23. Ibid.

24. Samuel A. Stouffer et al., *Studies in Social Psychology in World War II*, vol. 2, *The American Soldier: Combat and Its Aftermath* (Princeton, N.J.: Princeton University Press, 1949), 197–200; Kennett, *G.I.*, 145–46; and Mullins, *Neuropsychiatry in World War II*, 20.

25. Mullins, *Neuropsychiatry in World War II*, 999–1000, 1024–25.

26. Ibid., 281–83; USFET, *Reports*, no. 91, 7–11.

27. Mullins, *Neuropsychiatry in World War II*, 286–88, 311, 347; and USFET, *Reports*, no. 91, 10.

28. Ruppenthal, *Logistical Support of the Armies*, 2:316, 465.

29. Ibid., 337–43.

30. Ibid.

31. U.S. War Department, Operations Division, Combat Analysis Section, "Replacement Orientation," *Combat Lessons*, no.7 (n.d.): 8.

32. Ruppenthal, *Logistical Support of the Armies*, 2:337–43.

33. Ibid., 310, 461–63, 468–69.

34. Pergrin, *First across the Rhine*, 21.

35. Wilson, *If You Survive*, 20–21.

36. Ibid.

37. U.S. War Department, Morale Services Division, "What Officers Think of Their Own Training," *What the Soldier Thinks*, no. 3, 13–14; and "What Combat Veterans Think of Army Training," *What the Soldier Thinks*, no. 4, 1–5.

38. Stouffer, *American Soldier*, 228–31.

39. "What Combat Veterans Think of Army Training," *What the Soldier Thinks*, no. 4, 1–5.

40. 12th Army Group, "Battle Experiences," no. 14, 1–2.

41. AGF Obs. Bd., ETO, Rept. no. 481, "Training of Infantry Division during a Lull in Combat," 3.

42. AGF Obs, Bd., ETO, Rept. no. 807, "Assault Operations," 2, 4.

43. Marshall, *Men against Fire*, 56.

44. Patton, *War as I Knew It*, 320–21.

45. John E. Kelley, "Shoot, Soldier, Shoot," *Infantry Journal*, January 1946, 47–48; and War Department Pamphlet 20–17, 12–14.

46. AGF Obs. Bd., ETO, Rept. no. 481, 1–3.

47. Ibid.

48. AGF Obs. Bd., ETO, Rept. no. 633, "State of Training of Reinforcements," 1–2; "Replacement Orientation," *Combat Lessons*, no. 7, 11–12; and Headquarters, ETO, U.S. Army, Immediate Report no. 44 (Combat Observations) "Division Reinforcement Training Center," 3 February 1945, 1–2.

49. Ibid.

50. John Ellis, *The Sharp End: The Fighting Man in World War II* (New York: Charles Scribner's Sons, 1980), 10.

51. Stouffer, *American Soldier*, 169.

52. Ibid., 220–24.

53. "How Officers Combat Fear among Their Men," *What the Soldier Thinks*, no. 6, 11–16.

54. Ibid.; and Stouffer, *American Soldier*, 201.

55. Paul Fussell, *Wartime* (New York: Oxford University Press, 1989), 278.

56. Stouffer, *American Soldier*, 201–2.

57. Ibid., 231–41; and MacDonald, *Company Commander*, 89.

58. Headquarters, CCA, 7th Armored Division, U.S. Army, "Reconnaissance by Fire," 9 February 1945, 1; and "How to Stay Alive in Combat," *What the Soldier Thinks*, no. 11, 10–14.

59. Ibid.

60. Ibid.

61. "Worries of Combat Troops," *What the Soldier Thinks*, no. 5, 10–11.

62. "Things Which Tend to Make or Break Morale," *What the Soldier Thinks*, no. 15, 3–6; and "What is Morale?" *What the Soldier Thinks*, no. 1, 1–7.

63. Kennett, *G.I.*, 146.

64. Stouffer, *American Soldier*, 158.

65. "Hatred of the Enemy," *What the Soldier Thinks*, no. 7, 9.

66. Stouffer, *American Soldier*, 158.

67. Ibid., 162; Duckworth, "Operations of Company F, 23d Infantry," 24; and MacDonald, *Siegfried Line Campaign*, 262.

68. Kennett, *G.I.*, 151.

69. Harold P. Leinbaugh and John D. Campbell, *The Men of Company K: The Autobiography of a World War II Rifle Company* (New York: William Morrow and Company, 1985), 164.

70. MacDonald, *Siegfried Line Campaign*, 438; and USAARMS, "Remagen Bridgehead," ii.

71. Linebaugh and Campbell, *Men of Company K*, chaps. 2–6 passim. All factual material on the attack of Company K, 333d Infantry, is from the cited reference.

CHAPTER 10: THE SCHOOLHOUSE OF WAR

1. David Brinkley, *Washington Goes to War* (New York: Alfred A. Knopf, 1988), 74–75.

2. Headquarters, AGF, "Report of Activities of the Army Ground Forces in World War II," 10 January 1946, 5–15; and "AGF Job: To Build Units Fit to Fight," *Infantry Journal*, June 1946, 17–23.

3. USFET, *Reports*, Study no. 15, "Organization, Equipment, and Tactical Employment of the Infantry Division," 12.

4. 12th Army Group, "Battle Experiences," no. 1, 1.

5. USFET, *Reports*, Study no. 15, Foreword.

6. Dennis J. Vetock, *Lessons Learned: A History of United States Army Lesson Learning* (Carlisle Barracks, Pa.: USAMHI, 1987), 61–64.

7. MacDonald, *Company Commander*, 254–55.

8. Martin Blumenson, *The Patton Papers*, 2 vols. (Boston: Houghton Mifflin, 1972–1974), 2:616, 620.

9. Bruce I. Gudmundsson, *Stormtroop Tactics: Innovation in the German Army, 1914–1918* (New York: Praeger, 1989), chaps. 9 and 10 and Conclusion passim; and Timothy T. Lupfer, *The Dynamics of Doctrine: The Changes in German Tactical Doctrine during the First World War*, Leavenworth Papers, no. 4

(Fort Leavenworth, Kans.: Combat Studies Institute, U.S. Army Command and General Staff College, 1985), Introduction and chaps. 1 and 3 passim.

10. David M. Glantz, *Soviet Military Operational Art: In Pursuit of Deep Battle* (Portland, Ore.: Frank Cass, 1991), Preface and chaps. 1, 4, and 5 passim.

11. Weigley, *Eisenhower's Lieutenants*, Epilogue.

12. USFET, *Reports*, Study no. 15, 1–16.

13. Ibid.

14. Ibid.

15. H. J. Matchett, "Let's Teach Battlefield Training," *Infantry Journal*, January 1946, 49.

16. Frederic Smoler, "The Secret of the Soldiers Who Didn't Shoot," *American Heritage* 40, 2 (March 1989): 37–45; Roger J. Spiller, "S. L. A. Marshall and the Ratio of Fire," *RUSI Journal*, Winter 1988, 63–71; and F. D. G. Williams, U.S. Army, *SLAM: The Influence of S. L. A. Marshall on the United States Army* (Fort Monroe, Va.: Office of the Command Historian, U.S. Army Training and Doctrine Command, 1990), Introduction.

17. USFET, *Reports*, Study no. 60, "Organization, Equipment, and Tactical Employment of Tank Destroyer Units," 12–29; and Gabel, *Seek, Strike, and Destroy*, 64–65.

18. Ibid.

19. USFET, *Reports*, Study no. 54, 15.

20. Linebaugh and Campbell, *Men of Company K*, 89.

21. USFET, *Reports*, Study no. 15, 14–15.

BIBLIOGRAPHY

PERSONAL PAPERS AND INTERVIEWS

Chester B. Hansen Diaries, U.S. Army Military History Institute, Carlisle Barracks, Pa.
Harry W. O. Kinnard, transcript, oral memoirs (1983), U.S. Army Military History Institute, Carlisle Barracks, Pa.
Charles B. MacDonald Papers, U.S. Army Military History Institute, Carlisle Barracks, Pa.
Arthur S. Nevins Papers, U.S. Army Military History Institute, Carlisle Barracks, Pa.
Elwood R. Quesada, transcript, oral memoirs (1975), U.S. Army Military History Institute, Carlisle Barracks, Pa.
William C. Sylvan Diaries, U.S. Army Military History Institute, Carlisle Barracks, Pa.

SPECIAL REPORTS AND STUDIES

Allied Force Headquarters. Training Memorandum no. 50, "Lessons from the Sicilian Campaign," 20 November 1943.
Army Air Forces Evaluation Board, ETO, U.S. Army Air Forces. "The Effectiveness of Third Phase Tactical Air Operations in the European Theater, 5 May 1944–8 May 1945." August 1945.
Campbell, William R. "Tanks with Infantry." Fort Knox, Ky.: Advanced Officers' Class no. 1, U.S. Army Armor School, 1947.
"Combat Interviews." Records of the Adjutant General's Office, Record Group 407. Entry 427, World War II Operations Reports, 1940–1948.
Committee no. 3, Advanced Officers' Class no. 1. "Employment of 2d Armored Division in Operation COBRA." Fort Knox, Ky.: U.S. Army Armor School, 1950.
Committee no. 7, Advanced Officers' Class 1948–1949. "Armor in the Huertgen Forest." Fort Knox, Ky.: U.S. Army Armor School, 1949.
Committee no. 17, Advanced Officers' Class 1952–1953. "A Critical Analysis of the History of Armor in World War II." Fort Knox, Ky.: U.S. Army Armor School, 1953.
Creamer, Forrest W. "Operations of the XIX U.S. Army Corps in Normandy." Fort Knox, Ky.: Advanced Officers' Class no. 1, U.S. Army Armor School, 1947.
Daniel, Derrill M. "Capture of Aachen, Germany, 10–21 October 1944." Combined Arms Research Library Report N-2253.17. Fort Leavenworth, Kans.: U.S. Army Command and General Staff College, 1947.
_____. "The Operations of the 2d Battalion, 26th Infantry at Dom Butgenbach,

Belgium, December 16–21, 1944." 9 June 1958. Found in the Charles B. Mac-Donald Papers, U.S. Army Military History Institute, Carlisle Barracks, Pa.

Doubler, Michael D. *Busting the Bocage: American Combined Arms Operations in France, 6 June–31 July 1944*. Fort Leavenworth, Kans.: Combat Studies Institute, U.S. Army Command and General Staff College, 1988.

Duckworth, George H. "Operations of Company F, 23d Infantry Regiment at Brest, France, 8–14 September 1944." Fort Benning, Ga.: Advanced Officers' Class no. 1, U.S. Army Infantry School, 1948.

Folsom, Charles D. "Hedgerow Fighting near Carentan." Fort Knox, Ky.: Advanced Officers' Class no. 1, U.S. Army Armor School, 1948.

Gabel, Christopher R. *Seek, Strike, and Destroy: U.S. Army Tank Destroyer Doctrine in World War II*. Leavenworth Papers, no. 12. Fort Leavenworth, Kans.: Combat Studies Institute, U.S. Army Command and General Staff College, 1985.

Gendron, Thomas J. "Operations of the 2d Battalion, 26th Infantry at Dom Butgenbach, Belgium, 18–21 December 1944." Fort Benning, Ga.: Advanced Officers' Class no. 2, U.S. Army Infantry School, 1949.

Greenfield, Kent R. *Army Ground Forces and the Air-Ground Battle Team Including Organic Light Aviation*. Study no. 35. Fort Monroe, Va.: Historical Section, Army Ground Forces, 1948.

Hancock, William F. "The Operations of the 1st Battalion, 9th Infantry, in the Hasty Defense against an Armored Attack North of Rocherath, Germany, 17–18 December 1944." Fort Benning, Ga.: Advanced Officers' Class no. 1, U.S. Army Infantry School, 1949.

Harmon, Ernest N., "Notes on Combat Experience during the Tunisian and African Campaigns," n.d. Manuscript collection. U.S. Army Armor School Library, Fort Knox, Ky.

Headquarters, 12th Army Group, Air Effects Committee, U.S. Army. "Effects of Air Power on Military Operations, Western Europe." 15 July 1945.

Headquarters, XIX Corps, U.S. Army. "XIX Corps Demonstration: 2d Armored Division in the Tank-Infantry Assault of a Tactical Locality and 30th Infantry Division in the Infantry Assault of a Fortified Village." 10 December 1944.

Headquarters, XIX Corps, U.S. Army. "Breaching the Siegfried Line." 12 January 1945.

Headquarters, XX Corps, U.S. Army. "The Reduction of Fortress Metz, 1 September–6 December 1944, An Operational Report." 1945.

Headquarters, Army Ground Forces, Plans Section, U.S. Army. "Study of AGF Battle Casualties." 25 September 1946.

Headquarters, Army Ground Forces, U.S. Army. "Report of Activities of the Army Ground Forces in World War II." 10 January 1946.

Headquarters, Combat Command A, 4th Armored Division, U.S. Army. "The Nancy Bridgehead." n.d.

Headquarters, First Army, U.S. Army. "Battle Experiences." 1944. Carlisle Barracks, Pa.: U.S. Army Military History Institute, 1944.

_____. *Report of Operations, 20 October 1943–1 August 1944*. 7 vols. Carlisle Barracks, Pa.: U.S. Army Military History Institute, 1945[?].

_____. *Report of Operations, 1 August 1944–22 February 1945*. 4 vols. Carlisle Barracks, Pa.: U.S. Army Military History Institute, 1945[?].

Headquarters, Mediterranean Theater of Operations, U.S. Army. Training Memorandum no. 2, "Lessons from the Italian Campaign," n.d.

Headquarters, Office of the Theater Historian, ETO, U.S. Army. *Order of Battle, United States Army in World War II—European Theater of Operations*. December 1945.

Historical Branch, Programs Division, U.S. Army G-3 Staff. "Historical Survey of Army Fire Support." 1963.

Lupfer, Timothy T. *The Dynamics of Doctrine: The Changes in German Tactical Doctrine during the First World War.* Leavenworth Papers, no. 4. Fort Leavenworth, Kans.: Combat Studies Institute, U.S. Army Command and General Staff College, 1981.

McCain, Francis Marion III. "Mobility Support of Offensive Maneuver: First U.S. Army Attack on the Siegfried Line—1944." Master's thesis, U.S. Army Command and General Staff College, Fort Leavenworth, Kans., 1985.

Mortensen, Daniel R. *A Pattern for Joint Operations: World War II Close Air Support, North Africa.* Washington, D.C.: Office of Air Force History and U.S. Army Center of Military History, 1987.

Mullen, James J. "Operations of Company E, 317th Infantry, in the Establishment of a Bridgehead Across the Moselle River, vicinity of Dieulouard, France, 5–14 September 1944." Fort Benning, Ga.: Advanced Officers' Class no. 1, U.S. Army Infantry School, 1950.

Ney, Virgil. *Evolution of the U.S. Army Division, 1939–1968.* Fort Belvoir, Va.: Combat Operations Research Group, Headquarters, U.S. Combat Developments Command, 1969.

Observer Board (ETO), U.S. Army, Army Ground Forces. *Reports of the AGF Observers Board, ETO.* 6 vols. Carlisle Barracks, Pa.: U.S. Army Military History Institute, 1944–1945.

Randall, Frank J. "Operations of the 1st Battalion, 39th Infantry in the Huertgen Forest, Vicinity of Germeter and Vossenack, 10–14 October 1944." Fort Benning, Ga.: Advanced Officers' Class no. 2, U.S. Army Infantry School, 1949.

Thompson, Clarence A., Jr. "The Operations of the 1st Battalion, 502d Parachute Infantry at Champs, Belgium, 25 December 1944, 0330 to 0900." Fort Benning, Ga.: Advanced Officers' Class no.1, U.S. Army Infantry School, 1947.

U.S. Army Armor School. "The Remagen Bridgehead." Fort Knox, Ky., n.d.

U.S. Army Infantry School. *The Infantry School Quarterly,* Fort Benning, Ga.

———. *The Mailing List,* Fort Benning, Ga.

U.S. Forces. European Theater. *Reports of the General Board.* 131 vols. Carlisle Barracks, Pa.: U.S. Army Military History Institute, November 1945.

Warmbrod, Karlton. "Operations of the 2d Battalion, 317th Infantry in the Crossing of the Moselle River and the Establishment of a Bridgehead at St. Genevieve, France, 5–12 September 1944." Fort Benning, Ga.: Advanced Officers' Class no. 2, U.S. Army Infantry School, 1950.

U.S. WAR DEPARTMENT PUBLICATIONS

Combat Lessons. 9 vols. Washington, D.C.: Operations Division, Combat Analysis Section, 1944–1945.

FM 5-6. *Operations of Engineer Field Units.* Washington, D.C.: Government Printing Office, 23 April 1944.

FM 6-20. *Field Artillery Tactics and Technique.* Washington, D.C.: Government Printing Office, 1940.

FM 7-20. *Rifle Battalion.* Washington, D.C.: Government Printing Office, 28 September 1942.

FM 17-36. *Employment of Tanks with Infantry.* Washington, D.C.: Government Printing Office, 7 July 1944.

FM 17-36, Supplement No. 1. *Employment of Tanks with Infantry, Illustrated Problems*. Washington, D.C.: Government Printing Office, 7 July 1944.

FM 31-15. *Operations in Snow and Extreme Cold*. Washington, D.C.: Government Printing Office, 18 September 1941.

FM 31-50. *Attack on a Fortified Position and Combat in Towns*. Washington, D.C.: Government Printing Office, 31 January 1944.

FM 70-15. *Operations in Snow and Extreme Cold*. Washington, D.C.: Government Printing Office, 4 November 1944.

FM 100-5. *Field Service Regulations: Operations*. Washington, D.C.: Government Printing Office, 22 May 1941.

FM 100-20. *Field Service Regulations: Command and Employment of Air Power*. Washington, D.C.: Government Printing Office, 21 July 1943.

Lessons from the Tunisian Campaign. Washington, D.C.: Government Printing Office, 1943.

War Department Pamphlet no. 20-17. *Lessons Learned and Expedients Used in Combat*. Washington, D.C.: Government Printing Office, 1945.

What the Soldier Thinks. 15 vols. Washington, D.C.: Morale Services Division, Army Service Forces, February 1944–July 1945[?].

BOOKS AND ARTICLES

"AGF Job: To Build Units Fit to Fight." *Infantry Journal*, June 1946, 17–23.

Baily, Charles M. *Faint Praise: American Tanks and Tank Destroyers during World War II*. Hamden, Conn.: Archon Books, 1983.

"Battle Casualties." *Infantry Journal*, September 1949, 18–21.

Beck, Alfred M., et al. *The Corps of Engineers: The War against Germany*. United States Army in World War II. Washington, D.C.: U.S. Army Center of Military History, 1985.

Blair, Clay, and Bradley, Omar N. *A General's Life*. New York: Simon and Schuster, 1983.

Blumenson, Martin. *Breakout and Pursuit*. United States Army in World War II. Washington, D.C.: U.S. Army, Office of the Chief of Military History, 1961.

Boesch, Paul. *Road to Huertgen—Forest in Hell*. Houston: Gulf Publishing Company, 1962.

Bradley, Omar N. *A Soldier's Story*. New York: Rand McNally, 1951; reprint ed., New York: Rank McNally, 1978.

Butler, James J. "Individual Tank-Infantry Communications." *Armored Cavalry Journal*, July–August 1947, 43–45.

Cole, Hugh M., *The Ardennes: The Battle of the Bulge*. United States Army in World War II. Washington, D.C.: U.S. Army, Office of the Chief of Military History, 1965; reprint ed., Washington, D.C.: U.S. Army Center of Military History, 1988.

———. *The Lorraine Campaign*. United States Army in World War II. Washington, D.C.: U.S. Army, Office of the Chief of Military History, 1950; reprint ed., Washington, D.C.: U.S. Army Center of Military History, 1984.

Coll, Blanche D.; Keith, Jean E.; and Rosenthal, Herbert H. *The Corps of Engineers: Troops and Equipment*. United States Army in World War II. Washington, D.C.: U.S. Army, Office of the Chief of Military History, 1958; reprint ed., Washington, D.C.: U.S. Army Center of Military History, 1969.

Cottingham, Levin B. "Smoke over the Moselle." *Infantry Journal*, August 1948, 15–19.

Craven, Wesley F., and Cate, James L., eds. *The Army Air Forces in World War II*. Vol. 3, *Europe: Argument to V-E Day, January 1944 to May 1945*. Chicago: University of Chicago Press, 1951; reprint ed., Washington, D.C.: Government Printing Office, 1983.

Ellis, John. *The Sharp End: The Fighting Man in World War II*. New York: Charles Scribner's Sons, 1980.

Ewing, Joseph H. *29 Let's Go! A History of the 29th Infantry Division in World War II*. Washington, D.C.: Infantry Journal Press, 1948.

Fussell, Paul. *Wartime*. New York: Oxford University Press, 1989.

Gavin, James M. *On to Berlin: Battles of an Airborne Commander, 1943–1946*. New York: Viking Press, 1978.

Glantz, David M. *Soviet Military Operational Art: In Pursuit of Deep Battle*. Portland, Ore.: Frank Cass, 1991.

Greenfield, Kent R., Palmer, Robert R., and Wiley, Bell I. *The Organization of Ground Combat Troops*. United States Army in World War II. Washington, D.C.: U.S. Army, Office of the Chief of Military History, 1947.

Gudmundsson, Bruce I. *Stormtroop Tactics: Innovation in the German Army, 1914–1918*. New York: Praeger, 1989.

Hains, Peter C., III. "Tanks in Tunisia." *Cavalry Journal* 52 (July–August 1943): 13–17.

Hall, William C. "Bridging at Thionville." *Military Engineer*, April 1948, 169–73.

Harrison, Gordon A. *Cross-Channel Attack*. United States Army in World War II. Washington, D.C.: U.S. Army, Office of the Chief of Military History, 1950; reprint ed., Washington, D.C.: U.S. Army, Office of the Chief of Military History, 1977.

Hastings, Max. *Overlord*. London: Michael Joseph, 1984.

Headquarters, 5th Infantry Division, 5th Division Historical Section, U.S. Army. *The Fifth Infantry Division in the ETO*. n.p.: 1945.

Hechler, Ken. *The Bridge at Remagen*. New York: Ballantine Books, 1957.

Hewitt, Robert L. *Work Horse of the Western Front: The Story of the 30th Infantry Division*. Washington, D.C.: Infantry Journal Press, 1946.

Huston, James A. "Tactical Use of Air Power in World War II: The Army Experience." *Military Affairs* 14 (Winter 1950): 171–75.

Kelley, John E. "Shoot, Soldier, Shoot." *Infantry Journal*, January 1946, 47–48.

Kemp, Anthony. *The Unknown Battle: Metz, 1944*. London: Frederick Warne, 1981.

Kennett, Lee. *G.I.: The American Soldier in World War II*. New York: Charles Scribner's Sons, 1987.

Leinbaugh, Harold P., and Campbell, John D. *The Men of Company K: The Autobiography of a World War II Rifle Company*. New York: William Morrow and Company, 1985.

MacDonald, Charles B. *The Battle of the Huertgen Forest*. New York: Jove Books, 1963.

_____. *Company Commander*. New York: Bantam Books, 1982.

_____. *The Last Offensive*. United States Army in World War II. Washington, D.C.: U.S. Army, Office of the Chief of Military History, 1973.

_____. *The Mighty Endeavor*. New York: William Morrow, 1986.

_____. *The Siegfried Line Campaign*. United States Army in World War II. Washington, D.C.: U.S. Army, Office of the Chief of Military History, 1950; reprint ed., Washington, D.C.: U.S. Army Center of Military History, 1984.

_____. *A Time for Trumpets: The Untold Story of the Battle of the Bulge.* New York: Bantam Books, 1985.

MacDonald, Charles B., and Mathews, Sidney T. *Three Battles: Arnaville, Altuzzo, and Schmidt.* United States Army in World War II. Washington, D.C.: U.S. Army, Office of the Chief of Military History, 1952; reprint ed., Washington, D.C.: U.S. Army Center of Military History, 1985.

Marshall, S. L. A. *Bastogne: The Story of the First Eight Days.* Washington, D.C.: Infantry Journal Press, 1946.

_____. *Men against Fire: The Problem of Battle Command in Future Wars.* Gloucester, Mass.: Peter Smith, 1947; reprint ed., Gloucester, Mass.: Peter Smith, 1978.

Palmer, Robert R., Wiley, Bell I., and Keast, William R. *The Army Ground Forces: The Procurement and Training of Ground Combat Troops.* United States Army in World War II. Washington, D.C.: U.S. Army, Office of the Chief of Military History, 1948.

Parrish, Monte M. "The Battle of Aachen." *Field Artillery Journal* 44 (September–October 1976): 25–30.

Patton, George S., Jr. *War as I Knew It.* Boston: Houghton Mifflin, 1947; reprint ed., New York: Bantam Books, 1981.

Pergrin, David E., and Hammel, Eric. *First across the Rhine: The 291st Engineer Combat Battalion in France, Belgium, and Germany.* New York: Ballantine Books, 1989.

Pogue, Forrest C. *The Supreme Command.* United States Army in World War II. Washington, D.C.: U.S. Army, Office of the Chief of Military History, 1954.

Rosen, Milton L. "Forest Fighting." *Infantry Journal,* April 1945, 8–10.

Ruppenthal, Roland G. *Logistical Support of the Armies.* 2 vols. United States Army in World War II. Washington, D.C.: U.S. Army, Office of the Chief of Military History, 1953, 1959; reprint ed., Washington, D.C.: U.S. Army Center of Military History, 1985, 1987.

Ruse, C. H. "Smoke—Tactical Weapon of World War II." *Armored Cavalry Journal,* January–February 1947, 52–54.

Smoler, Frederic. "The Secret of the Soldiers Who Didn't Shoot." *American Heritage,* March 1989, 37–45.

Spiller, Roger J. "S. L. A. Marshall and the Ratio of Fire." *RUSI Journal,* Winter 1988, 63–71.

Stanton, Shelby L. *Order of Battle, U.S. Army, World War II.* Novato, Calif.: Presidio Press, 1984.

St. Lo. American Forces in Action Series. Washington, D.C.: War Department, Historical Division, 1946; reprint ed., Washington, D.C.: U.S. Army Center of Military History, 1984.

Stouffer, Samuel A., et al. *Studies in Social Psychology in World War II.* Vol. 2, The American Soldier: Combat and Its Aftermath. Princeton, N.J.: Princeton University Press, 1949.

Utah Beach to Cherbourg. American Forces in Action Series. Washington, D.C.: Department of the Army, Historical Division, 1947; reprint ed., Washington, D.C.: U.S. Army Center of Military History, 1984.

Van Creveld, Martin. *Fighting Power.* London: Arms and Armour Press, 1983.

Walker, Fred L., Jr. "Siege Methods: 1945." *Infantry Journal,* January 1945, 10–15.

Weigley, Russell. *Eisenhower's Lieutenants.* Bloomington: Indiana University Press, 1981.

Whiting, Charles. *The Battle of the Huertgen Forest*. New York: Pocket Books, 1990.

Williams, F. D. G. *SLAM: The Influence of S. L. A. Marshall on the United States Army*. Fort Monroe, Va.: Office of the Command Historian, U.S. Army Training and Doctrine Commmand, 1990.

Wilson, George. *If You Survive*. New York: Ivy Books, 1987.

Wright, Charles E. "Moselle River Crossing at Cattenom." *Armored Cavalry Journal* 57 (May–June 1948): 50–53.

INDEX

Aachen, 229; fight for, 81, 96–101
AAF. *See* Army Air Forces
Abrams, Creighton, 152; at Dieulouard, 263; at Moselle, 153
ACC missions. *See* Armored column cover missions
Adaptation, 2, 8, 28–29, 58–59, 84, 266, 297; analyzing, 278–79, 285; battlefield, 57, 59–60, 226, 269, 273, 278, 279; decentralized, 227, 279, 280–82; importance of, 298–99; societal values and, 5–6; tactical/technical, 4–5, 7, 107, 108, 168, 206 (photo), 223, 227, 268–69, 271, 272, 282, 289, 298. *See also* Problem solving
Aerial resupply, 220, 225, 271
Afrika Korps, 11
Aid stations, 158, 245
Air-ground operations, 63, 84, 292; adaptation in, 73, 83, 289; defensive, 219–20; improving, 3, 29, 65, 73, 74–75, 85, 225, 267, 273; problems with, 20–21, 65–66, 67–68; success of, 295. *See also* Close air support
Air-Ground Operations Center, 66–67
Air power: adaptations in, 3, 289; flexibility of, 64, 85; imprecision of, 235; tactical, 20, 63, 295–96. *See also* Bombers
Air superiority, 20, 64, 85, 112
Air support, 220, 296; improving, 281; morale and, 84
Allen, Terry, 17, 253
Anderson, Glen H., 190, 191
Anderson, Harry, at Driant, 132
Anderson, Harry, leadership of, 237
Antiaircraft, 164, 268, 285; countering, 73–74, 84
Antitank crews, 105; casualties for, 14; effectiveness of, 212
Antitank defenses, 116, 199, 286, 301; overcoming, 305, 306
Antitank guns, 28, 199, 210, 213, 224; towed, 286
Antitank warfare: problems in, 17–18; revisions in, 29, 92
Ardennes, 88, 197, 198–226, 271; adaptation in, 222–24, 226; counteroffensive in, 171, 198, 199, 201–2; defensive battles in, 280; terrain of, 201. *See also* Battle of the Bulge
Armed Forces School (Fort Knox), 15, 101
Armored column cover (ACC) missions, 70, 71, 81; controlling, 84; number of, 72
Armored divisions, 170, 302; adaptations for, 108; combat days for, 235, 237 (table)
Armored forces, 139, 302; adaptations by, 222; casualties for, 240; training for, 268–69
Army Air Forces (AAF): AGF units and, 64; coordination with, 20, 21, 77; replacements from, 248
Arnaville, 158, 171
Artillery, 13–14, 68, 233, 235, 250; defense by, 225; effectiveness of, 19–20, 41; firepower of, 306; flexibility of, 18–19, 230; forest combat and, 195; improving, 48, 286; pillbox attacks and, 125; Soviet, 277; tank-infantry forces and, 306; urban combat and, 107
Artillery units, 301, 302; adaptation by, 19, 223; casualties for, 240
Assault boats, 142, 154, 255 (photo); handling, 158–59, 171. *See also* Support rafts
Assault formations, 177; casualties for, 14; developing, 112
Attack in Position Warfare, The, 274
Attrition, 283, 295, 297

B-17 Flying Fortresses, on D-Day, 77
B-24 Liberators, on D-Day, 77
B-29 Superfortresses, 296
B-52 Stratofortresses, 296
Bacon, Robert L., 135, 136
Bangalore torpedoes, 124, 131, 292; using, 119, 122, 134
BAR. *See* Browning automatic rifle
Barrage balloons, 82, 83, 164
Barton, Raymond O., 187, 189
Bastogne, 271, 295; air support at, 220–21, 225; defense of, 214–18, 215 (map), 220–21

Battalions: attacks by, 232; composition of, 301
"Battle Experiences," 270
Battle of the Bulge, 74, 198–226; CAS at, 221; close combat in, 259. *See also* Ardennes
Bayerlein, Fritz, 1–2
Bazookas, 99, 210, 292; training with, 252; using, 119, 122, 123, 286
Bazooka teams, 93, 207, 208, 209; effectiveness of, 212, 224
Bocage. *See* Hedgerows
Bombers, coordination of, 77, 82, 268. *See also* Fighter-bombers; Heavy bombers; Medium bombers
Bomb safety zones, 79, 233; problems with, 68, 83. *See also* Short bombings
Bradley, Omar N., 10, 11, 35, 39, 57, 69, 88, 201; air-ground coordination and, 65, 78–79; at Bulge, 215; COBRA and, 78, 79–80; cold weather casualties and, 241; combat exhaustion and, 244; on hedgerows, 36, 46; at Normandy, 32; on Quesada, 66
Brest, capture of, 90
Bridgeheads: antitank capabilities at, 268; counterattacking, 144; securing, 141–45, 150, 169, 170
Bridges, 143, 144, 151, 152, 166, 169, 170; laying, 141, 156–57, 165
Brittany Peninsula, breakout from, 57, 72, 87
Browning automatic rifle (BAR), 51, 93, 250, 251, 301
Bunching, avoiding, 257, 261, 290
Bush warfare, 33. *See also* Hedgerows, defense of

C-47 transports, at Bastogne, 220
Cameron, A. D., 147
Carpet bombing, 235
CAS. *See* Close air support
Casualties, 26; fighting power and, 288; friendly fire, 291; marching fire and, 251; minimizing, 228, 256–57, 263, 264, 269, 271, 272, 287, 292, 297; numbers/types of, 237, 239–40, 293. *See also* Cold weather casualties
Cavalry Journal, The, 15
Champs, defense of, 218–19
Chateau Leerodt, 260, 261, 262
Chemical troops, crossings and, 168
Cherbourg, fall of, 35
Churchill tanks, 114, 115
City combat. *See* Urban combat
Clarke, Bruce C., 152, 153
Clearing teams, 108, 109

Close air support (CAS), 2, 66, 67, 71, 72–73, 75, 81, 102, 199, 295; absence of, 20, 29; analysis of, 85, 281; at Bulge, 220–21, 224, 225; defensive, 223; development of, 63, 65, 70, 83, 84, 230, 271, 273; forest combat and, 172, 195; German, 64–65; in Normandy, 68; river crossings and, 149. *See also* Air-ground operations
Close combat, 173, 174, 195, 218, 229, 281, 293; adaptation for, 223; experiences with, 259; matériel advantages and, 272
Cody, George R., 219
Cold weather casualties, 240–41; preventing/treating, 225, 241–42, 267. *See also* Casualties
Collins, J. Lawton, 41, 80–81, 116, 166, 182, 297; on air support, 63; on hedgerows, 36; at Huertgen, 175, 192; at Normandy, 35
Combat days, average number of, 235
Combat exhaustion, 126, 148, 186, 188, 195, 262; example of, 243–44, 261; losses from, 187, 189, 242–43; preventing/treating, 26, 61, 242–45, 253, 264, 267
Combat lessons, gathering/disseminating, 269, 270, 278, 279, 297
Combat Lessons, 270–71
Combat power, 8; concentrating, 230, 285, 289, 292, 297
Combined arms forces: defensive, 199; improving, 140, 264; Soviet, 276, 277
Combined arms operations, 2, 8, 9, 289, 297, 302, 304; artillery firepower and, 306; defensive, 200, 224; improving, 28, 217, 271, 272–73, 281, 284, 293; problems with, 13, 20; urban combat and, 101, 106; winter, 224
Combined arms tactics, 298; defensive, 218; development of, 106–7; urban combat and, 109; village fighting, 108
Combined arms training, 28; need for, 17, 18; problems with, 60
Combined Chiefs of Staff, mission statement of, 31
Command and control, 22–23, 39; improving, 46–47, 107, 267, 268; maintaining, 106–7, 230, 232, 293; problems with, 92–93, 172, 235; Soviet, 277
Commanders: adaptation by, 267, 269; artillery planning by, 19; fire discipline and, 250, 263; force massing by, 230; leadership by, 25–26, 254–55, 266–67; morale and, 257–58; pressure on, 230, 238, 239; replacing, 27–28; training and, 23, 252
Communications, 92; improving, 48, 224,

268; maintaining, 293; problems with, 46–47, 80, 173; Soviet, 277

COMZ, 246, 247; replacements from, 248

Coordination, 273, 284, 304–5; importance of, 13, 24, 258; problems with, 16, 60

Corlett, Charles H., 35, 48, 118

Cota, Norman D., 31, 49, 181, 189; at Bulge, 202; hedgerow tactics and, 58; at Huertgen, 180; at Schmidt, 184–85, 186

Cotentin Peninsula, 34

Craig, Louis A.; at Huertgen, 175–76; at Schmidt, 176

Creveld, Martin van; analysis by, 287–89; on German army, 6–7

Culin, Curtis G., hedgerow cutting device by, 45–46, 58, 269

Daniel, Derrill M.: at Aachen, 97–101, 109; on artillery/mortars, 87; at Bulge, 211–12, 213

D-Day, 12; casualty rates for, 240

Deep battle doctrine, 276, 277, 278–79

Defensive tactics, adaptation to, 199–200, 224

Demolition teams: training for, 252; work of, 92, 93

Depot system: improving, 288; replacement and, 246–47

DESERT STORM, air-ground coordination in, 297

Devers, Jacob L., 88

Dietrich, Josef "Sepp," 202, 203, 213

Dieulouard, 150, 152; crossing at, 170; fight for, 154

Dispersing, importance of, 257, 261, 290

Divisions: effectiveness of, 7; organization of, 301. See also Triangular divisions

Division training centers, quality/scope of, 253

Doctrine, 8; air-ground operations and, 268; changes in, 4, 268, 279, 281, 298; offensive/defensive, 266, 268; problems with, 267; soundness of, 29, 266–68, 281

Douhet, Giulio, 295

Dozer tanks, 53, 54, 120, 131, 138; hedgerows and, 56; modifying, 43. See also Tanks

Drabik, Alex, 163, 260

Duckworth, George H., 94–96

Eddy, Manton S., 20, 149; at Moselle, 145, 150, 152; at Nancy, 126–27

Eisenhower, Dwight D., 10, 20, 129; air support and, 21, 77; Bulge and, 215, 216; broad front strategy of, 88, 287; European invasion and, 31; heavy bombers and, 80, 86; on training, 25

Eisenhower's Lieutenants (Weigley), 6; analysis in, 282–87

Elsenborn Ridge: attacking, 203–4; defense of, 204 (map), 205, 207–9, 211–13, 225

Engeman, Leonard, 160, 162

Engineers, 96, 121, 124, 271, 306; bridges and, 143, 170; casualties for, 240; coordination with, 179, 194; forest campaigns and, 172; river crossings and, 151 (photo), 168; Soviet, 277; support from, 2, 57, 108, 111–12, 114, 115, 158

Engineer School (Fort Belvoir), 121

Engineer schools, training at, 121, 294

Envelopments, 275, 304; penetrations and, 305

FAC system. See Forward air controller system

Falaise-Argentan, battle at, 87

Fear, 290; coping with, 254–56, 264

Field Artillery School (Fort Sill), 18

Field Manual 17-36, "Employment of Tanks with Infantry," 101, 305

Field Manual 31-50, "Attack on a Fortified Position and Combat in Towns," 89, 111, 112

Field Manual 100-5, "Field Service Regulations, Operations," 12, 89, 112, 147, 200; on bridgeheads, 142; on defense, 199, 224, 225; doctrine from, 266, 304, 305; on forest combat, 172–73; on fortification reduction, 111, 139; on offensive operations, 297, 304–5; on river crossings, 143, 144, 167, 169, 170

Field Manual 100-20, "Command and Employment of Air Power," 64, 84

Field of fire, 8

Fighter-bombers: adaptation by, 66; artillery barrages and, 68; coordination of, 20–21, 22, 65, 69, 70, 74, 84, 268; support by, 63, 66, 72, 73, 75, 125, 295; targeting by, 139, 233

Fighting Power (Creveld), 6–7; analysis in, 287–89

Firepower, 8, 141, 227, 228, 301; at close quarters, 291–92; concentration of, 104, 232–33, 234 (diagram), 250, 263, 264, 285, 289; defensive, 223; effectiveness of, 13–14, 291, 298; increasing, 284, 286, 297; infantry, 250–51; limits on, 291; maneuver and, 104, 108, 263; reliance on, 289, 291; small arms, 14

Flail tanks, 138

Flamethrowers, 93, 100, 114, 123, 124, 131, 292; training with, 252; using, 119, 134, 138

Flamethrower tanks, 113, 138

Fleig, Raymond E., 184
Flexibility, 18–19, 64, 85, 230, 267, 285; lack of, 12; mobility and, 284; in problem solving, 279
Flood, Albert, 183, 184
FO. *See* Forward observers
Folsom, Charles D., 36
Forest combat, 281, 291, 292; adaptations for, 268, 280; doctrine for, 172–73; maneuver and, 229; problems with, 172–73
Fort Driant: attacking, 129–34; surrender of, 137
Fortifications: attacking, 109, 111, 112–13, 121, 138–39, 280, 281, 287, 290, 292, 294–95; categories of, 111; defense of, 140; maneuver and, 229; training for, 121, 134, 292. *See also* Pillboxes
Fort Montbarey, 113–15, 138
Fort St. Julien, 136, 137
Forward air controller (FAC) system, 69, 102, 273; communicating with, 268; development of, 21, 74
Forward observers (FO), 56, 74, 102, 124; aerial, 47–48; artillery, 57; casualties for, 240; coordination with, 19, 20, 57; shortage of, 47
Foxholes, 222, 257
Fragmentation bombs, 73, 80
Frontal assaults, 111; hedgerow defense and, 42
Frostbite, preventing, 222, 241
Fuller, J. F. C., 295

G-3 air staff, 67, 74
Gaffey, Hugh M., 1
Gavin, James M., 36
Geilenkirchen, 260, 262
Gendron, Thomas J., 214
General Board: on adaptation, 298–99; reports by, 270
General Headquarters (GHQ) tank units, 302
Generals: criticism of, 287; pressure on, 230
Gerhardt, Charles H., 43, 48, 49, 52
German army: adaptation by, 273–75, 280; authoritarian traditions of, 6–7
Gerow, Leonard T., 53, 186, 187, 202; at Bulge, 204, 205, 210; at Huertgen, 180; at Normandy, 35, 36; at Schmidt, 181
GHQ tank units. *See* General Headquarters tank units
Gieszl, George, 260–62
Ginder, P. D., 192
Grant, Ulysses S., 282
Green, Charles B., 44

Hains, Peter C., 15
Harmon, Ernest N., 102, 118; fire and movement principle and, 104; at West Wall, 124
Hart, B. H. Liddell, 2, 295
Haste, speed and, 24, 106
Hatred, lack of, 258–59
Hatzfeld, Colonel, 185
Hausser, Paul, 32
Hazlett, Robert T., 183, 184
Headquarters companies, 301, 302
Headquarters sections, 301
Heavy bombers: advantages/disadvantages of, 86; COBRA and, 78–79; on D-Day, 77, 78; fortifications and, 139; ground support by, 22, 63, 78–81, 83–86, 295, 296; targeting by, 233
Heavy weapons companies, 301
Hedgerows: combat in, 43–44, 61, 272, 291, 292; adapting to, 58, 280; training for, 251; cutters, 45 (photo), 46; defense, 37 (diagram), 48; complexities of, 34, 36–39; overcoming, 41–42, 44–46, 49, 51, 56–59, 109, 273, 281; tactics, 59, 61; improving, 51, 54, 56
Hentges, John A., 250
Hickey, Doyle O., 54, 56
Hill 182, capture of, 230
Hill 192, fight for, 53, 54, 59, 68
Hill 382, 151; fight for, 147, 153
Hill 385, fight for, 147
Hill 609, fight for, 13
Hitler, Adolf, 127; Western Front and, 32–33, 108, 116, 198, 200–201
Hobbs, Leland S., 104–5; training session by, 105; at West Wall, 118, 120, 124
Hodges, Courtney H., 108, 166, 171, 180, 182, 189, 229, 242; at Aachen, 96; at Rhine, 159
Hoge, William M., 160, 162
Holmlund, Robert, 132–33
HORSEFLY system, 289, 297; development of, 21, 29, 65, 74, 75, 84
Hostrup, Bruce M., 183
Howard, Michael, 2
Huebner, Clarence R., 78, 97, 192
Huertgen Forest, 57, 88, 171, 172, 174–75; battles in, 177–78, 179, 195–97, 259, 272, 281; casualties in, 196; combat exhaustion in, 243; defenses in, 273; lessons from, 194–96; reserve problems in, 235; tank-infantry coordination in, 178–79

Infantry, 295, 301, 306; casualties in, 14, 240, 264; coordination with, 57; doctrine

for, 40, 305; hedgerows and, 41; mobility for, 287; shortcomings of, 7, 40
Infantry-artillery coordination, 19–20, 41; improving, 100, 271, 274. *See also* Tank-infantry coordination
Infantry battalions, 286, 301, 305
Infantry divisions, 301, 302; adaptation by, 108; casualties of, 239; combat days for, 235, 236–37 (table)
Infantry in Battle, 8–9
Infantry Journal, 111, 290
Infantry School (Fort Benning), 8–9, 121; on attack preparation, 139
Infantry schools, 8–9, 121, 139, 294
Infiltration tactics, 278; development of, 273–74, 275
"Information Bulletin," 270
Innovation. *See* Adaptation
Intelligence, 125; collecting/disseminating, 26, 84, 138; improving, 75–76, 171; problems with, 149
Irwin, S. LeRoy, 129, 130, 131, 134
Italian campaign, 11; air-ground coordination in, 20–21, 22

Kasserine Pass: defeat at, 11; lessons from, 25
King, Howard, 125
Kinnard, Harry W. O., 220, 221, 217
Koenigsmacher bridgehead, securing, 154–57
Kogenbroich, 261, 262
Kommerscheidt: defense of, 184, 185, 186; lessons from, 196
Krinkelt-Rocherath, 295; defense of, 208, 209, 210

Larsen, Harold, 160
Lauer, Walter, 202, 203
Leadership, 3–4, 7, 269, 304; of authoritarian armies, 5; challenges of, 230, 238, 293–94; coordination and, 13; criticism of, 287; improving, 29, 237; morale and, 263; qualities for, 22–23; style of, 237–38, 262, 294; teaching, 23, 235, 237, 248, 254–55
"Lessons Learned and Expedients Used in Combat" (War Department pamphlet), 1
Liaison officers, 74, 84, 273
Light tank companies, 285, 302
Linebaugh, Harold, 262
Lines, fortified, 111, 113
Lines of communication (LOCs), 76; disrupting, 20, 73
Localities, fortified, 111, 113
Logistics, 272, 284; improving, 88, 107;

problems with, 110, 126, 127, 145, 147, 173, 287; Soviet, 277
Lorraine campaign, 127; river crossings during, 145
Luckett, James S., 187, 188
Ludendorff bridge, 160, 162, 162 (photo), 163, 170; capture of, 166–67; collapse of, 166; protecting, 164–65, 168
Luftwaffe: CAS by, 64–65; at Remagen, 164, 166

McAuliffe, Anthony C., 216, 220, 221
McBride, Horace L., 145, 149, 150, 151, 152
MacDonald, Charles B., 238
McKinley, William D., 206–7, 208, 209
McNair, Lesley J., 80
M1 Garand rifles, 250, 301
M10s, 209, 210, 218, 295; panzer attacks and, 217
Maginot Line, 88
Maintenance sections, adaptations by, 222–23
Maneuver, 8, 29, 104, 285, 304; changes in, 23; doctrine/practice of, 231 (diagram), 283; employing, 13, 141, 227, 228, 229; firepower and, 263; problems with, 24, 39, 40, 229, 283, 284; training for, 251. *See also* Mobility
Manpower: conserving, 228, 263, 287; problems with, 7–8, 196, 227, 246, 273, 288, 289
Marching fire, 250–51
Marksmanship training, 290
Marshall, George C., 227, 304; on *Infantry in Battle,* 9
Marshall, S. L. A., 7; analysis by, 289–91; on firepower, 250, 290
Martinville, 51, 52, 59
Massed formations, 229, 267
Matériel superiority, 108, 272, 282
Mechanized units: maneuver by, 283; Soviet, 276
Medical aid stations: establishing, 158; treatment at, 245
Medium bombers: ground support by, 22, 295; pillbox attacks and, 125; targeting by, 233
Men against Fire (Marshall), 7, 289–91
Metz, 229; attack on, 125–40; capture of, 128 (map), 140; fortifications around, 128–29
Middleton, Troy H., 108, 202, 215; at Brest, 90, 91, 230; at Bulge, 216; at Normandy, 35
Millikin, John, 159, 163, 166, 167

Minefields, 90, 199, 210, 249; overcoming, 26, 112, 114, 138, 305, 306
Mobility: adaptations in, 48; defensive, 223; doctrine/equipment for, 112; flexibility and, 284; importance of, 138, 229, 260, 286–87; problems in, 283, 284, 287; tactical, 42. *See also* Maneuver
Model, Walter, 202
Monte Cassino: air-ground coordination at, 22; artillery at, 19; bombing of, 77
Montgomery, Bernard L., 11, 32, 88, 129, 201
Morale, 286, 287; casualty rates and, 237; improving, 235, 251, 291, 293, 298; leadership and, 263; maintaining, 257–58, 273; problems with, 255, 258
Mortar crews, 51; adaptation by, 223; casualties for, 14
Moselle River: crossing of, 141, 145, 146 (map), 150, 155–56; defense of, 88

Napalm, 73, 80, 223
Normandy, 12, 33 (map), 229; adaptation at, 61–62; air support at, 86; breakout from, 87; German defense of, 36–39; training for, 60
North Africa, invasion of, 10, 11, 28
"Notes on Woods Fighting" (Operations Memorandum Number 23), 188

Offensives, 228, 229, 305; preference for, 282; series of, 276
Officers: casualties and, 237, 239; leadership by, 238–39, 293–94; number of, 266; problem solving by, 280; safety concerns about, 238, 294
Old sergeant syndrome. *See* Combat exhaustion
Operation COBRA, 57, 58, 291; air support for, 69, 70, 78–79, 85, 233; mobility and, 229; short bombing during, 79, 80–81, 84
Operation MARKET-GARDEN, 116, 141
Operation OVERLORD, 31–32, 283; preparatory bombings for, 85
Operation QUEEN, 81–83, 125; adaptation for, 86; air support in, 83, 85, 233
Operations Division (War Department), publications by, 270–71
Operations Order No. 20, air-ground operations and, 69–70
Operation TORCH, design for, 10
Operation WACHT AM RHEIN, 198
Ordnance Section (First Army), hedgerow cutters and, 46
Oyler, Al, 227

P-47 Thunderbolts, 67, 71 (photo), 184, 271; ACC missions by, 70, 72; CAS missions by, 72; communication with, 74, 75; support from, 70, 73, 177, 220–21
Panzers, 209; attacking, 68–69, 212, 225. *See also* Tanks
Parker, James E., 220–21
Patrolling techniques, training for, 252
Patton, George S., Jr., 1, 11, 26, 88, 135, 229; on 90th Division, 157; Brittany breakout and, 57, 72; combat exhaustion and, 244; on marching fire, 251; at Metz, 125, 126, 129, 285; shortages and, 272; on small arms firepower, 14; support for, 72, 85; on trench foot crisis, 241
Peace Offensive (1918), 275
Penetrations, 304; envelopments and, 305
Pentagon, building, 265–66
Performance, 288; analysis of, 6, 282–87; improving, 25–26, 28, 267, 298; maintaining, 273; problems with, 29, 249–50, 290
Pergrin, David E., 248; on bridge building, 141; at Remagen, 165
Perimeter defense, coordinating, 271
Pershing, John J., 282
Pershing tanks, 162, 295
Personnel system, shortcomings in, 288, 289
Personnel turnover, rate of, 239
Pillboxes, 90; attacking, 110, 112, 116, 119–25, 139, 286, 291, 294. *See also* Fortifications
Pipe devices, 44, 49
Piper Cubs, 47, 118
Planning, 109; artillery, 19; importance of, 24–25; for river crossings, 140, 141, 142, 169–70; for urban combat, 88–89, 106–7, 292
Platoons, configuration changes for, 93–94
Ploger, Robert R., 43, 44
Pont-a-Mousson, 149; bridgehead at, 145, 147; crossing at, 169, 170
Pooling concept, 284, 285
Preiss, Herman, 127
Prisoners of war, handling, 258, 293
Problem solving, 298; centralized, 263; decentralized, 58–59, 280, 282; flexibility in, 279; low-level, 138, 194–95, 223–24, 269, 281; tactical, 58–59, 267. *See also* Adaptation

Quesada, Elwood R. "Pete," 66–67, 69, 85, 269

RAF. *See* Royal Air Force
Ramcke, Herman B., 90, 91

Reconnaissance: aerial, 21, 76, 92, 125, 289; collection/dissemination of, 76; by fire, 70, 123, 257, 268; photo, 69, 76, 125, 268; problems with, 21, 149; training for, 252; visual, 69, 76; weather, 80
Regiments, attacks by, 232
Reinforcements. *See* Replacements
Remagen: bridgehead at, 159–60, 161 (map), 162–65, 162 (photo), 167, 235; combined arms operations at, 271
Replacements, 61, 188–89, 195, 262–63, 274, 284, 286, 287; infantry, 248; morale of, 27–28, 247; number of, 266; problems with, 27–28, 110, 243; sources of, 246–47; training, 247–48, 252–53, 257, 264, 288, 292
Replacement System, 246, 263; problems with, 247, 281, 286, 287–88
Reserves, 177; maintaining, 25; problems with, 235, 288
Rhine-Marne Canal, 147; fight for, 148
Rhine River: crossing, 141, 165; defense of, 88, 201
Rhino tanks, 46
Rifle battalions: casualties for, 240; supporting elements of, 303
Rifle companies, 301, 305
Riflemen: casualties for, 240, 241; training, 250, 264
Rifle platoons, 14, 301
River crossings, 144, 281; adaptations for, 168–69; advantages/disadvantages of, 141; combined arms at, 168, 169; command and control of, 158; doctrine/tactics for, 142, 143 (diagram), 144, 160, 167, 169; haste/speed in, 170–71; planning/coordinating, 140, 141, 142, 169–70; tactical/technical problems with, 157–58, 168; training for, 171; weather and, 154–57
Roberts, William, 216, 217
Robertson, Walter M.: at Bulge, 203, 205–6, 207, 211; hedgerow combat and, 52–53; at Krinkelt-Rocherath, 210
Rommel, Erwin, 32
Roosevelt, Franklin D., TORCH and, 11
Royal Air Force (RAF), QUEEN and, 81–82
Rudder, James E., 228
Ruhr industrial area, defense of, 201
Rundstedt, Gerd von: at Bulge, 202; mobile defense and, 32

Ste. Genevieve, 151, 153
St. Lo, 229; attack at, 51, 52, 52 (map), 57
Satchel charges, using, 119, 122, 123, 124, 134
Schmidt, Hans, 177, 181

Schmidt: attack on, 175–76, 176 (map), 177–78, 180–82, 193, 195; capture of, 183, 184–85; lessons from, 196
Searby, E. W., 153
Security measures, 22–23, 171
Selective Service System, 27
Self-inflicted wounds, 261, 262
Self-propelled artillery, 139, 268, 286; fortress reduction and, 291; problems with, 18
Service companies, 301, 302
SHAEF, 36
Shell shock. *See* Combat exhaustion
Sherman tanks, 1, 120, 132, 153, 191, 208, 209, 210, 213, 302; hedgerows and, 42–43, 53; modification of, 16 (photo), 43, 44, 45, 45 (photo), 46, 49; panzer attacks and, 217
Shortages, 110, 287; problems with, 7–8, 272
Short bombings, 79, 81, 83; preventing, 80, 82, 86. *See also* Bomb safety zones
Sicily, invasion of, 11
Siegfried Line. *See* West Wall
Signals, 47, 188
Singling, assault on, 1–2
Ski troops, 200, 225
Smoke generators, 158, 168, 169
"Snake" explosive devices, 131, 132 (photo), 134
Snowsuits, 206 (photo), 222
Soviet army: adaptation by, 273, 280; authoritarian traditions of, 6; counteroffensives by, 277; transformation of, 275–78
Soviet General Staff: analysis by, 276, 280; deep battle and, 278, 279; gathering/disseminating by, 277, 278
Special units, 292; fortification attacks and, 139
Speed, 109; haste and, 24, 106; problems with, 23
Squads, configuration changes for, 93–94
Stalin, Josef, 279
Stinson Sentinels, 21, 47; air-ground control by, 75; HORSEFLY and, 74
Strategic campaigns, 63, 64
Strategic weapons systems, maintaining, 296
Strategy, 8
Stroh, Donald A., 189, 190
Stuart light tanks, 302
Suicide Point, bridge at, 165
Support rafts, 144, 169. *See also* Assault boats
Support troops, 108, 109, 177, 301
Suppression, 8
Supreme Headquarters Allied Expeditionary Force (SHAEF), 36

Survivability, 256–57; improving, 271, 298

Tactical Air Command (TAC), 85, 296
Tactics, 8; adaptation in, 107, 264, 272,
281, 298; practicing, 269, 292
Tank armies, Soviet, 276, 277
Tank battalions, 285, 286, 302; at Huertgen,
194; infantry support by, 15; organizational weaknesses of, 15–16
Tank companies, 302
Tank Destroyer Center (Camp Hood), 295
Tank destroyers (TD), 96, 102, 103, 124,
139, 267, 268; development of, 269; effectiveness of, 212; elimination of, 285,
295; failure of, 17–18; role of, 18, 210,
224, 291; support from, 108, 199; urban
warfare and, 107, 112, 114–15
Tankers, casualties for, 240
Tank-infantry coordination, 29, 48, 102,
179, 194, 260, 269, 292; hedgerows and,
273; improving, 42–43, 46–47, 57, 108,
250, 251, 267, 271; problems with, 15–
17, 41, 48–49; Soviet, 277. See also Infantry-artillery coordination
Tank-infantry teams, 212; artillery and, 306;
firepower by, 104, 105; maneuver by,
101–2, 104, 105; signals for, 47; village
fighting and, 106
Tank platoons, 302
Tanks: air attack on, 68–69; in forests, 173;
hedgerows and, 40, 41; role of, 224, 302;
winter camouflage for, 223. See also
Dozer tanks; Panzers
Target identification, 20, 82, 83, 84, 86,
120, 233, 273; problems with, 66
Task Force (TF) Bacon, 135–36; at Metz,
137, 139
Task Force (TF) Engeman, 168; at Remagen,
160, 163
Taylor, Maxwell D., 216
TD. See Tank destroyers
Terrain: capture of, 229; problems with,
287
Tiger tanks, 209
Timberwolf Reinforcement Training Center,
253
Time-on-target (TOT) volley, 19, 67
Timmerman, Karl H., 162, 163
Training, 252–53, 264; combat exhaustion
and, 242; combat zone, 4, 25, 28, 60, 119
(photo), 139–40, 248–49, 251–52, 262,
273, 278, 279, 292, 297, 298; doctrines
for, 305; fear and, 255, 256; peacetime,
248–49, 292–93; problems with, 26–27,
39, 40, 248–49, 250, 290, 298
Transportation systems: improving, 288;
problems with, 27–28

Treadway bridges, 143, 144, 152, 169; laying, 156–57, 165
Trench foot, 261, 262; preventing/treating,
222, 241–42, 249; problems with, 186,
187, 241
Triangular divisions, 301; adaptation and,
285; armored support for, 302; mobility
of, 284. See also Divisions
Tukhachevsky, Mikhail N., 276, 277

Units, reorganization of, 108
Urban combat, 140, 272, 291; adapting to,
107, 108, 109, 268, 280; demands of, 92–
93, 101; doctrine for, 87, 89–91, 107;
German, 90–91, 108; maneuver and, 229;
planning for, 88–89, 106–7, 292; problems with, 108–9. See also Village combat

Valletta, Lawrence, 218
Van Fleet, James A., 154, 155, 166
Village combat, 101, 102–6; adapting to,
109; doctrine for, 107. See also Urban
combat
Villiers-Fossard, 59; capture of, 56–57
Von Manteuffel, Hasso, 202, 214, 218

Walker, Walton H.: at Driant, 130, 131; at
Koenigsmacher, 154; at Metz, 127, 129,
135, 137, 287; reserve problems for, 235
Wall-busting strategies, 96, 99, 101, 106,
108, 109; effectiveness of, 93
Ward, Herbert A., 114
War Department: battlefield lessons and,
270; on hatred, 258; offensive doctrines
by, 305; publications by, 270–71; shortages and, 272
War-fighting philosophy, 266, 267–68; conventional views on, 228–29; tenets of,
228
Warming tents, 158, 222, 242
Warner, Henry F., 212–13
Water barriers. See River crossings
Weapons: adaptation of, 16 (photo), 107,
132 (photo), 264, 268–69, 272, 297, 298,
299; reliance on, 289
Weapons platoons, 301
Weather, 73; adapting to, 280; influence of,
34–35, 174; maneuver and, 229, 284;
manpower problems and, 227; problems
with, 174, 179, 195, 196, 200, 201, 223,
225, 240–41, 287; river crossings and,
154–57
Weaver, William G., 172
Weigley, Russell, 6, 282–87
West Wall, 96; attacking, 81, 88, 89 (map),

116, 118, 117 (map), 140, 294; defense of, 88, 110–11, 127, 198
Weyland, Otto P., 71, 72
Wilck, Gerhard, 97, 100
Wilson, George, 248
Winter warfare, 200, 224
Wood, John S. "P.," 145, 152
Wurm River, assault at, 119–20

Zones, fortified, 111, 113, 125

Military Units

First Army (France), 88
First Army (U.S), 88, 235, 248, 284; at Aachen, 97; adaptation by, 58–59; air support for, 66, 67, 81; cold weather casualties for, 241; combat exhaustion and, 242–43, 245; forest combat and, 195; at Huertgen, 175, 180–81, 196–97; at Normandy, 29, 32, 33, 35, 36, 62; publications by, 270; at Rhine, 159; special units of, 139; training for, 60; urban combat for, 98–99; at West Wall, 140, 171, 175
1st Engineer Combat Battalion, at Bulge, 213
1st Infantry Division, 36, 108; at Aachen, 97, 98, 99 (photo), 100, 235; at Bulge, 203, 211, 212; casualties for, 239; combined arms operations and, 17; at Huertgen, 192–93
I SS Panzer Corps, at Bulge, 202–3
2d Armored Division, 36, 45, 69; CAS for, 71; fire and maneuver tactics of, 103 (diagram), 104; village fighting and, 102–3; at West Wall, 118, 121, 124, 229; at Wurm River, 170
II Corps: artillery of, 19; in North Africa, 11, 13
2d Engineer Combat Battalion, 53
2d Infantry Division, 36, 53–54, 59; at Brest, 90, 91, 94–96, 94 (photo), 113; at Bulge, 203, 204–5, 207–11, 212; hedgerow combat and, 52–53; at Hill, 68, 192; at St. Lo, 230
2d Marine Division, casualties for, 193
2d Parachute Division: at Brest, 90; defense by, 94
2d Ranger Battalion, combat exhaustion for, 243
II SS Panzer Corps, at Bulge, 203
3d Armored Division, 36, 59; CAS for, 71; combat zone training for, 60; hedgerow tactics of, 54, 54 (diagram), 55, 56; turnover rate for, 239; at Villiers-Fossard, 68
Third Army, 88, 145; in Brittany, 57, 87; cold weather casualties for, 241; combat

exhaustion in, 243, 245; at Driant, 285; logistics problems for, 126, 127, 145; at Metz, 125, 129; special units of, 139; support for, 71–72, 85; tank battalions for, 92
3d Cavalry Group, at Moselle, 155
III Corps, 159; air defense by, 164; casualties for, 166; at Remagen, 160, 163
3d Infantry Division, casualties for, 239
3d Panzer Grenadier Division, 151; defense by, 147, 149
4th Armored Division, 150; at Bastogne, 221; breakout by, 170; at Moselle, 145, 152, 153
4th Infantry Division, 35, 36, 45, 187; at Bulge, 202; casualties for, 239; at Huertgen, 188–89, 193, 259–60; training for, 188
5th Armored Division, 189, 190–91, 198; at Huertgen, 193
Fifth Army: in Italy, 11, 12; at Monte Cassino, 13, 22
V Corps, 36, 53, 189, 190, 230; air defense by, 164; at Bulge, 202, 205, 207, 212; at Huertgen, 180–81; at Normandy, 35
5th Infantry Division: adaptation by, 132 (photo); at Driant, 130–31, 134, 137, 140, 285; at Metz, 127, 129, 135, 137; at Moselle, 158
Fifth Panzer Army, at Bulge, 202, 214
6th Armored Division, turnover rate for, 239
6th Army Group, 88
Sixth Panzer Division, at Bulge, 213
7th Armored Division: at Metz, 127; training memorandum of, 238
Seventh Army (German): at Bulge, 202; at Normandy, 32, 35, 51, 57, 78
Seventh Army (U.S.), 88; combat exhaustion in, 245; support for, 73
VII Corps, 41, 45, 78, 118, 182, 190; at Aachen, 97, 98; air support for, 79, 297; at Bulge, 210–11, 212; casualties for, 166; at Huertgen, 175, 180; at Normandy, 35; at Remagen, 166; short bombings and, 79, 80–81; at West Wall, 116, 124
Eighth Air Force, 66; adaptations by, 80, 82; bombing mishap by, 79; communication with, 83; at Normandy, 77–78; QUEEN and, 81–82; support from, 86
Eighth Army: in Italy, 11; at Monte Cassino, 13
VIII Corps, 108, 215; at Bastogne, 220; at Brest, 90, 91, 113; at Normandy, 35; tank battalions of, 92
8th Infantry Division, 35, 189; at Brest, 90, 91, 113; at Huertgen, 191, 192, 193

Ninth Air Force, 84; at Bulge, 221–22; in Brittany, 87; D-Day and, 65; liaison/intelligence teams of, 76; organization of, 296; QUEEN and, 81–82; saturation bombing by, 120; support from, 73, 150, 297
9th Armored Division, 167; at Bastogne, 215; at Bulge, 202, 216; at Remagen, 159, 163, 170
Ninth Army (U.S.), 88, 260; air support for, 73, 81; at West Wall, 140
9th Infantry Division, 35, 36, 181, 188; at Bulge, 205–6, 212; casualties for, 180, 239; at Huertgen, 175–76, 193; at Remagen, 163; at Schmidt, 176–77, 179–80; training program of, 20
IX Tactical Air Command (TAC), 56, 67, 69; at Aachen, 98; at Bulge, 221; coordination with, 82, 83; D-Day and, 65, 66; reconnaissance by, 118; at Schmidt, 181, 183; support by, 70, 71, 73, 75, 125; at Villiers-Fossard, 68
10th Armored Division: at Bastogne, 221; at Bulge, 215, 216; at Koenigsmacher, 229; at Metz, 135
10th Tank Battalion, at Huertgen, 191
11th Infantry, at Driant, 130, 131
12th Army Group (U.S.), 88, 201, 235; combat lessons by, 270; forest combat and, 195; support for, 75, 81–82
XII Corps, 159; at Moselle, 145; at Nancy, 126–27
12th Infantry, 187, 189, 190; at Huertgen, 188
12th SS Panzer Division, 207; at Bulge, 203, 205, 209, 212
12th Volks Grenadier Division, at Bulge, 212, 213
XIII SS Corps, at Metz, 127–28
14th Tank Battalion, at Remagen, 160, 162
Fifteenth Army (German), at Bulge, 202
15th Panzer Division, at Bastogne, 218
16th Antiaircraft Artillery Group, at Remagen, 164
17th SS Panzer Grenadier Division, 127
18th Army Group (British), in North Africa, 11
18th Infantry, at Bulge, 213
XIX Corps, 48, 125, 230; hedgerow tactics and, 54; maps by, 118; at Normandy, 35, 51; preparations by, 139; at West Wall, 116, 118, 120, 121, 123, 124, 139
XIX Tactical Air Command (TAC): at Bastogne, 220; coordination with, 74; D-Day and, 65; support from, 71–72, 73, 75, 130

XX Corps, 131; Koenigsmacher and, 154; at Metz, 127, 128 (map), 129, 134–37, 139; training for, 140
20th Engineer Combat Battalion, 183
21st Army Group, 201
XXII Tactical Air Command (TAC), support from, 73
23d Infantry, at Bulge, 205
26th Infantry Division: at Aachen, 97; at Bulge, 211–13
26th Volks Grenadier Division, at Bastogne, 218
27th Armored Infantry, at Remagen, 160, 162
28th Infantry Division; at Bulge, 202; at Huertgen, 180, 181, 187, 193, 194; at Kommerscheidt, 184; at Schmidt, 182, 186–87, 193, 195
29th Infantry Division, 36, 43, 45, 48–49, 56, 59; at Brest, 90, 91, 113, 115; casualties for, 60, 239; hedgerow fighting and, 48, 50 (diagram), 51–53, 58, 232; at Montbarey, 113, 139; at St. Lo, 52 (map), 57, 230; training for, 60–61, 251
XXIX Tactical Air Command (TAC), support from, 73, 75
30th Division, 36, 104–5, 170; bombing mishap for, 79; pillbox reduction tactics by, 121–22, 122 (diagram), 123–24; training for, 118–19, 119 (photo), 124, 251; at West Wall, 118, 120, 121, 124, 229, 232, 235
32d Armored Infantry Regiment, 54
34th Infantry Division, Hill 609 and, 13
35th Infantry Division, 36; at Moselle, 145
36th Armored Infantry Regiment, 54
37th Tank Battalion, at Moselle, 152, 153
38th Infantry, 53, 198; at Bulge, 205, 207–8; at Hill 182, 230
39th Infantry, at Schmidt, 176
44th Infantry Division, river crossing by, 151 (photo)
47th Armored Infantry, 190
XLVII Panzer Corps, at Bulge, 215
48th Division, 127
51st Combat Engineer Battalion, at Linz, 165
53d Armored Infantry Battalion, at Moselle, 152, 153
60th Infantry: casualties of, 180; at Huertgen, 178–79; at Schmidt, 176
78th Division, training memorandum of, 250
79th Infantry Division, 35
80th Infantry Division: at Dieulouard, 232;

at Moselle, 145, 146 (map), 147, 150, 152, 153–54
82d Airborne Division, 35, 36, 215
83d Infantry Division, 35, 45; training for, 253
84th Chemical Company, 158
84th Division, 260
89th Division (U.S.), 255 (photo)
89th Infantry Division (German): at Kommerscheidt, 185; at Schmidt, 181, 183, 184
90th Infantry Division, 35, 284; at Koenigsmacher, 154, 155, 168, 229; at Metz, 127, 135; at Moselle, 156, 157; training for, 134, 154, 171, 252
95th Infantry Division, 136; at Driant, 134; at Metz, 135, 137
99th Infantry Division, 284; at Bulge, 202–5, 210, 212
101st Airborne Division: at Bastogne, 214–18, 220, 221, 286; at Champs, 219
102d Cavalry Reconnaissance Squadron, 45
104th Division, training for, 253
105th Combat Engineer Battalion, 119–20
106th Infantry Division, at Bulge, 202
109th Infantry, 187; at Huertgen, 180, 182
110th Infantry, 187; at Huertgen, 180, 182
112th Infantry, 196; casualties for, 187; at Huertgen, 182; at Kommerscheidt, 184, 185; at Schmidt, 180, 183, 186, 232
116th Infantry, 51, 52, 232; at Montbarey, 113; at St. Lo, 230
116th Panzer Division, 181, 183
117th Infantry: pillbox reduction tactics by, 123; training for, 118–19; at West Wall, 120, 121
119th Infantry, 110; training for, 118–19; at West Wall, 120, 121, 123
120th Infantry, training for, 118–19
121st Engineer Combat Battalion, 51; hedgerow demolition by, 43; at Montbarey, 113
121st Infantry Division, at Huertgen, 189–90, 191, 192
141st Tank Regiment (British), at Montbarey, 114
146th Engineer Combat Battalion, 185; at Huertgen, 194
175th Infantry, tank-infantry coordination and, 48–49
179th Engineer Combat Battalion, at Moselle, 157
180th Infantry, in Sicily, 14
183d Volks Grenadier Division, training memorandum of, 197

246th Grenadier Division, at Aachen, 97, 99, 100
275th Division, at Schmidt, 177–78, 181
277th Volks Grenadier Division, at Bulge, 203, 205, 209
291st Engineer Combat Battalion, bridge by, 165
305th Engineer Combat Battalion, 147, 149, 150
317th Infantry, 150–51, 152; at Moselle, 148–49; at Pont-a-Mousson, 147
318th Infantry, 150, 151; at Moselle, 152
319th Infantry, at Moselle, 153
327th Glider Infantry, at Bulge, 216, 218, 219
333d Infantry: attack by, 260–63; casualties for, 262
343d (Static) Division, at Brest, 90
357th Infantry, 154
358th Infantry, 154
359th Infantry, 154
377th Infantry, at Metz, 135
378th Infantry: at Metz, 135; at St. Julien, 136
394th Infantry, at Bulge, 203
462, Division Number, 127; at Metz, 129
501st Parachute Infantry, at Bulge, 216
502d Parachute Infantry, at Bulge, 216, 218–19
506th Parachute Infantry, at Bulge, 216
559th Volks Grenadier Division, 127
612th Tank Destroyer Battalion, at Bulge, 209
613th Tank Destroyer Battalion, at Bulge, 213
633d Antiaircraft Artillery Battalion, 150
634th Tank Destroyer Battalion, at Bulge, 211
644th Tank Destroyer Battalion, 209; at Bulge, 205, 207, 210; at Montbarey, 113
703d Tank Battalion, 45
705th Tank Destroyer Battalion, at Bulge, 216, 218, 221
707th Tank Battalion, 181, 182, 183, 184, 185
709th Tank Battalion, at Huertgen, 192
735th Tank Battalion, at Driant, 130
741st Tank Battalion, 53; at Bulge, 205, 208, 209, 210
745th Tank Battalion, 41; at Bulge, 211
746th Tank Battalion, at Huertgen, 178–79
747th Tank Battalion, 43, 51; hedgerow demolition and, 44, 45; tank-infantry coordination and, 48–49

801st Tank Destroyer Battalion, at Bulge, 209

818th Tank Destroyer Battalion, at Driant, 130

991st Engineer Treadway Bridge Company, adaptations by, 156–57

1117th Engineer Combat Group; bridge by, 151–52; support from, 150

1139th Engineer Combat Group: at Koenigsmacher, 154; at Moselle, 156

1171st Engineer Combat Group: at Huertgen, 194; at Schmidt, 180, 181